Planning the
Great Metropolis

As the Regional Plan Association embarks on a Fourth Regional Plan, there can be no better time for a paperback edition of David Johnson's critically acclaimed assessment of the 1929 Regional Plan of New York and Its Environs. As he says in his preface to this edition, the questions faced by the regional planners of today are little changed from those their predecessors faced in the 1920s.

Derided by some, accused by others of being the root cause of New York City's relative economic and physical decline, the 1929 Plan was in reality an important source of ideas for many projects built during the New Deal era of the 1930s.

In his detailed examination of the Plan, Johnson traces its origins to Progressive era and Daniel Burnham's 1909 Plan of Chicago. He describes the making of the Plan under the direction of Scotsman Thomas Adams, its reception in the New York Region, and its partial realization.

The story he tells has important lessons for planners, decision-makers and citizens facing an increasingly urban future where the physical plan approach may again have a critical role to play.

David A. Johnson, FAICP, is Professor Emeritus of Planning at the University of Tennessee, Knoxville. He is a past President of the Fulbright Association of the United States and has directed educational projects in Slovenia, Brazil, and Portugal. Professor Johnson also has served on the staffs of the Boston Redevelopment Authority, the Washington National Capital Planning Commission and the Regional Plan Association of New York.

Planning, History and Environment Series

Editor:
Ann Rudkin, Alexandrine Press, Marcham, UK

Editorial Board:
Professor Arturo Almandoz, Universidad Simón Bolivar, Caracas, Venezuela and
    Pontificia Universidad Católica de Chile, Santiago, Chile
Professor Nezar AlSayyad, University of California, Berkeley, USA
Professor Scott A. Bollens, University of California, Irvine, USA
Professor Robert Bruegmann, University of Illinois at Chicago, USA
Professor Meredith Clausen, University of Washington, Seattle, USA
Professor Yasser Elsheshtawy, UAE University, Al Ain, UAE
Professor Robert Freestone, University of New South Wales, Sydney, Australia
Professor John R. Gold, Oxford Brookes University, Oxford, UK
Professor Michael Hebbert, University College London, UK

Selection of published titles

Planning Europe's Capital Cities: Aspects of nineteenth century development by Thomas Hall

Selling Places: The marketing and promotion of towns and cities, 1850–2000 by Stephen V. Ward

The Australian Metropolis: A planning history edited by Stephen Hamnett and Robert Freestone

Utopian England: Community experiments 1900–1945 by Dennis Hardy

Urban Planning in a Changing World: The twentieth century experience edited by Robert Freestone

Twentieth-Century Suburbs: A morphological approach by J.W.R. Whitehand and C.M.H. Carr

Council Housing and Culture: The history of a social experiment by Alison Ravetz

Planning Latin America's Capital Cities, 1850–1950 edited by Arturo Almandoz

Exporting American Architecture, 1870–2000 by Jeffrey W. Cody

The Making and Selling of Post-Mao Beijing by Anne-Marie Broudehoux

Planning Middle Eastern Cities: An urban kaleidoscope in a globalizing world edited by Yasser Elsheshtawy

Globalizing Taipei: The political economy of spatial development edited by Reginald Yin-Wang Kwok

New Urbanism and American Planning: The conflict of cultures by Emily Talen

Remaking Chinese Urban Form: Modernity, scarcity and space, 1949–2005 by Duanfang Lu

Planning Twentieth Century Capital Cities edited by David L.A. Gordon

Planning the Megacity: Jakarta in the twentieth century by Christopher Silver

Designing Australia's Cities: Culture, commerce and the city beautiful, 1900–1930 by Robert Freestone

Ordinary Places, Extraordinary Events: Citizenship, democracy and urban space in Latin America edited by Clara Irazábal **(paperback 2015)**

The Evolving Arab City: Tradition, modernity and urban development edited by Yasser Elsheshtawy

Stockholm: The making of a metropolis by Thomas Hall

Dubai: Behind an urban spectacle by Yasser Elsheshtawy **(paperback 2013)**

Capital Cities in the Aftermath of Empires: Planning in central and southeastern Europe edited by Emily Gunzburger Makaš and Tanja Damljanović Conley **(paperback 2015)**

Lessons in Post-War Reconstruction: Case studies from Lebanon in the aftermath of the 2006 war edited by Howayda Al-Harithy

Orienting Istanbul: Cultural capital of Europe? edited by Deniz Göktürk, Levent Soysal and İpek Türeli

Olympic Cities: City agendas, planning and the world's games 1896–2016, 2nd edition edited by John R. Gold and Margaret M. Gold

The Making of Hong Kong: From vertical to volumetric by Barrie Shelton, Justyna Karakiewicz and Thomas Kvan **(paperback 2014)**

Urban Coding and Planning edited by Stephen Marshall

Planning Asian Cities: Risks and resilience edited by Stephen Hamnett and Dean Forbes **(paperback 2013)**

Staging the New Berlin: Place marketing and the politics of reinvention post-1989 by Claire Colomb

City and Soul in Divided Societies by Scott A. Bollens

Learning from the Japan City: Looking East in urban design, 2nd edition by Barrie Shelton

The Urban Wisdom of Jane Jacobs edited by Sonia Hirt with Diane Zahm **(paperback 2014)**

Of Planting and Planning: The making of British colonial cities, 2nd edition by Robert Home

Healthy City Planning: Global health equity from neighbourhood to nation by Jason Corburn

Good Cities, Better Lives: How Europe discovered the lost art of urbanism by Peter Hall

The Planning Imagination: Peter Hall and the study of urban and regional planning edited by Mark Tewdwr-Jones, Nicholas Phelps and Robert Freestone

Garden Suburbs of Tomorrow? A new future for cottage estates by Martin Crookston

Sociable Cities: The 21st-century reinvention of the Garden City by Peter Hall and Colin Ward

Modernization, Urbanization and Development in Latin America, 1900s–2000s by Arturo Almandoz

Planning the Great Metropolis: The 1929 Regional Plan of New York and Its Environs by David A. Johnson **(paperback 2015)**

Planning the Great Metropolis

The 1929 Regional Plan of New York and Its Environs

David A. Johnson

For RPA, carry on!

David A. Johnson

Routledge
Taylor & Francis Group

LONDON AND NEW YORK

First published 1996 by E Spon

This paperback edition first published 2015
by Routledge
2 Park Square, Milton Park, Abingdon, Oxfordshire OX14 4RN

and by Routledge
711 Third Avenue, New York, NY 10017

Routledge is an imprint of the Taylor & Francis Group, an informa business

© 1996, 2015 David A. Johnson

This book was commissioned and edited by Alexandrine Press, Marcham, Oxfordshire

The right of the author has been asserted in accordance with sections 77 and 78 of the Copyright, Designs and Patents Act 1988.

British Library Cataloguing in Publication Data
A catalogue record of this book is available from the British Library

Library of Congress Catalog Card Number 95-74647

ISBN: 978-0-419-19010-3 (hbk)
ISBN: 978-1-138-88572-1 (pbk)
ISBN: 978-1-315-71495-0 (ebk)

Typeset in Times by PNR Design, Didcot

Printed and bound in the United States of America by Publishers Graphics, LLC on sustainably sourced paper.

CONTENTS

PREFACE TO THE
PAPERBACK EDITION

This book is about the making and impact of an audacious plan for America's greatest metropolis, the New York, New Jersey and Connecticut metropolitan area. Privately funded and independent of government, the Regional Plan of New York and Its Environs had considerable impact on the subsequent development of the region as well as on the theory and practice of planning. In the final analysis, though, the 1929 Plan tried, but failed, to straddle the great fault line in American society between wealth and commonwealth, between the primacy of property or of people. Nowhere was this more evident than in the war of words between Lewis Mumford, the urban critic, and Thomas Adams, the British planner who directed the making of the Plan. Mumford took the view that the city and the urban region existed to provide a decent life for its people and should be planned accordingly. Adams, following the lead of his business-dominated Committee on the Regional Plan, had little choice but to work within the realities of the American economic and legal system. Not that the regional planners were oblivious to social needs. The 'Progressive' reform movements of the late nineteenth and early twentieth centuries sought not to remake the society according to utopian formulations but rather to remedy and regulate the excesses of a raw market economy. The people supporting the making of the Regional Plan followed in direct lineage the liberal reformers who were leaders in the slavery abolitionist movement and in later institutional reforms such as the creation of the American Red Cross, the Federal Reserve System, and the Port of New York Authority. The banking and philanthropic sponsors of the Regional Plan embraced the concept of *noblesse oblige*, the notion that elites should give back something in civic amenities, educational improvement or economic melioration of poverty. While *noblesse oblige* was no substitute for the structural reforms needed to address the disparities and injustices of the social and economic order, it helped to shape Franklin Roosevelt's New Deal depression relief programmes.

It is timely to see a reissue of this book since the New York Metropolitan region today faces many of the same problems identified by the planners of the 1920s:

◆ a shortage of affordable housing;

◆ areas of the city and region poorly served by public transportation resulting in excessively long commuter trips for many workers;

◆ how best to realize the potential of underutilized waterfronts;

◆ how to control the clustering and heights of buildings in business districts;

◆ restructuring the economy to reduce growing social inequalities;

◆ the need to protect natural areas for environmental and recreation needs;

◆ a deficiency of Hudson River crossing capacity for rail and transit.

It is pathetic that one of the world's great cities has not been able to build new desperately needed trans-Hudson transportation capacity even though the need was clearly evident as long ago as the 1920s. By contrast, in the nineteenth and early twentieth century New York implemented a number of bold development moves. These included the 1811 Commissioners' Plan which gave Manhattan its real estate-friendly gridiron, the Croton and Catskill Water systems, a great Central Park, consolidation of the Greater City in 1898, and multiple bridge and tunnel crossings of the East River, all still in use. By contrast, today's public infrastructure maintenance and development are neglected. While other world cities such as Paris and London are able to move ahead with bold plans, New York and its region struggle merely to keep its old facilities functioning. The decay of public urban infrastructure is striking evidence of political paralysis and of misplaced national priorities. The New York metropolitan region has for decades been limited in its ability to shape its development destiny. Key transportation decisions are made in Washington and in the distant capitals of the three states of the region. Getting these actors to work together has always proved difficult and sometimes impossible.

The Regional Plan Association (RPA), created in 1929 to implement the 1929 Regional Plan and still actively at work in the Region, has announced a project for a Fourth Regional Plan. The Second Regional Plan was released by RPA in 1966 and the Third Regional Plan, in 1996. These successor plans had important impacts on the Region and helped shape public discourse on development needs and priorities.

The Second and Third Regional Plans tended to emphasize general policies rather than the comprehensive detailed physical plan approach of the 1929 Plan. It will be interesting to see whether the Fourth Regional Plan moves towards an environmental planning approach that utilizes the computer-based geo-design techniques that are revolutionizing regional and metropolitan planning.

The future of the planet and our descendants will, for better or worse, be an urban future. Are we capable of shaping that future so it is sustainable and favourable to human habitation? Can we shape large urban agglomerations so that they function efficiently and are environmentally sustainable? How do we anticipate and use emerging technologies to achieve those ends? Whose values and whose power to decide will shape the future? These are all questions the regional planners faced in 1929. We still face them.

David A. Johnson, FAICP
Professor Emeritus, University of Tennessee
Asheville, North Carolina, USA

November 2014

PREFACE

Twenty-five years ago, I was Senior Planner for the non-profit Regional Plan Association and was involved in studies for an ambitious new Second Regional Plan for the New York Metropolitan Area. It was an audacious undertaking by this unique private research association which has been working for the better development of the New York Region since 1929. My involvement in the Second Regional Plan naturally stirred my curiosity about its predecessor, the Regional Plan of New York and Its Environs, published in 1929 by the Committee on the Regional Plan of New York, the forerunner of the Regional Plan Association. The files of the Committee on the Regional Plan of New York and the records and drawings of its staff rested in a storeroom near my desk in a mid-town Manhattan skyscraper. Occasionally, I would thumb through the old reports and papers to see how a previous generation of planners had approached problems not unlike those with which we grappled. After forty years, the first Regional Plan has, of course, long since ceased to be very useful as a source of concepts or proposals. But tantalizing questions remained: how had the 1929 Regional Plan taken shape? Who were the people behind the Plan? Whose interests were being served? And what impact did the Plan have on the subsequent development of New York and the surrounding counties?

It was not possible at the time to search out answers to those intriguing questions. Then, quite by coincidence, both I and the voluminous files and records of the 1929 Regional Plan of New York moved at about the same time to Cornell University: I to resume graduate studies in planning, and the papers to be deposited in the Olin Library Collection of Regional History. The opportunity to answer those questions proved irresistible. The questions, I hope, have been answered in this book. But in the chapters that follow, there is more than simply the fulfilment of a long-standing personal interest. I have sought to shed additional light on an important American experience, the thrust toward metropolitan reform, and more generally, on the decade immediately after World War I, a period too often characterized as a hiatus in social change in the United States. During the 1920s the reforms of the Progressive Era were transformed to become the foundations of the emergent Administrative State. It was a decade of vitality and movement, a small but significant episode of which is chronicled here.

This book goes further, though, than merely presenting a chronicle of events, however interesting they may be. It attempts a systematic evaluation of the impact of a major regional plan. There have been few, if any, previous efforts to analyze, after the fact, the long-term effects of comprehensive metropolitan plans. The activities described in these pages may therefore be of interest to today's urban and regional planners who wish to know something about the origins of their profession – if only to transcend them. A great deal of current planning behavior, for better or worse, can be traced to what happened in the New York Region in the

1920s. Indeed, the Regional Plan Association is at the time of writing completing a *Third* Regional Plan for the New York ,New Jersey, Connecticut metropolitan region. The challenge of shaping this complex cosmopolitan area is just as great today as it was in the 1920s, perhaps more so. Contemporary regional planners can learn much from their predecessors.

Many people contributed to the research on which this book has been based. The primary sources for the study were the papers of the Committee on the Regional Plan of New York, the papers of the Regional Plan Association, and the John Nolen papers, all of which are now part of the Olin Library Collection of Regional History at Cornell University. Interviews and assistance granted by six men, all now deceased, who were central figures in the events described in this book, were of inestimable help: Robert Moses, Lawrence M. Orton, and Harold M. Lewis each provided information unavailable elsewhere. Flavel Shurtleff and C. McKim Norton also furnished helpful comments and materials. Lewis Mumford kindly gave permission to quote his private correspondence concerning the Regional Plan. Responsibility for the interpretations made of the information furnished by these men is solely my own. I doubt that each would have agreed with all of my conclusions regarding the Regional Plan of New York, though I hope they would have regarded my use of the material provided as fair and accurate.

At Cornell University, Kermit C. Parson, Barclay G. Jones, John W. Reps, Edward S. Flash and the late Stephen W. Jacobs, provided very helpful direction and encouragement during the gestation of this work. Jameson W. Doig, John P. Keith, William B. Shore, and Richard T. Anderson offered valuable ideas and advice. I would also like to express my gratitude to the Regional Plan Association for additional materials and maps and to the Syracuse University Geography Department Cartographic Laboratory for making its facilities available. Thanks go also to The University of Tennessee, Knoxville, which provided a faculty leave grant making it possible to conduct additional research in New York. Victoria Johnson and Heather Ewing provided superb typing and editorial review. Ann Rudkin, of Alexandrine Press, provided the kind of outstanding editorial oversight and help all authors yearn for. My wife, Eleanor Stephens Johnson, provided indispensable advice, criticism, assistance, and support during the long evolution of this project. For whatever quality may be found in this work, the credit is theirs, The mistakes and shortcomings are my own.

David A. Johnson
Knoxville, Tennessee
September 1995

(Note: A portion of this book was previously published as chapter 7, 'Regional Planning for the Great American Metropolis', in Daniel Schaffer (ed.) (1988) *Two Centuries of American Planning*. London: Mansell.)

The New Yorker of 1965 will have plenty of room, if he wants it. He will not spend so much of his time sitting in stationary motor cars in congested traffic, unless he really wishes to. He will not have to brave the perils of the open streets so often. He will be able to get around the 5,000 square miles of the region far more easily than now. But he will not have so much occasion to do so. His job, his recreations, his stores, his children's schools will be much more conveniently situated with respect to where he lives than they are now.... Easy transit in 1965 will really be easy, not the present struggle against crowds. The suburban resident may choose to live far out. If he does he will find it possible to reach Manhattan by belt lines, similar to the trunk belt lines of the main railways, which will carry him, without need of changing cars, from a point near his home to within walking distance of his office.... Double-decked and triple-decked streets, gardened terraces, lofty footpaths, perhaps built of glass so as to permit light to penetrate to the lower levels, and towers shooting a thousand feet and more into the clouds, like miniature mountain peaks, are features of this idea. In such buildings the residents might, if they choose, live out their entire lives without setting foot on ground.... A process of re-building will have gone on all over Manhattan, the old tenements will have disappeared, garden apartments will have taken their places, parked motor cars will have disappeared from the streets, into sub-surface garages, or sky-scraper storage buildings, the smoke evil will have been done away with and the community will have progressed far towards the ideal of a spotless city.

'New York in 1965', *The Morning Bulletin*
(Rockhampton, Queensland, Australia)
September 6, 1928

1

INTRODUCTION

Between 1910 and 1929 regional plans were initiated by citizens' groups for a number of large metropolitan areas in the United States, the most notable, New York and its environs. Metropolitan regional planning in this period linked Progressive era planning and reform movements to the thrust towards administrative efficiency and to the responses evoked by the beginning of mass ownership of the automobile. Reforms at the national level, such as the creation of the Federal Reserve System, and the emergency administrative measures taken during World War I prompted calls for similar centralizing administrative reforms at the metropolitan level. The spread of urban development beyond city boundaries produced by the automobile and the demand for remedies to growing traffic congestion created an unstable political vacuum into which the planner-reformers hoped to move.

In the New York area the planners' response took the form of a monumental Regional Plan of New York and Its Environs. Ultimately, some 1.2 million dollars was spent on its preparation, making it perhaps the most costly planning endeavor ever undertaken in the United States.[1] Privately organized by businessmen and financiers and funded by the Russell Sage Foundation, the Plan provided a blueprint for transforming New York into a physically integrated metropolis of twenty million people by 1965. Completed in 1929, the Plan had considerable impact on the development of highways, parkways, and open space. Studies made for the Plan contributed many new techniques and concepts to urban and regional theory, including economic base theory, advances in population projection techniques, and the concept and term, 'freeway'. The Plan also changed the character of the urban planning profession by establishing the need for a greater knowledge of social science as a foundation for physical planning. The creation of separate departments of city and regional planning in institutions of higher education can also be traced to activities related to the Regional Plan of New York.

The non-governmental regional planner-reformers were not the only groups that emerged to fill the political vacuum created by the growth of the New York Region. State-sponsored bodies under Robert Moses and the Port of New York Authority were initiated during this period and carried out many of the proposals of the Regional Plan, or, alternatively, made proposals that were incorporated into the Plan.

Constrained by political and institutional realities and the fiscally cautious and efficiency-oriented philosophy of its sponsors and organizers, the Plan took on a cautious, project-oriented cast, embodying the values and enhancing the interests of a growing, suburbanizing, affluent upper-middle class. The Plan emphasized highway construction and acquisition of outlying parklands. It made few proposals to provide for the needs of the urban poor, failing especially to cope with the problem of low-and moderate-income housing.

A general, integrating, upward social mobility was implicitly assumed in the Plan. An evaluation of the impact of the Plan indicates that to the extent to which upward class movement by the children of the urban ethnic poor occurred, the Plan worked to redistribute regional social wealth. For its contemporary generation, however, the Plan largely reflected efficiency rather than equity values.

Though its target year was 1965, the Plan's period of relevance and influence was short – only about ten years – and by the outbreak of World War II in 1941 it was for most purposes obsolete. The successful implementation of many proposals in the Plan was achieved by several means: by the inclusion of pre-existing, long-standing proposals, by endorsement and incorporation of proposals made by public authorities with their own development capabilities, or through consultation between the technical staffs of the Plan and the regional authorities. The subsequent proposals of these technicians often conformed to proposals that had been made in the Regional Plan. The transfer of proposals between parallel, special-function technical staffs such as the highway engineers seems to have been a particularly effective means of placing unofficial Plan proposals on the public agenda.

The Regional Plan of New York and Its Environs was a flawed development guide, which nevertheless had a profound impact on the New York Region and on planning thought and practice, and therefore should be regarded as a major event in American urban history. Given the significance of the Regional Plan of New York and Its Environs, it seems an oversight that to date, little major research or analysis has been undertaken on the making of the Plan and its subsequent impact on American urbanism. The most detailed review was that of the critic, Lewis Mumford, which was published shortly after the appearance of the final Plan volume in 1932. Mumford, in a trenchant and detailed analysis, attacked the Plan for its acceptance of metropolitan growth and congestion as inevitable, a reflection, he thought, of the exploitative values of its business and philanthropic sponsors.[2]

In the decade after the Plan was published, three successive progress reports were prepared by the Regional Plan Association, the private advisory group created to carry out the proposals in the Regional Plan of New York and Its Environs.[3] But these compendia of accomplishments could hardly have been expected to take an impartial view of the proposals contained in the Plan.

It was not until 1963 that the Plan captured the interest of several writers, who were prompted, no doubt, by a renewed concern for the plight of the cities. Roy Lubove took a fresh look at efforts in the 1920s to cope with the problems of metropolitan regional development.[4] His focus was primarily on the Regional Planning Association of America, the loosely knit but influential group of intellectuals and architects which included Lewis Mumford, Henry Wright, Clarence Stein, and Benton MacKaye, among others. Lubove compared the work of the Regional Planning Association of America with that of the Regional Plan of New York and Its Environs and found the latter far less heroic and humane, though more powerful. Lubove nevertheless recognized the significance of the Regional Plan of New York and Its Environs for subsequent developments in the New York Region:

> The RPNYE constituted a landmark in planning history for the collaboration in a single project of planners, architects, engineers, lawyers, economists, social workers, and other specialists. The Plan they devised, moreover, was significant for its practical influence. It was eminently successful, if measured by the number of proposals subsequently adopted by local government agencies. The Russell Sage Plan, finally, greatly stimulated the growth of both local and county planning organization in the Metropolitan Region. Particularly important in this respect was the Regional Plan Association Inc., established in 1929 and still active.[5]

Lubove's tempered but generally negative conclusions about the work of the Committee on the Regional Plan were not entirely shared by Forbes B. Hays, who undertook a brief history of the Regional Plan Association, published in 1965.[6] Hays' major interest was the emergence of the Regional Plan Association as a civic leadership group guiding public opinion on regional issues. He emphasized the importance of the Plan as a factor in shaping the subsequent commitments of the Association to regionalism, comprehensiveness, and physical planning. Hays' focus, as a political scientist, was on organizational development for implementing the Plan rather than on an assessment of the Plan itself. He concluded, however, that the Plan was 'an integral conception, attempting to relate systematically several major factors of regional development, starting from a statement of the problems and a set of priorities that were a compound of what the survey research revealed and what the planners' judgment and intuition suggested.'[7]

By 1933, twenty-eight of the fifty-one proposals in the Plan that were classified as urgent had been carried out or officially adopted, suggesting a high rate of accomplishment. Hays correctly concluded that to attribute all of these successes to the influence of the Plan was to risk a *post hoc* fallacy. Many of the proposals had been suggested or developed by others, as the makers of the Plan readily admitted. Nevertheless, the Plan, in Hays' view, could at least be credited *prima facie* with having synthesized and coordinated these proposals and, thereby, having helped to bring them to completion. But Hays carefully and quite properly avoided making excessive claims for either the virtues of the Plan or its direct impact on subsequent decision-making.

Christopher Tunnard, in his 1968 survey, *The Modern American City*, lavished praise on the Plan, labeling it 'a bold stab at the task of metropolitan development along orderly lines, and an important influence.[8] Tunnard rejected the Mumford criticisms of excessive growth and congestion, and suggested that Mumford has 'ignored the Plan's quest for livability in the giant region's surroundings, an approach which was advanced for its day.'[9]

Mel Scott, in his 1969 history, *American City Planning Since 1890*, skilfully placed the Regional Plan of New York and Its Environs in the perspective of the larger trends that shaped American planning thought in the first three decades of the century. Scott's chronicle of the development and implementation of the Plan is woven into the warp of the municipal and housing reform movements, the 'scientific management' concept, and the changing technologies of urban life. In contrast to Tunnard, Scott was less than enthusiastic in assessing the impact of the Regional Plan. While he concluded that Charles Dyer Norton, the driving force behind the inception of the Plan, was ahead of his time in envisioning the need for a regional approach, Scott looked on the Plan that eventually resulted from that vision as unnecessarily conservative and orthodox. Particularly serious, according to Scott, was the Plan's failure to come to grips with fundamental economic and social issues, most notably, housing for low-income groups.[10]

But Scott did not underestimate the impact of the Plan. He noted the conclusion of Melvin Webber that the Plan offered 'the first product of a "systems approach" to urban transportation planning in the United States.[11] Scott also noted the important events connected with the Plan that led to the establishment of the first school of instruction in city planning, established at Harvard in 1929.[12] But the Plan's actual impact on the physical shape of the New York metropolitan region was not elaborated by Scott. He noted simply that 'much of the plan was translated into reality, with initial successes greatest in highway and railroad improvements and in the expansion of the regional park system.'[13]

Harvey A. Kantor provided us with an outline of the origins of the Regional Plan of New York and Its Environs and a useful biographical sketch of Charles Norton, the initiator of the Plan.[14] Kantor concluded that the Plan was significant for urban planning history not only for its sheer size, but for its consequences for the growth of the New York area. Kantor credited the Plan with furthering urban congestion because it 'in effect planned *for* growth rather than attempting to direct it in any way.' He suggested that through emphasis on the private automobile as the major means of transportation, mass transit was relegated to a secondary role. Finally, in a more positive vein, Kantor concluded that the Plan was an early promoter of the concept of regionalism. Thus, like Lubove and Scott, he assessed the record of the Plan's accomplishments as a mixed one, in which the Plan itself was defective, but the larger concepts it embodied and its organizational legacies were tangible and progressive contributions.[15]

More recent critics, such as Jason Epstein, Robert Fitch and Michael Heiman, have attributed the decline in New York's relative status to the impact of the Plan, charging that it was responsible for the departure of New York City's manufacturing sector and subsequent economic distress – a charge others have challenged.[16] Other analysts, such as Jameson Doig, have argued that the Plan was largely irrelevant and had relatively little direct impact on the New York Region.[17] Whatever its effect on the physical shape of the Region, the importance of the Regional Plan in the evolution of the planning tradition in the United States has generally been acknowledged by scholars writing in the field.

The broad outlines of criticism of the Plan have been sketched and a number of assessments have been made. But the details on the canvas are hazy and their significance ambiguous. The present work seeks to clarify matters. Drawing on records and files of the Committee on the Regional Plan, it has been possible to determine the steps through which the Plan evolved. The historical record of the making of the Plan, set in the context of the emergence of planning in New York, is laid out in some detail in the pages that follow. It makes for a fascinating history.

More is required than historical fact, however, to assess the significance and place of the Plan in American urban social history. The Plan should be viewed as part of a larger reform movement, and its sponsors and guiding spirits were connected with a number of related activities concerned with governmental efficiency and societal integration. Indeed, there is a thread of reform continuity here which links the regional planning movement through a few families and individuals to the pre-Civil War abolitionist movement, and, later, to the establishment of the Federal Reserve System, the American Red Cross, and the Institute of Governmental Research (which subsequently merged with another institute to become the present-day Brookings Institution).

The Regional Plan was published in the inter-war period, but its origins lay in the Progressive Era, those formative years between 1890 and 1917, during which America reached urban and industrial maturity, and so many of our political and economic structures came to seem settled business. Social and economic historians have sought in the Progressive Era the roots of our present national domestic condition. While historians writing in the period between the two World Wars, such as Harold Faulkner, accepted the Progressive reforms at face value as the fruits of a successful fight between the citizenry and the trusts, later interpreters such as Eric F. Goldman, Richard Hofstadter, and Robert H. Wiebe reached a somewhat different conclusion: that the chief beneficiary of Progressive reform and its aftermath was corporate business.[18] This conclusion was presented, however, without normative judgments as to whether this outcome was particularly good or bad as far as democratic processes were concerned, but rather was viewed as the inevitable consequence of the growth in the scale of business, technology, and population.

Later historians agreeing with the conclusion that big business promoted and reaped the benefits of reform have argued that the consequent loss of representative democracy was not inevitable, that America had a choice between a more responsive form of industrial democracy and what ultimately evolved: a centralized tri-partism among big business, big government, and big labour, with the business group dominant. This is the argument of Gabriel Kolko and James Weinstein, among others.[19]

Among political scientists a similar re-examination occurred, which, though not specifically addressed to the Progressive period, has relevance here. The enduring debate between pluralists, such as Robert Dahl and Nelson Polsby, and those who subscribed to a theory of elites, such as the late C. Wright Mills and Floyd Hunter, subsided some time ago.[20] Few would now argue that elites do not exist. Nor would many argue that single, monolithic elites dominate the process of political decision at either national or metropolitan levels. The debate now centers on two more substantial questions: how do political decisions get made in an arena characterized by a multiplicity of sometimes competing, sometimes cooperating elites? And secondly, what are the ethical issues raised by reliance on a system of interacting elites? In other words, can such a system be regarded as legitimate in terms of a democratic ideal?

A later group of political scientists, including Peter Bachrach and T.B. Bottomore, sharply challenged the pluralist argument on the basis of ethics rather than process. Bachrach, while implicitly accepting pluralist arguments, argued that American political decision-making can be characterized as democratic elitism, elite because decision-making is concentrated among a number of small powerful groups, and nominally democratic because it is premised on the notion of equality of circulation into elites, a concept originating in the work of Vilfredo Pareto. Bachrach's argument holds that equality, to be ethical, requires equality in the sharing of power, not merely in the opportunity to become powerful at the expense of others. Bottomore's thesis is similar.[21]

While it would be simplistic to try to condense this stream of social criticism into a brief summary, a number of recurrent themes stand out. (1) Western industrial society has been dominated by a drive toward the centralization of power with a resultant diminution of the power vested in sub-groups. (2) The major thrust of development has been towards order, uniformity, and unity at the expense of democracy and equality. (3) This thrust has been characterized by a consequent move toward non-legislative control. (4) There has been an increasing separation of the functional and moral realms. (5) Social scientists have with varying degrees of awareness tended to reinforce the prevailing distribution of social power and have been guilty of reification, empty empiricism, scientism, and technicism.

It is not surprising then that social historians such as Kolko and Weinstein attempted to find the roots of these contemporary tendencies in the American past, and particularly in the formative years of industrial organization in the Progressive era. That they have emerged with unambiguous indictments, unlike their predecessors, is to be expected. Their basic argument is with the distribution of power in an industrial society, and the Progressive era clearly concentrated power. Certainly this was true at the national level. Kolko, for one, contended in his study of the reorganization of banking that the assumption of regulatory power by the national government from the states weakened responsiveness to local needs and control. He charged that state banks were not as inefficient and unstable as the Progressives believed, were more keenly aware of local conditions, and more competitive than the nationally-organized financial system created through progressive reform.[22] This argument has particular relevance to the present study. The thrust toward metropolitan regionalism in the 1910s and 1920s paralleled that towards national organization. The arguments that Kolko made for the national level should therefore find support at the metropolitan level. This should especially be true in the New York Metropolitan Region, where many of the wealthy regionalists were the very same individuals instrumental in achieving national banking reform through the creation of the Federal Reserve System. Elihu Root, Charles Norton, and Frederic Delano stand out, but there were others as well.

There is, of course, an apparent inconsistency that must be satisfied before the Kolko thesis concerning national reform can be said to hold for metropolitan reform. If the Progressive thrust was toward national concentration, how then can we explain the regionalists' desire to strengthen planning at the metropolitan level? The facts presented in this study show that there is little inconsistency. A primary motivation behind metropolitan planning in New York was a desire to rationalize the development of the Port of New York, a national as much as a regional goal. The creation of a stable climate for business was the primary aim both of the regionalists and of the national reformers. Concern for the welfare needs of the population was an enunciated but clearly secondary motive.

This is not to say that the metropolitan planners did not have worthy objectives. It would be grossly unjust to characterize them as self-serving manipulators. They accomplished much of value, particularly in the acquisition of open space. They prided themselves on being both idealists and realists, claiming that they could not hope to make over society but only improve things incrementally. But in the end they did help remake society by inadvertently reinforcing the latent tendencies of an urbanizing society to concentrate power in the absence of institutions to control that power.

It would be an error, however, to credit the regionalists with more power than they actually possessed. The emergence of metropolitan areas at the beginning of the twentieth century created a political vacuum which a number of groups came forward to fill, the most noteworthy in the New York area being the Port of New York Authority and Robert Moses, both drawing their power from the state rather than from local or regional sources. The regionalists worked to influence these potential competitors and the conflicts that arose among them were not over fundamental issues – there was substantial agreement here – but over detailed matters of how to achieve objectives held in common. In the end, however, it was the Port Authority and Moses who made the important decisions, not the foundation-supported regional planning groups.

It is perhaps a moot point to ask whether there were real alternatives possible for the organization of metropolitan society in the first decades of the century. If there were they certainly were not perceived by the regionalists. And it is not at all certain, had the regionalists not appeared on the scene, that other, less centralized entities could have filled the power vacuum. Socialist and labor groups offered no alternative visions of the possible re-organization of urban areas. They were much too concerned with the bread and butter issues of daily life to think about the possibilities of the future. And the political machines of the cities were typically regarded as corrupt or self-serving, and indeed, many were, though some have argued that the machines were more responsive to the needs of the masses than were the well-meaning but aloof reformers. The alternatives to existing political organization seemed limited to citizens' groups and independent commissions and authorities, and both approaches were used with varying results.

The two central ideas of the regionalists were metropolitanism and comprehensiveness. How appropriate were these notions as origin points for policy-making? Were there really any region- wide metropolitan problems or merely aggregates of local problems potentially resolvable at the local level? What was meant by comprehensiveness? Was it simply a cover for special interests thirsting for power but hoping to appear value-neutral?

By 1920 there were indeed problems which could be called regional in scope. These were largely in the areas of transportation and recreation. But there were also serious local problems with important regional implications, such as the provision of decent housing for workers, which the regionalists chose to ignore because their scope was already too diffuse and because their *status-quo* ideology could not embrace radical innovation. The metropolitan regionalists' definition of comprehensiveness was, as a result, rather narrow and abstract.

None of the foregoing gainsays the contributions the regionalists made to an understanding of urban phenomena and to the betterment of the regions they attempted to mold. There *were* real achievements. The Regional Plan of New York and Its Environs was a pivot point in the development of the planning tradition in the United States. Well-financed by the Russell Sage Foundation, the project drew together some of the best minds of the time, such as Edward M. Bassett, the lawyer who originated zoning, the economist Robert Murray Haig, Nelson P. Lewis, the engineer, and Frederick Law Olmsted, Jr., the landscape architect. The work they did together in applying their disciplines to the problems of an earlier 'urban crisis' laid the groundwork for subsequent progress in population projection technique, urban economic analysis (particularly economic base theory), the legal basis of zoning, and transportation engineering. And both the profession of planning and planning education in the universities were greatly influenced by the experiences of these early researchers.

Many of the proposals of the Regional Plan of New York and Its Environs were realized, in contrast to the fate that befell other metropolitan planning efforts such as in Philadelphia and Los Angeles. Secrets of success in the implementation of plans, no matter from what era, should be highly valued. It would be illuminating to know just what ingredients were required to convert plans into realities – and at what price. The key questions then were what impact did the Regional Plan have and how was that impact realized? But there are important subsidiary questions as well.

Though in the 1920s social conditions and the technological setting were clearly different from what currently prevails (more radically changed than the early planners anticipated), the planners and the policy-makers of that era faced issues much like those which concern us today. The literature of the policy sciences continues to be dominated by such questions suggested by these early planners as:

- How does technical information enter and shape the decision process?
- What are the roles of technical elites in policy formulation, and what power do they possess by virtue of their expertise and reputation?
- Where does political power reside in communities, how is it employed, and how is it identified?
- Whose values are invoked in the making of public policy, and how can these values be identified?

The current planning literature contains related questions:

- What issues, elements, sectors or functions should metropolitan-scale planning properly be concerned with?
- How are alternative metropolitan plans and policies to be evaluated?
- How are the economic issues of externality and the social discounting of the future to be accommodated in the formation of public plans and policy?

- How should planning activity respond to risk and uncertainty?
- What are the virtues, if any, of the holistic, comprehensive approach which has characterized the ideology if not the practice of planning?
- What effects do plans as imageable documents have on the making of public policy?
- What is the expectable viable lifetime of regional planning proposals?
- What levels of specificity are appropriate for regional planning policies?

All of these questions currently confront contemporary urban policy-makers. And they can, with profit, also be addressed to the past, as this study attempts to do.

There are those who reject the usefulness of the past as a source of analogs for the future, and, strictly speaking, they are correct.[23] Too many variables are at work for the past to repeat itself exactly. Even so, all anticipations of the future derive in the end from past experience. History is a rich source of clues and suggestions to guide present behaviour. Given the present parlous state of our urban areas, we can use whatever help we can find. As E. H. Carr has put it, 'history should be a dialogue between the events of the past and progressively emerging future ends.'[24] This study is an attempt to conduct such a dialogue.

The events surrounding the making of the Regional Plan of New York can only be comprehended and analyzed within the context of its place and its time. Chapters 2 and 3 help establish that context. Chapter 2 briefly summarizes the evolution of urban development in New York and its surroundings prior to the Regional Plan. Chapter 3 is a description and analysis of the major attempts by reformers to plan and control the physical growth and development of the New York Region. Out of these efforts a distinctive planning tradition emerged. The Regional Plan of New York represented both a continuation of this tradition and an attempt to consolidate previous plans into a single grand scheme.

Chapter 4 focuses on the events leading up to the decision to undertake the Plan and the relationship of the Regional Plan of New York to the Plan of Chicago. Chapters 5, 6 and 7 describe and analyze the process by which the Regional Plan was made and the substantive proposals contained in it. Chapter 8 comprises three case studies of significant development decisions made while the Plan was in preparation. The case studies shed light on the nature of the political relationships between the Regional Plan Committee and the principal regional decision-makers, the Port of New York Authority, Robert Moses, and the City of New York.

Chapters 9 and 10 analyze the extent to which the Plan was carried out and the reasons for its successes and failures. Chapter 11, the concluding chapter, presents a theory of reform and evaluates the Plan in terms of its distribution of social and economic benefits. Tentative hypotheses for a theory of planning reform behaviour are presented.

NOTES

1. The Plan was published in two volumes: *Regional Plan of New York and Its Environs. Volume I. The Graphic Regional Plan.* New York: Committee on the Regional Plan, 1929; *Regional Plan of New York and Its Environs. Volume II, The Building of the City.* New York: Committee on the Regional Plan, 1931.

2. Mumford, Lewis (1932*a*) The Plan of New York. *The New Republic*, LXXI, June 15, pp. 121–126; (1932*b*) The Plan of New York, II *The New Republic*, LXXI, June 22, pp, 146–153. Mumford's criticisms are discussed on pages 185–194.

3. Regional Plan Association (1933) *From Plan to Reality*; (1938) *From Plan to Reality, II*; (1942) *From Plan to Reality III*. New York: Regional Plan Association.

4. Lubove, Roy (1963) *Community Planning in the 1920s: The Contribution of the Regional Planning Association of America.* Pittsburgh: University of Pittsburgh Press.

5. *Ibid.*, pp. 116–117.

6. Hays, Forbes B. (1965) *Community Leadership: The Regional Plan Association of New York.* New York: Columbia University Press.

7. *ibid.*, pp 20–21.

8. Tunnard, Christopher (1968) *The Modern American City.* Princeton: D. Van Nostrand.

9. *ibid.*

10. Scott, Mel (1969) *American City Planning Since 1890.* Berkeley: University of California Press, pp 290–292.

11. Quote from Webber, Melvin M. (1967) Transportation planning for the metropolis, in Schnore, Leo F. and Fagan, Henry (1967) *Urban Research and Policy Planning.* Beverly Hills: Sage Publications, p.391.

12. Scott, *op. cit*, p.265.

13. *ibid.*, p.294.

14. Harvey, Kantor A. (1973) Charles Dyer Norton and the origins of the Regional Plan of New York. *Journal of the American Institute of Planners*, **XXXIX**, No.3, pp. 35–41.

15. Scott, *op. cit.*, p.294.

16. Epstein, Jason (1992) The tragical history of New York. *New York Review of Books*, April 9, pp.45–52; Fitch, Robert (1993) *The Assassination of New York.* London and New York: Verso, pp. 56–90; Heiman, Michael K. (1988) *The Quiet Evolution: Power, Planning, and Profits in New York State.* New York: Praeger, pp. 30–64.

17. Jameson W. Doig in correspondence with the author. Doig's book on the Port of New York Authority is forthcoming.

18. Faulkner, Harold U. (1931) *The Quest for Social Justice, 1898–1914.* New York: The Macmillan Co.; Goldman, Eric F. (1952) *Rendezvous with Destiny: A History of Modern American Reform.* New York: Alfred A. Knopf; Hofstadter, Richard (1955) *The Age of Reform.* New York: Vintage; Wiebe, Robert H. (1962) *Businessmen and Reform.* Cambridge: Harvard University Press.

19. Kolko, Gabriel (1963) *The Triumph of Conservatism.* New York: The Free Press; Weinstein, James (1968) *The Corporate Ideal in the Liberal State: 1900–1918.* Boston: Beacon Press.

20. See, for example, Dahl, Robert A. (1960) *Who Governs? Democracy and Power in an American City*. New Haven: Yale University Press; and Polsby, Nelson W. (1963) *Community Power and Political Theory*. New Haven: Yale University Press; for the pluralist view. For the classic statements of the elite theory, see Mills, C. Wright (1956) *The Power Elite*. New York: Oxford University Press; and Hunter, Floyd (1953) *Community Power Structure*. Chapel Hill: University of North Carolina Press. A good bibliography of the voluminous literature of pluralist-elitist controversy can be found in Hawley, Willis D. and Wirt, Frederich M. (1968) *The Search for Community Power*. Englewood Cliffs: Prentice-Hall, pp. 367–379.

21. Bachrach, Peter (1967) *The Theory of Democratic Elitism*. Boston: Little Brown; Bottomore, T.B. (1964) *Elites and Society*. Baltimore: Penguin Books.

22. Kolko, *op. cit.*, pp. 139–158.

23. For such a view see Dror, Yehezkel (1971) Planning in the United States - some reactions as a foreign observer. *Public Administration Review*, **XXXI**, May-June, p. 402.

24. Carr, Edward Hallett (1961) *What is History?* New York: Vintage Books, p. 164.

2

THE MAKING OF THE NEW YORK METROPOLITAN REGION

URBAN BEGINNINGS

At the beginning of the nineteenth century there was, of course, no New York urban region but simply a small, compact mercantile city of 60,000 people mostly clustered in a square mile at the southern tip of Manhattan Island. Beyond the edge of the city in the counties surrounding Manhattan lay smaller harborside cities and a vast agricultural hinterland of towns, villages and farms with a total population of nearly 300,000 people, most of whom had only indirect ties to the City. The daily life of New York City was for the most part self-contained and independent of that of the numerous towns and villages in the surrounding area. What intercourse occurred between settlements was mostly over water routes, land travel being slow and difficult.

Table 2.1. Population of Manhattan, New York City and the New York Metropolitan Region, 1800 to 1920

	Manhattan	*New York City*[a]	*New York Metropolitan Region*[b]
1800	60,515	79,216	291,186
1810	96,515	119,734	364,885
1820	123,706	152,056	424,654
1830	202,589	247,278	551,333
1840	312,710	391,114	756,860
1850	515,547	696,115	1,163,141
1860	813,669	1,174,779	1,835,176
1870	942,292	1,478,103	2,374,576
1880	1,164,673	1,911,698	3,026,367
1890	1,441,216	2,507,414	3,966,378
1900	1,850,093	3,437,202	5,384,734
1910	2,331,542	4,766,883	7,466,942
1920	2,284,103	5,620,048	8,979,055

(*a*) The area of the present five boroughs.
(*b*) As defined in 1921 by the Committee on the Regional Plan comprising all or parts of twenty-two counties in New York, New Jersey and Connecticut.

Source: Regional Plan of New York and Its Environs (1929) *Regional Committee Survey, Vol. II. Population, Land Values and Government.* New York: Regional Plan of New York and Its Environs p. 71.

The New York of 1800 was above all a pedestrian's city. From the center of settlement just south of City Hall one could walk to almost any point in less than ten minutes. The street patterns inherited from the Dutch and English were laid out, not by meandering cows, as legend has it, but in logical fashion parallel to the waterfronts which gave the town its livelihood. Adjacent to the waterfronts were located the various wholesale markets and exchanges – the seeds of the future mercantile and financial success of the City. The real center of civic and social life, however, was to be found not on the water, but in the heart of the settlement, along Broadway, the southern terminus of the Boston Post Road. Here were clustered the shops, the theater, the hospital, the important public buildings, and, above all, the churches, their tall spires dominating the skyline. Even while moving north over the subsequent years, the heart of the City would continue thereafter to occupy the center of the island, for here would always be the most accessible of places.

MID-CENTURY: THE RAILROAD ARRIVES

In the first half of the nineteenth century the eastern seaboard cities turned their attention to the development of the interior. First, turnpikes, then canals and railroads were pushed through mountain gaps to western farmlands. While historians generally agree that New York's pre-eminence among American cities pre-dates the opening in 1825 of the upstate Erie Canal, the canal undoubtedly accelerated the growth of New York.

Several canals were also built in what is now the metropolitan area: the Delaware and Raritan Canal and the Morris Canal in New Jersey, the Delaware and Hudson Canal in New York State, and the Farmington Canal in Connecticut. While several of these carried freight as late as the early twentieth century, their initial promise was never fulfilled, owing to the almost concurrent appearance of the faster, more versatile railroads.

For passenger travel, the steamboat was the fastest, cheapest, most popular mode in the period between 1830 and 1860. But the railroad, which made its first appearance in the New York area in the 1830s, overtook the steamboat's supremacy by the eve of the Civil War.

The rapid growth of New York City and of the twin harborside cities of Brooklyn and Williamsburgh immediately after 1850 was due to their advantageous situations for waterborne commerce, which favored the ice-free East River over the Hudson. But it was the railroad that opened up for the urban area around the port a true hinterland, pulling into its orbit outlying centers such as Hempstead, Paterson, and White Plains. Instantaneously, the overland travel time to points newly linked to New York by rail was cut to almost a fourth of what it had been. It became faster, by 1850, to travel by rail and ferry from lower Manhattan to Hempstead than by horse from lower Manhattan to the vicinity that was about to become Central Park.

This great breakthrough in urban accessibility was not lost on those city dwellers who sought and had the means to find residential retreats in the open countryside near the rail lines. In 1852, some twelve miles from Manhattan, Llewellyn Park was laid out by a New York businessman in Orange, New Jersey, near the tracks of the Morris and Essex Railroad. It was probably the first American suburb spawned by a railroad.[1]

The railroads for the most part chose routes through the open countryside, bypassing the old turnpike crossroad settlements. The objective of the new lines was to be the first to link New York to distant cities in Upstate New York and in the expanding Midwest. Little concern was given to serving the smaller towns surrounding New York City. Newark, Elizabeth, Paterson, New Brunswick, Bridgeport, Jamaica, and a few others were considered important enough to receive the benefits (and the problems) of rail lines slashed through their centers. Hempstead, bypassed by the main progenitor company of the present Long Island Railroad, was tied in by means of a branch spur. Princeton and several other smaller towns were similarly served. Thus, by the eve of the Civil War the future destinies of the outlying towns were sorted out between haves and have-nots.

River valleys usually provided the easiest routes for new rail lines. Crossing the rivers was another matter. The waters surrounding Manhattan Island, so essential to the early development of the city, became barriers in the early years of rail development. Routes from the south and the west terminated at the western shore of the Hudson, requiring elaborate ferrying arrangements for the trip to Manhattan. By 1852 only two routes, both from the north, had been able to penetrate the developed part of the city to terminals not far from City Hall. In 1851 the New York and Hudson Railroad began operations over a right-of-way that hugged the eastern shore of the Hudson, and in 1852 the New York and Harlem Railroad occupied rights-of-way along Fourth Avenue. Both lines offered local passenger service between lower Manhattan and points further north on the Island, as well as to more distant places outside the city.

By 1850 population growth had pushed Manhattan's urban development north to about 23rd Street along the lines of a rigid gridiron of streets laid out by a State Commission in 1811, establishing a physical pattern that was followed in cities across the country. The Commissioners' Plan, as it came to be known, intended that Broadway should be obliterated north of Canal Street. But the tenacious ancient spine of the city continued to attract development and was too well established to be denied.

Three important concentrations of commercial and institutional activities had emerged along Broadway by 1850, the most important of which was the cluster just north of the City Hall area. Here were located the city's most important shops, cultural activities, schools, city government, and the southernmost terminals of the two rail lines leading to the north. A smaller group of mercantile, customs and other port-related activities remained clustered near the Battery.

Long before 1850, the city had ceased to be traversable from one end to the other on foot. By mid-century a full hour was required to walk to the Battery from the fashionable new residential edge of the city north of 23rd Street. The city responded to its growth with improved north-south transportation. The world's first horse cars on tracks began operation in 1832, sharing the route of the New York and Harlem Railroad. A few years later steam replaced horse power on this route. But horse car operations continued to expand and by the middle of the century lines had been established on Third, Fourth, and Sixth Avenues.

Improved accessibility from the new residential areas to the older centers in south Manhattan did not preclude the emergence of an important new business cluster just north of Cooper Square. A center developed at this point because of its proximity to stations of the steam rail line. The prestige and traffic of Broadway also played a role. Moreover, Cooper Square was sufficiently far from the cluster around City Hall not to have to compete with that older center for the newly developed market area within ten minutes' walking time. There is also some evidence that land was held vacant in this area for some time after all around it had been developed for residence. These factors – centrality to an emerging market, accessibility to older established central points, and the availability of vacant land – were the indispensable conditions required for the appearance of new centers.

THE REGION EMERGES

The half-century between 1850 and 1900 saw an unprecedented rate of technological, economic, and social change in the large urban centers of the world. It is not necessary to describe the well-chronicled progression of revolutionary mechanical and electrical inventions, the rise of corporate capitalism, the waves of immigration from Europe. All worked to change the rural nation of 1850 into an urban nation by 1900, with New York its foremost metropolis. Historians have called the latter part of the nineteenth century the period of 'the rise of the city.'[2] But this was also the period when the broad outlines of the metropolitan region began to appear. Between 1850 and 1900 the population of the metropolitan area quadrupled – from 1.6 million to 6.2 million. Between 1860 and 1900, 120 square miles of land were developed for urban uses, more than three times the area that had been urbanized in 1850.

The physical growth of the Region in this period was shaped by three powerful transportation forces: the railroad, street railways, and, in New York City, elevated rapid transit. The railroad opened up large quantities of raw land for residential development in the vicinity of stations and engendered concentrations of commercial development at the major terminal points in outlying areas. The street car and elevated rapid transit had the same effect on a local scale.

The railroads greatly influenced the Region's response to population growth. Two phenomena were particularly evident: the center of urban gravity in the Region shifted westward towards New Jersey; and satellite towns grew along the lines radiating from the core cities around the harbor, establishing corridors of development still important today.

The shift of the Region's center of gravity westward was a response to the rail accessibility advantage with which cities west of the Hudson were endowed. Freight from Manhattan and Brooklyn destined for points west and south had to be floated across the harbor to rail heads on the Jersey side, a costly inconvenience that industry tended to avoid by locating west of the Hudson. Port activities in this period also were drawn westward from their East River orientation to the Hudson shores and the Jersey rail terminals. As a result of the growth in jobs and industries, the New Jersey portion of the Region grew three-and-a-half times in the period between 1860 and 1900, whereas the New York portion grew but two-and-a-half times. The second notable effect of the railroad on physical growth in this period was the emergence of satellite cities and towns along the rail lines radiating from the center of the Region (figure 2.1). Strings of urban settlements grew around the major stations of the principal rail lines, particularly those built along the Connecticut shore, the south and north shores of Long Island, south of the Watchung ridges, and along the main line to Philadelphia in New Jersey. While a few of these cities and towns developed as service and commercial centers for local populations who commuted to Manhattan and Newark, most were relatively independent places such as Bridgeport, Danbury, and Paterson, old towns expanded around industrial activities newly established or spun off from the increasingly congested core cities.

Most of the industrial growth in the core cities occupied sites along waterfronts in order to be near the many rail lines which had taken water or riverfront rights-of-way so as to serve extant industry originally oriented to shipping or water power. Water routes were also selected because they made for the easy grades railroads require through areas of rough terrain. In urban areas residences and institutions retreated from the amenities of the water's edge, yielding to economic pressure and repelled by the noise and nuisance of industry.

The impact of the railroad on regional development was duplicated on a smaller scale in and around the Region's cities and larger towns by the development of street car systems. By the turn of the century, every important outlying city and town had several trolley lines radiating from its downtown to its outskirts. A few lines reached far out into the open countryside to recreation areas of new residential subdivisions in which the traction compa-

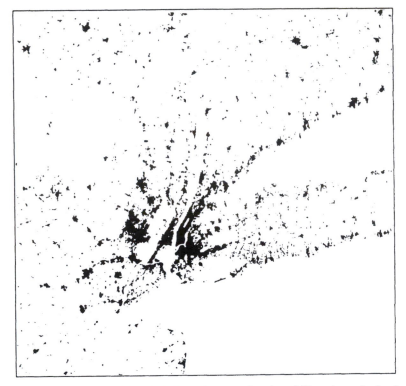

Figure 2.1. Urbanized land, 1900. (*Source*: Regional Plan Association)

nies frequently had an interest. The lines were built to serve existing development but inevitably they shaped new growth. New subdivisions grew up within walking distance of the major routes. On either side of the most important lines long strings of local shops were built to serve the new neighborhoods. Street car track was laid in the Region's cities at a high rate from 1860 to 1900. The peak rate occurred between 1890 and 1900, spurred by the replacement of horse power with steam and electric power in the late 1880s. Cable cars were first used in Manhattan in 1885 and electric trolleys in 1887.

While the railroad made possible the growth of industrial activities in decentralized cities, the street car opened up land in those cities for workers' housing. While little change in the Region's residential density had occurred between 1820 and 1860, so much new land was opened up by street car lines that by 1900 average residential density in the Region was two-thirds of what it had been in 1860, even while the Region's population was tripling over that period.

Just as workers were freed by the street car from the need to be within walking distance of their factory jobs, factories were freed from the need to

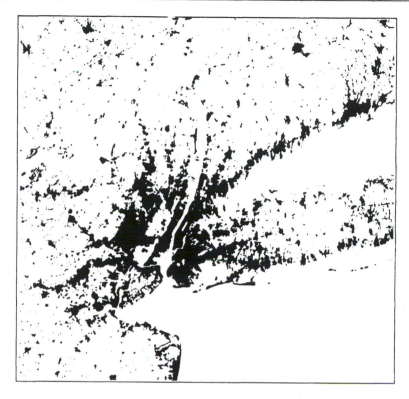

Figure 2.2.   Urbanized land, 1935. (*Source*: Regional Plan Association)

be near workers' housing. New plants could bypass older industrial areas in the immediate vicinity of the old downtown in favor of industrial districts somewhat removed from the center.

Though the street car spurred the spread of homes and factories, it had the opposite effect on retail and office activities. Most of the Region's important downtowns outside Manhattan grew rapidly in the street car era. The appearance of downtown department stores in the 1870s and 1880s in such places as Newark, Brooklyn, Elizabeth, Bridgeport, Newburgh, White Plains, and other such centers can be traced to the development of radial street car systems which opened up new markets and focused them on downtown. Local offices and banks followed a similar pattern.

In 1850 half of the Region's population lived on Manhattan Island. By 1900, less than a third of the population lived there. However, the consolidation of Greater New York, effected under the Charter of 1897, united Brooklyn, Queens, and Richmond with Manhattan and the Bronx and brought 3.4 million of the Region's 5.4 million people under a single New York City government, making New York the world's largest city at the time.[3] The consolidation set the stage for subsequent large-scale extension of the rapid transit systems begun in the late 1870s and 1880s. These elevated and subway line extensions helped preserve Manhattan's primacy as the Region's commercial and employment focus.

The political consolidation of greater New York was realized in part because of the growing interdependence of Manhattan and adjacent counties resulting from the rapid expansion of street car lines, most notably the Brooklyn Bridge cable car line, which began operation when the Bridge was completed in 1883.

By 1900, Manhattan had numerous street car lines, many of which were operating under electric power. But surface congestion due to pedestrians and horse-drawn vehicles (as well as from more than a few curious automobiles), together with the relatively slow speeds and frequent stops of surface lines gave rise to the construction of railways with separate elevated rights-of-way to serve the spreading city. The first experimental 'el' had opened on Greenwich Street in 1868, and in 1878 the Sixth Avenue line was opened from Rector Street to Central Park. By 1900 four elevated lines ran from lower Manhattan to the northern reaches of the Bronx, straddling for much of their length in Manhattan, Second, Third, Sixth and Ninth Avenues, from which they took their names.

Significantly, the elevated lines in Manhattan occupied routes at the edge of the principal shopping and entertainment district, which by 1900 lay between 14th and 23rd Streets and Third and Sixth Avenues. Broadway, still the business spine of the Island, did not receive the mixed blessing of an elevated structure, probably because of the resistance of local merchants. Rail transit below ground was more acceptable in the central business district. Digging for the City's first subway, now part of the East Side IRT line, began in 1900, and the line was opened in 1904 between City Hall and 145th Street.[4]

Spurred by transit, by the elimination of passenger rail service south of 42nd Street to the old Grand Central Depot in 1871, and by the northward movement of the center of population, several new centers of business and cultural activity had emerged by 1900 in Manhattan. By this time, the cluster just north of City Hall had ceased to exist and the cluster near Cooper Square was in its declining years. The effect of rapid transit had been to pull central activities northward and to separate them into distinct, specialized districts: a financial and office district in lower Manhattan, a major shopping cluster centered on Sixth Avenue and 23rd Street, a new theater and club district between 34th and 42nd Streets along Broadway just north of the retailing center, a loose group of educational, cultural, and medical institutions along the southwest edge of Central Park, and, far to the north on Morningside Heights, on the fringe of the built-up area of the Island, a cluster of educational institutions relocated from more crowded sites in the center of the City. Prominent among these was Columbia University, which had moved in 1897 from the 50th Street site on which Rockefeller Center now stands and to which the university had previously removed in 1857, having first occupied a campus in lower Manhattan at Church Street and Park Place. This leapfrogging to the edge of development was typical of many institutions whose space needs outweighed their need to be at the heart of the business area growing up around them.

An expanded transit system spurred the development of new centers uptown. But its major impact was felt where the various lines converged – in the original center in lower Manhattan. In the final five years of the nineteenth century the old commercial center changed radically as dozens of new office buildings were built to accommodate the growing corporate and financial activities of the country. The tall office building was made possible through the innovations of the steel frame and passenger elevator.[5] But that so many were able to cluster so as to function as a unified, compact financial district was due to the intense local accessibilities created by the rapid transit system. Only rapid transit could deliver thousands of workers to such a small area in the short interval of a rush hour.

In the first few decades of the twentieth century still more and taller office structures were required to serve the growing national office complex. The streets of lower Manhattan were transformed into a web of dark canyons where sunlight rarely penetrated. The subways, which had stimulated the concentration of office towers, became dangerously overcrowded. While most new office space was attracted to the cluster in lower Manhattan, an increasing share was located farther uptown on sites near Madison and Times Squares and in the vicinity of the new Pennsylvania and Grand Central Stations.

The northward growth of the city in the latter decades of the nineteenth century had forced the closing of surface rail terminals south of 42nd Street, except for ferry connections to the New Jersey railroads. The original Grand Central Depot, opened in 1871, was the sole rail terminus south of Central Park until 1910, when the vast Pennsylvania Station complex was constructed astride a great tunnel route under Manhattan and the Hudson and East Rivers, linking New Jersey to Long Island and later to New England via the Hell Gate Bridge, opened in 1917. In 1913, the old Depot was replaced by the present Grand Central Terminal, a spectacular example of the possibilities for integrating multiple-function buildings and transportation.

The rapid growth of Manhattan's central business district after 1900 was made possible by additional river crossings, which provided more access between the center and surrounding communities. While several rail and vehicular bridges spanned the relatively narrow Harlem River in 1900, the Hudson and East Rivers remained the domain of the ferry except for the Brooklyn Bridge, which stood in solitary grandeur for twenty years until the Williamsburgh Bridge was built in 1903. In the decade of intense building activity between 1903 and 1913, another eleven bridges and tunnels were completed. Of the twenty-five river crossings in use today, half were built in this decade. Of these, three were bridges and nine were tunnels. Eight of the facilities crossed the East River, three, the Hudson. All carried some form of rail transportation. Three were railroad facilities, five carried only public transit, and four carried both transit and private vehicles.

The new bridges and tunnels were both symbols and manifestations of the emergence of the metropolitan region as a unified, functional entity whose parts had come to share a common destiny transcending city, county, and even state boundaries.

THE 1920s: A TURNING POINT

The 1920s marked a turning point in the urban development of the New York Region. Between 1915 and 1920 New York City built 250 miles of rapid transit track, but between 1920 and 1925 almost no new track was laid. Construction of housing boomed, however. Transit had opened up vast areas of land for residences in the Bronx, Brooklyn, and Queens.

Between 1920 and 1930 the Region grew by about 2.6 million people — more than in any other decade before or after. One point three million, about half of the Region's total increase, occurred in New York City, also setting a record rate there. Between 1920 and 1930 the Bronx, Brooklyn, and Queens each gained about a half million people, while Manhattan, astonishingly, was losing a like number, a loss of about 18 per cent in ten years.[6] Residential density in Manhattan decreased rapidly after 1920, having reached a peak around 1910. This vast turnover and growth was possible only because transit improvements had opened up large areas in the outer boroughs.

The period between the end of World War I and 1920 was a watershed in other ways. All-time peak use of public rail and transit facilities occurred in this period: peak trolley ridership occurred in the Region around 1918; trolley systems reached their most extensive point in number of track miles in New York City in 1920; peak railroad mileage in the three states of the Region was also reached in 1920; a peak in rapid transit ridership occurred in 1929, to be equaled afterwards only in 1947, and then because of temporary postwar shortages of automobiles and housing.

The 1920s also saw Manhattan's share of the Region's total retail sales reach a zenith. Manhattan was already beginning to lose ground to other parts of the Region as stores followed the spread of homes.

The significance of peaks is not that they are high points, but rather that they are the beginnings of decline. In the case of public rail, transit, and trolley, the peaks of the early 1920s reflected a new competitive force at work: the internal combustion engine. By 1920 the Region had some 540,000 motor vehicles registered. The automobile, truck, and bus had, of course, been in use for twenty years prior to 1920, but in such small numbers and operating at such slow speeds as to have little impact on physical development. By 1920, however, the effects of the motor vehicle began to appear. On weekdays, downtown business streets became extremely congested with autos, trucks, horse-drawn vehicles, and trolleys. On weekends, radial roads leading to the countryside became jammed for miles with the Model A s and Model T s of a growing urban middle class. In 1900, urban development along the railroads resembled beads spaced along a string. By 1920, the spaces between the beads filled in, leaving wedges of undeveloped land between the rail corridors. In contrast to the millions living in the cities, those living in the corridors were never very far from the countryside (figure 2.2).

Some of this corridor development was also influenced by the last stages of trolley line construction between 1900 and 1920, which emphasized long-distance routes linking towns as a supplement to the local radial systems developed in the 1880s and 1890s. Newark and Hackensack, for example, were linked by a trolley line built shortly after 1900. Following this policy, trolley routes were built in many places parallel to rail lines, in some instances providing a local service to complement longer-haul rail service. In other situations inter-city trolleys simply competed with the railroads for passengers. In either case, the trolley parallel to the railroad reinforced the established corridor pattern.

The automobile also played an important role in shaping the outlying urban corridors in this period. Numbered state highway systems were adopted just after World War I, in response to the growing numbers of motor vehicles and a need to articulate and rationalize what had been a fairly casual system of roads. The routes selected for upgrading were usually those that paralleled the main rail lines, linking the centers of the old rail-oriented corridor towns on which the new development depended for local shopping and services. This had the effect of adding to the pressures that the trolley lines created for development of the open land along the old radial rail corridors.

In the 1920s, Manhattan, the heart of the Region, experienced great change and development. While the lower Manhattan office complex did grow substantially between 1901 and 1925, it decreased in its share of Manhattan's corporate executive offices from 64.6 per cent to 39.4 per cent. In the same period, the area between 34th Street and 59th Street was increasing from 2.6 per cent to 29.9 per cent. By 1920 the Midtown office district had become firmly established.

The general movement of population and jobs northward in pursuit of space and better transit had also continued to pull the major retailing center uptown. By 1920, Fifth Avenue north of 34th Street had emerged as the prime retailing street of the country. The theater district had also completed its move to its present location just north of Times Square. Though a distinct area, the theater district continued to share a common vicinity with the major shopping district, explained partly by a shared need for similar situations of high accessibility and partly by the natural linkage that existed between entertainment and shopping activities.

Just south of Times Square on Seventh Avenue a new intensive industrial district for the manufacture of clothing was emerging by 1920, replacing part of the notorious old entertainment district known as the 'Tenderloin'. This concentration of factories, offices, and showrooms for a single industry came about when department stores on Fifth Avenue successfully opposed the growth of the garment industry into their neighborhood. The stores, worried that crowds of garment workers would congest sidewalks and discourage customers, brought pressure to bear on the manufacturers in the form of the nation's first zoning ordinance in 1916. Garment industry leaders responded by organizing the present intensely developed center.

By 1920 the development problems facing the New York area seemed clear: how to reduce subway crowding; how to provide for the intolerable congestion due to growing numbers of trucks and cars; how to rationalize the railroad service of the port, whose chaos had become all too apparent in the intensified activity of World War I; how to prevent the intrusion of undesirable uses into established residential and commercial areas; how to control future suburban developments so that the mistakes of the city would not be repeated; and how to provide for the airplane, which was undoubtedly going to play an important role in the future. There were other problems as well: the wretched housing conditions of the millions of immigrant poor, conditions at which some reformers had pointed an accusatory finger as the source of crime, disease, disorder, and Bolshevism.

Business and philanthropic reformers were convinced that these problems could not be resolved by the existing city machine governments, which they regarded as corrupt, or, at best, too short-range in their orientation to carry out long range policy. Nor could their problems be left to the *laissez-faire* marketplace to solve, as had been done in the past. An alternative approach was required, one which would recognize the inter-relationships among the problems and deal with them comprehensively in a regional context. Above all, better planning seemed essential. For the most part New York and the surrounding area had developed incrementally without conscious public planning. There were important exceptions, however, and out of these a planning tradition had begun to develop.

NOTES

1. Tunnard, Christopher (1953) *The City of Man*. New York: Charles Scribner's Sons, pp. 183–186

2. Schlesinger, Arthur M. (1933) *The Rise of the City 1878–98*. New York: The Macmillian Co.

3. The three eastern towns of Queens County, which in 1897 extended to the present

Suffolk County western boundary, voted not to join New York but instead formed a new county: Nassau. Parts of the Bronx had earlier been annexed by New York from what was then Westchester County in 1832 and 1875. The Bronx did not become a separate county until 1913.

4. An experimental pneumatic tube subway was built by Alfred Ely Beach in 1870 beneath a few blocks of lower Manhattan, but was operated in a limited way for only four years.

5. New York was not as innnovative in building technology as in transportation, lagging at least five years behind Chicago in the introduction of steel-framed building. The first steel building in New York was the eleven-story Tower Building erected at 50 Broadway in 1888–1889, four years after the erection of Chicago's pioneering Home Insurance Building, designed by William Le Baron Jenney, See: Condit, Carl, W. (1964) *The Chicago School of Architecture*. Chicago: University of Chicago Press, pp. 80–81.

6. Manhattan's population loss between 1920 and 1930 has never been equaled, even in the most recent post-war decades of rapid suburbanization.

3

THE EMERGENCE OF
A PLANNING TRADITION

THE LEGACY OF FREDERICK LAW OLMSTED

Systematic planning played little part in the surge of the New York region to national primacy in the last quarter of the nineteenth century. Development had occurred mostly through the accretive results of market forces or political deals. Planning for the use of land was limited mostly to the layout of streets, usually in mechanical imitation of the gridiron introduced in the 1811 Commissioners' Plan. Social planning was an even more remote concept. The Social Darwinism of Herbert Spencer and Yale's William Graham Sumner, to which the nineteenth-century business elite of New York largely subscribed, had little place for collective public action. State intervention could only disrupt the natural processes of evolution by which virtuous men demonstrated their superiority through economic achievement. Drawing on the ideas of Spencer, Sumner and his followers waged a constant struggle from the 1870s through the early 1890s against reformism, protectionism, socialism, and government interventionism. Gradualism and voluntarism were held to be the only ethical means for achieving social change.[1]

The dominant philosophy of mercantile *laissez-faire* did not go entirely unchallenged, however. New York as early as 1842 had demonstrated a capacity for collectively solving large-scale civic problems when the extraordinary Croton waterworks system was completed. But it was the landscape architect, Frederick Law Olmsted, who with a small band of reformers first offered the city a comprehensive and humane vision of what it could become. It was with Olmsted's work that the reform planning tradition in New York can be said to have begun. Olmsted's greatest achievements were his parks, but his vision extended far beyond the simple provision of open space.

Central Park had been acquired in 1856, Prospect Park between 1864 and 1869, and Riverside Park in 1872. Subsequently, the Central Park Commission and its successor, the Department of Public Parks, was designated to plan the northern part of Manhattan and the western part of the Bronx.[2] Olmsted, who became chief landscape architect of the Department of Parks in 1869, designed street patterns adjusted to the uneven terrain of the area and proposed low-density neighborhoods in which shops, schools, public gardens, and transit facilities would be integrated. But Olmsted's vision was unfortunately incompatible with the Wickham administration's desire to develop the area quickly at conventional densities and patterns. Olmsted was fired in 1877, his neighborhood concept discarded.[3] Olmsted had somewhat more success with his grand plan to link the major parks and shore areas of Manhattan and Brooklyn by means of a system of parkways. First proposed in 1868, the plan contained a variety of proposals, many of which would be repeated in subsequent plans and ultimately carried to completion. The central idea of the plan was that large parks should be established throughout the city and should be inter-connected by parkways to form a natural framework for the growth that was to follow. Following this design principle, Olmsted proposed a great loop parkway extending from the Brooklyn side of the Narrows, with an extension to Prospect Park, connected through Queens to a proposed bridge over the East River at Ravenswood, thence through the east side of Manhattan along a park strip at 59th Street to the southern edge of Central Park and on across the island to Riverside Park on the Hudson side. The parkways were to serve as green spines through the otherwise undifferentiated, interminable gridiron which was spreading through the city. While only fragments were carried out, Olmsted's 1868 scheme was the first definitive step toward regional environmental planning in the New York area.[4]

Olmsted's regional park and parkway proposals were looked on favorably by Andrew Haswell Green, a businessman reformer and the dominant figure on the Central Park Commission. A sympathetic state legislature sought to prevent Tammany Democrats from exploiting the expansion and improvement of the city, and, had Green remained in control, Olmsted's proposals might have received constructive attention. But Green was stripped of his power when Tammany took control of City Hall in 1866 with the election of A. Oakley Hall as mayor. In 1869 a new city charter was pushed through by the Tammany forces, which radically reorganized municipal administration, centralized responsibility, and granted the city vastly increased powers to implement public works, including unlimited borrowing powers. William M. Tweed, the boss of Tammany, arranged to be appointed superintendent of public works by his puppet, Mayor Hall.[5]

As Seymour Mandelbaum has emphasized, Tweed was a master communicator. He was responsive to the needs of both business and the slum dweller, and his group moved quickly to develop and exploit the expanding city.[6] Thus it was during the Tweed era, in 1869, that the decision was made to go ahead with John A. Roebling's proposals to link Brooklyn and New York by means of a daring suspension bridge.

Tweed formulated impressive plans to rebuild the chaotic docks, develop rapid transit lines, and improve water and sewer systems, all of which the city desperately required. The Tweed machine offered an effective alternative structure to satisfy the unfulfilled needs of diverse groups.[7]

Tweed's interest in public works was, of course, hardly altruistic. He skimmed more than $40,000,000 from bloated city contracts, for which he ultimately paid in a prison cell. But he was keenly aware of his constituents' priorities and these did not include those of Olmsted's parks and parkways reform enthusiasts. Funds for Olmsted's schemes were diverted to developing and improving smaller urban parks closer to congested neighborhoods where the votes were to be had.[8] Olmsted's notion of *rus in urbe,* the country in the city, was not compatible with Tammany's approach to the distribution of public bounty.

Had Tweed not become greedy, he might have served the city and himself not altogether badly. But the heavy public indebtedness he had incurred as he pursued his criminal scheme of contractor kickbacks outraged public sensibility. By late 1871, his illicit activities exposed, Tweed was out of power, and in the election of 1872, the economy-minded reform administration of William G. Havenmeyer took over City Hall.

When Andrew Green returned to public office as comptroller in Havemeyer's administration, prospects for implementing Olmsted's plans appeared brighter. But the Tweed revelations had drastically changed business attitudes towards city development. Havemeyer, an aging businessman who had previously been mayor in the Jacksonian era, was opposed on principle to municipal spending for capital improvements. The city's financial crisis created by Tweed simply reinforced Havemeyer's inclinations. Green, who had always favored gradual, planned development, concurred with Havemeyer's demand for fiscal austerity and shelved the Tweed proposals for dock, transit, and street improvements. Despite his sympathetic interest in civic improvement and adornment, Green could not support Olmsted's regional plan for parks and parkways in a period of austerity. These would have to be postponed for nearly thirty years, pending the successful outcome in 1897 of Green's lifelong battle to achieve the consolidation of Greater New York, and the election of the reform administration of Seth Low.[9] Tweed's 1870 charter, giving the city the power to undertake vast public projects, was replaced by the legislature in 1873 with a compromise charter under which development power was decentralized among a variety of bipartisan boards. This system of confused checks and balances effectively stymied the efforts of both speculative private developers who wanted rapid growth and those elements of the reform movement who wanted fiscally prudent, controlled development.[10]

The Yankee virtue of fiscal economy failed to meet the needs of a rapidly industrializing city. The economy-minded reformers, who vehemently opposed the building of the Brooklyn Bridge and the annexation of the Bronx, could offer no alternative positive program for development which either recognized the growing interdependence of the separate parts of the region or accommodated the demands of merchants, manufacturers, and speculators. The consequence was a return to power of the Tammany machine, which had at least demonstrated its ability to do the latter. Under Tammany leadership the Brooklyn Bridge was finally completed in 1883, and elevated rapid transit constructed over the length of Manhattan Island and northward into the annexed portion of the Bronx. The park movement gained new momentum, and Van Cortlandt, Pelham Bay, and Bronx Parks were acquired in the 1880s. Tammany's dominance of city affairs lasted until the end of the century when it was once again toppled by revelations of a committee of the State Legislature created by Republicans to investigate the corruption of another Tammany Boss, Richard Croker. With the election of Seth Low the reform cycle in New York had crested again, this time as part of the Progressive movement which was sweeping the nation. This cycle was to produce a number of planning activities of significance to the development of the New York Region.[11]

THE NEW YORK CITY IMPROVEMENT COMMISSION

In December 1903 the Board of Aldermen and reform Mayor Seth Low approved the creation of a New York City Improvement Commission, whose mandate was to prepare a comprehensive plan for the development of the newly consolidated city. Francis K. Pendleton was appointed chairman of the group, which was comprised of prominent businessmen, architects, and artists, including sculptor Daniel Chester French and Whitney Warren, the architect. An advisory committee was also designated, consisting of three municipal engineers, Nelson P. Lewis, John A. Bensel, and O. F. Nichols, and a landscape architect, Samuel Parsons, Jr. Lewis, who was secretary to the commission, was to play a leading role in later regional planning efforts. He had been Chief of the Bureau of Local Improvements for the City of Brooklyn, a position to which Alfred T. White, housing philanthropist and Commissioner of City Works, had appointed him in 1894. In 1898, Lewis became Chief of the Brooklyn Bureau of Highways. Mayor Low, noticing Lewis' achievements in Brooklyn, appointed him as the first Chief Engineer of the Board of Estimate and Apportionment, a post he held until 1920.[12]

The Commission, given an impossible mandate to return with a completed comprehensive plan within a year, presented instead a preliminary report in 1905, which emphasized urban aesthetics and city beautification.[13] A final report, presented in 1907 as a general plan for the City, addressed the more fundamental planning questions of parks, highways, and the location of city buildings (figure 3.1)[14]. The basic feature of the plan was an elaboration of Olmsted's parkway system linking the City's largest parks:

> The salient feature of the general plan as it affects the City as a whole is to afford adequate, proper and suitable avenues of connection between the different parts of each borough, as well as between the different boroughs themselves and the outlying districts . . . [and to] connect as far as possible the parks of the different

Figure 3.1. New York City Improvement Commission (McClellan) Plan, 1907. (*Source*: New York City Improvement Commission, *Report to the Mayor*, 1907)

boroughs with each other by suitable parkways so as to make them all parts of one harmonious whole.[15]

The Commission obviously looked on the integrated parkway system as an expression of the unity of the consolidated city.

The proposed parkway system contained much of what was first proposed by Olmsted in 1868. This was not surprising, since Olmsted Brothers, successors to the firm of the elder Olmsted, were consultants to the McClellan Commission. The bridge proposed by the elder Olmsted over the East River at Ravenswood to link Central and Prospect Parks was already under construction and would be opened to vehicles in 1909 as the 'Queensborough Bridge'. Shore Road in Brooklyn, another part of the loop, had also been completed. The Commissioner's plan recommended that the missing pieces of Olmsted's plan be completed: the connection from the East River to Central Park and across to Riverside Park; a link from a grand bridge plaza in Queens, skirting Williamsburgh on the east and connecting to both the Shore Road and Prospect Park over existing streets, which were proposed to be embellished as parkways.

The Commissioners' scheme extended Olmsted's basic ideas to other parts of the city. Parks were to be acquired along the waterways and wetlands of Queens. The three large islands in the East River, Wards, Blackwell's, and Randall's, would also become parks, and a bridge connecting Queens and the Bronx was to complete the links between parks in the four boroughs east of the Hudson. Parks were proposed for Flushing Meadows, Rockway, and Bayside, all to be linked by a great shore loop encircling the greater city near its boundaries. While Nelson Lewis could complain in 1914 that the Commissioner's plans had largely been ignored, a similar statement could not be made by 1950, for this was the blueprint from which Robert Moses drew many of his proposals for park and parkway projects in New York City.

While the Commission plan's central notion was the park and parkway system, other significant proposals were made, some of which were quietly executed. Among these were plans for widening Fifth Avenue and other streets in Manhattan and the disruptive cutting through of Sixth Avenue in Greenwich Village to facilitate traffic movement to lower Manhattan. Proposals were also made to control the architectural features of new piers, some of which were suggested for recreational use. The Commissioners opposed a projected elevated street along the Hudson waterfront – to no avail, as it developed – and called for acquisition of waterfronts not needed for commercial purposes to be developed as parks. In Brooklyn a proposal was made for a bridge plaza where the Williamsburgh and Brooklyn Bridge approaches intersected, to be the future site of a grand civic complex for that borough.

The Commissioners had little to say about the most crucial planning issue of the period: the development of additional rapid transit facilities. The problem was cursorily noted, however, in the context of a rivalry with New Jersey:

> The question of increased transit facilities between Manhattan and Brooklyn should receive the closest attention by the City authorities. It is a matter of prime importance both to the convenience of residents of the borough and in the interest of the City at large, which requires that the population should be kept in the State of New York and nothing done which might encourage a drifting across the North River.[16]

The plan, following the then current ideas of the City Beautiful Movement, called for the clustering of the larger public buildings to form civic centers in the various boroughs. The same concept at a smaller scale was proposed for neighborhoods where schools, libraries, and police stations were to be concentrated at a single focal point on a square, park, or important highway. This was an early progenitor of the neighborhood idea to be advanced later by Clarence Perry and others.

The plan also rather boldly called for the elimination of all railroad crossings at grade and the use of excess condemnation to capture for the public increases in land values resulting from public developments.

Controls for advertising signs were also suggested, the report noting that signs became large and extravagant when one sign competed with another nearby. Control, it was asserted, would simply change the rules of the game to no one's disadvantage and to the public's ultimate benefit.

The Report of 1907 was an extraordinarily influential document in the development of the city. A curious blend of Olmsted's regional vision and City Beautiful formalism, it was both broad in scope and sufficiently precise in its proposals to provide a foundation for subsequent planning and development.

THE BROOKLYN CITY PLAN

Seven years after the New York City Improvement Commission report, a private group of businessmen commissioned a new plan for the Borough of Brooklyn. The plan was prepared by Edward H. Bennett, a Chicago architect, for the Brooklyn Committee on the City Plan and published in a special supplement of the *Brooklyn Daily Eagle* of January 18, 1914. The Plan had its origins in a series of sermons on 'Great Cities' delivered in October of 1911 at historic Plymouth Church, where Henry Ward Beecher had preached abolition a generation earlier. The Reverend Dr. N. D. Hillis, describing his observations of European planning, ventured the opinion that 'only apoplexy and Greenwood Cemetery would cure the short-sightedness of some of our public officials.' In his last sermon of the series Dr. Hillis outlined his ideas for 'A More Beautiful Brooklyn'. He proposed the improvement of principal streets and drives and emphasized transportation links from Brooklyn to eastern Long Island which, he anticipated, would be 'the entrance to the country', with the construction of a great new port there.

At the suggestion of Hillis, Daniel Burnham, the principal author and architect of the Plan of Chicago, was invited to come to Brooklyn to inspire and advise the Brooklyn City Plan movement. A citizens' committee was assembled and officially appointed by the Brooklyn Borough President to meet Burnham on his arrival in the city on December 16, 1911.

The aged Burnham toured Brooklyn by automobile, then stirred his Hamilton Club audience with admonitions and cautions:

> You propose to take up the making of a plan for this city. Now there are two ways of going about it. The one which is the easiest comes to very little. This is to plan for those things you are now ready to pay for, to go no further than your pocket-book in its present state will allow you to go. It is not worth your while individually to plan for Brooklyn if you are going to limit yourselves in this way.
>
> The other way of planning is to look upon the city as a place of residence and business for those who will come after you. This is the unselfish side, the side of those who are willing to sacrifice for the future.

Burnham offered stirring visions of a Brooklyn embracing all of Long Island and a sense that those present were part of a world-wide planning movement:

> The City Planning Movement means that men have arrived at a certain level of intelligence, and having arrived there they inevitably desire to have good air. The first sign in that direction is the feeling that they must have their town in good order. Their streets, their transportation, their sewer and water facilities must be in good order.
>
> Now shall all these elements be allowed to go on and develop in their own way? No, they are to work together and be welded into a logical whole. That's what town planning means.
>
> If you do the work as you should do it, it must take a long time. Moreover, it is going to take the heart and brains of your best men . . . working together without selfish motives.
>
> In the matter of your plan here you cannot go too far. My own opinion is that when you get down to it you are likely to take in the entire Long Island . . . If there is any feasible way of uniting it to the city, a way that is beneficial to both, that ought to be recorded in your diagram.

Burnham proposed that the Brooklynites begin at their bridge approaches, create a large civic center and include in their scope all Long Island to Montauk Point.

With the citizens' committee as a nucleus, the Brooklyn Committee on City Plan was formed of 250 prominent men in the borough. Burnham declined the position of architect and adviser which the committee had proffered, and at his suggestion his associate Edward H. Bennett was chosen for the position. In his plan for Brooklyn, completed in 1914, Bennett endorsed the Burnham proposals for a civic center and for the development of the approaches to the East River Bridges (figure 3.2).

Bennett's Plan, which envisioned an ultimate Brooklyn population of 5,000,000, contained in addition to Burnham's suggestions a number of other

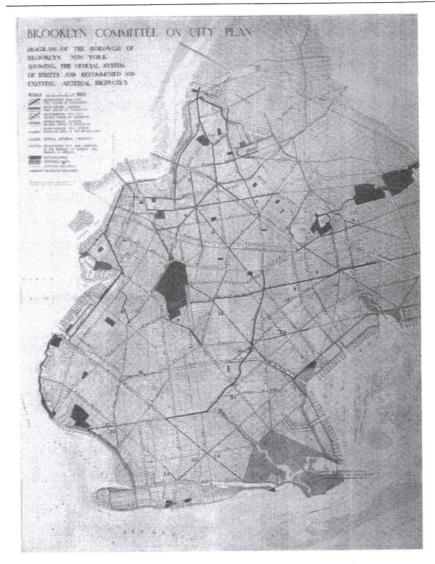

Figure 3.2. Brooklyn Committee on City Plan: Plan for streets and highways, Edward H. Bennett, 1914. (*Source:* City Plan Number, *Brooklyn Daily Eagle*, January 18, 1914)

proposals. Kings Highway, an old colonial road which had survived the official-map gridiron, was proposed to be widened into a partial circumferential. Several dozen other diagonal arteries were also to be cut, Chicago Plan-style, through existing areas to facilitate movement through Brooklyn's interminable gridiron. An enormous waterfront park was proposed for the South Brooklyn site which later became Floyd Bennett Field. An extraordinary scheme for converting Jamaica Bay into a great harbor and port com-

Figure 3.3. Brooklyn Committee on City Plan: Plan for business and highways, Edward H. Bennett, 1914. (*Source:* City Plan Number, *Brooklyn Daily Eagle*, January 18, 1914)

plex, first espoused by the New York City Commission of Docks and Ferries, was incorporated by Bennett into his plan, though slightly reduced from the original proposal.

Vast areas 'in which industrial development may be expected' were designated in locations lining the waterfront from Newton Creek to the Narrows and adjacent to the circumferential rail line linking the new Hell Gate Bridge to the lighterage pier at 65th Street (figure 3.3). This allowed for more area than could ever be needed by industry, a gesture perhaps, to the industrialists on the Committee.

Bennett gave considerable attention to the need for local parks and playgrounds, laying out in detail close to a hundred sites.

Of great interest in the Bennett Plan is his proposal, following Burnham's suggestion, for three great boulevards 'running the entire length of Long Island along each shore and through the center, the latter labeled "Grand Central Boulevard"'. This, along with several other Bennett proposals, would continue to appear in planning proposals and would eventually be realized fifteen years later by Robert Moses in modified form as the Long Island parkway system.

THE COMPREHENSIVE PLAN OF NEWARK

On the other side of New York Port, the City of Newark was at the same time preparing a plan for its future development. In 1915 Newark's City Plan Commission published its detailed comprehensive plan prepared by George B. Ford, with Ernest P. Goodrich and Harland Bartholomew as associates. The plan was largely the work of Bartholomew, a young engineer who was later to become a nationally prominent planning consultant.[17] The Newark Plan, dealing with a considerably smaller area, was far more detailed than the Brooklyn scheme and included sections on metropolitan planning as well as a far-sighted financial program. The plan emphasized solutions to the problem of downtown traffic congestion, proposing that new streets be cut through or old ones be widened. Bartholomew and his staff de-emphasized the aesthetic axial boulevard approach and played down the importance of a civic center, although the report did argue for the clustering of public buildings.

Improved rail terminals were suggested and a large industrial-residential community was proposed for the flats south of the city adjacent to a projected harbor development (which eventually was realized as the massive Port of Newark terminal facility). A metropolitan network of improved arterials was also proposed for the area around the City of Newark. These proposals were to have an important impact on subsequent planning and development for the Newark area.

THE JAMAICA BAY PORT SCHEME

In 1914, the Committee on Industrial Advancement of the Brooklyn League, a group of businessmen, some of whom were associated with the Bennett Plan. published a remarkable little book by Harvey Chase Brearly called *The Problem of Greater New York and Its Solution*. The 'problem' cited was the need for more port facilities, less constricted than the old piers surrounding

Manhattan, and thought to be essential to cope with greatly increased port commerce anticipated as a consequence of the opening of the Panama Canal. Concern was also voiced that Newark's scheme for a large harbor on the Jersey Meadows would attract many of the city's industrial firms. The solution proposed was the creation of an enormous 'auxiliary harbor' in Jamaica Bay, an idea which Bennett had made part of his Brooklyn Plan. In support of his arguments for this vast scheme, Brearly invoked the image of population congestion, quoting Lawrence Veiller's 1905 report to the Tenement House Committee that at their extreme, New York's densities approached those of Calcutta.[18] By decentralizing port facilities and residences, port and industry workers could live at more humane densities. But it was the problem of commercial congestion and local boosterism that primarily motivated the Brooklyn businessmen.

While nothing was to come of the Jamaica Bay scheme except some preliminary channel dredging, the concept eventually spurred the creation in 1921 of a Port of New York Authority, whose task would be to rationalize and integrate the various improvement schemes proposed for New York Harbor.

THE BIRTH OF ZONING, 1911–1916

Shortly after the turn of the century, two forces were at work that would radically alter the character of New York City: one was the presence of two million foreign-born immigrants, many from Eastern and Southern Europe, slowly working their way into the life and the economy of the city; the second was the rapid expansion of the city subway system, whose tentacles now radiated outward from lower Manhattan to the four western boroughs. The activities of the immigrants and the construction of the subways produced rapid changes in the physical pattern of Manhattan, resulting in two severe conflicts between the owners and users of land. Firstly there was the inexorable movement of the city's high-class department stores northward up Fifth Avenue, pulled by the shift of their customers toward Central Park and pushed by the growing stores. The store owners were appalled to discover that the sidewalks on which their display windows and entrances faced had become increasingly jammed with immigrant, lower-class, foreign-speaking workers. Fearing the loss of their trade, they founded the Fifth Avenue Association to fight the garment loft situation.

Concurrently, another problem was developing further south in the financial district in Manhattan. The new subways had made lower Manhattan a locale of extraordinary accessibility, with some twenty subway stations located within a half square mile area. This concentration had produced in turn a new cycle of skyscraper construction which had overwhelmed the capacity of sub-surface stations, had severely congested the sidewalks, and had blocked light and air from older lower buildings.

By 1912 the skyscraper and loft problems had opened a new wedge for the planning reform forces to mount a drive to increase the City's power to control its own development – and to carry out their plans, which up to this time had gone largely unrealized. This drive would eventually lead to the enactment of the nation's first comprehensive zoning law.[19]

The fusion of reformers and regular Republicans that had elected Seth Low in 1901 but had collapsed in 1903 was revived in 1909. Though William J. Gaynor, the Democratic candidate, won the mayoralty in that year, two reformers won important lower offices. George McAneny, a lawyer and journalist active in civil service reform and in subway planning, won the borough presidency of Manhattan. John Purroy Mitchel, who would later become Mayor, was elected president of the Board of Aldermen.

McAneny had developed a keen knowledge of the city's physical development problems as President of the City Club, a watchdog reform group, and chairman of its Committee on City Planning. His interest in subway planning had brought him into close contact and friendship with several influential men who shared his concerns for the future development of the city. Edward Murray Bassett, lawyer, former Independent Democratic congressman from Brooklyn, and member of the State Public Service Commission, worked closely with McAneny in formulating plans for the subway system.[20]

Two other men worked with McAneny and Bassett. Lawson Purdy, like Bassett a lawyer, had long been interested in urban tax reform, an interest developed from his tenure as secretary of the New York Tax Reform Association. Later, Purdy became City Assessor and president of the city's Tax Commission and, in 1913, president of the National Municipal League. Nelson P. Lewis, the chief engineer of the Board of Estimate, had also long been concerned with the city's physical development and worked closely with McAneny and Bassett on plans for the city.[21]

McAneny and Bassett had become deeply concerned that the construction of subways tended to aggravate rather than solve the problems of residential crowding and of sidewalk congestion in the business areas. Purdy was concerned that the value of business real estate would be reduced by the overcrowding of skyscrapers in a small area. Lewis saw the development problem largely in terms of providing more through arterials to cope with growing vehicular traffic and preserving future thoroughfare rights-of-way in the new residential areas spawned by the subways. All agreed that to plan for transportation was not enough to guide the total development of the city. A mechanism was needed to control the intensity and nature of the use of land.

Bassett, on a trip to Germany in 1908, was impressed with the extent to which Werner Hegemann and other German town planners had devised and carried out improvements in public buildings, parks, and streets. Bassett was particularly taken with the German method of reducing residential densities through districting.[22]

Through 1911 and 1912, the Fifth Avenue Association pressed Borough President McAneny for a solution to the loft problem. McAneny's response was to appoint a quasi-official Fifth Avenue Commission consisting of Nelson P. Lewis and six members of the Fifth Avenue Association. The Commission delivered a report calling for height limitations which would in effect preclude loft construction but not retail stores. McAneny duly submitted the report to the Board of Estimate, but the Board, concerned with the questionable legality of the proposal, took no action on it.[23]

McAneny, seeing the Fifth Avenue Association problem as part of the larger dilemma of controlling land development, persuaded the Board of Estimate, in February of 1913, to appoint an unpaid Advisory Committee on City Planning to take up the general question of building regulation along the lines of the districting concept that Bassett had thought so effective in German cities. Appointed to the Committee, which subsequently became the Advisory Commission on the Height and Arrangement of Buildings, were realtors, architects, builders, and businessmen, and, representing the City, Lawson Purdy and Nelson P. Lewis. Edward Bassett was selected as chairman, and Purdy, vice-chairman.[24] The Committee assembled a small staff to gather information, including George B. Ford, an architect, Robert Whitten, a sociologist, and attorney Frank Backus Williams. Williams was dispatched to Europe to gather further information on precedents there.[25]

On December 5, 1913, the commission submitted its draft report, largely the work of Bassett, to McAneny, who had, a month before, been elected president of the Board of Alderman in a hard-fought Fusion victory, in which John Purroy Mitchel had won the mayoralty. The Commission's report emphasized the regulation of high buildings and districting of uses, or 'zoning', as it had come to be called. The loft problem on Fifth Avenue was played down as being only a special case of a larger problem. The report called for a city charter amendment by the State Legislature to permit building and use regulation under the police power. On February 21, 1914, the bill was passed in both houses of the legislature with bi-partisan support and was signed into law on April 21, 1914.[26] The first round had been won.

With the election victory of the Fusionists in 1913 the Board of Estimate was comprised of reformers sympathetic to proposals to improve the city's physical development. Though zoning enabling legislation was now on the books, it remained for Bassett and McAneny to gain support for a city-wide zoning ordinance. To achieve this end, McAneny moved a resolution through the Board of Estimate creating a 'Commission on Building Districts and Restrictions'. The membership of this second zoning commission was nearly identical to that of the original commission, with Bassett and Purdy again chairman and vice-chairman. The commission set to work on two tasks: gathering technical data on land use in the city and generating support for its activities. After two years of work a tentative plan was completed which divided the city into four types of districts: residential, business, unrestricted, and undetermined. Specific height limitations were laid down for the first two categories. On the basis of this tentative proposal, hearings were held throughout the city. Bassett and his staff spoke at countless business and neighborhood meetings on behalf of the measure. The Fifth Avenue Association added its support to the proposal with full-page ads in the local newspapers urging zoning as a way to 'Save New York'. After considerable debate and juggling of boundaries to accommodate local groups, the Board of Estimate, on July 25, 1916, approved the resolution adopting city-wide zoning regulating the height, bulk, and uses of buildings. The vote was nearly unanimous, 15 to 1, the lone dissenter being the borough president of Staten Island, who felt that his borough had been left with too little protection since much of the undeveloped part of the Island had been designated as unrestricted. It was significant that for all the rhetoric about the use of zoning to control future development, the final revision had emphasized the protection of existing areas. The open areas, which were most in need of control over development, went largely unprotected.

The vote of July 25, 1916, established zoning as the primary means of American land development control. From this precedent, set by the efforts of a few determined reformers, zoning would spread quickly across the country, and a decade later the U.S. Supreme Court would remove any lingering doubts as to its constitutionality. But the reformers realized soon after their success in 1916 that they had won only a partial victory. Two serious problems remained. First, zoning had gained legal acceptance while the planning on which it was to be based had not. The next battle that had to be fought appeared to be to achieve legitimacy and authority for planning. But a second problem had emerged that seemed to block solutions to the first, at least in New York: what would happen in the metropolitan area if each locality devised its own separate zoning ordinance without coordinating with its neighbors? And what would happen if all the communities in the metropolitan area decided to zone out the vital but unpleasant activities such as industries and garbage dumps, on which the life of all the communities depended? The battle for zoning had been won by the turning of a specific conflict into a general reform issue, by careful technical study and attention to detail, and by personal communication with local interests. The question for Bassett and his colleagues was how the campaign strategy that had won the battle for zoning could be used to achieve planning on a metropolitan scale.

THE PORT OF NEW YORK AUTHORITY PLAN

One of the most significant events in the development of planning activities in the New York Region was the creation of the Port of New York Authority in 1921. The establishment of the Port Authority was the result of years of promotional effort by prominent business groups, mostly on the New York side of the harbor. Port development had become a passion in cities on both coasts following the opening of the Panama Canal in 1914. The Canal symbolized the achievement of industrial supremacy by the United States and demonstrated in a dramatic way the practical fruits that could be produced by the combination of public capital, engineering skill and military discipline, brought together under a governmental administration attuned to the needs of business. The Canal also held out the promise of greatly increased trade through the Port of New York.[27]

The importance of the port had been recognized by successive New York City administrations which between 1870 and 1914 had spent over $100 million to improve pier and dock facilities.[28] In 1914, New Jersey, hoping to attract a larger share of total port trade, established a permanent New Jersey Harbor Commission with power to approve all plans for the development of its waterfront. All but two of the intercontinental railroads had terminals on the Jersey waterfront, from which freight was carried by lighter across the harbor to trans-shipment points or terminals in Manhattan. Through the Interstate Commerce Commission, New York had managed to obtain an equalized shipping cost throughout the harbor. In effect, this meant that the shipments originating or terminating in New Jersey were subsidizing New York shipments that required lighterage across the harbor. The New Jersey Harbor Commission initiated litigation to obtain a reduced rate for shipments terminating on the west side of the Hudson. Since the majority of trunk lines terminated there, it was hoped that the cost differential would attract industries that might otherwise settle on the New York side.

This posed an ominous threat to New York business interests, who were already distressed over the chaotic condition of the multiple rail freight terminals. Transfer of cars between lines was not easily made and incurred surcharges. Pickups of less than car load shipments were delayed, and drayage in general was difficult because of the narrow configuration of the old lighterage piers. Compared to the well-planned harbors of Europe, New York harbor was chaos, hardly a fitting terminus for ships traversing the magnificent Panama Canal.

The early years of World War I, during which neutral America was prospering on the war demands of Europe, saw an unprecedented volume of freight move through the harbor, and further revealed the glaring inefficiencies of the port in coping with trans-shipment of rail freight. The rail coordination problems had become so bad nationally that the Federal government had stepped in to manage the railroads and had demonstrated the efficiency possible in unified operations. The case for a rational approach to port development seemed self-evident to New York businessmen, particularly in light of New Jersey's entrepreneurial threat. When the Interstate Commerce Commission denied New Jersey's brief for rate differentials, it urged that the two states join to solve the problems of the port in their mutual interest. New York State Chamber of Commerce president Eugenius H. Outerbridge, who was instrumental in shaping the ICC outcome, proposed the creation of a bi-state commission to study the problems of port development. With Republicans sympathetic to business interests in control in both states, the New York, New Jersey Port and Harbor Development Commission was established by the two legislatures in 1917. General George W. Goethals, the builder of the Panama Canal, was retained as consulting engineer, and Julius Henry Cohen as counsel. Cohen had successfully argued the Interstate Commerce Commission case for New York against New Jersey on behalf of the New York State Chamber of Commerce.

The Commission reported back a year later with a recommendation that an autonomous port authority be established for New York harbor similar to the Port of London Authority. To substantiate the need for such an authority, the Commission devoted the next three years to an exhaustive study of the geography, history, and condition of the port. In a monumental five-hundred-page report issued in 1920, it concluded that the basic problem of the harbor was that of rail freight. With the report a comprehensive plan was offered for the rationalization of the rail chaos, including proposals for several circumferential belt lines along the waterfront and at the fringe of urbanization a tunnel linking New Jersey and Brooklyn to eliminate lighterage, as well as an underground, automatic electric goods delivery system for Manhattan (figures 3.4 and 3.5).[29] The plan was well-researched and buttressed the claims to technical competence of the proponents of an authority.

The legislatures of the two states strongly supported the proposed Port Authority compact, but the large waterfront cities violently opposed it. New York City's Board of Estimate filed a stongly-worded memorandum in opposition before the Judiciary Committee of the New York State Senate on April 20, 1920. The Board's memorandum was, as it turned out, rather prescient in its concern for political accountability:

> The creation or incorporation of irresponsible commissions is contary to the very fundamentals of our government. The highest responsibility and the greatest powers under democracy are to be exercised only by those who are elected by and directly responsible to the people; and the worst evils that have grown up in this country are those incident to the performance of governmental functions by boards and commissions not responsible to the electorate and who hold . . . appointments for indefinite or overlapping terms and therefore cannot be reached or held accountable by the Governor or other executive or elective

officers to whom their appointments were originally due. Such commissions or corporations once created go on forever.[30]

The Board of Estimate was not impressed with the protection clause in the proposed compact, which provided that 'no city within the Port district shall be bound by the comprehensive plan unless and until it has approved of the same . . .' The Board was sanguine about the political uses of a comprehensive plan:

> It is argued from these and other provisions that the making of the Treaty would be entirely harmless because the Port authority could not effectively function unless and until its proposed comprehensive plans were approved. But this is fallacious to the highest degree. It is easily within the power of the Port Authority to prepare 'a comprehensive plan' that shall be so attractive and so promising in its provisions that no member of the Legislature or other public officer would hesitate for an instant to approve such a plan. The approval of such a plan is a very different thing from having a treaty or compact with the State of New Jersey providing the manner and time in which it shall be carried into effect. In other words, a highly attractive comprehensive plan upon which the consent of the Legislature of the local authorities of any city might be procured would mean nothing whatever in the way of obligation as to when the parts vitally affecting the City of New York would be carried into effect. This is a matter that would rest wholly within the discretion and control of the so-called Port Authority and it might postpone the New York improvements for an indefinite period.
>
> It is to be observed, moreover, that the Port authority is not required to account to the City or State of New York, or to anyone, for the avails of the bonds or other securities that it may issue or mortgages that it may make. Such sums may be expended in any manner that the Port authority deems fit. There is not even any provision of law by which their contracts are required to be let at public bidding. There is no provision whatever that the surplus or other accumulations that may be amassed from time to time shall ever be distributed or divided or in any way apportioned to the State and the City of New York. In other words, perpetual accumulation and other profits or the avail of borrowing may go on without limit or restraint and subject only to such use as the unbridled discretion of the Port authority may dictate.[31]

New York City's objections were ignored in the final draft of the bill establishing the Port of New York Authority, passed in 1920 by both houses of the New York Legislature, which split along party lines with the Democrats in opposition. New Jersey's legislature also approved the bill, almost unanimously, over-riding the veto of Governor Edwards, whose objections reflected the opposition of Jersey City's mayor, Frank Hague, an ally and supporter of Edwards.

New York's Governor Nathan Miller signed the bill, appointing Louis H. Pounds, Alfred E. Smith (who had previously been Governor but had lost to Miller in the 1920 Republican landslide), and Eugenius Outerbridge, President of the State Chamber of Commerce, as New York's three original Commissioners. The New Jersey Legislature, not trusting Governor Edwards

Figure 3.4. The Jamaica Bay Port Scheme, 1913. *(Source*: Thomas E. Rush (1920) *The Port of New York*. New York: Doubleday, Page and Company)

to make sympathetic appointments, specified the names of three men from the ranks of New Jersey business leadership. The U.S. Congress, which constitutionally must approve interstate agreements before they can take effect, shortly thereafter approved the compact with little debate.

The legislation creating the Port Authority specifically required it to propose a physical plan for port development. To assist General Goethals a technical advisory board of prominent consulting engineers was formed by the Port Authority to confer with the railroad engineers to determine which projects should be undertaken.[32] The plan proposed by the board was almost identical with the 1919 Comprehensive Plan of the New York, New Jersey Harbor Development Commission (figure 3.5).

The successful implementation of the plan was dependent on two factors: the cooperation of the eleven railroads, which at first seemed to be forthcoming, and the economic feasibility of the individual projects in the plan, since the Authority was legally required to pay its bonds out of revenues and could not levy or receive tax moneys. By 1922 it had become evident that the railroads would not support any of the Port Authority's proposals for belt line connections. Each railroad was reluctant to give up the local monopoly it enjoyed along its own right-of-way for the benefit of operating as a system. The railroads were eager, however, to get out of the unprofitable but growing passenger commuter business and it appeared that a *quid pro quo* might have been effected, with the Port Authority assuming some responsibility for the

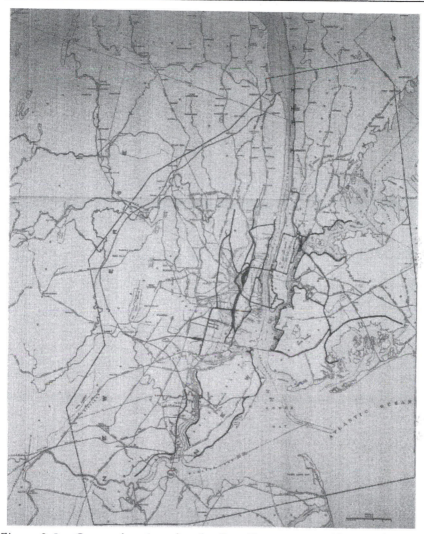

Figure 3.5. Comprehensive plan for Port Development, New York, New Jersey Port and Harbour Development Commission, 1916. (*Source*: New York, New Jersey Port and Harbour Development Commission)

rail commuter problem. But the Authority saw freight as its prior concern and declined to cooperate on the basis suggested by the railroads. The result was an impasse which appeared to be insurmountable, the consequences of which would prove most unfortunate for the long-term development of the Region. What seemed to be required was a planning authority which could look at the whole regional problem in all its aspects and interrelationships, an agency or group whose scope could go far beyond the narrow legislative mandate of the Port of New York Authority and yet work closely with the Authority. This was exactly what Morgan banker Charles Dyer Norton, just at that moment, was attempting to create with his project for a regional plan of New York. The successful sequence by which the Port Authority had been established – research. plan, publicity, and then implementing institution – suggested to Norton the way to realize a regional plan of New York and its environs. What was needed, Norton suggested, was a plan to put all the various plans for New York together and a 'Plan of New York Authority' to carry them out.[33]

NOTES

1. Hofstadter, Richard (1955) *Social Darwinism in American Thought*. Boston: Beacon Press, pp. 51–66.

2. Regional Plan of New York and Its Environs (1929) *Physical Conditions and Public Services*, VIII. New York: Committee on the Regional Plan of New York, pp. 164–165.

3. Mandelbaum, Seymour J. (1965) *Boss Tweed's New York*. New York: John Wiley, pp. 116–117

4. Fein, Albert (ed.)(1968) *Landscape into Cityscape: Frederick Law Olmsted's Plan for a Greater New York City*. Ithaca: Cornell University Press, pp. 158–159.

5. Mandelbaum, *op. cit.*, p.69.

6. For an illuminating account of how a ward boss furthered city development for the interests of business, his constituents, and himself, see Riordon, William L. (1963) *Plunkett of Tammany Hall*. New York: E.P. Dutton, pp. 61–64 (first published in 1905).

7. For an exposition on the functions of a machine boss, see Merton, Robert (1957) *Social Theory and Social Structure*. New York: Free Press (rev. enl. ed), pp. 71–82.

8. Mandelbaum, *op. cit.*, pp. 70–75.

9. *Ibid.*, pp. 87–104

10. *Ibid.*, pp. 106–110.

11. For a thoughtful analysis of reform cycles in New York politics in this century, see Lowi, Theodore J. (1964) *At the Pleasure of the Mayor*. New York: The Free Press of Glencoe, pp. 175ff.

12. American Society of Civil Engineers (1924) Memoirs of Nelson Lewis. *Transactions of the American Society of Civil Engineers*, March 30.

13. Olmsted, Frederick Law (1914) The town planning movement in America. *Annals of the American Academy of Political and Social Sciences*, LI, January, pp. 172–181.

14. New York City Improvement Commission (1907) *Report to the Honorable George B. McClellan, Mayor of the City of New York*. New York: City Improvement Commission, p.36.

15. *Ibid.*, p.9.

16. *Ibid.*, p.22.

17. City Plan Commission, Newark (1915) *Comprehensive Plan of Newark*. Newark: City Plan Commission.

18. Brearly, Harvey (1914) *The Problem of Greater New York and Its Solution*. New York: Committee on Industrial Advancement of the Brooklyn League.

19. The emergence of zoning in New York has been examined in detail in two works: Toll, Seymour (1969) *Zoned America*. New York: Grossman Publishers, pp. 143–210; Makielski, S.J. (1966) *The Politics of Zoning: The New York Experience*. New York: Columbia University Press, pp. 7–40.

20. Makielski, *op. cit.*, p.10.

21. Toll, *op. cit.*, p.148.

22. *Ibid.* p.144.

23. Makielski, *op. cit.*, p.13.

24. Bassett, Edward M. (1936) *Zoning: The Laws, Administration and Court Decisions during the First Twenty Years*. New York: Russell Sage Foundation, p.11.

25. Toll, op. cit., p.152

26. Makielski, *op. cit.*, pp. 22–23.

27. For a contemporary description of the significance of the Panama Canal, see: Rush, Thomas E. (1920) *The Port of New York*. Garden City: Doubleday, Page and Co. For a later view see: Julien, Claude (1971) *America's Empire*. New York: Random House, chapter 3.

28. This section draws on Bard, Erwin Wilkie (1942) *The Port of New York Authority*. New York: Colombia University Press, chapters 1 and 2.

29. New York, New Jersey Port and Harbor Development Commission (1920) *Joint Report with Comprehensive Plan and Recommendations*. Albany: The Development Commission.

30. Bard, *op. cit.*, p. 492.

31. *Ibid.*

32. The consulting engineers were Nelson P. Lewis, the former chief engineer of the New York Board of Estimate, Morris R. Shepherd, who held a similar post in Newark, and Francis L. Stuart, former chief engineer for the Erie and Baltimore and Ohio Railroads.

33. Minutes of the Committee on the Regional Plan of New York and Its Environs, October 30, 1922.

4

FIRST STEPS TOWARDS A METROPOLITAN REGIONAL PLAN

CHARLES NORTON AND THE PLAN OF CHICAGO, 1893–1909

Had Charles Dyer Norton not elected to leave Washington for Wall Street, it seems likely that there would never have been a Regional Plan for New York and Its Environs. Norton had been a driving force behind the preparation of Daniel Burnham's 1909 Plan for Chicago and in his short tenure in Washington had observed the implementation of Burnham's plans for the Macmillan Commission. Norton decided in 1911 to resign his post as President William Howard Taft's secretary to accept a position as vice-president of J.P. Morgan's First National Bank of New York. Norton had been close to the raging issue of national bank reform, and the Morgan interests wanted a man who could help shape Federal banking policy. It was more than a sentimental journey that Norton made in 1911 from Washington to New York, entraining near the rising Union Station designed by his friend Burnham, and debarking in the magnificence of the just-completed Pennsylvania Station, designed by Charles McKim, to whom he was related by marriage. With ambitious plans underway in Chicago and Washington, New York's lack of a plan offered a challenge to Norton's avocation in planning.

Though not a wealthy scion like many of his fellow New York bankers, Charles Norton could claim direct descent from Roger Williams, the founder of Rhode Island. His father, Franklin Burroughs Norton, was a minister in Oshkosh, Wisconsin, where Charles Norton was born in 1871. At the age of fourteen Charles began working for the Mutual Life Insurance Company in Milwaukee, carefully saving his earnings for a period of four years until he had enough to pay for college tuition. After his graduation from Amherst in 1893, he joined the staff of Scribner's Magazine. Then in 1895 he returned to the Mutual Life Insurance Company in Milwaukee, but soon left to become a partner in the Chicago insurance and financial firm of Kimball and Norton. The firm was successful, serving for a time as general agents for the State of Illinois, an activity that placed Norton in a strategic position to influence public policy.

The early 1890s were heady years in Chicago. Great fortunes were being consolidated by men clever enough to ride the crest of Midwest growth which the confluence of railroads focused on Chicago. The 1893 World's Columbian Exposition, rejected by New York, was welcomed by Chicago, whose business elite saw in it an opportunity to announce Chicago's emergence as a national metropolis. It also furnished Chicago's new wealthy families with an opportunity to demonstrate respectability in their taste for the fine arts. The robust, but home grown, Chicago building tradition was discarded in favor of a refined neo-Classical style more fitted to an expression of wealth and aristocracy. A new generation of Eastern architects had emerged from the ranks of the rising wealthy families, trained in the ateliers of Paris in the 1860s and 1870s, and returned to mingle business, wealth, and art to produce an 'American Renaissance'. But if New York was the principal point of debarkation of the classical tradition, Chicago's leading firms were not slow to adopt it. Chairman of the Exposition's Committee of Architects was Daniel Burnham, a partner in one of these leading firms, and an early convert to the glories of classicism. While most of the designers of the Fair's buildings were prominent New York architects, such as Charles Follen McKim and Richard Morris Hunt, it was Chicagoan Burnham who orchestrated the pieces into a *tout ensemble* and set in motion an enthusiastic movement to beautify and classicize every large and small city in the country.

As general agent for the State of Illinois, Norton had been involved with the planning of the Fair. It was through this connection that he had met Katherine McKim Garrison, a niece of Charles Follen McKim and a daughter of Wendell Phillips Garrison, editor of the *Nation,* and granddaughter of the abolitionist, William Lloyd Garrison. Their marriage in 1897 brought Norton closer to both the reform and the architectural traditions and into a prominent New York family. Katherine's uncle was Henry Villard, the railroad financier. Her cousin was Villard's crusading socialist son, Oswald Garrison Villard, editor in the 1920s of the *New York Post* and the revitalized *Nation,* which Katherine's father had earlier edited for many years.

Katherine brought Charles into a world he had known only from a distance. Through the McKims and the Villards he was brought close to the accepted leaders of American architecture and art at the century's turn.[1] It was this contact that converted Norton to an advocate of planning, for planning was at that juncture largely a matter of aesthetics and taste. In a paper he prepared in 1922, Norton described how in 1901 he first became a devotee of planning on the porch of Augustus Saint Gaudens' summer house at Cornish, New Hampshire:

> Saint Gaudens came up from his studio for tea after a hard day's work, and he entranced us all by his glowing vision of what he and Burnham, McKim and [Frederick Law] Olmsted hoped to accomplish in restoring and developing L'Enfant's Plan of Washington. He exacted a promise from me of active effort with refractory Illinois Congressmen, who, among others in Washington, were threatening to place the new Agriculture Building athwart the Mall in a way to ruin L'Enfant's Plan. That was the beginning of my interest in City Planning.

In the effort to fulfil my promise to Saint Gaudens I found a new and fascinating hobby.[2]

Norton rose rapidly in Chicago financial circles, becoming a member of the Merchants Club, a group of young, public-minded businessmen, filled with the spirit of *noblesse oblige:*

> When a man was asked to join the Merchants Club he was asked quite bluntly whether or not he would respond to any call for public service at the Club's command – whether he would give not merely his money and his influence, but himself. If he accepted election he enlisted. It came as an honor, a much prized distinction, an opportunity for service with a powerful, congenial, inspiriting group. Presidents of railroads, of packing houses, merchants and bankers found themselves on committees charged with responsibility for the opening of schools at night to the public, for organizing honest pawn shops, for cleaning the streets, for a score of projects to which they gave without a stint of their personal time and strength, as well as money.[3]

In 1906, at age thirty-five, Norton was elected president of the Club. Secretary of the Club was Frederic A. Delano, born in Hong Kong, Harvard graduate, and a member of an old Hudson River Valley family related to the Roosevelts. Delano had worked his way up through the executive ranks of the Chicago, Burlington, and Quincy Railroad Company, becoming general manager at the age of forty. He had held this position until 1905, leaving then to become a consulting engineer for the United States War Department, advising in the financing and construction of railroads in the Philippines. It was the beginning of a long career in the public service.

Delano, through eight years his senior, found he had much in common with Norton. Both had the financier's sense of the importance and permanence of capital investment. As businessmen with public connections, both saw government as a positive force to rationalize the growth and development of the cities. Both were deeply committed to the progressivist good government that was gaining momentum after Lincoln Steffens' 1902 revelations of municipal corruption. Both embodied that combination of reform sentiment and aesthetic sensibility which gave the City Beautiful movement its driving force.

Through 1905 and 1906 Norton and Delano, along with Edward B. Butler, became interested in having Burnham develop a city-wide plan of Chicago similar to those he had drawn up for Washington and San Francisco. Ten years earlier, at the close of the Fair, Chicago Park Board President, James W. Ellsworth had persuaded Burnham to draft for the Commercial Club a scheme for recapturing the waterfront from the site of the 1893 Exposition at Grant Park to Jackson Park, eight miles to the south. But as a result of the panic and depression that followed the close of the Fair, the plan had been put aside. Norton and Delano had no intention of simply reviving this plan, but visualized a proposal covering not only the waterfront but the whole city of Chicago. Early in 1906, Delano and Norton broached their idea to the aging

Burnham at a lunch at the Chicago Club. Burnham was reluctant to proceed under Merchants Club auspices out of loyalty to Franklin MacVeagh who, as chairman of a Commercial Club committee, had strongly supported the Ellsworth-Burnham scheme of 1895. Moreover, Burnham was a member of the Commercial Club, a group of businessmen somewhat older and more established than those in the Merchants Club of which he was not a member. But MacVeagh released Burnham from his obligation to the Commercial Club, and on July 6, 1906, Burnham announced to Norton that he was ready to begin work on the plan. Norton promptly assembled the Merchants Club members at the Union League Club and asked for pledges to a $20,000 fund. Norton apparently was persuasive, as he recalled some years later:

> I made an incoherent but earnest effort to expound the doctrine of comprehensive City Planning, and I remember Charles Dawes' pungent remark: 'I don't understand what it is that Charlie Norton wants, but I'm for it and I'll subscribe' and so did everyone else.[4]

Norton raced over to tell Burnham to begin and that money was in hand, but Burnham was still reluctant and appeared to be in serious distress: 'It is wonderful, Charles, but I am afraid it is no use. My doctor has just been here to tell me that I have a mortal disease – that I have at most three years to live'. Norton stood stunned and after a painful silence blurted out, 'But Mr. Burnham, that is just time enough; it will take only three years.' Burnham looked startled, then breaking into a laugh, said, 'You are right. I will do it.'[5]

The plan did in fact take three years, consuming most of Burnham's time and a good deal of his own money. Norton believed that Burnham's joy in his plan helped prolong his life, for he lived not three more years, but six.

Shortly after Burnham's acceptance the Merchants Club merged with the Commercial Club, and the project was continued under the sponsorship of the combined organization. Burnham, with the assistance of his protege, Edward Bennett, and others labored in their atelier overlooking the lake front for some thirty months, meeting periodically with Charles Norton, Frederic Delano, Charles Wacker, and other members of the Club to make progress reports. Finally, in 1909, the conception was considered complete, and the plan was presented by the Commercial Club to the City of Chicago in the form of a magnificently printed quarto volume filled with colored drawings and the renderings of Jules Guerin, a skilled watercolorist brought from Paris for the project by Burnham. The Plan was presented with a suggestion that a commission be appointed to study it and recommend such portions of it as should be carried out. The suggestion was duly accepted by Mayor Fred A. Busse, and on November 1, 1909, the Chicago City Plan Commission was created, largely from the membership of the Commercial Club. Charles Wacker was appointed chairman.

Burnham's plan was extraordinary, a strange combination of metropolitan regionalism and baroque splendor, more European than anything in Europe.

The central elements contained in the original 1896 proposal were preserved: the recapturing of the lake front for a continuous park and drive and the cultural ensemble at the edge of the Loop. But grand new elements had been added: a gargantuan civic and governmental center west of the Loop crowned by an enormous, pompous, domed structure intended to be Chicago's secular equivalent of London's St. Paul's and Rome's St. Peter's. From this center grand diagonal boulevards were proposed to radiate in six directions, to be carved in Hausmannian fashion out of the existing drab, gridiron neighborhoods. Special projects were called for at other important junctions: an opera house at Michigan and Washington Avenues, strikingly reminiscent of Garnier's Paris Opera; special treatment of the waterfront along the Chicago River, with Michigan Avenue to be widened and double-decked in that vicinity; and a masterful reconstruction and consolidation of the main railroad passenger terminals between the Loop and the proposed civic center, a proposal drawn largely from earlier studies made by Frederic Delano in 1904.

The plan paid little attention to the nondescript residential areas between the center of the city and the developed fringe. But in the suburbs the newly emergent idea of metropolitan regionalism was given its due in the form of proposals for a radial-concentric grid of highways intended to link together the scattered constellation of suburban villages spawned by the commuter railroads. A green belt was also proposed to link projected sizable wedges of park land. This was designed at a scale not previously attempted even by Burnham. Norton later recalled how the scheme was evolved:

> Our first half year was practically wasted on a scheme to develop La Salle Street as an axis: to make a square at La Salle and Washington Streets opposite the proposed new Court House and City Hall. The scheme involved removing the Board of Trade Building, and other huge difficulties like that, and we were speedily lost in details. Burnham was the first to recognize the error of beginning at an arbitrarily located center, instead of at the circumference of the whole area, and then working in toward the true and logical civic center. Drawing on our office wall map the great Waukegan, Elgin, Aurora, Gary, Michigan City circle, he sounded this bugle blast: 'Make no little plans: they have no magic to stir men's blood and probably themselves will not be realized. Make big plans: aim high in hope and work, remembering that a noble, logical diagram once recorded will never die, but long after we are gone will be a living thing, asserting itself with growing intensity.' This was for us all the beginning of correct thinking.[6]

This may have been the beginning of 'correct thinking' for the Commercial Clubmen, but the 1909 conception of a regional network of parks and highways was not entirely original. In 1903, Cook County had created a commission on the Outer Belt, and in 1905 the State of Illinois had passed legislation establishing a Forest Preserve District around Chicago. And the proposed road network was largely in existence prior to the Plan. Burnham simply selected segments for upgrading and boulevarding.

Thus, the Burnham Plan was in many ways a collage of earlier proposals from various sources, with some additions, to be sure. By assembling these pieces into a whole, Burnham and his associates could claim rationality, comprehensiveness, and metropolitan scope. These would be powerful virtues in the quest for public support of the plan.

The Burnham Plan was, in fact, focused largely on those areas that were of interest to the commercial elite who sponsored it: the city center where they worked and the suburbs where many of them lived. Its aim was largely to manipulate public lands and public buildings into efficient rationalized systems and to provide the wealthy with symbolic representations of their power and their civic virtue. The needs of the common citizen in his own neighborhood were largely ignored. He would instead benefit from wage and employment spillovers from a more efficient local economy and as an awed spectator contemplating in wonder the monumental edifices proposed for government and culture. Nevertheless Norton had confidence that the man in the street would be able to identify with the plan and particularly with its Hausmannian diagonals:

> These is no way to interest the man in the street in a City Plan for a community of millions of people unless the Plan includes all of the area in which the city workers live. Men and women are interested in Plans that include their homes, their gardens, the environment in which they and their children dwell. When we went out to that circumference we found at once the eleven great existing diagonals, the old trails and country roads that led originally to Fort Dearborn . . . and these diagonals, properly extended to new encircling streets with a broadened and extended Michigan Avenue as a solid foundation, quickly became the framework of the Chicago Plan. We found that we already possessed much of what Hausmann had created in Paris, and that we needed only to develop our assets to be rich.

Norton's grand vision of the plan as a joint responsibility of business and government elites who would have to shape public opinion to achieve their ends was eloquently expressed in a speech he delivered at a dinner given by the Commercial Club in honor of the newly created Chicago Plan Commission:

> . . . A hundred million of people will look to this city as their capital, their center in which to trade, to hear music, to see pictures, to enjoy themselves. This places a high responsibility upon the men who control public and private business in Chicago. They have instinctively recognized that responsibility from the date of the first settlement here. This dinner marks a great event in our civic history, for the responsibility for the development of the Plan of Chicago passes tonight literally into the hands of the city of Chicago. The Chicago Plan Commission, in the truest and best sense, represents the people of this city. Public confidence must be secured ward by ward, street by street. The people must be shown what the Plan of Chicago means to them so that there may be had an irresistible public opinion behind this great movement. Upon recognition of this great opportunity depends to a large extent the respect and regard not merely of the citizens of

Chicago but of the millions of the Mississippi Valley who are thus being directly served. The commission should not be bound in its vision of what it may accomplish by anything which has been accomplished in the past. The Plan of Chicago offers a closely reasoned, carefully studied, well-balanced solution which provides generously alike for all of the community.[7]

The man in the street was to be the final judge of the plan's impact. His vote on bond referenda was essential to finance the proposed projects, and it was not altogether certain how he would react. A successful means of eliciting popular support was devised by the Chicago Plan Commission; Walter D. Moody, managing director, would prepare a school text version of Burnham's plan. Moody surmised that not only children but their parents as well would read the well-illustrated book, the famous *Wacker's Manual*, and he was proven right when large majorities of citizens voted for the first projects – mostly street widenings and new bridges.[8]

While many cities were commissioning city plans at this time, the Chicago Plan effort became the paradigm of business-elite plan-making. The Plan was to be more than a noble design. It was to be an article of faith and an equivalent of law. A public or private decision could be judged as to its worthiness according to its compatibility with the Plan. The Plan was to reign as an unarguable summation of the highest goals of the urban leadership; no need to refer directly to civic objectives, for the Plan subsumed these objectives. The Plan was to be an authoritative substitute for authority.

The Chicago Plan demonstrated to many that effective civic action was possible only through private initiative and leadership. Planning required money, technical knowledge, and persuasive powers, none of which urban machine governments appeared able or willing to provide. But with the stimulus of private action, urban governments could be persuaded to assume the task of planning once it had been successfully established. This could best be accomplished by creating an independent planning commission composed of business and civic leaders.

The Chicago Plan also demonstrated that the comprehensiveness of geographical space could be substituted for the larger comprehensiveness of the political process. By expanding the scope of geographic consideration and dealing with key urban functions at their highest order of abstraction, both political legitimacy and scientific rationality could be claimed, despite the fact that, because it originated in the business elite, it inevitably reflected the values of only a narrow spectrum of the population. The plan was designed to produce coalition among groups seeking to reduce friction and uncertainties in their commercial environments.

Charles Norton was not in Chicago to see the first effects of the plan he had brought to fruition. He had moved to Washington in 1909, when the Taft administration had taken office, at the behest of Taft's Treasury Secretary, Franklin McVeagh, Chicago's leading wholesale financier. McVeagh, who had been active in both the planning of the Fair and the work of the Plan committee of the Commercial Club, appointed Norton Assistant Secretary of the Treasury in charge of fiscal bureaus.

Norton went to Washington only out of public-spiritedness, sacrificing a salary of $50,000 a year for the meagre $4,500 of an Assistant Secretary. He served in this capacity for less than a year, though even in this short period he was able to introduce reforms which reportedly saved the department thousands of dollars annually.[9] President Taft also credited him with the creation of the Efficiency and Economy Commission, the progenitor of the Bureau of the Budget, and with the establishment of a private Institute for Governmental Research 'to assist the Government by disinterested examination and report on better methods.'[10] The Institute later merged with another research organization to become the Brookings Institution.

Taft, recognizing Norton's talents for organization and innovation, appointed him to the position of presidential secretary in June of 1910. At the time Taft was embroiled in the controversies over reorganization of the national banking system, and Norton played an important role in the conception of the plan put forward by Senator Nelson Aldrich to create fifteen regional banking associations under a central bank board in Washington. a somewhat modified version of this plan was passed by Congress in 1912, establishing the Federal Reserve System.[11]

Norton's familiarity with the banking reform issue soon resulted in an offer of a vice-presidency in the First National City Bank of New York, one of the elements of the vast Morgan financial empire. Norton accepted in January, 1911, and resigned his position in the White House to go to Wall Street.[12] Norton's move was to have great significance for the subsequent planning and development of New York and its environs.

THE ADVISORY COMMITTEE ON THE CITY PLAN OF NEW YORK, 1914

Not long after his arrival in New York Charles Norton was asked to assume a major role in planning for his adopted city. In January 1914, when the reform administration of Mayor John Purroy Mitchel took office, George McAneny, the Borough President of Manhattan, persuaded the Board of Estimate and Apportionment to establish a standing Committee on the City Plan. This committee was intended to carry on the studies of the Heights of Buildings Commission, which had just completed its report on the possibility of creating zoned districts of protected land uses.[13] The Committee on the City Plan, consisting of the various borough presidents and the President of the Board of Aldermen, was mandated to consider all larger questions of public improvements. It was expected that the Committee would eventually formulate a general scheme for improvement with which all local improvements would be coordinated and which might provide a planning basis for the creation of use and density zones. To assist the Committee in its work, and, not incidentally, to add stature to its unavoidably controversial deliberations, an Advisory Committee on the City Plan was created, with many prominent architects, lawyers and engineers in its membership. A number of its members had also been members of the Heights of Buildings Commission. Charles Norton was Chairman, and Frederic B. Pratt, Vice Chairman. Members included Edward M. Bassett, the Brooklyn lawyer who, with George McAneny, was then actively seeking passage of New York State legislation which would permit the city to zone itself. Other members included Frank B. Williams, another lawyer prominent in zoning affairs, Arnold W. Brunner, the architect, Richard M. Hurd, the real estate specialist, C. Grant LaFarge, the artist, Daniel L. Turner, the transportation engineer, Eugenius H. Outerbridge, and Irving H. Bush, a development-minded businessman who had built the vast Bush Terminal in Brooklyn. Robert H. Whitten, a social scientist, was Secretary, and George B. Ford, an architect-planner, was Consultant to the Committee. All of these men would later become associated with the Regional Plan project.[14]

With men of such reputation working within the benign ambience of Mitchel's reform administration, New York seemed at last about to realize the benefits of rational city planning. An estimable beginning was made with the publication of a comprehensive analysis of the current situation in city planning in December of 1914. Previous planning efforts were reviewed, including the work of the McClellan Commission and the Brooklyn Committee on the City Plan. Ernest P. Goodrich analyzed the port and terminal problem. Nelson O. Lewis reported on his work on the official city map. Daniel C. Turner discussed the transit situation, and George B. Ford summarized 'present city planning needs'. Ford emphasized the need to control private development, noting that the city could legally restrict character of occupancy and the height of buildings for the welfare of the citizens and to stabilize property values. He urged the development of a comprehensive plan for physical development:

> The development of every tract should be determined upon which is best not only for itself but for the neighboring tracts and for the City as a whole. Then the whole circulation system and the lot, block, and open space units should be designed so as to secure to the City the best uses of its parts, both now and far into the future. The comprehensive city plan should not stop at the City boundaries but include the whole commuting belt, so as to bring the entire region that is related to and dependent on the City into one perfectly coordinated plan.[15]

The 'commuting belt' was defined as 'the area that may be reached within one hour by the most rapid means of communication at present developed for the transportation of passengers.'

How a New York City advisory committee could hope to influence the course of development in so large and politically diverse an area was not indicated. But the Committee's definition of the region as the proper unit of analysis was undoubtedly justified in an era of metropolitan expansion and economic integration.

In 1915, Charles Norton prepared a proposed public statement to be issued by the Executive Committee of the Advisory Plan Commission. In this statement Norton further elaborated his ideas for a metropolitan plan:

> No American city is so rich in competent personnel. None has so superb a situation, or presents so great an opportunity for a noble city plan. Comprehending and applauding the successful efforts of Washington, of Chicago, Detroit, Cleveland, of scores of American cities which have caught from France, England, and from Germany the spirit of city planning, New York has no plan . . . The reason is not hard to find.
>
> No plan has ever been projected here on a scale vast enough to capture the interest and the imagination of this group of cities, towns and villages which is New York . . .
>
> No plan of New York will command recognition unless it includes all the areas in which all New Yorkers earn their livelihood and make their homes.
>
> From the City Hall a circle must be swung which will include the Atlantic Highlands and Princeton; the lovely Jersey hills back of Morristown and Tuxedo; the incomparable Hudson as far as Newburgh; the Westchester lakes and ridges, to Bridgeport and beyond, and all of Long Island.[16]

Norton left little doubt that his Chicago experiences had provided the model for his proposals for New York:

> Let some Daniel H. Burnham do for this immense community what Burnham did for Chicago and its environs; spend the best years of his life studying all the varied possibilities which lie within an area so infinitely attractive physically with a population so dense, a commerce so great – let him show how the isolated Palisades Park with its thirty square miles of wilderness, and the East Side of New York only six miles away, with its million and a half of tenement dwellers, may be brought together, how the commuters of small income in Jersey or the Bronx may more easily reach the beaches; how the merchants and the railroads and the public authorities may combine to reduce the cost of handling goods and maintain the supremacy of this port; where markets and parks may be created. Let him demonstrate with unfailing logic where the civic centers of this vast population really are, and how they should be developed and embellished.[17]

Recalling the success of the Chicago Commercial Club in eliciting support for the plan, Norton proposed an assembly of a hundred men and women to support the plan:

> This group should enlist for at least five years of study and it should occasionally dine together as a group and receive reports. It should select a chairman and a small executive committee. It should raise $200,000 in voluntary cash contributions for expenses. It should have quarters high up in one of the city's towers. It should find and employ a planner, and then at the cost of endless labor and patience, the Executive Committee should see to it that all the varied important interests of New York – commercial, social, industrial, artistic – are studied.[18]

Norton's blueprint was drawn directly from his Chicago experiences, even to the desire to duplicate Burnham's atelier high above the city. These were lofty sentiments resembling a political campaign speech. But Norton was not merely running for office. He was attempting to create one. Indeed, he was in effect proposing a quasi-government of the technical and business elite, capable of generating and influencing regional public opinion and of flanking the existing fragmented government structure. What Andrew H. Green had accomplished through the legislative consolidation of the City in 1898, Norton hoped to achieve through influence and persuasion.

But Norton's vision was not shared by all of his fellow members on the Advisory Committee. John B. Pine warned of 'overplanning' for too large an area. And Frederic B. Pratt expressed a reluctance to become a vice-chairman of the committee of a hundred, because he had only mild feelings about the desirability of the project.[19] These reservations made little difference, however. Norton's high hopes for the Advisory Committee were not to be realized. The 1914 Report was both overture and finale to its efforts. Though the World War temporarily diverted attention from planning activities in the city, it was Mitchel's coolness toward the planner-reformers, together with the opposition of the borough presidents who felt threatened, which doomed the Committee. Another set-back occurred when the driving force behind the Committee, George McAneny, resigned as Borough President of Manhattan to become an editor of the *New York Times*. Finally, with the defeat of Mayor Mitchel in 1917 by John F. Hylan, a Hearst-supported candidate who was unsympathetic to patrician planner-reformers, the Committee was disbanded, its work unfinished.[20]

Norton later noted somewhat bitterly that: 'Our Advisory Committee met in a beautiful room in the City Hall once or twice and wisely resolved to give our advice only when it was asked for, which was never.'[21]

The failure of the Advisory Committee undoubtedly reinforced the conviction of Norton and his colleagues that planning was best pursued, at least initially, outside the political arena. That was how it had been done in Chicago and that was apparently how it would have to be done in New York.

INITIATION OF RUSSELL SAGE FOUNDATION SUPPORT, 1917–1921

With the entry of the United States into the World War, Charles Norton was again called to Washington. President Woodrow Wilson had asked his predecessor, William Howard Taft, to help organize an American War Council to manage the wartime activities of the American Red Cross. Norton, in his previous period in Washington, had been instrumental in getting the Red Cross established and was a logical choice for a leading role on the Council, to which he was appointed on May 10, 1917. Typically, Norton threw himself into the work, touring the war zone in late 1917.[22]

His work on the War Council brought him into close association with Robert DeForest, a wealthy New York lawyer and philanthropist who was also a member of the Council. DeForest, who was president of the Charity Organization Society and the Russell Sage Foundation, as well as a director in a score of banks, railroads, and insurance companies, was sufficiently impressed with Norton's abilities to tender a membership on the Sage Foundation of Trustees, which Norton accepted in November 1918.[23] The Sage Foundation, created in 1907 by Mrs. Russell Sage, had focused its efforts in social reform particularly in the areas of housing, social work, and public health. The Foundation had underwritten the establishment of the National Housing Association in 1910 and had sponsored the influential Pittsburgh Survey in 1907–1909, under the direction of Shelby M. Harrison and Paul U. Kellogg. It had also initiated work in 1911 on Forest Hills Gardens, a planned middle-class residential community in Queens.

Shortly after joining the Sage Foundation trustees, Norton was asked by DeForest to study the Foundation's affairs and make suggestions for new projects. Noting that under the terms of the Sage bequest, at least a fourth of the Foundation's income was to be spent exclusively for the benefit of the city of New York and its vicinity, Norton saw an opportunity to carry out the aborted work begun by the Advisory Commission on City Planning.

In December, 1918, Norton prepared a draft memorandum for the trustees of the Foundation much like the one he had addressed to the Advisory Planning Committee. Alfred T. White, a fellow trustee who had long been involved in Brooklyn public affairs and philanthropy, encouraged Norton to pursue his vision of a regional plan through the auspices of the Russell Sage Foundation. White, a graduate of Rensselaer Polytechnic Institute, and former Commissioner of City Works of Brooklyn, had been highly active in efforts to improve the tenement situation. In 1877 he privately constructed a block of model tenements in Brooklyn to demonstrate that new housing could be provided for working-class families and still earn a profit of five per cent.[24] White's success spurred others to construct model tenements. But by 1918 it was evident that private-enterprise, philanthropic housing had made little impact on the congested housing situation in New York. White, like many others concerned with housing matters, increasingly looked on metropolitan planning as a means to decongest the city, by building housing on the fringe close to decentralized industries.

In February 1919 White, DeForest, and John Glenn, Executive Director of the Foundation, met with Norton at the Century Club to discuss the possibilities of organizing and financing a New York City Plan and agreed that Norton should submit his memorandum at the next meeting of the Board. The memorandum as submitted outlined the need for and possibilities of a plan and suggested that a grant of $300,000 be spent on its preparation under the direction of a committee of five to be appointed by DeForest. The Board was not receptive, however, because the amount requested represented a major share of the Foundation's anticipated income and the scheme was dropped from consideration.[25]

That might have been the end of the idea had Alfred White not taken the initiative of inviting Norton, DeForest, Glenn, and Nelson P. Lewis to a luncheon conference at the Downtown Association on December 10, 1920, to discuss the possibility of reopening the question of Russell Sage support for a city plan. Lewis had just retired from his position as Chief Engineer of the Board of Estimate and Apportionment. No other individual knew the city as Lewis did, and few engineers were as respected in the field of city planning. His book, *The Planning of the Modern City,* published in 1916, had brought him international fame.[26] If Lewis could be persuaded to lend his talents to the project, perhaps the board of trustees might change their views. Lewis was agreeable, as was DeForest.[27]

White and Norton continued their conferences through January 1921, in preparation for a new presentation of the project to the trustees at their January 31st meeting. At their meeting on Saturday morning, January 29th, at Norton's bank, they agreed on the wording of their proposal, and White departed for a weekend of ice-skating at the Harriman Estate in Central Valley, New York. That afternoon, White drowned when the ice under him gave way.[28]

The meeting set for January 31st was postponed to February 7th. White's death meant the loss of a helpful ally on Norton's project, but it may also have prompted the trustees to decide to carry out Alfred White's wishes. Not all of the trustees were yet convinced of the project's feasibility, however.

On the eve of the meeting scheduled for January 31st, John Glenn set out in a memorandum to Norton his lingering doubts about a commitment beyond the initial $25,000. Glenn, still concerned about devoting so large a share of the Foundation's income to the project, raised a number of serious questions about the undertaking. Glenn asked whether the proposed expenditure was socially valuable and the best way for the Foundation to spend its money. He also saw difficulty in obtaining the funding for the project:

> I see only three ways in which the necessary money may be provided:
> (1) from the income of the remainder of Mrs. Sage's bequest which has not been paid to the Foundation; (2) from the release of funds now tied up in Forest Hills; (3) by cutting off some of the work which is now supported by the Foundation directly or indirectly.[29]

None of these alternatives seemed feasible to Glenn. The additional Sage bequest was intended for investment, the sale of the Sage-owned middle-income suburb at Forest Hills could not be counted on, and the cutting off of other projects was not a desirable course of action. He concluded:

> I think we should proceed, but proceed with deliberation, get the most
> competent advice before embarking in any such large and dazzling enterprise.[30]

Glenn's desire to proceed slowly prevailed at the meeting of February 7th.
By unanimous vote the Board adopted a motion authorizing the expenditure
on preliminary work of $25,000 and the appointment of a City Plan Commit-
tee. At the same meeting two new trustees of the Foundation were elected,
Dwight Morrow, a J.P. Morgan lawyer and chairman of the New Jersey
Prison Commission, and Norton's close friend and Chicago Plan associate,
Frederic A. Delano.[31] With Norton, Glenn, and DeForest, these men were to
comprise the original Committee on the Regional Plan of New York.

The proposal which the Board accepted emphasized a preliminary reconnaissance and survey:

> It is hoped that ultimately the Committee can find the man to plan for New York
> as L'Enfant planned for Washington or Burnham for Chicago. In the meantime,
> it is proposed that the Committee make progress by arranging at once for
> reconnaissance of the entire field to be covered. Such a survey would lay solid
> foundations of fact as a basis for future planning.[32]

Norton's proposal for the reconnaissance was spelled out in detail: Nelson
Lewis would visit each municipality in the Plan area, mapping and recording
existing local conditions and plans and interviewing local officials and
interested citizens who later might be organized into a larger group or
advisory committee representing the whole area.

Shelby M. Harrison of the Sage Foundation Staff would study and report
on the social aspects of the proposed Plan of New York,

> so that from the outset of the work the Committee will be alive to the needs of
> the masses of the people – particularly of those in congested areas, who are less
> fortunately housed and environed.[33]

Frederick Law Olmsted, Jr., a consultant and son of the famous landscape
architect, would indicate problems which required further investigation,
study park and other recreational facilities, and advise whether it was feasible
to find locations for garden cities similar to Letchworth in England.

Frederic A. Delano would look into the railroad and harbor problems and
the solutions already proposed. Ernest P. Goodrich, another planning consultant, would report on transportation and transit facilities and their relation to
street traffic.

Edward M. Bassett, the lawyer who had written the nation's first zoning
ordinance for New York in 1916, would report on existing provisions affecting the regulation of the height, size, and use of buildings.

Laurence Veillier, Secretary of the National Housing Association, would
study and advise the Committee on existing housing conditions and on the
possible sources of relief from congestion. Lawson Purdy, an attorney and
former president of the New York Department of Taxes and Assessments,

would study the relation of the proposed plan to the municipal and other taxing bodies.

In addition, the Committee of the Plan of New York would invite one or more men from the various professions, and artists, business, and labor groups to advise it in its work.[34]

After approving the $25,000 of preliminary funds, the trustees voted to request Norton to call together the men mentioned in his memorandum and ask their opinion as to the practicability of the project. Norton had achieved his first victory, but the trustees still needed reassurance before a major commitment could be made.[35]

On February 11th, Norton called a confidential meeting in his apartment at 4 East 66th Street of the group he hoped would carry out the planning work he had outlined in his memorandum to the Sage Trustees. In addition to Norton, Glenn, and DeForest, in attendance were Frederic Law Olmsted, Jr., George McAneny, Lawrence Veillier, Edward Bassett, Frederic B. Pratt, Lawson Purdy, Ernest P. Goodrich, and Shelby Harrison. Norton read aloud his bold proposal for a new plan of New York and outlined his scheme for a preliminary survey on which the plan would be based. The reactions of those present were enthusiastic. Several made comments which would later prove useful to the Committee as it deliberated on where to begin the monumental task it had set for itself. Bassett, the zoning lawyer, urged that a planning staff be set up and maintained for ten to twenty years to study the social and physical conditions in the metropolitan region. The planning future could not be limited simply to the making of the plan. Bassett also propounded a principle that was to be a guiding philosophy of the Regional Plan: let the cooperating public officials take all the credit they could for any plan. The purpose of the Committee ought to be to secure results, not to win public praise and recognition for itself.

Olmsted, the landscape architect, like Bassett, stressed the need for staff continuity over a long period, at least twenty-five years, to follow up without intermission the opportunities which would arise and to bring pressure to bear in the interest of the whole community. He also called for greater stress upon studying the basic economic and social conditions of the problem and proposed the study of primary ancillary industries, perhaps the first formulation of the important distinction between basic and non-basic industries.[36]

In the weeks that followed Norton received suggestions from other leaders in the planning movement among whom he had circulated his proposal for a regional plan of New York. Charles Moore, Chairman of the Fine Arts Commission in Washington, D.C., and author of the published version of the Chicago Plan, urged Norton to search for a new Daniel Burnham:

> The prime consideration is to find a mastermind to look at the whole problem – someone who can cover fifty years with his vision.[37]

Moore proposed Cass Gilbert, the architect of the Woolworth Building, to become the New York Burnham:

> I believe Gilbert's ideas as to main thoroughfares and railroad disposition are bigger, more far-reaching and more comprehensive than those of any other man with whom I have come in contact. Of course, Gilbert has his limitations in his temperament, in the antagonisms he has created, in the jealousies that have sprung up . . .
>
> The subdivision of work that has arisen, the new conceptions that human needs have developed, all have tended to make specialists. But it needs a supreme commander just the same. And this is what we get back to – the one man to dominate the job.[38]

Moore had raised a vital question which Norton was not yet prepared to answer: should a dominant single individual be placed in charge of the making of the plan, and, if so, who was it to be? The question was put aside, and Olmsted's suggestion was followed that all eight preliminary investigators act as a unified technical committee working under the informal chairmanship of Nelson Lewis.[39] Lewis himself believed that it was vain to hope for a Burnham to guide the development of the plan. Nor was it desirable:

> The problem is so much bigger and so much more complex that it will doubtless prove too great for any one man to grasp in its technical details . . . it might even be safe to say that he could maintain a better balance in the whole scheme if he were not a man technically trained in any one of the professions.[40]

Frederic Delano greeted Norton's proposal for a plan with the enthusiasm of their Chicago Plan days. But he had no illusions about the difficulties in making tangible changes in the fabric of a city, especially Manhattan.

> . . . what appalls one are the enormous difficulties in the way. In New York we do not begin our plan with a clean sheet of paper, nor can we say that the City is without a plan. The truth is that the plan was made many years ago and that the City has been built in accordance with it . . .
>
> The problem of the future as it has been for at least 50 years, is largely a problem of transportation; for if we cannot create additional parks and playgrounds on the island of Manhattan, we must facilitate access to those we can create.[41]

Delano, noting that serious proposals to solve Manhattan's congestion included the costly opening of a new north-south avenue between Fifth and Sixth Avenues and the creation of new subways, suggested several specific alternatives. He proposed elevated concrete highways along the East and Hudson Rivers and vehicular viaducts over Lexington, Seventh, and Eighth Avenues. These were examples of the kinds of specific proposals he thought should be included in the plan. As for the overall approach,

> The imperialistic method of a strongly centralized government is not open to us and the only means which can be considered is one which involves
> 1. Careful study
> 2. So taking the public into our confidence that it will progress as we progress

3. Arousing public interest and sympathy with the problem

4. Appealing to those men and women and to those organizations already interested in certain phases of the work to cooperate with us

5. Carefully avoiding the suggestion that the project is the aim of any one man or group of men, that it is to be financed chiefly or wholly by any foundation or group.

In other words, the true object of the Russell Sage Foundation, in this as in any other undertaking, must be limited to helping our citizens to help themselves. If we can open a door and point a new way out, we shall have done a work worth doing.[42]

Shelby Harrison was an enthusiastic as Delano about the proposed plan. But Harrison, who had guided the work of the Pittsburgh Survey, emphasized social welfare as the real objective of plan-making:

I should covet for this project the distinction of having gone far in working out the social or sociological bases for the constructive plans to be drawn up – farther than previous cities have gone.[43]

Harrison raised the question of the future growth of New York:

Many facts seem to indicate that New York City is too large for the welfare of all concerned – at least that it should not grow larger by adding people and activities to the congested areas of Manhattan and Brooklyn. How then can the concentration be stopped or relieved to a degree?[44]

Concentration, for Harrison, meant more than the traffic congestion that Lewis was concerned with or the skyscraper clusters that concerned Bassett. Concentration was seen as a primary source of slum evils. Harrison quoted Thomas Adams, the British town planner, as saying that 'in practice it is found that the improved environment converts men and women of the slums into decent and respectable citizens.'[45] High on Harrison's list of solutions was the planning of suburban or satellite areas at the fringe of the city, an idea imported from the English Garden City movement and the German industrial suburbs built by Krupp and other large firms. To determine what character industrial satellite suburbs might take in the New York area, Harrison urged studies of both the character and trends in industries in New York and of the residential and neighborhood needs of working and poor people. He suggested that existing ethnic or racial areas be studied and compared with what he termed 'promise' communities, working-class areas characterized by a general upward mobility. But Harrison also emphasized the desirability of looking into the needs and problems of the public infra-structure: water supply, waste disposal, air pollution control, health centers and hospitals, public schools, parks and playgrounds, prisons, and even public 'comfort' stations. And he called for an inquiry into the shocking incidence of street traffic accidents in the city. Harrison's views carried considerable weight. Trained as a social worker, he was a staff member of the Russell Sage Foundation and had earned a reputation in planning on the basis of his Pittsburgh Survey work. More than any of the other experts in the study group he was concerned with the social welfare aspects of planning. But as his list of study desiderata revealed, social welfare questions often involved analysis and policy at a scale far below the coarse grain of metropolitan analysis. This raised a dilemma which was to preoccupy the Committee and its staff throughout its efforts: which public concerns were metropolitan in scope, and which were not and therefore should be excluded from the survey and plan?

In the following months Harrison pursued the question of what a regional social survey should comprise and how it should relate to a prospective plan. By June he had revised his conception of the social survey. '. . . "social" is not really a separate category because all studies made for purposes of drafting the plan are social studies,' he wrote to Norton.[46] Harrison continued to urge that the studies and plan be based on social welfare interest, particularly the interests of the poor.

> It is not that the social worker has the social welfare and social interests of the community any more at heart than say, the city planner, but merely that the social worker, because of his fairly consecutive and immediate contact with all groups in the community and particularly with those carrying the heaviest burdens, is likely to help in keeping these considerations to the fore in all planning for the future; and for that reason he has a distinct contribution to make to the City Plan.[47]

Harrison's revised proposal for a social survey was both comprehensive and ambitious. He emphasized a general empirical study of the distribution and movement of population, 'including data upon the present boundaries of the different neighborhoods having decided racial or natural characteristics.' A survey of Harlem was a priority project:

> We have within the city's borders this big Negro population – upwards of 75,000 people. What about them in planning for the future? Is it not important to find out whether there are not factors in their welfare that need to be taken into account in the fairly immediate as well as the more distant development of the future city? Is this to be a permanent Negro community: If so what are its special needs as to parks, housing, civic centers, schools, hospitals, etc?[48]

For African-Americans and ethnic groups, Harrison proposed studying an extensive list of conditions:

> Growth and distribution of the population group.
> Organization, social, economic, religious and political.
> Relations with the Police, Street Cleaning, and Tenement House Departments.
> Housing and home conditions.
> Health and sanitation.
> Cost of living and work opportunities.
> Wages and income situation in relation to normal family life.
> Recreation and leisure time opportunities.

Opportunities for participation in the activities of the district.
Constructive agencies and forces of the district.
School and other educational needs.[49]

Harrison also proposed to learn more about the actual impact of a policy of decentralization, and how best to realize benefits which might result from a greater dispersion of jobs and housing. He suggested a case study of the build-up of the Brownsville area, which followed the construction of the Williamsburgh Bridge. What, he asked, were the social effects of the new access to a less populated region and what safeguards should be kept in mind if the full social results of the new developments were to be gained?

Harrison was not entirely certain that all the groups in the congested areas would welcome decentralization. He proposed to look closely at the Lower East Side to determine whether there might not be any favorable sides to life there. Would the average family there really want to leave the congested center to live in a suburban or rural home?

Moreover, the suburbs did not always offer uniformly good environments. Some had problems as serious as those found in the city. Harrison was skeptical about the social panacea of simply reducing densities.

> Here and there, in spite of the fact that ground space is not limited and of other favorable influences, communities have grown up in which living conditions are inexcusably bad.[50]

An outlying section of Brooklyn known as 'Pigtown' offered possibilities for a case study, Harrison suggested.

Harrison's questions were highly pertinent, and he proposed to obtain answers through sound empirical and case study techniques. The problem remained, however, of just how the planners might make use of Harrison's answers in their formulations. But the prospect of linking social research to regional planning was an exciting one.

Charles Norton was elated at the generally favorable reception of his project for a Russell Sage plan. He felt certain that the Foundation would, with the additional bequest of Mrs Sage in hand, find the $300,000 he needed. Then in March of 1921, he fell seriously ill while visiting in Baltimore. Undaunted, he wrote from a Johns Hopkins hospital bed to Charles Wacker in Chicago of his plans for New York.

> I'm getting well fast and hope to escape shortly but I've something on my mind and I'll scribble it . . . this is very private and personal. I've got a lot of money for a New York Plan [plenty of money!] and am going to organize something along our old Merchants Club lines when I get up and out of here.
>
> I want to invite Robert DeForest and half a dozen others to visit Chicago very quietly and privately and look at the Chicago situation. Will you give us at least part of a day and show us the works?
>
> I've been quite sick. Felt pretty badly when I saw you last and felt worse when I got home. Guess I was walking around with a mild typhoid. Now I'm fat and

brown and having a happy convalescence under Dr. Llewellyn Barber's able hand. Charlie, good doctors and good nurses will all be angels in heaven.[51]

Norton's confidence was apparently justified. The trustees voted on May 17, 1921, to amend the February 7th resolution to authorize the expenditure of $300,000 on the plan. The trustees also accepted DeForest's suggestion that Norton be made chairman of the Committee on the Plan.[52]

NOTES

1. Henry Villard had aspirations as an urban reformer which may have influenced Charles Norton. Villard, unhappy with the typically narrow townhouse imposed by the Manhattan Street plan and with the dearth of squares and places, commissioned. Charles McKim's architectural firm, McKim, Mead, and White, to design a group of townhouses in the form of a single Renaissance villa with a courtyard. The group was completed in 1886. Villard hoped that his model would inspire others to develop whole Manhattan blocks in a similar fashion. This, of course, did not happen. Ironically, a mob protesting economic conditions in 1893 menaced the railroad financier and his family at his townhouse, mistaking the palatial group of houses for a single residence. Charles Norton was a frequent visitor at the Villard Houses between 1897 and 1923. For an account of the life at Villard House, see: Villard, Oswald Garrison (1939) *Memoirs of a Liberal Editor*. New York: Harcourt Brace & Son.

2. Charles D. Norton, prepared for the history of the Merchants Club of Chicago, June, 1992, Regional Plan Papers.

3. *Ibid.*

4. *Ibid.*

5. *Ibid.*

6. *Ibid.*, p.3.

7. Moody, Walter D. (1919) *What of the City?* Chicago: A.C. McClurg and Co., pp. 363–364.

8. Moody, Walter D. (1920) *Wacker's Manual of the Plan of Chicago*, 3rd ed. Chicago: Chicago Plan Commission. The manual was named for Charles Wacker, who had succeeded Norton as Chairman of the Commercial Club's committee on the Plan of Chicago and went on to become the first chairman of the Chicago Plan Commission.

9. *New York Evening Post*, March 6, 1923. One of Norton's interesting innovations was the installation of machines to wash dirty currency. Previously currency had been disposed of by burning. This was a literal case of saving the treasury money.

10. Letter of William H. Taft, *New York Times*, March 10, 1923.

11. Kolko, Gabriel (1963) *The Triumph of Conservatism*. New York: The Free Press, pp. 170–189.

12. *New York Times*, March 7, 1923.

13. Report of Heights of Buildings Commission, City of New York, December 23, 1923.

14. City of New York Board of Estimate and Apportionment: Committee on the City Plan (1914) *Development and Present Status of City Planning in New York City*. New York.

15. *Ibid.*, pp. 72–76.

16. Norton memorandum of November 27, 1915, quoted in the Committee on the Regional Plan of New York and Its Environs, *The Plan of New York with References to the Chicago Plan*, Letter from Charles D. Norton to Frederic A. Delano. New York, May, 1923, Regional Plan Papers.

17. *Ibid*

18. *Ibid*

19. Quoted in Scott, Mel (1969) *American City Planning Since 1890*. Berkeley: University of California Press p. 177.

20. Mitchel, a reform Democrat who had won in 1914 on a Republic-Fusion ticket, was denied the Republican nomination in 1917, which went to the obscure William M. Bennett. Mitchel ran on the Fusion ticket but lost when the Socialist Candidate Morris Hillquit polled nearly 150,000 votes. With the votes split four ways, the Democratic candidate, Hylan, was the chief beneficiary and victor. Sayre, Wallace S. and Kaufman, Herbert (1960) *Governing New York City*. New York: Russell Sage Foundation, pp. 692–694.

21. Quoted in Adams, Thomas (1927) *Planning the New York Region*. New York: Regional Plan of New York and Its Environs, pp. 33.

22. Soule, George (1947) *Prosperity Decade: From War to Depression, 1917–1929*. New York: Holt Rinehart and Winston, p.10; *New York Evening Post*, March 6, 1923.

23. Glenn, John M. (1947) *Russell Sage Foundation*, II, 1907–1926. New York: Russell Sage Foundation, p. 438.

24. Lubove, Roy (1962) *The Progressives and the Slums*. Pittsburgh: University of Pittsburgh Press, pp. 34–39.

25. Committee on the Regional Plan of New York and Its Environs, *The Plan of New York with References to the Chicago Plan*, p.10.

26. Lewis, Nelson P. (1916) *The Planning of the Modern City*. New York: John Wiley and Sons.

27. Committee on the Regional Plan of New York and Its Environs, *The Plan of New York with References to the Chicago Plan*, p.10

28. *Ibid*

29. John M. Glenn to Charles D. Norton, January 31, 1921, Regional Plan Papers.

30. *Ibid*

31. Charles D. Norton, Memorandum of January 31, 1921, Regional Plan Papers. Frank L. Polk, a prominent lawyer and former secretary of State under Wilson, joined the Committee on October 31, 1921.

32. *Ibid.*

33. *Ibid.*

34. *Ibid.*

35. *Ibid*

36. Abstract of comments on Norton memorandum, April 29, 1921, Regional Plan Papers.

37. Charles Moore to Charles D. Norton, February 8, 1921, Regional Plan Papers.

38. *Ibid.*

39. Frederick Law Olmsted, Jr to John Glenn, February 21, 1921, Regional Plan Papers.

40. Nelson P. Lewis to Charles D. Norton, March 24, 1921, Regional Plan Papers.

41. Frederic A. Delano to Charles D. Norton, April 4, 1921, Regional Plan Papers.

42. *Ibid.*

43. Shelby Harrison to John M. Glenn, March 9, 1921, Regional Plan Papers.

44. *Ibid.*

45. *Ibid.*

46. Shelby M. Harrison to Charles D. Norton, June 11, 1921, Regional Plan Papers.

47. *Ibid.*

48. *Ibid.*

49. *Ibid.*

50. *Ibid*

51. Charles D. Norton to Charles Wacker, April 12, 1921, Regional Plan Papers.

52. Committee on the Regional Plan of New York and Its Environs, *The Plan of New York with References to the Chicago Plan.*

5

THE SEARCH FOR
SCOPE AND SUBSTANCE

FOUR SURVEYS

On the basis of reactions to the proposal of February 11th, Norton, in a memorandum prepared on November 3, 1921, outlined four inquiries to be undertaken by the Committee as part of its survey work: (1) an economic and industrial survey, which would analyze the fundamental reasons for the existence of New York, and would attempt to forecast its future development, an inquiry into economic activities that create populous districts and those that follow population; and a study of land values and taxation; (2) a physical survey, under the direction of Nelson Lewis, which would map existing topographic and physical conditions, including man-made facilities such as highways and railroads; (3) a legal survey under Edward Bassett, which would look into existing law as it would affect the plan, including an analysis of zoning, excess condemnation, official maps, and public rights to shore-lines and land under water, and (4) a social and living conditions inquiry under Shelby Harrison, which would 'bring to the attention of the planners those factors which have direct bearing upon human values and social welfare, and work for healthful and satisfactory housing and home surroundings.'[1]

Lewis set to work to assemble and prepare the maps and charts describing the physiognomy of the metropolitan area, working from material collected by the Brooklyn Committee on the City Plan, that of the defunct Advisory Committee, and his own files. In this work he was aided by his son, Harold M. Lewis, a civil engineering graduate of Rensselaer Polytechnic Institute who was appointed chief assistant to the Physical Survey. In September 1921, Nelson Lewis submitted a report outlining the area that should be defined as the New York Metropolitan Region. It was agreed that the Region should consist of all or parts of twenty-two counties in New York, New Jersey, and Connecticut within two hours rail commuting time of Manhattan. An exception was Suffolk County, included so that all of Long Island would be part of the study area. The region, as Lewis defined it, encompassed 5,527 square miles and contained a population in 1920 of 8.98 million people[2] (figure 5.1).

Figure 5.1. The New York Metropolitan Region as defined by the Committee on the Regional Plan of New York, 1921. (*Source:* Regional Plan Papers)

In his report, Lewis outlined what he considered to be the key physical development categories which the Physical Survey should investigate:

(*a*) The railway transportation system, whether by trunk line railroads or by rapid transit lines for the accommodation of both passengers and freight.

(*b*) The closely related questions of shipping facilities and their coordination with those for railway transportation.

(*c*) The main highway system of the entire area, including the bridges over, and tunnels under, waterways.

(*d*) The park and recreation facilities, including existing open spaces, such as cemeteries, and a study of the areas which should be secured and preserved for public recreation.

(e)   The location of public and semi-public buildings.

(f)   An investigation of the possibility of establishing industries outside of existing congested areas, with provision for the suitable housing
of employees in such industries.

Both Lewis' definition of the areal dimensions of the region and his proposed
scope of investigation were accepted by the Committee and would have
significant influence on the subsequent development of the Regional Survey
and Plan.

Bassett set about collecting the zoning ordinances of the many municipalities and villages in the Region which had enacted restrictions in the five years
following the adoption by New York of the first such ordinance.

After six years of discussion and setback, work on the surveys had begun.
From these surveys it was hoped would issue the great Plan to guide New
York's regional destiny for decades. Norton's dream was at last becoming a
reality. But problems remained. Norton was keenly aware from his Chicago
Plan and Red Cross experiences that technical studies alone, no matter how
competent, would make only ripples when what he needed was a tidal wave
of support. Norton was not thinking of mass support – that would have to
come later through such means as a *Wacker Manual* based on the complete
Plan – but support among the influential leaders of the Region. Actually,
there were two leadership groups that Norton sought to involve: the notables
in business and politics, and the leading technicians and practitioners in the
subject areas of the surveys. He drew on his Washington experience with the
Federal Reserve System. 'We must,' he wrote,

> approach our problem very much as Senator [Nelson] Aldrich approached the
> problem of monetary reform: that we must organize a series of well-defined
> fundamental inquries, deliberately undertaken, staffed by the ablest men and
> women, the reports carefully edited for brevity and clarity, and published in
> attractive form, and that we should announce the project at a meeting of
> architects, artists, engineers, and other citizens to be addressed by Mr. [Elihu]
> Root and Mr. [Herbert} Hoover.[3]

Through the last months of 1921 Norton threw himself into the tasks of
organizing the survey advisory committees and preparing for the public
meeting at which the proposed work would be announced. Norton was
particularly concerned with the composition of the general committee to
advise on the economic and industrial survey, for here was an opportunity to
draw into the project the business interests which to a large degree controlled
the economic destiny of the Region. By involving business leaders he hoped
to educate them in the need for the Plan, solicit their advice in its preparation,
and enlist them in carrying out the various proposals that would come out of
the work. Norton's business connections were undoubtedly helpful in this
effort, but only his personal enthusiasm and talent for persuasion could have
won the cooperation of such a powerful and prestigious group of people.

Among those who accepted were Darwin P. Kingsley, President of the New York Chamber of Commerce, William Fellows Morgan, President of the Merchants Association, E.H. Outerbridge, Chairman of the Port of New York Authority. A.C. Bedford, Chairman of the International Chamber of Commerce, Herbert Hoover, the Secretary of Commerce, Frederic B. Pratt, Brooklyn industrialist and promoter of the Brooklyn City Plan, and former Governor Alfred E. Smith.[4]

For the legal survey, Norton enlisted a prestigious group of lawyers, including James Pyne, President of the Association of the Bar of the City of New York, Charles Evans Hughes, Harding's Secretary of State and a former Governor of New York and Supreme Court Justice, Julius Henry Cohen, Counsel for the Port of New York Authority, Issac Mills, a prominent attorney, and Chancellor James F. Fielder of New Jersey. Formation of the Advisory Committee on the Social and Living Conditions Survey was placed largely in the hands of Robert DeForest and Shelby Harrison, who recruited Lawson Purdy, former New York City Tax Commissioner, Felix Warburg of the banking family, Porter R. Lee, Director of the New York School of Social Work, the Reverend Harry Emerson Fosdick, Joseph Lee, President of Community Services, Inc., and Father Keegan, a leader in Catholic charity work.

Harrison had selected three special topics for study: public health and hospitals, play and leisure time, and correctional and custodial institutions, and had lined up advisors in each field. For the hospitals study he would call on Homer Folks, Secretary of the State Charities Aid Society, Dr. Herman M. Biggs, Commissioner of the New York State Department of Health, Dr. Winford H. Smith of Johns Hopkins Hospital, Dr. S.S. Goldwater, Director of Mt. Sinai Hospital, Dr. Thomas W. Salmon, Medical Director of the National Committee for Mental Hygiene, Dr. Lindsay Williams of the Rockefeller Institute, with Dr. Harry Emerson and Michael Davis of the Committee on Dispensary Development providing leadership. These men would organize a pathbreaking study of health and hospital needs of the region and propose new facilities.

The Play and Leisure Time Study would be directed by Lee F. Hanmer, Director of the Department of Recreation of the Russell Sage Foundation, and his associate Clarence A. Perry, with an advisory committee consisting of Mr. V. Everit Macy, George H. Bell, Otto Kahn, H.S. Brancher, Joseph Lee, President of Community Services, Inc., Dr. J.E. Roycroft, head of Physical Education at Princeton University, Mrs Charles Farnsworth, Chairman of the Recreation Committee of the Women's City Club, and Mrs Kate Oglesbey of the Drama League.

The correctional and custodial institutions study would be advised by Dwight W. Morrow, Burdette Lewis, Commissioner of Correction of New Jersey, Dr. George W. Kuckeney, former warden of Sing Sing Prison, Bernard Gluck, Professor of Mental Hygiene at the New York School of Social

Work, Orlando F. Lewis, Secretary of the New York Prison Association, and Hastings H. Hart, Director of the Department of Child Health of the Sage Foundation.[5]

The physical survey presented a problem with which Charles Norton had been concerned since his Chicago years: how to bring the engineers and architects together. DeForest expressed his apprehensions about the role of the architects.

> I think it is important in our program to keep art and artists and city beautiful distinctly in the background. I think they are associated in the lay mind largely with impracticable schemes of the 'blue sky' order.
>
> I would want to emphasize in every way that our program related to the city wholesome, the city of homes, and to let the artistic largely take care of itself.[6]

As a result of DeForest's concern, the physical survey, under Nelson Lewis, was separated from the work of the architects, for whom a project committee would later be organized. Lewis's advisory committee was comprised almost entirely of engineers: D.L. Turner, Consulting Engineer, Rapid Transit Commission, B.F. Cresson, Jr., Chief Engineer of the Port Authority, Frederick Law Olmsted, Jr., Landscape Architect, Jay Downer of the Westchester County Parks Commission, Morris R. Shepherd, and Professor George C. Whipple. To this group would later be added Henry M. Brinckerhoff, consulting engineer, and Charles U. Powell, Engineer in Charge of the Topographic Bureau of the Borough of Queens.[7]

Additional staff was needed to coordinate the work of the advisory committees, and in November, 1921. Flavel Shurtleff was hired to act as secretary of the Committee on the Regional Plan. Shurtleff, an energetic young Boston lawyer who had been drawn into planning by Frederick Law Olmsted, had authored a book in 1914 for the Sage Foundation titled *Carrying Out the City Plan*.[8] At the time Shurtleff was serving as Secretary of the National Conference on City Planning, which he had helped organize and which was supported and located at the Sage Foundation Building at 130 East 22nd Street in Manhattan.

Shurtleff was a capable and vigorous young man. But Norton wanted a permanent Executive Secretary with more maturity, whose experience and credentials approximated those of the members of the several advisory committees. The man he had in mind was Frederick P. Keppel, then with the International Chamber of Commerce in Columbia College and former Assistant Secretary of War. Keppel had also been associated with Norton in his work with the American Red Cross during World War I. In January 1922 Keppel agreed to leave his Paris position to join the staff of the Regional Plan Committee on a part-time basis. But a permanent move could not be made before September. In the interim, Shurtleff, who would serve as his assistant, would carry on the duties of Secretary. Henry James, a Wall Street lawyer, volunteered to serve on the Committee's staff without pay. It was the consensus that he would work well with Shurtleff and Keppel, particularly in the area of building community support for the Plan.

Norton was well aware that the work of the Committee would be of considerable historic importance in the planning movement, and one of the duties of the Executive Secretary would be to keep the record or history of the Plan. To this end Norton enlisted the aid of I. N. Phelps Stokes, author of the remarkable *The Iconography of New York*, Charles Moore, who wrote the report of the Chicago Plan, and Bruce Rogers, an Englishman who was regarded as 'the best printer in the world.'[9]

With staffing complete and the scope of the four surveys in hand, Norton was ready to make the public announcement of the project:

> So many people are now in our confidence that we must consider the probability of publicity. I suggest, therefore, that . . . we call a small but very important conference of engineers, architects, artists and public spirited citizens. . .
>
> The one man we must have if possible by reason of his interest and knowledge of the whole subject is Mr. [Elihu] Root. No one can state the case for the need of city planning as he can, and he will be accepted as representative by the artistic group. For the engineers, Mr. [Herbert] Hoover would be glad to speak.[10]

The meeting was scheduled for the evening of May 10, 1922, at the auditorium of the Engineering Societies Building. The guest list of notables grew to eight hundred, of whom about six hundred accepted. Dress for the occasion was the dinner jacket.[11]

Charles Norton, the first speaker, outlined the project for a Regional Plan of New York and the surveys that would be undertaken as a basis for planning. Noting that the Regional Plan would make proposals for a large area comprised of twenty-two counties in three states, Norton recalled how the Commissioners of the 1811 Plan for Manhattan had worried that their report would be a subject of merriment for having planned for a population 'greater than is collected at any spot this side of China.'[12]

Norton explained why a regional plan was needed, and the problems it would attempt to solve:

> Deep-seated structural defects leave masses of the population in an environment ill suited for human happiness and welfare. Traffic in existing streets is congested to the point where it places intolerable burdens upon commerce and endangers human life. . .
>
> Many admirable local plans have been developed, but no inspiriting vision of the future guides us in our present expenditures of money and civic effort. Without a guiding plan, what of New York one hundred years hence? Momentous decisions are being constantly made, decisions that are local, piecemeal and unrelated to the larger trends. The time has come for unified planning in the interest of the whole people.[13]

Norton added that a regional plan, though an expensive undertaking, would pay for itself in the long run. The plan, Norton suggested, would not call for large new expenditures but rather would coordinate projects which would have to be undertaken even without a plan:

> It can be shown that without a plan hundreds of millions of dollars have been wasted in and near New York during the past century in desultory or ill-considered public improvements. As time passes, a plan of New York can become a reality by the expenditure of the very funds which will be expended in any event.[14]

The next speaker, Herbert Hoover, then Secretary of Commerce, commended the Russell Sage Trustees for undertaking a survey and comprehensive plan for New York and Its Environs. Hoover asserted that the cities were not contributing all that they should to the national character and economy:

> The enormous losses in human happiness and in money which have resulted from lack of city plans which take into account the conditions of modern life, need little proof. The lack of adequate open spaces, of playgrounds and parks, the congestion of streets, and misery of tenement life and its repercussions upon each new generation, are an untold charge aginst our American life. Our cities do not produce the full contribution to the sinews of American life and national character. The moral and social issues can only be solved by a new conception of city building.[15]

Elihu Root, the former Secretary of State, also praised the efforts of the Sage Committee. Root thought that the existence of a Plan, even one without official standing, could guide development in proper directions:

> This project is to get an intelligent idea of how the growth of the city in the future may be directed, with common and general judgment about the way in which it is desirable that it should grow, so that it will meet as fully as possible the difficulties that are inseparable from mass human life. I think the project is practicable. I think that the existence of plans known to everybody will give just enough direction to the movement of the multitude of separate impulses to lead the growth along the right lines.[16]

Other speakers followed, including Lillian Wald, Charles Dana Gibson, and Mrs. August Belmont; and each warmly praised the conception of a Regional Plan and the men who had undertaken it.

The reception of the project at the meeting of May 10, and the widespread endorsement which ensued, spurred the Committee in its efforts to refine the scope of the four surveys and to gain public acceptance of the proposals that would emerge from the plan. The Sage Trustees were equally enthusiastic and at a meeting the following day approved Grosvenor Atterbury's plan to add a story to the Sage Building for permanent quarters of the Regional Plan Committee and its staff.[17]

Through the first months of 1922 Norton continued to urge the involvement of artists and architects and suggested that a dramatic architectural proposal would attract additional attention:

> We must have early in our work a 'stunt,' and I have from Mr. [Edward] Bennett

an estimate on the study and architectural sketches for the widening of 59th Street and an elevated shorefront rolled around Manhattan Island from 59th Street.[18]

Delano expressed concern for the reaction of New York architects on employing Bennett. 'It will be a case of too much Chicago with Mr. Norton, Mr. Delano, and Mr. Bennett,' he wrote. Glenn noted that Bennett had produced the Brooklyn City Plan. But Norton accepted Delano's counsel: 'Chicago and Brooklyn planning New York will cause a riot.'[19] The Bennett proposal was dropped and architectural studies put aside for the moment. Norton, observing that previous plans had begun with architectural schemes, agreed that the Regional Plan should break new ground:

> We spent in Chicago $325,000 in three years, sold the plan to the public by various publicity methods, including a school text book, and with this public support flanked the politicians, and yet we missed entirely a great opportunity to study the social and living conditions in the city and the fundamental reasons for Chicago's existence.[20]

Norton agreed with Olmsted's definition of planning, expressed in a conference a few weeks earlier:

> City planning, like other planning, includes in the first place the recognition and adoption of certain objectives to be attained, and in the second place the devising of practicable mechanisms for attaining them. Since actually fruitful results from planning are apparent only in so far as the mechanism itself is devised and is seen to be practicable, the emphasis in city planning is apt to be upon the devising of the mechanism.
>
> In a great deal of planning the objectives are so obvious and so familiar, in a general way, that people of common sense spend little time in academic definitions of those objectives; preferring rightly to concentrate their efforts on the problem of devising the most practicable mechanism for attaining them. The emphasis can never safely be withdrawn from the latter problem, and it is with no thought of so withdrawing it that we would concentrate for a time on a consideration of objectives.
>
> If we look at any human affairs in a sufficiently large way we have to admit that 'We don't know where we're going but we're on our way.' And we have to devote most of our energies to making the going as good as we are able without worrying because we can't see much of the road ahead, and without withdrawing too much energy from the job of dodging the obstacles immediately in front of us in an effort to peer further ahead. At the best we can forecast the more distant future only in a very uncertain way. But whether we forecast it well or ill we cannot avoid the responsibility that the course we steer today will largely determine whether the ship gets into the shallows or into clear sailing tomorrow.
>
> When it comes to dealing with city planning on the scale of such a metropolis as New York, common sense requires us to take a larger perspective than in most jobs of planning; and out of the enormous amount of effort which must be expended on the whole job if it is to come to anything at all, an amount of effort large in itself, even if relatively no larger than usual, ought to be devoted to scrutiny of the less obvious and more distant objectives. That scrutiny means a

study of the more important economic and social conditions, tendencies and possibilities of the community. Before attempting in any large way to exercise deliberate control over *what* New York is physically to become, we ought to have as clear an understanding as we can reasonably get of the answer to the question, never completely to be answered, *'Why is* New York?'[21]

Thomas Adams, the Scottish planner who had worked with Ebenezer Howard on the garden cities of Letchworth and Welwyn and had recently served as a consultant to the Canadian government, also attended the meeting. Adams concurred with Olmsted's view on the need to distinguish local from non-local activities and proposed to find ways to control the location of manufacturing.

> The manufacturer usually builds his factory and is not dependent on local trade. He can be influenced to go wherever the facilities for carrying on his business are best without regard to a local market for his produce. He originates the demand for land for housing purposes, the need of schools and local improvements. Cities try to attract industries to get an increase of population. They do not need to attract retail merchants or doctors. These come after the population.[22]

Norton concluded that the key to the successes of the plan and the solution to problems of congestion and bad housing lay in the control of the location of industry. If the economic study could identify the industries which might be relocated, decentralization might be possible.

> The Economic Study must be a combination of the practical and the academic. The Director of the Inquiry must be one who can compel the attention of businessmen . . . The job seems clear but who is the man? He must have, or must develop, a vision of New York based on its economic factors.[23]

When Norton approached Nicholas Murray Butler, the President of Columbia University, for suggestions, he immediately recommended a member of the economics faculty, Robert Murray Haig. Butler thought Haig would be best, but other possibilities at Columbia were Roswell McCrea and Wesley C. Mitchell. Others suggested E.M. Hopkins, President of Dartmouth, and Leonard Ayres, formerly of the Sage Foundation. It was decided that a proposal for the economic study would need to be drafted over the summer, then Haig would be approached. Haig agreed to accept the direction of the Economic Survey, with McCrea as consultant. Because of other commitments, however, the Columbia economists could not begin work for several months. In the interim Professor Walter W. Stewart of Amherst College was commissioned to survey the economic factors that would need to be considered.

The work of the Spring had exhausted Norton, and he decided to vacation in Europe in August. Characteristically, he determined to combine work with leisure by inspecting the regional planning work in London and Paris. Keppel would accompany him and examine other cities. Perhaps the Old World had some answers that could profitably be brought back to New York. After three weeks of travel Norton reported to Delano from aboard the *S.S. Majestic* on what he and Keppel had seen:

The outstanding thing in Paris is the study now going on of the area encircling Paris now dedicated to fortifications. These are to be abandoned as such, and Monsieur Bonniere and his very able and enthusiastic group of architects, engineers and artists are studying this huge windfall of new land with zeal and high intelligence. Some of the land is to be sold off: for villas, for tenements, for various types of housing projects, and a great deal is to be dedicated to 'sport' : to parks and playgrounds, stadium for games, etc, etc. We spent a long time in that office [the Prefecture of the Seine] and two things interested us most: the fine spirit of group effort which was shown; and the skill and beauty with which their schemes are 'rendered.' They have an instinct for showing their plans well. I asked them why they gave so much thought to that phase of it. They said frankly they were trying to interest the city fathers who decide what shall be done and who control the purse . . .

In London our friend Thomas Adams was most kind. He did the most generous thing an Englishman can do - came in to town to meet us on a bank holiday – and later took us through the Middlesex county where he is designing and building great new arteries 100 feet wide to open up the southern approaches and also to several of the latest London County Council housing schemes, near Putney and Hammersmith and also to see the *first* housing scheme – now a matured Forest Hills affair of prosperous and handsome homes. To the north, near Hampstead, Raymond Unwin took us in tow and first showing us quite thoroughly Hampstead Gardens – the best subdivision of suburban land ever I saw or heard of – and a charming bit of architectural design as well – he then took us to his own house on the top of Hampstead Heath, one of the most ancient houses in London, where he had a comfortable and spacious studio and garden, and where he gave us no end of useful suggestions, showed us no end of interesting schemes now going forward in every part of Europe, and with the kind and hospitable aid of his wife, gave us a delightful afternoon and evening.

He is to give us a week of his time in New York – and we can learn much from him. Adams struck me as harder headed, more practical, a man to do things and do them well. Unwin more of the philosopher and idealist, but no one can say that Hampstead Gardens is not a practical and admirable solution of that problem. Unwin is now in the Ministry of Health and has turned over to other architects the further development of Hampstead Gardens. I may perhaps be allowed to remark that the newer work is less good.[24]

While in Paris, Norton had learned of Mayor John Hylan's destructive plans to build recreational facilities in Central Park. In an angry letter to Frank L. Polk, a member of the Committee, he revealed again his ability to go to the heart of a problem:

. . . I read in New York papers of Hylan's plans for War Memorial and swimming pools in Central Park. The attacks on Central Park are incessant. They grow out of real popular demand and crying needs. No use in hammering Hylan as 'stupid'; and it isn't true [as the Post claims] that the sea beaches are 'accessible' in New York. They are, for the poor, remote, expensive, difficult. The real trouble is that the Playground crowd in New York have not been vigorous enough in finding solutions; Chicago has found them; Paris is finding them. The difference between a park and a playground is thoroughly understood by the many experts interested in playgrounds in New York, but they have never successfully educated the public about this.

There is *plenty* of vacant land in the Ghetto for playgrounds. A small place, near the house, is what the poor mother and her child need. A small place with equipment for play -gravel, sand, swimming or wading pool, an area for swings and slides these children can swarm over happily . . . They should be scattered about every two or three blocks, where people congest in flats. It is suicidal to try to transport children away over the Central Park to *play*. Central Park is about as useful to a Broome Street mother as a playground in the Bronx is to you and me. She doesn't need something that costs a day's excursion in time and a day's wages in money to enjoy.[25]

As a result of the Central Park controversy Norton invited Jacques Lambert, a noted French landscape architect, to come to New York to study Manhattan's park and playground problem. And despite Norton's reservations about Raymond Unwin's lack of hard-headedness, he too was invited to come for a series of lectures and discussions at the Sage Foundation.

Unwin, who was fifty-seven, was then Chief Technical Officer of the British Government for Building and Town Planning and was regarded as the international dean of town planners and housing experts. Trained as an engineer, he had, with Barry Parker, helped plan Letchworth, the first garden city laid out according to the principles of Ebenezer Howard. In 1913 he was one of the founders, under the leadership of Thomas Adams of the Town Planning Institute and had served as its president in 1915. His best known piece of writing was his 1912 essay, 'Nothing Gained by Overcrowding,' which urged the lowering of densities through larger lots in garden city suburbs linked to city centers by fast railways. As Frederick Osborn later observed, 'Unwin's is a cardinal name in planning and housing history, because he combined three distinguished qualities – proficiency as a technician, sociological insight, and the ability to explain.'[26]

In September 1922 Unwin arrived in New York to share his insights with the Regional Plan Committee. During the ten days Unwin devoted to the Regional Plan, he delivered three well-attended talks at the Sage Building and prepared a number of papers containing his recommendations for the planning of the New York Region. In his talks and reports Unwin generally endorsed the proposals for the physical, economic, social, and legal surveys. But he urged that the surveys be based on certain provisional hypotheses. Otherwise, the surveys would tend to be unfocused and would result in the collection of data not essential to the major thrust of the Plan. As provisional hypotheses he suggested the following:

1. Increased transportation facilities would not cure congestion but might stimulate further congestion, unless accompanied by the restriction of the concentration of excessively high buildings.

2. More natural arteries of communication were needed between important places, more streets should be restricted from through traffic in residence areas, and main avenues should have fewer interruptions by cross traffic.

3. Extensive use of streets by private cars might need restraint, and more natural routing of traffic should be promoted by prescribing definite routes for main streams of traffic.

4. Instead of multiplying traffic facilities, consideration should be given to eliminating unnecessary movement by means of decentralization and improved localization as a guiding hypothesis based on:

   (a) dispersal of certain industries or other functions from Manhattan;

   (b) improved location of functions involving needless movement;

   (c) creation of new suburbs or garden cities;

   (d) prevention of haphazard development in open areas in the environs.[27]

In a talk given at the Sage Building on September 25, Unwin explained his views:

> The first aim of your new plan must be to stop the crowding, to distribute your population properly, and having distributed them, your second aim must be so to localize their lives, that they will, in your own expressive words, 'stay put.'[28]

Unwin, here, departed somewhat from the idea he had expressed in 'Nothing Gained by Overcrowding,' of substituting good transportation to outlying suburbs for higher densities closer to the city center. Most people, he argued, had little need to go to Manhattan. Therefore, the way to solve Manhattan's problems and also to provide better living conditions for the masses was to try to isolate them in self-contained satellite suburbs. The way to do this would be by limiting the amount of transportation into the center and by introducing a conscious program for decentralization of industries into new garden cities, which would contain all the local facilities one could need.

Though it was hardly noticed at the time, Unwin had raised here what would become the most controversial issue of the plan. In effect, he was proposing a conscious, planned return through environmental design to the *Gemeinschaft* or village form of life, albeit one embedded in the metropolitan region characterized by a highly mobile, industrial, *Gesellschaft* way of life. Unwin was implicitly denying the significance of the metropolitan-region scale for the great majority of the Region's people. There is, he suggested,

> a constant reaction between the place folk live in and the life they lead. It is action and reaction, environment on character, character on environment. The desire for the group life promotes the neighbourhood centre and causes people to gather round it. But also the planning of the group centre and the provisions there made for the social, cultural and recreational life to be gathered round that centre, in turn stimulates and enlarges the community life. Here is the greatest opportunity of the city planner. He can help that which is bent on the best in

civic life to find its fullest expression . . .

Follow out this clue and it will gradually bring order, efficiency, design and beauty out of the present confusion in which the commerce, industry, domestic life and distraction of some millions of people jostle and obstruct each other in their struggle to expand.[29]

Unwin proposed that the Regional Plan Committee start an experimental new garden suburb as soon as a suitable site could be found, to demonstrate how industry might be decentralized and a re-orientation of civic life effected.

Was this a romantic, very English manifestation of environmental determinism, or was it a real alternative to be considered by the Regional Plan Committee? Did it contradict the very reasons for the existence of the metropolis: access to opportunities unavailable in smaller settlements? And was the notion of reducing rather then enhancing accessibility to opportunity through well-greased transportation channels contrary to the obvious desire of the populace to possess and use the private automobile? Unwin's idea that individual human opportunity could be enhanced by reducing mobility and economic opportunity appeared ambiguous to the cosmopolitan regional planners of New York.

Unwin's proposals for the organization of the planning studies were more favorably received than his substantive proposals for the Plan itself. He urged that the economic studies focus on industries that could easily be removed from Manhattan to outlying sites. Some of the proposed surveys, particularly the social surveys proposed by Harrison, he felt would not have a direct bearing on the design of the Plan and might be postponed or dispensed with. As an architect he emphasized physical design rather than social policy as the salient output of the project. For all the surveys to be relevant to the making of the plan, he suggested that a city planner direct the survey work:

I am inclined to think that you need on your staff in some capacity the technical city planning mind, constantly revising the work and reporting on the proposals of the various specialists so as to determine between essentials and non-essentials . . . it occurs to me that this might be done in two ways. First by appointing a town planning advisor . . . to give to you and the committee advice from this point of view on all matters. Second, by making the post of Director of Research . . . filling it with a man who would give the city planning direction and point of view to all investigations and to the working staff. On the whole this would seem to be the safest plan if you can find a suitable man who has the right outlook as city planner and has enough knowledge of survey working to direct and co-ordinate the various surveys.[30]

Unwin urged the physical planning get underway immediately and that the geography of the New York region would permit planning for separate areas:

In New York, while the broad distribution of the parts and the outline of development must be determined for the city as a whole, the conditions, particularly the intervening waterways, practically decree that the actual planning will have very largely to be carried out for each of the parts separately.

It will not be possible to produce any complete symetrical [*sic*] design for the whole city, such as was adopted for Chicago. And therefore, it seems to me that it will be quite practicable to hand over, for example, Manhattan Island to one man; Brooklyn to another; and the New Jersey side to another; etc.: provided that their work is properly coordinated by one presiding city planner, who would maintain the unities in all respects. This would have several advantages, it would separate the work in a number of competent hands, secure probably greater adaption [*sic*] of each plan to its particular area and bring out a greater amount of variety in the details of the work. A variety which would legitimately arise out of the varying conditions of the various parts.[31]

Unwin's proposals for procedure and organization were very influential and were subsequently followed in most particulars. The effect of his visit was to concentrate the attention of the Committee on the key issues of population and industrial distribution, and on the desirability of physical proposals as the ultimate expression of the Regional Plan.

Unwin's visit highlighted a busy fall for the Committee and its staff. On September 26 the staff had moved into temporary quarters in the East Hall of the Russell Sage Buildings, pending completion of a new roof-top story which the architect Grosvenor Atterbury had been commissioned to design. Norton would have his Burnham-style atelier after all. In October Norton received an invitation from London to become a member of the Executive Committee of the International Garden City and Town Planning Association, which he accepted. Also in October, the Committee reported that a projected biography of the elder Frederick Law Olmsted was nearly ready for the pens of Frederick L. Olmsted, Jr. and Theodora Kimball. The Committee had underwritten the project with an appropriation of $4,000, in recognition undoubtedly, of the legacy of the elder Olmsted to the planning of the New York Region.[32] Unwin's reports and the enthusiastic activity of the staff convinced the Sage trustees of the need for and the feasibility of a new Regional Plan. After considerable debate they agreed to increase the Russell Sage Foundation commitment to $500,000, with no more than $100,000 to be expended in any one year. This was a strong vote of confidence in Norton's concept, for it represented a large share of the foundation's income.[33]

In December 1922, Raymond Pearl of Johns Hopkins delivered a report on regional population projections, the first substantial piece of survey research commissioned by the Committee.[34] Pearl predicted that by 1965 the Region would have about twenty million people, more than twice its 1920 population of nine million. Norton was pleased with the professional quality of the study and suggested it serve as a model for future reports. The predicted growth that seemed to lie ahead further confirmed for Norton the importance of the great project in which they were engaged. At the December meeting of the Committee, he summarized where matters stood and outlined the next steps that should be taken:

We are reaching the stages where we would welcome a chief architect, a chief planner. But we are not in position to adopt the simple method of turning the job over to a competent man. Our finances do not permit of employment of such talent.

Probably this is fortunate. We might select the wrong man and so lose time. Adopting the more laborious method described below, if successful, we get an immense amount of volunteer work free, arouse widespread interest and enthusiasm in professions, and later the 'Master Minds' will disclose themselves in action. It has been argued that we need unity of command from the start. That certainly would be easiest for this Committee. But to select a general before public sentiment is roused to the point where troops will volunteer to fight, involves us in financial commitments in excess of our resources.

So the 'command' must for the present rest in our Committee in our Executive Secretary.[35]

With the Sage money in hand, Norton was eager to get on with the planning work. He proposed that architects, city planners, and engineers be organized and left to work in separate groups. Later they could be brought together in a common effort to coordinate the studies.

Norton had approached a number of distinguished New York architects and obtained their commitment to work on several problem areas. The Manhattan City Hall and Court House group, already at work, consisted of Cass Gilbert, Guy Lowell, Lawrence S. White and W. Welles Bosworth. The 59th Street group included Burt L. Fenner, Arnold Brunner, Harvey Corbett, and Charles U. Platt. Norton proposed that other groups be organized to work on Central Park, and the Hudson, Harlem, and East River waterfronts.

The city planners would be organized in the same way, with groups to investigate five sectors of the region:

> Obviously we cannot ask or expect City Planners to make detailed plans of large areas and finished reports without compensation. That comes later. But by allocating each sector to the men who now understand it best, we can easily get their generalizations based on previous study – and can assemble and coordinate these generalizations and after free discussion [in which 'master minds' will appear] can later decide where and how to spend our money on actual planning. For instance, Bartholomew of St. Louis, one of the best men, formerly lived in Newark and worked on the Newark Plan.[36]

Then Norton exhorted the group with words which echoed those of Burnham in Chicago:

> Thus Architects, Planners, Engineers, will attack the Regional Plan problem just as similar groups cooperated in the creation of the World's Fair in Chicago. That was the first time such groups ever cooperated on a vast scale in America. We offer them their first chance to cooperate on a regional Plan. And there are so many projects to be studied that we can give every good man a chance whether he is able to work in a group or temperamentally must work as an individual.
>
> Now while all this goes forward our staff proceed with their Economic and other inquiries. Our Secretarial Staff will develop a standard technique for organizing citizens into Regional Plan groups throughout the area. For

educating them, or rather helping them educate themselves, lectures will be written, lantern slides assembled. The main problem of the Secretary is to create a widespread public interest in *Regional* Planning: to teach everyone in the Region to think of New York and Its Environs as a unit. On this basis many minds will be studying, we shall be raising an army of volunteers ready to obey our 'Master Minds' when we discover them.

As a sure test, I have put this program frankly before men like Cass Gilbert, [William] Wilgus, [Frederic A.] Delano and [Chester H.] Aldrich, [Thomas] Hastings, Unwin – dominant men who usually expect a free hand in anything they do – and without exception they subscribe to it and are ready to work it out with us. It calls for tact and diligence, fairness and courtesy on our part to thus assemble and hold in a common effort what is probably the ablest group of architects, engineers, and planners in the world, many of them residents of New York and thus vitally interested in the solution of the problem.

But what about Borough President Miller's new street plans or Commissioner Harris's crosstown double deck street plan? These men are official. What shall we do about them? Nothing – except of course to encourage every sincere effort. It's a splendid thing that these officials are alive to the problem. The more suggestions and solutions that are projected the better. They will collide with each other, they will be terribly discouraged as they learn that headlines are transitory and don't get results.

But if they hit on some good scheme that the public will support, none should cooperate more generously or heartily than we.

Meantime we will grind ahead steadily and carefully, remembering that we are the only group with funds, with officers and with a highly competent staff, which realizes that New York is really all that you can see from the Woolworth Tower, that no official body has jurisdiction on this area, that no Plans will be true solutions that fail to serve the whole Region: that no widespread public support can be assembled until we get *all* the good local schemes coordinated into a unit so that every man in the street will find *his* local problem a part of the Regional Plan we are developing.

And if we grind ahead steadily, asking nothing of credit, involving ourselves not at all in political projects, encouraging freely and handsomely all citizens and officials who are working on the right lines . . . we shall increasingly attract and hold the cooperation of the ablest men and women. Deep in the hearts of every architect, every engineer, and planner, of everyone of us lies an intense longing so to direct our thought and effort that New York will no longer be 'the worst place in the world for a poor man to live in.'[37]

By the end of 1922, the Committee could no longer postpone its most difficult task: organizing and staffing up for the physical planning of the New York Region. There was no one of the stature of Daniel Burnham in New York, and Burnham was dead. Besides, the mood of the times had changed. The single genius-formgiver had been replaced by the team leader orchestrating a medley of experts. But the man to lead the orchestra was not yet in evidence. Norton proposed that a planning board be selected from the best men available, an idea that the British town planner Thomas Adams had suggested to him in August, and which Raymond Unwin had also urged.[38] Delano responded favorably and proposed the creation of an executive board of no more than five men, residents of New York, and a somewhat larger group to serve as an advisory board. Delano expressed the hope that the planning board 'may prove the true stepping stone towards the selection of a final man.'[39]

Norton called a meeting at the Century Club on December 31, 1922, to discuss his idea for a planning advisory group. John Glenn of the Sage Foundation, Frederick Law Olmsted, Frederick Keppel, and Flavel Shurtleff joined Norton for the session. Norton explained the method of allotting studies to teams of architects, and raised the possibility of following the same method with city planners: divide the Region outside the congested area into six or seven sectors, with each advisory planner taking responsibility for a sector.

The suggested work program for the city planners, probably prepared by Keppel and Nelson P. Lewis, set out a bold array of matters to be dealt with. Under the heading of uses of land and zoning the planners were to consider the general scope of industrial, business, and residential development with 'indications of probable future tendencies and changes'. They were also to consider restrictions on use, height, and area of occupancy for areas not yet zoned and were to consider the rather radical possibility of regional zoning.

They were also to consider the desirability of encouraging industrial dispersal in satellite centers and to recommend locations for new centers of business and social life. Methods of controlling subdivisions outside of boundaries of cities were also to be developed.

Proposals for improvement of radial and circumferential highways of state or regional importance, as well as observations regarding rail, waterway, and terminal facilities, and recommendations for classifying main arterial roads were to be made.

Problems of safety and traffic were noted: congestion, grade crossings, and the need for public garages were to be considered.

Open spaces to be considered were of two kinds: the present and proposed park and parkway systems and recommendations for improvement, and reservation of cultivated areas adjacent to cities or of afforested areas in the neighborhood of water supplies.

Olmsted's reaction was decidedly favorable, but John Glenn was concerned with problems of coordination with the surveys already under way to gather facts about the Region. Olmsted's response was that careful administration might avoid some waste of time but even so, the risk of overlap was worth taking. Olmsted explained his conception of planning at the meeting:

> In city planning there are two different methods of approach (1) the research method, finding facts and making conclusions (2) the arriving at intuitive 'hunches' as a result of an unanalyzable mental process. The latter method, of course, must be checked up. Both methods must be used in the New York work in combination or in alternation or in compromise; the danger in the team or in the sector plan is in individuals getting wedded to a 'fine idea.'[40]

Olmsted added his recommendation that the sector investigation not be labeled a study in city planning, 'but rather a scouting party to list opportunities and dangers.' Olmsted pointed to the influential study for a park and parkway system for Queens made by his firm for the McClellan Commission as an example of a 'scouting study.'[41]

Olmsted suggested that two lines of research would be of importance to the study and would interest city planners, because 'both would advance the science of city planning.' One piece of research proposed was a comparison of the consequences of population densities associated with the walk-up tenements found in the Bronx, the one-family house, and possible combinations, to discover the economic and social advantages of each, including the cost per family of housing and cost per family of local improvements and utilities. The other research direction proposed by Olmsted was a study of neighborhood facilities such as stores, banks, etc., to discover the type that requires a center like Manhattan, or that requires a density of population but not a metropolitan center, or that can exist in suburban or garden city conditions. Olmsted obviously wanted some solid evidence on which to build a policy of decentralization.[42]

There followed a discussion of planners who might be asked to become involved and sectors which might be studied. Mentioned were Adams, Olmsted, the George B. Ford–E.P. Goodrich team, Harland Bartholomew, John Nolen, Edward Bennett, and Arthur Comey, undoubtedly the most illustrious group of planners active in the United States at the time.

Out of this discussion came the following agreement:

> Adams should take Westchester, Ford–Goodrich, that part of New Jersey which they preferred; Bartholomew and Nolen, other portions of New Jersey, and that a sector should certainly be given to Bennett.[43]

A follow-up meeting was held on January 22, 1923, at Charles Norton's apartment. Norton, however, had taken sick and could not be present. Adams and Olmsted reported that they had discussed the sector idea and had agreed that 'it was a sound and desirable method of tackling the planning problem in the Region.'[44] They suggested, however, that rather than publish five or six separate reports, a group of planners organize and appoint a chairman who would act as a 'convenor' or 'moderator' with no authority except to call the group together and draft material for consideration by the group, and that a secretary be appointed to keep the work on schedule. The two planners realized that cooperation was essential, but were not ready to place control in the hands of any one member of the group.

Adams and Olmsted proposed a program of study for the group with work to commence immediately and be completed by October 1, 1923:

1. Organization of an Advisory Planning Group and selection of chairman and secretary.

2. Several days of careful study of the material collected by Nelson P. Lewis.
3. Division into sectors and allotting of sectors to individual planners.
4. The adoption of standard specifications for each of the sector studies.
5. A survey of the field by motor, to take at least ten days.
6. Frequent conferences either of the whole group or between members of the group.
7. Drafting of the report for each sector.
8. The assembly of these reports into a joint report to be signed by all the members of the group.

Following the report, the group would act as an advisory council because of its members' intimate knowledge of the Region to be gained in the study, and because of their habit of working together.

By message Norton notified the assembled group that the Committee on the Regional Plan had agreed to devote up to $25,000 for the study, noting 'the importance of participation in the development of the Plan by a city planning group.' Norton's apparent desire was to help the new profession to become known and not leave the making of the plan simply to engineers, economists, and architects.[45]

The next day, January 23, the group reassembled at the Sage Foundation Building and, on the motion of George B. Ford, elected Thomas Adams as chairman. Adams agreed to serve 'only if he were the choice of any others who should join the group.' The question was also discussed as to whether a seventh city planner should be added to the group to serve as secretary and as a connecting link between the group and Nelson Lewis's division. Pending a decision, Flavel Shurtleff agreed to act as secretary.

Between February 12 and 15, 1923, a series of important meetings was held, attended by both the Advisory Planning Group and the Plan staff, including Bassett, Haig, Lee Hanmer, Harrison, Keppel, Lewis, Roswell, McCrea, Shurtleff, and Frank B. Williams (figure 5.2). Norton was not present. He had suffered a recurrence of serious illness and was in the hospital. Keppel wondered whether Delano would be able to devote much time to the plan, given his duties in Washington as a governor of the Federal Reserve Board, but hoped that the group could 'go ahead without loss of momentum.'[46]

Adams, in his new role as chairman of the Advisory Group, succinctly presented the objectives of the planners and asked for preliminary reports from the staffs of the Economic, Social, and Legal Inquiries to assist them. Adams then outlined the six sectors and named the individuals who would work in them and the matters they would be expected to deal with (figure 5.3). The final assignments were:

Figure 5.2. Advisory Planning Group, meeting at Sage Foundation Building, February 14, 1923. Left to right: Frank B. Williams, Edward M. Bassett, Frederick L. Olmsted, Jr., (unidentified), John Nolen, Hale Walker, Edward H. Bennett, (unidentified), Thomas Adams, Chairman, Harland Bartholomew, Henry Hubbard, Nelson P. Lewis, Ernest P. Goodrich, H.T. Frost, (unidentified), Flavel Shurtleff, and George B. Ford. (*Source:* Regional Plan Papers)

1. Frederick Law Olmsted – Nassau and Suffolk Counties and undeveloped portion of Queens;
2. Thomas Adams – area north of city and west of Hudson including Westchester County, and part of Putnam and Fairfield Counties;
3. John Nolen – area to west of Hudson comprising parts of Bergen, Rockland, and Orange Counties, and on east of Hudson comprising parts of Putnam and Dutchess Counties;
4. Harland Bartholomew – Passaic County and parts of Orange, Bergen, Morris, Essex, and Hudson Counties in New Jersey;
5. George B. Ford – Union County and parts of Essex, Hudson, Middlesex, Somerset and Morris Counties.
6. Edward H. Bennett – Richmond County and parts of Middlesex, Monmouth, and Somerset Counties.[47]

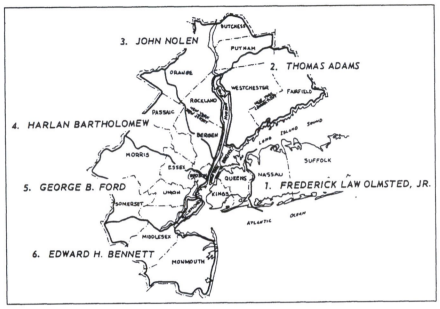

Figure 5.3. Sector assignments, Advisory Planning Group, 1923. (*Source:* Based on drawings in Regional Plan Papers)

The general scope of the study was outlined by Adams:

> . . . to ascertain the Regional and City Planning problems that need to be dealt with in each Sector and to indicate the character of possible and desirable solutions of these problems and the order of importance and urgency.
>
> . . . to suggest the kind of data needed to supplement information already available as the basis for more detailed consideration of solutions, and the degree of importance to be attached to different lines of social and economic inquiry.[48]

Within this scope Adams proposed to deal with four issues in each sector:

1. Uses of land and densities (zoning), including decentralization.
2. Subdivision and land development, including housing.
3. Circulation or means of communication.
4. Open spaces and recreation.[49]

Adams summarized his views on centralization, decentralization, and congestion, a matter which would later provide the major controversy of the plan:

> Perhaps the general considerations can be accepted in advance. These are first, that while some relief of the problems of congestion and economic waste due to decentralization may be both practicable and desirable, permanent relief can be achieved by greater decentralization of both industry and population; and second, that while transportation is a problem of the highest importance and urgency, no project has been put forward that can be accepted as certain either

to be carried out or to solve the problem if carried out. In regard to both these matters the studies of the group may help to indicate new directions in which both problems of centralization and transportation [necessarily interdependent] can be solved.[50]

Adams then asked for status reports from the Economic, Legal and Social Survey directors. Haig reported on his work first. He made clear that his concern was with industrial production and his approach an empirical one:

> Our objective is to discover the best use of given areas from an economic viewpoint. Brief sections of our report will be taken up with the historical view, with the economic geography of the region and with the region's relation to world economy.
>
> The heart of the economic problem is an analysis of the businessman's costs divided into the elements of
>
> (a) Accessibility or transportation facilities.
> (b) Land value.
> (c) Transportation costs of workers.
> (d) Transportation costs of raw materials and finished products.
> (e) The costs of time spent on transportation.
> (f) Special ancillary factors.
>
> Our approach to the problem is a study of industry after industry. A base map showing land value will be prepared; then the essential facts about an industry will be shown on a transparent medium which will be superimposed on the base maps: such facts as location and amount of land used. By repeating this process for several five year periods, we hope to discover significant industrial trends and to make generalizations as to the industries which can best stand the high land values.[51]

Following Haig's presentation, Shelby Harrison gave the status report of his Social and Living Conditions Survey. Harrison's emphasis was on the needs of local populations:

> The Social and Living Conditions Survey is divided into five parts and for each a preliminary report has been made:
>
> *Housing* (1) A survey of the trends of housing development during recent years, that is, types of houses built; number of rooms per house, the density of population. This survey has been completed by Mr. Wayne Heydecker under the supervision of Mr. Lawson Purdy. It is now being done for the whole region. Mr. Bassett suggested that while Mr. Heydecker was in the field he might add a few inquiries to his list and make substantially a zoning survey. (2) A study of the types of houses best adapted to the various zoning regulations of the region.
>
> *Recreation* (1) Present recreation facilities. (2) Adequacy in number and size of various types of recreation areas and a general plan for locating new facilities. (3) The elements of local community units – Mr. Hanmer and Mr. Perry are working on this. (4) Apartments and tenement house sites in relation to opportunities for play on the premises. Mr. Hanmer expects to make a progress report soon on this subject.
>
> *Health* (1) Water supply and polution [sic]. Mr. Lewis has prepared maps showing sources of water supply and polution of water by sewage. (2) Air

polution. (3) Refuse collection and disposal. (4) Site requirements for hospitals and other agencies caring for the sick. (5) Location of cemeteries.

Schools (1) Existing facilities. (2) Plan for future school sites. (3) Types of school site requirements.

Public Welfare Buildings (1) Location and site requirements of correctional institutions.

In addition to these five groups, a study of street accidents has been given a place on our program and a spot map of the accidents throughout the region is contemplated.[52]

Harrison's emphasis on social welfare needs provided a counterweight to Haig's emphasis on the needs of business. Bassett's group on the legal survey thus held the balance of the direction the surveys were likely to take. Bassett reported the work of the Legal Department:

(1)   To discover the shortcomings in legal powers.

(2)   To draft suggestions for the improvement of the law and administrative procedure which will assure more orderly city planning.

(3)   To draft reports on legal topics as submitted by the staff. Reports have already been made on excess condemnation and intermediate reports on open spaces, congested areas, a regional planning authority. A report on land under water will be finished in two or three days.

(4)   To conduct 'experimental stations' on city planning *(a)* work with the New York Charter Revision Commission particularly on the stabilization of official maps *(b)* work with the Charter Revision Commissions of Nassau and Westchester Counties *(c)* Mr. Williams has drafted the city planning sections for the proposed charters *(d)* drafting of zoning law for villages and townships *(e)* a study of state and town lands.[53]

Each sector planner was asked to prepare a map of his sector showing present and future uses of land including land adaptable for agriculture, forests, parks, other kinds of open areas, residential development, and industrial/commercial developments. Sites adaptable for satellite cities were also to be shown, as well as a generalized indication of land values in the sector. It was agreed that the data collected by the staffs of the surveys would be made available to the sector planners. But no further coordination was envisioned. The integration of the two approaches to planning, the intuitive and the analytical, would have to await a later synthesis.

CHANGE IN LEADERSHIP, 1923

By the Spring of 1923 the planning work was at last underway. Then tragedy struck. Charles Norton died on the 6th of March, at the age of fifty-three. The influenza he had contracted in January had resulted in a rare type of septic poisoning for which there was no cure. Tributes poured in from Norton's former associates, who were shocked by the untimely death of their cherished and admired colleague. Former President William Howard Taft, in a letter to the *New York Times,* recalled Norton's service to him as presidential secretary:

> He was a cultured high-minded patriotic American citizen and gentleman. He had real brilliancy and genius for progressive, constructive tasks, and a strong sense of responsibility prompting devotion of his talents to the public interest. I knew him and loved him . . . [54]

Norton had combined a lifetime of public service with a remarkably successful business career. At his death he was not only chairman of the Committee on the Regional Plan and a trustee of the Russell Sage Foundation, but trustee of the American Academy in Rome, the Metropolitan Museum of Art, the American Federation of Arts, and the Institute for Government Research. He was President of the First National Bank of New York, having moved up from Vice-President. He was also President of the First Security Company, the Coal and Coke Railway Company, and the New Gaulery Coal Corporation, Vice-President of the West Virginia Coal and Coke Company, and a director of numerous corporations, including the American Railway Express Company, Equitable Life Assurance Society, Montgomery Ward and Company, Delaware, Lackawanna and Western Coal Company, Tide Water Oil Company, and the American Telephone and Telegraph Company. Norton epitomized the spirit of American business and civic *noblesse oblige,* and now he was gone. The *New York Evening Post* declared that 'no better memorial could be erected in his honor than the completion of the [Regional] plan.'[55]

Norton's death deprived the Committee of the leadership and vision of the man who had been the driving force behind the Plan. His sorrowing friend, Frederic Delano, seemed the logical choice to carry on as chairman. During Norton's illness, Delano had spent one week a month in New York, and for the rest had important things referred by mail. 'I cannot in any way take Mr. Norton's place,' he informed the staff.[56] Delano's Washington duties as a Federal Reserve Commissioner seemed to preclude his assuming the position of permanent chairman of the Regional Plan Committee. When his name was put forward at a meeting of the Committee in late May, Keppel raised a number of serious objections:

> Delano is not a New Yorker and lacks the instinctive knowledge of local conditions and local points of view. This might embarrass his relations with local officials and reduce his effectiveness at public meetings and in raising funds.[57]

Keppel also objected that because Delano resided in Washington and frequently traveled, he would be unable to devote adequate time to the Plan and would be inaccessible in emergencies. Keppel further objected to Delano's penchant for proposing his own schemes:

> Mr. Delano does not really understand what the Committee is for . . . We must regard the Committee as charged primarily with financing the enterprise,

organizing a group of experts who shall, under a direction which is general and not specific, formulate a Regional Plan and educate the public to accept it.

While the members of the Committee may of course suggest local improvements they should not press these forward without reference to the orderly evolution of the Plan as a whole. This is precisely what Mr. Delano, in his enthusiasm and his very great personal interest in certain projects, is constantly tempted to do. I admit that Charles Norton did it too, but his unique usefulness as chairman was, in my judgement, in spite of this rather than because of it.[58]

Keppel noted, however, that agreeing on someone else would be very difficult, and that the negative aspects of the appointment of Delano might be outweighed by 'his distinguished abilities, his experience in Chicago and by his devotion to carrying through the enterprise as a memorial to Norton.' Keppel, supported by Morrow and Polk, urged that DeForest be appointed temporary chairman. But John Glenn thought it inappropriate for the president of the Sage Foundation to hold the position. With no alternative in sight, sentiment ruled, and the Committee voted on May 29 to designate Delano as Norton's successor.[59]

Keppel's admonitions may not have carried great weight for the reason that he had been tapped by Nicholas Murray Butler for the presidency of the Carnegie Corporation, an important foundation largely oriented to matters of education, and was scheduled to leave the Regional Plan by the end of September to assume his new duties.

Delano realized that he would need a deputy to carry on the work. Keppel's departure, together with Delano's own duties in Washington, would leave a large gap in leadership. Delano fixed on Thomas Adams as a good candidate for the position of 'Deputy Chairman' or 'Chief Advisor to the Committee.' It was clear that Delano did not look on Adams as the Burnham of the Regional Plan, bur simply as the best man around to represent him in his absence.

Both Keppel and the rest of the staff were very skeptical as to the desirability of taking on Adams in a directory capacity. Keppel wrote confidentially to John Glenn of his reasons for opposing Adam's appointment:

1. Because it would give too much prominence to a single professional planner at this stage, and particularly to a non-resident and non-citizen. Neither the Committee nor the public should get the idea that The Planner has been selected. Mr Adam's present position as chairman of a group [the Advisory Planning Group], selected as such by his own professional associates, is far better strategically and gives him, I feel confident, all the authority he needs.

2. Because it makes no logical place in the organization for the building up of local planning groups and contact with those already in existence.

3. Because it also neglects the problem of educating the public to understand and support the Regional Plan. It is true that at this stage work in this field is necessarily preliminary, but it is none the less vital for the success of the enterprise that it be taken up under the best possible conditions.

4. It does not seem to me to make proper recognition of what Mr. Shurtleff has done and is capable of doing.[60]

Keppel's candidate was his assistant, Flavel Shurtleff, who with Nelson Lewis had through 1922 been laying the groundwork for acceptance of the plan by addressing numerous civic groups and chambers of commerce around the Region. Keppel's opposition to Adams was unanimously shared by the rest of the staff, he reported to Glenn.[61] It is not clear why this opposition was so strong, although it is likely that Adams, a Scotsman, may have been regarded as having too little knowledge of the American scene.

The Committee did not share the views of its staff. The ever formal Bassett observed that 'Mr Adams' only disadvantage is that necessarily he cannot think in terms of the Constitution of the United States.'[62] The Committee, at its meeting of May 29 accepted Delano's condition that he would serve only if he had full time assistance from 'some qualified planning expert of proved executive ability.' A resolution was passed offering Adams a nine-month appointment at $18,000 a year. Adams, in fact, would stay with the project for nearly six years as General Director of Plans and Surveys.

Delano's first act as chairman was to propose a drastic re-organization and reorientation of the studies. He proposed that six distinct divisions be created out of the four survey divisions:

- the survey of existing conditions, by a group to be made up largely of engineers;
- architectural problems, by a group largely of architects;
- town planning, with special reference to the environs, to be made up chiefly of town planners and landscape architects;
- social and living conditions;
- completion of economic studies;
- public relations.

Delano also proposed that Bassett's Division on Legal Survey be dropped and that Bassett perform as a staff counselor to Adams. Bassett had irritated both Committee and staff with his narrow views of what regional planning should be.[63]

Delano's proposal clearly set a new course for the staff, one that would lead to fragmentation of effort. Nelson Lewis reacted very negatively to the reorganization. Lewis observed that the history of city planning in the United States demonstrated that to be successful a plan had to be the result of group effort in which engineers, architects, and landscape architects must all take a hand. He predicted that if independent studies were made and independent conclusions were reached much time would be wasted in trying to reconcile the different plans.[64] Though Delano's reorganization plan was realized only in part, Lewis' prediction turned out to be accurate.

Toward the end of 1923 Adams, now General Director of Plans and

Surveys, made a few minor changes in the existing organization which shifted the orientation of the staff towards engineering and public relations. The Division of Physical Survey was renamed the Engineering Division and six engineers were added to its Advisory Committee.[65]

To augment the public relations work begun by Lewis and Shurtleff, Henry James was appointed Research Secretary, Lawrence M. Orton, a young economist who had just graduated from Cornell, was appointed Field Secretary, and Flavel Shurtleff was designated Field Secretary with the status of Director of Planning Services. Leslie S. Baker was appointed Assistant to the General Director. At about the same time, the Committee on the Regional Plan was enlarged by the addition of three new members: Keppel, who was now president of the Carnegie Corporation, Frederic B. Pratt, the businessman who had been associated with the Brooklyn City Plan, and Lawson Purdy, former Tax Commissioner of New York City.[66]

With these changes in staff, Adams had set the direction for the work to be accomplished in 1924. In his new capacity as General Director, he turned his attention to the reports of the Advisory Planning Group, which had been submitted by the consultant teams.

SECTOR PLANS FOR THE ENVIRONS

Long Island: Frederick Law Olmsted, Jr.

Frederick Law Olmsted Jr, assisted by Henry V. Hubbard, reported on the fast-growing Long Island Sector east of the built-up portion of Queens. He predicted three kinds of growth occurring on Long Island: new large estates developed on farm land, older estates, closer to the city, divided into smaller properties, and, on the fringes of the city's developed area, detached, but crowded, single-family houses.

> built so poorly as to fall much farther below good standards for detached houses in suburban communities than it is possible for tenement houses under the 'new law' to fall below good standards for a multiple-house community.[67]

Olmsted was greatly concerned with the effects such mass-produced housing would have on the existing development:

> It is not improbable that if really good standards for detached house suburban developments could be maintained by zoning and other means of public control the cost would be such as to put them beyond the reach of most of the people who constitute the market for the present cheap development. This incoming type of cheap development, and still more the type into which it will tend to change as small industries follow the labor supply, does not mix well with those which have been up to the present typical of the sector. Even a better regulated growth economically adapted to the same market, so far as intended to a large extent among the high grade commuting residential development typical of the

sector, would almost certainly be fatal to the continued maintenance of the latter.[68]

Olmsted suggested that segregative regional zoning be established on radial lines in connection with selected transportation routes to prevent the 'fatal' outcome:

> Wedges of sub-sectors of relatively open residential use with relatively high standards of amenities should be protected by every suitable means as corridors from outlying areas devoted to highgrade commuting residence use toward the center of the city, and that any expansion of the industrial and residential areas of a more intensive sort, the occupants of which are much less generally engaged in work which *must* be done in the central district, should be directed into separate and district subsectors, the more outlying expansion of which might even approximate to industrial satellite cities.[69]

Olmsted did not wish to keep lower and middle income housing out of Nassau and Suffolk altogether. He envisioned such housing as developing in the form of a central wedge separated from the more open, affluent development on the north and south shores of the island by corridors of farms, forests and recreation space. These corridors were to extend the network of open spaces and parkways the Olmsted firm had conceived for Queens in the 1907 McClellan Commission report. In addition to parkways on the north and south, Olmsted called for a major relief road in the center of the Island, essentially the scheme Burnham had suggested to the Brooklyn Committee on the City Plan in 1911. He also called for a new circumferential from Oyster Bay to a proposed park at Jones' Beach, ideas which Robert Moses would draw on a decade later.

Olmsted noted the necessity for the environs to provide open space for the metropolis as a whole:

> With the exception of Jamaica Bay, the marshes extending eastward from Cedarhurst, Rockaway Beach, and perhaps portions of Long Beach, there is no area on Long Island near to New York which could be developed as a large metropolitan park without being a serious detriment to its neighborhood and without taking land which would be very useful indeed for some other purpose. If within the areas just named Long Island contributes substantially for this purpose . . . The remaining necessary amount of metropolitan parks within twenty miles or so of New York can best be found in other sectors about the city.[70]

These were unlikely sentiments from the son and namesake of the designer of Central Park. Olmsted, however, did call for the protection of places of special scenic value or examples of typical landscape beauty. The salt marshes west of Great South Bay were proposed for recreation use and the great barrier beaches on the ocean side of the Island were proposed to be 'rendered more accessible.' Interestingly, Olmsted did not propose outright public acquisition of the waterfronts except for a few small areas on both coasts.

Westchester-Fairfield: Thomas Adams

Thomas Adam's report on Sector II, Westchester and Fairfield Counties, was the best organized and most comprehensive of the six sector reports. Adams viewed his sector in its regional setting, noting that despite its superior accessibility by rail compared to Long Island, it had been growing less rapidly. probably because the level terrain on Long Island was conducive to speculative development. Adams was in favor of increasing the population of Westchester and Fairfield as a means of reducing the congestion in the central part of the Region. 'The wider distribution of industry is the best way to promote the wider distribution of population,' he suggested.[71] But he also anticipated increased commutation from Westchester-Fairfield, emphasizing that this sector was the least desirable of the sectors for industrial growth, because of its topography and suitability for residence. He pointed to a few areas in the sector which he thought offered potential sites for creating garden cities and villages. Whereas Olmsted thought of satellite cities as fairly large cities with their own hinterland, Adam's view was that of the British Garden City movement which envisioned self-contained units of at most 25,000 people. The imageries of the two planners were quite divergent.

On the proper uses of the new device of zoning, there was more agreement. Adams noted that many communities had prepared zoning maps before a comprehensive plan had been completed. 'One city in Westchester, and perhaps others, have zoning plans that will have to entirely be changed wherever a complete city plan is prepared. This means that the money spent on zoning may have been entirely wasted.'[72] Adams little realized that what he was describing would become the rule rather than the exception, with zoning not only preceding planning but ultimately, in the view of the courts, substituting for it. Adams was aware of the problems created by many small jurisdictions devising their own zoning ordinances without reference either to their neighbors or to the region as a whole. His solution was a proposal for county-wide zoning for all of Westchester to be developed on the basis of a county plan.

Adams concluded that the five rail lines connecting the sector to Manhattan were adequate for future commuter needs. Highways were another matter. Adams called for additional cross county roads and a new highway along the Hudson to relieve the Albany Road. Both the Albany and Boston Post Roads required widening as well, according to his recommendations. A tunnel or bridge across the Hudson at Yonkers was also suggested. Acquisition of river valleys and reservoir areas was recommended as well as the greatest possible public purchase of land fronting on the Hudson River and Long Island Sound. Reservations for agricultural land were also proposed.[73]

Westchester by 1923 had achieved an elaborate system of parks and parkways developed or in planning, thanks to the efforts of the Westchester

County Park Commission. Adams endorsed the Westchester parks and parkways system and pointed to it as a model to be emulated.

Hudson Valley: John Nolen

John Nolen, assisted by his associate, Philip W. Foster, prepared plans for Sector III, which comprised all or part of Bergen County in New Jersey and Rockland, Orange, and Putnam Counties in New York (figure 5.4).

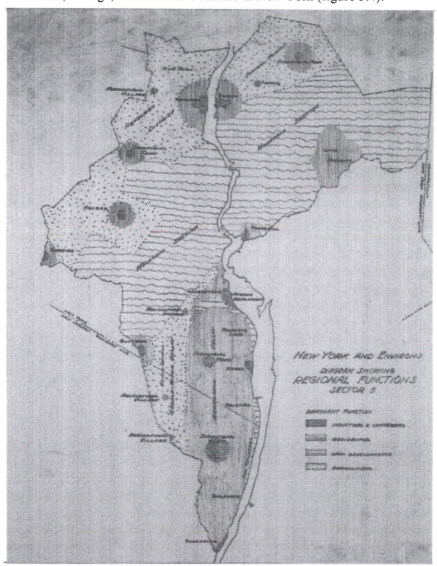

Figure 5.4. Plan for Sector 3, John Nolen, Advisory Planning Group, Regional Plan of New York and Its Environs, 1923. (*Source:* John Nolen Papers, Cornell University Library)

Nolen, more than any of his five colleagues, emphasized the concept of fiat satellite cities, proposing eleven new or enlarged cities for his sector.

- a large industrial city near Haworth;
- a smaller industrial city near Nanuet;
- an agricultural town near Paramus:
- an agricultural town north of Saddle River;
- a residential city near Sparkill;
- an agricultural town north of Pomona;
- a residential city near Congers;
- a mixed town for industry and agriculture: Washingtonville enlarged;
- an agricultural town near East Coldenham;
- an agricultural town: Fishkill enlarged;
- a mixed town for industry and an agricultural center: Hopewell Junction enlarged.

Nolen did not indicate the ultimate (1965) sizes he had in mind for his satellite cities, but they probably averaged around 50,000 to 100,000 each, given the population growth expected in the sector.

Having laid out his settlement pattern first, he structured his road scheme to suit it, rather than the reverse, the approach used by his colleagues. Nolen's road plan was designed with east-west connections as frequent as north-south routes, a homogeneous, if somewhat irregular, gridiron. Nolen was strongly in favor of a bridge between Yonkers and Alpine to carry the Port Authority's proposed belt line across the Hudson and to provide a by-pass for through traffic to New England. Nolen stuck by this recommendation despite a reminder of the commitment of the Port Authority to build a suspension bridge at 178th Street.

In the park category, Nolen's main proposal was an extension of the Bear Mountain Reservation, adding 47 square miles east of the Hudson. This would have more than doubled the area of the original park, a gift to New York State of the Harriman estate.[74]

Northern New Jersey: Harland Bartholomew

Harland Bartholomew's assignment was the sector comprising northern New Jersey south to Morris and Essex Counties, together with small portions of Rockland and Orange Counties in New York.[75] Bartholomew viewed his sector as consisting of four distinct parts: the Palisades Group, the Salt Meadows, an outer urban zone, and a mountain zone.

Bartholomew saw increased water-and rail-related industrial activity along the Hudson, resulting in a retreat of the extant residential development there. This should be encouraged, Batholomew wrote, because the old Jersey towns and cities along the river, such as Jersey City and Hoboken, were too congested and disorganized to provide suitable residential environments.

The largely unoccupied Hackensack Meadows offered an extraordinary opportunity for regional planning, Bartholomew recognized. A number of schemes had previously been proposed for the Meadows, including one by the Port of New York Authority for industrial and port development. Bartholomew did not attempt a plan for the area but urged that 'a definite detail plan' be devised to avoid piecemeal development. He did urge, however, that no residential development be permitted in the area and that industrial development be related to rail and to the Hackensack and Passaic Rivers.

The Outer Urban Zone seemed to Bartholomew to be rather disorganized, containing agricultural land, independent cities such as Paterson and Passaic, and suburbs tributary to Manhattan, such as Ridgewood. Bartholomew urged that the suburbs surrounding Paterson be encouraged to remain tributary to that city rather than becoming bedroom communities for Manhattan. Between some of the larger communities such as Hackensack and Ridgewood lay rich agricultural land which Bartholomew urged be preserved for truck gardens and orchards.

Bartholomew called for new radial and circumferential highways and a program of widening of existing routes. He argued that if it was decided that decentralization was to be encouraged it would be necessary to make Manhattan more accessible through additional Hudson crossings. He did not make specific recommendations as to such crossings, however, because the analysis required as a basis for such decisions was beyond the scope of his study. Bartholomew did call for an elevated roadway linking the tunnel then under construction (the Holland Tunnel) with the Jersey environs, a proposal that was later realized in the Pulaski Skyway.

Batholomew also called for several parkways in his sector, one along the Saddle and Passaic Rivers, reaching in the north to the Palisades Interstate Park and in the south linking up with the Essex County Park System. Another park and parkway route was proposed for the abandoned Morris Canal, so that it would be possible for a person to travel along the canal by motor as well as by canoe from Newark to Lake Hopatcong.

The Mountain Zone seemed highly appropriate to Bartholomew for regional open space, and he called for a system of mountain parks extending through the Wanaque Watershed, Greenwood Lake, and over mountain ridges to Green Pond and Lake Hopatcong, eventually to link up with the Bear Mountain Reservation.

Mid-New Jersey: George B. Ford and E. P. Goodrich

The Ford-Goodrich team examined the mid-Jersey sector encompassing all or parts of the counties of Essex, Morris, Somerset, Union, Middlesex, and Hudson (figure 5.5). Ford and Goodrich, who had specialized in this area in

Figure 5.5. Plan for Sector 5, George B. Ford, Advisory Planning Group, Regional Plan of New York and Its Environs, 1923. (*Source:* Regional Plan Papers)

their planning practice, produced the most detailed of the six sector reports. Their approach was an empirical one in which they sought to determine regularities in development phenomena which they then treated as standards to guide planning for future growth. Ford and Goodrich presented their findings in a summary way that was effective in quickly characterizing the situation:

> The present temper of commuters is that about one hour is the limit which they care to expend in travel.

> Communities which are largely inhabited by commuters are more advanced, with correspondingly higher tax rates than are others which do not have a large commuter population.

> The communities along the railroads which provide the best train service are most advanced.

> There seems to be a tendency on the part of existing industrial communities to hamper larger industrial growth because of a fear of a rise in wages.

> Land values for all classes of property increase in general in an exponential ratio with increase in size of community.

> Residential land is higher in value near New York and decreases with the distance from the city . . .

On the other hand, business and industrial property does not reveal this influence of proximity to the greater city.[76]

Ford and Goodrich, comparing development along the several railroads which traversed the sector, noted that the Lehigh Valley tracks were far less urbanized than the Lackawanna, the Jersey Central, or the Pennsylvania, due no doubt to the absence of passenger service on the Lehigh Valley line. The two planners proposed a 'linear city' to straddle the Lehigh Valley line for much of its length in the sector. There was ample precedent in the sector for this approach, for the Jersey Central had developed its corridor in linear city fashion by purchasing substantial land on either side of its right of way, laying out parallel arterials on either side of its tracks and attracting industry to the land closest to the rails, then business, with residences in the outermost blocks.

Ford and Goodrich accepted the desirability of decentralization, but unlike Bartholomew they did not feel better transportation was the best means to achieve dispersal and lower densities. Rather, the solution lay in encouraging the controlled speculative developer to build low-priced, low rent houses of the one- or two-family type.

> The provision of such housing would do more to draw away from the congestion of the large centers than would any other known decentralizing influences. Industrialists can rarely afford to supply homes. The speculative builder is the one toward whom we must turn to solve the problem.[77]

Ford and Goodrich made suggestions on improving the commuter rail facilities at Jersey City and elsewhere, and the usual recommendations that highways be upgraded for automobiles and more routes constructed. A parkway was proposed for the Morris Canal, and the purchase of park lands along the Watchung Range and in other steep areas was recommended.

With considerable prescience the planners predicted a rapid growth of 'aeronautics' over the coming two or three decades, hazarding the guess that long distance rail passenger service would be replaced by the airplane. They called for airfields for light craft to be spaced every ten miles or so in developed areas with larger fields for trans-Atlantic and transcontinental flights at intervals of 100 miles.[78]

Ford and Goodrich concluded by suggesting that functional surveys be conducted to complement the six sectors survey. Zoning, recreation, regional circulation, and land use could be understood and planned for only on a region-wide basis.

Staten Island and Southern New Jersey: Edward H. Bennett

Edward H. Bennett, who had worked with Burnham on the Chicago Plan and had devised the 1914 Plan for Brooklyn, supervised the study of Staten Island

and that portion of the Region in New Jersey south of the Raritan River.[79] He was assisted in the work by H.T. Frost.

Bennett and Frost were probably at a disadvantage working from a Chicago office. Their report was the shortest of the six and in some ways the weakest. Bennett's major proposals included bridges over Arthur Kill, Kill Van Kull, and from Staten Island to South Amboy, proposals which he had probably obtained from discussion with Port Authority planners. Bennett took no stand on the much-debated ship canal proposed by the State of New Jersey to cross the state from Raritan Bay to the Delaware River. Bennett did suggest, however, that, if the canal were built, a parallel highway and industrial development be channeled to its vicinity.

As for parks, Bennett followed the Olmsted precedent in suggesting acquisition of special areas such as swamps, woods, and hills, all to be linked by parkways. Bennett particularly urged the acquisition of the Fish Kill area on Staten Island.

Bennett's 1923 plan for Sector VI revealed the great changes which had occurred in planning theory over the nine years since he had produced his formalistic plan for Brooklyn. Gone were the diagonal boulevards, replaced by curvilinear networks of automobile highways. Formal urban parks were replaced by larger, more topographically related regional parks. Above all the scale was larger. City planning had expanded its horizons to encompass regional planning.

THOMAS ADAMS' SYNTHESIS

It was Adams' task to assemble the six sector reports into a unified statement. But the diversity of the points of view and the unevenness of the various plans resulted in a composite plan lacking both unity and coherence (figures 5.6, 5.7, 5.8). For example, new development seemed to be unduly weighted toward New Jersey. And Nolen's satellite towns stood out in contrast to the Ford-Goodrich proposals for corridors along the main transportation lines.

The best that Adams could do was to attempt a synthesis of the main questions raised by the consultants to serve as an introductory statement to the assembled reports. In a masterful summary of the issues to which the Regional Plan would have to respond he concluded that:

- Regional zoning should be established on the basis of a regional plan to serve as a guide to local zoning plans.
- Special agricultural zones in the shape of wedges should be established to provide more open space than could be provided through park or forest preserves alone.
- New transportation facilities should emphasize circumferential rather than radial movements to help ease congestion.

- Decentralization of activities should be encouraged where such activities did not need central locations; conversely, centralization was desirable for functions which could not be decentralized without loss to the Region as a whole.
- High buildings were generally not desirable as they did not pay the public costs they incurred in congestion and transportation requirements.
- More public open space should be acquired, particularly at river and harbor edges.

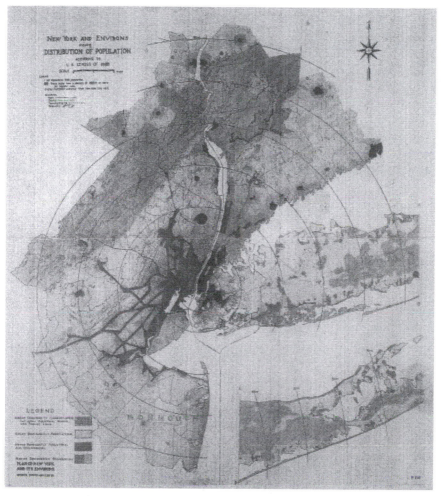

Figure 5.6. Thomas Adams's synthesis of Advisory Group Sector Plans, 1923. (*Source:* Regional Plan Papers)

T O W N   P L A N
RADBURN, N.J.

SCHOOLS	APARTMENTS	HOUSES	THEATRE
STORES	PLAYGROUNDS	PARKS	INDUSTRY

Courtesy of the City Housing Corporation

Figure 5.7. Plan for Radburn, New Jersey as featured in *The Building of the City.* (*Source:* Committee on the Regional Plan of New York and Its Environs. (1931*a*))

- Large sites should be acquired in advance for future airport needs.
- Subdivision design and location practice needed improvement, particularly the avoidance of the ubiquitous gridiron plat on hilly terrain and the coordination of subdivision development with sewerage and water facilities.

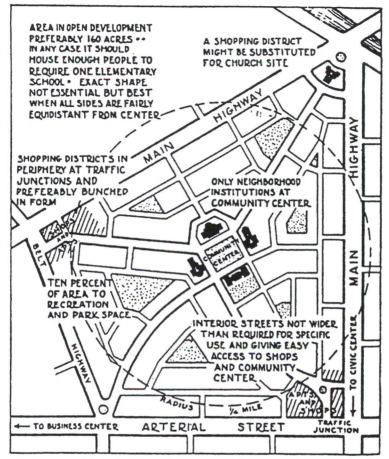

Figure 5.8. Neighborhood concept based on Clarence Perry's Neighborhood Theory. (*Source:* New York Regional Survey)

- A system was required to reduce the inequitable distribution of property taxes among industry-rich and industry-poor towns.
- Development corporations should be established to help industries relocate and to build satellite towns.

This was an early and extraordinarily comprehensive statement of the issues which would pre-occupy planners and far-sighted government officials for decades. Two crucial issues were neglected, however. How were the housing needs of the Region's populace to be met? And what steps should be taken to rebuild the decaying, substandard parts of the old cities?

The housing issue was postponed, Adams explained, until the results of the social survey were in hand. The redevelopment of obsolete areas was not included, because the sector reports dealt with the unbuilt environs, where, Adams rightly felt, planning could have its greatest impact.[80]

When Adams presented his summary and composite plan to the Advisory Planning Group, Delano was gratified at the progress that had been made. But several of the consultants were critical. Nolen felt that there was too much in the plan that was local, not regional. He also felt that the possibility of developing new satellite cities had not been examined adequately in several of the sectors.[81] George Ford felt that the report was too much like a composite of old theories, and that there was not the feeling that a solid research job lay behind the proposals. Ford hoped that out of the concurrent survey work would emerge an innovative approach to overall regional development.[82]

The joint report of the Advisory Planning Group was not published. Adams took the view that publication would be unwise because it 'would probably be misunderstood by the "man in the street" and of no real value as a guide to public bodies.'[83] But the report was to have a strong influence on the subsequent scope and substance of the Regional Plan, and many of the specific recommendations made by the consultants were incorporated into it.[84] If there were disagreements about details, the consultants were generally in accord about what the central issues facing the Region were and what remedies were possible.

FIRST ARCHITECTURAL STUDIES

While the Advisory Planning Group was conducting its studies through 1923, four committees of prominent architects who had been persuaded by Charles Norton to work without compensation were completing their sketch plans on specific Manhattan projects. Cass Gilbert, architect of the Woolworth Building, chaired a group charged with studying the City Hall area and also with preparing a general plan of Manhattan. D. Everett Waid, with the help of Chester H. Aldrich and William A. Delano, among others, would investigate possibilities for redevelopment along the East Side waterfront; the West Side waterfront was assigned to Thomas Hastings and three colleagues, including John Russell Pope; and the 59th Street development question, along with general traffic studies, were to be examined by Harvey Corbett with William A. Boring, Arnold W. Brunner, Burt L. Fenner, and Charles A. Platt. A number of other architects also participated in the work of the committees, including Hugh Ferris, Perry Coke Smith, Francis Swales, and E. Maxwell Fry.[85] It was a prestigious assemblage of architectural talent that Norton had recruited into the service of the Regional Plan. The older men represented for the most part the passing generation of neo-Classical, City Beautiful designers. The younger men, like Hugh Ferris and Maxwell Fry, espoused a romanticized modernism emphasizing movement and technology. With this diversity it was not surprising that several of the architects' committees would disagree about basic matters. It was the engineers, however, who became most skeptical of the architects' visionary proposals, especially after a meeting at Corbett's office on March 20, 1923. Corbett outlined the principles which had been agreed upon among the group as a basis for design:

1. New York and particularly Manhattan Island would continue to grow.
2. The bulk of buildings would continue to increase.
3. Present street capacity was no longer sufficient for present building bulk.
4. Streets were already one-third the total area of Manhattan and one-half the building area.
5. Consequently, no more streets should be provided, but the present street capacity should be increased in another way.
6. Double or triple decking was the only method of increase.[86]

Corbett concluded with a sweeping predication that Manhattan a hundred years hence would be almost entirely a business district raised on platforms above ground level. Even parks would be raised, he suggested, to permit traffic to move undisturbed on the surface. The transportation schemes that the architects had prepared on the basis of these principles and notices seemed far-fetched to the Regional Plan staff. The minutes of the meeting noted that it was the opinion of the members of the staff (Bassett, Nelson Lewis, McCrea, and Shurtleff) that for the most part the architects' transportation plans 'were entirely impractical and would not stand the light of day'.[87]

The committees of architects had produced a number of interesting proposals, particularly one by Ernest Flagg and Harvey W. Corbett, emphasizing the separation of vehicular and pedestrian traffic through progressive development of pedestrian bridges and arcades. For its time this was an advanced concept, though the transitional problem of getting the city to live on the second floor rather than the first made the scheme seem impossible of achievement.[88]

Monumental schemes for strategic sites also occupied the attention of the architectural committees. Cass Gilbert's team undertook a redesign of the City Hall-civic center area, long a focus of concern and controversy. Harvey Corbett's group also sketched a proposal for a prototypical bridge plaza for a proposed 57th Street Hudson River bridge, a project the Regional Plan Committee and staff would help to defeat a year later, substituting a proposal for a bridge away from the center, at 178th Street.

While the architects and engineers connected with the Plan had several disagreements, probably the greatest controversy swirled about the proposal which Nelson Lewis had made a year before, in 1922, for elevated roadways along the Hudson from 72nd Street south to the Battery, then north along the East River to 57th Street.[89] The idea was not entirely original with Lewis, since Charles Norton, undoubtedly thinking of Burnham's lakefront ideas for Chicago, had earlier proposed boulevards and parks around the perimeter of the island as a means to recapture the waterside amenities which had been lost to industry in the nineteenth century. Nelson Lewis, however, was more concerned about solving the Manhattan traffic congestion problem by moving through traffic to the edges of the island. Lewis thus was not greatly concerned about detrimental aesthetic or visual effects of elevated structures or their impact on adjacent buildings. But the West Side Waterfront Committee under the chairmanship of Thomas Hastings vehemently opposed the idea of an elevated highway along the Hudson south of Riverside Drive. Hastings and his group suggested instead that the West-side New York Central tracks on Tenth and Eleventh Avenues and West Street be placed underground, and that West Street be developed as a great artery on the ground level, a boulevard spine along which new parks, terraces, and residential blocks overlooking the water would be developed.[90]

Hastings' scheme would have recaptured the waterfront, as Norton had envisioned, through an integrated development of buildings, park, and roadway. Traffic flow would have been enhanced and dockside activities maintained. Hastings also provided for views of the river from new residential blocks and terraced gardens and parks, extending the elder Olmsted's Riverside Park southward. Hastings and his committee realized that marginal elevated highways would separate the city from the water when what was required was to make the river visually and physically accessible. Nelson Lewis, on the other hand, believed that a West Side elevated highway would provide vantage points from which to see a 'fascinating picture of the life of the harbor.' Thomas Adams later concluded that an elevated highway would have to be forty feet or more off the ground to provide general views of the river on the West Side.[91]

Nelson Lewis was appalled at the rail proposals for the West Side. 'Most objectionable,' he labeled them, in a letter to Adams, because the trackage would occupy part of the right of way he had proposed for his elevated highway. 'I had thought.' he continued in his note to Adams, written from a sickbed in his Brooklyn home, 'I might write you in some detail about these plans, but find that what I have already done has tried me a good deal so I must stop. I have not referred to the architect's plans for the west side as they appear to me chimerical.'[92] A few days after, the sixty-eight year old engineer-planner entered Brooklyn Hospital. Two months later, on March 30, 1924, Nelson Lewis was dead. The Regional Plan Committee and staff had suffered the loss of another of its key figures through death. Few had known New York and its problems as closely as Lewis. His knowledge and prestige would be missed. On April 15, Harold M. Lewis was appointed by the Committee to be 'Executive Engineer in Charge of the Office,' to carry on the work of his father. E.P. Goodrich and W.J. Wilgus were to act as consultants on engineering studies.[93]

Nelson Lewis did not live to see his concept for an elevated West Side highway accepted by the city, and the route of the elevated New York Central tracks shifted to permit the marginal road. Nor did he see Thomas Adams and the Regional Plan Committee vigorously oppose in public hearing the concept of his elevated highway, which, they claimed, would not relate well to the adjacent buildings and would subordinate local areas to the demands of through traffic. Hastings' plans for an integrated development came to be favored over the engineering conception of Lewis. When the first section of the elevated West Side Highway was completed in the mid 1920s, it was all too evident that the warnings of Hastings and Adams had been sound. The Miller Highway, as it was subsequently named, was an oppressive barrier to access to the waterfront, not at all the waterfront treatment that Norton had dreamed about ten years before. The engineering conception had won over the architectural, a dominance which was to be increasingly reflected in the work of the Plan. Adams' task was to try to synthesize the work of the architects and the engineers, but it was clear that they were speaking with very different vocabularies.

By the time the first round of studies by the four committees of architects had been completed, it was evident to Adams that greater control over output would be necessary if the detailed designs were to relate to specific projects which evolved from the basic conceptions of the Regional Plan. Adams decided to take on this part of the work himself, aided by Francis Swales, one of the architects who had assisted in the work of Cass Gilbert's committee. Between 1924 and 1929, Swales produced a series of designs which eventually constituted the core of the project proposals espoused by the Regional Plan.[94]

NOTES

1. Memorandum of Charles D, Norton, November 3, 1921, Regional Papers.

2. Nelson P. Lewis, 'A Plan for New York and Its Environs: A Preliminary Outline of the Problem', September 10,1921, Regional Plan Papers.

3. Committee on the Regional Plan of New York and Its Environs, *The Plan of New York with References to the Chicago Plan*.

4. Smith was out of office at the time, having served as Governor from 1918 to 1920. He was again elected Governor for three successive terms, from 1922 to 1928.

5. Memorandum of Charles D. Norton to Robert DeForest, October 12, 1921, Regional Plan Papers.

6. Robert DeForest to Charles D. Norton, October 27,1921, Regional Plan Papers.

7. Committee on the Regional Plan of New York, Record of the meeting of May 10, 1922, Regional Plan Papers.

8. Shurtleff, Flavel (1914) *Carrying out the City Plan*. New York: Survey Associates.

9. Charles D. Norton, Memorandum for the City Plan Committee, November 3, 1921, Regional Plan Papers.

10. *Ibid.*

11. Minutes of meeting, Committee on the Regional Plan of New York and Its Environs, May 3, 1922, Regional Plan Papers.

12. Quoted in 'Record of the Meeting of May 10, 1922', in the Committee on the Regional Plan of New York, *The Plan of New York with References to the Chicago Plan.*

13. *Ibid.*

14. *Ibid.*

15. *Ibid.*

16. *Ibid*

17. Minutes of meeting, Committee on the Regional Plan, May 11, 1922, Regional Plan Papers.

18. Minutes of meeting, Committee on the Regional Plan, February 24, 1922, Regional Plan Papers.

19. *Ibid.*

20. Minutes of meeting, Committee on the Regional Plan, March 3, 1922, Regional Plan Papers.

21. Frederick Law Olmsted, Jr., 'Memorandum for Conference at Century Club', New York, January 14, 1922, Regional Plan Papers.

22. Thomas Adams to Charles Norton, April 14, 1922, Regional Plan Papers.

23. Minutes of meeting, Committee on the Regional Plan, March 3, 1922, Regional Plan Papers.

24. Charles D. Norton to Frederic Delano, August 21, 1922, Regional Plan Papers. The 'first housing scheme' Norton refers to was probably Letchworth Garden City.

25. Charles D. Norton to Frank L. Polk, August 4, 1922, Regional Plan Papers.

26. Quoted in Creese, Walter L. (1967) *The Legacy of Raymond Unwin: A Pattern for Planning.* Cambridge: MIT Press, p.23.

27. Quoted in Adams, Thomas (1927) *Planning the New York Region.* New York: Regional Plan of New York and Its Environs, pp.42–43.

28. Address of Raymond Unwin, Sage Building, September 25, 1922, Regional Plan Papers.

29. *Ibid.*

30. Raymond Unwin, 'Report No. 3: Procedure and Organization', October, 1922, Regional Plan Papers.

31. *Ibid.*

32. Olmsted, Frederick L. Jr and Kimball, Theodora (1922) *Frederick Law Olmsted, Landscape Architect, 1822–1903.* New York: G.P. Putman's Sons.

33. Minutes of meeting, Committee on the Regional Plan, November 27, 1922, Regional Plan Papers.

34. Pearl, Raymond and Reed, Lowell J. (1923) *Predicted Growth of Population of New York and Its Environs.* New York: Committee on the Regional Plan of New York and Its Environs.

35. Minutes of meeting, Committee on the Regional Plan, December 16, 1922, Regional Plan Papers.

36. *Ibid.*

37. *Ibid.*

38. Frederic A. Delano to Charles D. Norton, November 3, 1922, Regional Plan Papers.

39. *Ibid.*

40. *Ibid.*

41. *Ibid.*

42. *Ibid.*

43. *Ibid.*

44. Minutes, 'Conference with City Planners, Mr Norton's Apartment', January 22, 1923, Regional Plan Papers.

45. *Ibid.*, p.2.

46. Minutes, 'Conference of Advisory Planning Group with the Staff', February 14, 1923, p.1., Regional Plan Papers.

47. *Ibid.*

48. Program of Conferences of Advisory Planning Group, February 12–14, 1923, Regional Plan Papers.

49. Minutes, Conference of February 14, 1923, p.2, Regional Plan Papers.

50. *Ibid.*

51. *Ibid.*, p.3.

52. *Ibid.*, pp. 4–5.

53. *Ibid.*

54. William Howard Taft, Letter to the Editor, *New York Times*, March 10, 1923.

55. *New York Times*, March 7, 1923' *New York Post*, March 7, 1923.

56. Committee Staff Minutes, February 27, 1923, Regional Plan Papers.

57. Frederick Keppel, Memorandum, May 23, 1923, Regional Plan Papers.

58. *Ibid.*

59. Frederick Keppel to John Glenn, telegram of May 23, 1923; John Glenn to Frederick Keppel, May 23, 1923; minutes of meeting, Committee on the Regional Plan, May 29, 1923, Regional Plan Papers.

60. Frederick Keppel to John Glenn, May 23, 1923, Regional Plan Papers.

61. Frederick Keppel to John Glenn, June 14, 1923, Regional Plan Papers.

62. Notes of conference of June 8, 1923; Frederick Keppel to John Glenn, June 14, 1923.

63. Frederic A. Delano, Memorandum, June 6, 1923, Regional Plan Papers.

64. Nelson P. Lewis to Frederick Keppel, June 12, 1923, Regional Plan Papers.

65. They were E.P. Goodrich, C.W. Leavitt, L.V. Morris, Arthur H. Pratt, M. Reynolds, and Amos Schaeffer. Minutes of meeting, Committee on the Regional Plan, November 23, 1923, Regional Plan Papers.

66. Minutes of meeting, Committee on the Regional Plan, October 18, 1923, November 20, 1923, Regional Plan Papers.

67. Committee on the Regional Plan of New York and Its Environs (1923) Reports on Sectors, Sector I. (MS) Regional Plan Papers.

68. *Ibid.*

69. *Ibid.*

70. *Ibid.*

71. *Ibid.*, Sector II, (1923), P.17. Adams was assisted by Hale J. Walker in the preparation of his report on Sector II.

72. *Ibid.*, p.19.

73. *Ibid.*, p.20.

74. *Ibid.*, Sector III.

75. Bartholomew was assisted by L.D. Tilton.

76. *Ibid.*, Sector V, p.13.

77. *Ibid.*, p.14

78. *Ibid.*, p.44.

79. *Ibid.*, Sector VI.

80. Draft Report of the Advisory Planning Group, November 12, 1923.

81. Minutes of meeting, Advisory Planning Group, October 19–20, 1923, Papers of John Nolen, Regional Plan Papers.

82. *Ibid.*

83. Thomas Adams, Memorandum to members of the Advisory Planning Group, November 12, 1923; also Minutes, Advisory Planning Group, November 21, 1923, Papers of John Nolen, Regional Plan Papers.

84. John Nolen to Thomas Adams, March 24, 1928, Papers of John Nolen, Regional Plan Papers.

85. Adams, Thomas (1927) *Planning the New York Region*. New York: Regional Plan of New York and Its Environs, pp.53–55.

86. Staff minutes, March 20, 1923, Regional Plan Papers.

87. *Ibid.*

88. Committee on the Regional Plan of New York and Its Environs (1931) *Regional Plan of New York and Its Environs*, Vol. II. *The Building of the City* (by Thomas Adams assisted by Harold M. Lewis and Lawrence M. Orton). New York: Regional Plan of New York and Its Environs, pp. 411–413.

89. *Ibid.*, pp. 299–301, Lewis also proposed an elevated cross-town connection on Canal Street between the Holland vehicular tunnel (under construction in 1923) and the Manhattan Bridge, providing a direct link between New Jersey and Brooklyn. This was the first proposal for the much-debated Lower Manhattan Expressway.

90. *Ibid.*, p. 349.

91. *Ibid.*, p. 357. Lewis' scheme for elevated marginal highways was not opposed by all the architects, however. The East Side Committee, chaired by D. Everett Waid, endorsed the concept for both the East and Hudson River waterfronts. The controversy over the future of the West Side was exacerbated when, in 1923, the New York Central Railroad proposed to elevate its dangerous two-track West Side surface freight line from Canal Street to Northern Manhattan, a project likely to cost more than $100,000,000, which the railroad had long been reluctant to undertake. Pressure from

the city administration and the prospect of having to place the route underground probably prompted the company proposal.

92. Nelson P. Lewis to Thomas Adams, January 28, 1924, Regional Plan Papers.

93. Committee on the Regional Plan of New York (1931), *op. cit.*, p.354.

94. Swales' proposals are discussed below, see pp.265–268.

6

TECHNICAL AND
IDEOLOGICAL INPUTS

THE REGIONAL POPULATION PROJECTIONS

An important formative element in the Regional Plan's approach to planning for future metropolitan density and population distribution was the population projections which were adopted in 1922. By the 1920s statisticians and statistically-minded engineers had discovered certain regularities in the growth of metropolitan areas. Consistent statistical relationships between past national growth and city growth were also observed. Such relationships inevitably suggested the biological analogy of urban growth that had long enjoyed popular currency even before Charles Darwin and Herbert Spencer's theories had reordered the ideology of man's social relationships. Urban growth was viewed as inexorable, natural, and most importantly, predictable to some degree.

The future metropolitan population was not a variable to be manipulated by the planner. Rather, it was seen as a given. In Adams' view the regional planner's job was to arrange the best possible receptacle to accommodate the additional inhabitants, not to set national urbanization policy, or to try to divert growth elsewhere. No group of experts really knew enough to set such policy, and even if a desirable policy could be determined, the extant political structure was neither able nor willing to carry it out. With some justification Adams could claim the twin virtues of being both scientific and pragmatic.

But the state of population forecasting was still more art than science in the early 1920s.[1] The Regional Plan staff's need for a reliable forty-year projection of metropolitan growth evoked not one but four separate estimates. Starting from a 1920 base of about nine million, two of the projections foresaw a 1965 regional population of about twenty-one million; the other two both settled on a 1965 estimate of about 14.5 million. (The 1965 population of the region turned out to be 16,860,000.)

The first of the four projections was prepared in 1922 by Nelson P. Lewis. Lewis employed the then standard method of plotting the curve of past growth on semi-logarithmic paper and extrapolating the curve into the future. Lewis simply assumed that the growth rate between 1910 and 1920 would remain constant to 1965. This assumption, which had been increasingly questioned after 1900, led Lewis to overestimate the eventual 1965 regional population by about four million.[2] A more sophisticated approach, which, however, yielded estimates close to those of Nelson Lewis, was that employed in 1923 by two professors at Johns Hopkins University, Raymond Pearl and Lowell J. Reed. Pearl, a biostatistician, had earlier devised a theory of population growth based on empirical observation of biological growth phenomena, such as the change of egg size with successive layings and the progressive weight increase of white rats.[3] Pearl hypothesized a similar growth process for whole nations and for their metropolitan areas. He posited a growth curve asymptotic to the X-axis at the beginning of the cycle and asymptotic to some stabilized ultimate limit determined by the observations of past trends. Pearl, in applying his formula to urban growth, looked on this asymptotic limit as a reflection of environmental constraints, such as a not unlimited food supply, and upper limits on tolerable population densities.

On the basis of their equations, Pearl and Reed calculated that the New York Metropolitan Region would reach an ultimate population of about thirty-five million in the year 2100. For 1965 they predicted a total population of slightly more than twenty-one million, a figure that seemed reassuring since it coincided with Lewis's prediction of a year earlier. Pearl and Reed were well aware that the smaller the area involved, the less reliable the projections became. But this did not deter them from predicting the population for each of three concentric groups of counties into which the region had been divided for purposes of analysis, and for New York City separately. Pearl and Reed anticipated a continued and large growth in the old core city areas from 6.7 million in 1920 to 14 million in 1965. New York City alone was predicted to grow from 5.7 million to 11.5 million in 1965, leveling off at 15.4 million after 2050.

These figures turned out to be astronomically high, of course. The old core areas did grow between 1920 and 1965 – but by two million rather than the predicted five million. And most of this growth took place between 1920 and 1930. The leveling off occurred 120 years ahead of schedule.

What Pearl and Reed neglected to note was that limiting factors were indeed at work, but they were not the factors they had in mind. What limited the incredible build-up of population implied by the Pearl-Reed figures was the simple availability of land. Their projections implied that the densities of Brooklyn in 1920, 35,000 persons per square mile, would prevail throughout Queens, Richmond and the other core counties by 1965. By the year 2000, densities in the entire core area were expected to equal those in Manhattan – over 50,000 persons per square mile – suggesting formidable intensification of population such as would be possible only through massive rebuilding of already developed areas, a highly unlikely prospect even in the urban halcyon days of 1923.

The Pearl-Reed 1965 density forecasts, therefore, turned out to be vastly overestimated for the region as a whole and for the two inner rings. Only the outer ring density was slightly underestimated.

Despite their authoritative tone, the Pearl-Reed estimates did not go unchallenged. Two Harvard University professors, Edwin B. Wilson of the School of Public Health and William J. Luyten of the Harvard College Observatory, looked carefully at the Pearl-Reed technique in 1924, after they had been called upon to make similar projections for the Metropolitan District of Boston in connection with planning for an adequate water supply for that region.

Wilson and Luyten attacked the Pearl-Reed technique on the grounds that it was not additive, i.e. that separate projections for the component parts of a county or region would not necessarily add up to the projections for the county or region as a whole. As an effective example demonstration, they showed that for the combined three-state area of New York, New Jersey, and Connecticut, the Pearl-Reed technique yielded an ultimate population lower by thirteen million than what had been predicted for the New York metropolitan region contained therein.

Wilson and Luyten proposed a simple way out of the dilemma: employ the Pearl-Reed technique for the U.S. as a whole, assume that the New York Metropolitan Region would continue to have its 1910 proportion of national population and work backwards from the resultant 'ultimate' (asymptotic) population. Using the Pearl-Reed national saturation figure of 197 million, Wilson and Luyten calculated an ultimate regional population of 16.7 million and a 1965 population of about 14.5 million. Because the Pearl-Reed national figure, which served as their base, turned out to be seriously underestimated, the Wilson and Luyten 1965 projection for the region was underestimated by 2.4 million.

A fourth estimate of population, by a New York City engineer, Ernest P. Goodrich, a consultant to the Regional Plan of New York, was based on his finding that the frequency distribution of cities by size tended closely to follow a binomial probability distribution.[4] Goodrich discovered that if the incorporated communities in the United States in 1920 were arranged by population size in groups the lower limit of which started at 2,500 and doubled with each step, the numbers of cities in each group corresponded almost exactly with the probability of drawing a sequence of, say, white balls from a bag containing equal numbers of black and white balls, drawing as many balls as there are total communities. Goodrich's figures are reproduced in table 6.1.

Goodrich converted his observations into a tool for predicting the region's future population by first calculating the future expected number of communities in the United States with more than 2,500 population. This figure he derived simply by extrapolating average growth in the number of such communities as reported in the censuses of 1890 to 1920. The projected

Table 6.1 Population projections for the twenty-two county New York Metropolitan Region, 1900–2000 and census figures, 1900–1990.

	Actual (U.S. Census)[a]	Nelson-Lewis Extrapolation	Pearl-Reed Logistic	Wilson-Luyten Logistic	Goodrich Rank Size	Goodrich Ratio	Projection selected by Engineering Staff, RPNYE
1900	5,385	–	5,460	5,584	–	–	–
1910	7,467	–	7,117	7,113	–	–	–
1920	8,979	–	9,122	8,755	–	–	–
1930	11,643	10,870	11,460	10,370	9,700	9,670	–
1940	12,518	13,253	14,070	11,840	11,000	11,000	13,253
1950	13,951	15,923	16,840	13,110	12,400	12,300	–
1960	16,140	19,295	19,650	14,130	13,600	13,820	19,295
1965[b]	17,325	21,067	21,000	14,510	14,350	14,625	21,000
1970	17,593	22,840	22,340	14,890	15,100	15,430	–
1980	17,121	26,788	24,810	15,460	16,400	16,850	–
1990	17,536	30,800	26,960	15,870	17,900	18,460	–
2000	–	34,698	28,760	16,160	19,200	19,780	–

(a) Census and estimates of actual population, 1930–90, are for a slightly larger region to conform to whole counties. The original region excluded the outer parts of Dutchess, Orange and Monmouth Counties.

(b) 1965 projections were interpolated from decennial figures.

Source: Pearl, Raymond, and Reed Lowell J. (1923) *Predicted Growth of Population of New York and Its Environs*. New York: Plan of New York and Its Environs; Regional Plan of New York (1965), *The Region's Growth*. New York; U.S. Census of Population, 1900–1990.

population of the largest community (New York City) was determined from the basic formula Goodrich had derived to express his version of the rank size rule. Then, by applying a system of ratios of region to city population, Goodrich developed a series of projections for the twenty-two county New York Metropolitan Region. His estimate for the year 2000 for the whole region was 19.2 million people. His projection for 1965 was about 14.5 million – precisely what Wilson and Luyten had arrived at by other means.[5] An approximate correspondence between the outcomes of the two techniques should not have been surprising, however, since both describe a highly-skewed J-shaped curve with a very long upper tail.

Goodrich also employed another, more empirical approach, the results of which appeared to confirm his first set of findings. This last approach derived small area projections through a sequence of ratios having as a starting point the future probable maximum population of the United States of 300,000,000 derived from a 1920 U.S. Department of Agriculture estimate of potential maximum food production.

Thomas Adams, when he assumed direction, was thus confronted with two pairs of widely divergent projections for the Region's 1965 population: the Lewis and Pearl-Reed estimates suggesting a population of about twenty-one million and the more conservative Wilson-Luyten and Goodrich projections, 14.5 million. The choice of projections was extremely important; projected high levels of growth would require higher levels of capital investment – and could be publicized to help mobilize regional development. Adams selected the higher figure. He recognized that the way population was to be distributed across the Region was at least as important as the aggregate Regional total. Both Lewis and Pearl-Reed had prepared projections for the three rings of the Region, amazingly in agreement; Wilson-Luyten and Goodrich had not. This made the Lewis distributions not only seemingly more scientific but more useful as well. Moreover, by 1925 a good deal of the Regional Plan staff outlook and activity had already been based on the Lewis projections prepared several years before the lower estimates had become available. Changing projections would have been awkward and disruptive. Besides, the temptation must have been present to rationalize the use of higher rather than lower figures on the grounds that planning errors due to underestimating population were likely to be more serious than errors of overestimation. Even if twenty-one million people were not in the Region in 1965, it was assumed that they would eventually be there.

In the aggregate, this was not an unreasonable view. The consequences of selecting a set of figures moderately high for the Region as a whole probably would not have been serious. But far more critical was the prediction of the future distribution of population across the three rings into which the regional total had been disaggregated. If the population of the Region as a whole was viewed as determined largely by external forces, the distribution of that population within the region was not. Presumably, it was a purpose of the Plan to recommend the use of zoning and subdivision controls to bend what was not altogether inevitable into what were deemed to be desirable directions. But the statistical projections for each of the counties did not explicitly derive from normative conceptions of suitable densities or of degrees of centralization and decentralization, the two white-hot issues which had dominated urban planning debate for twenty years prior to the undertaking of the Plan. Rather, they were offered as cool-headed, highly probable extrapolations of past trends, a starting point for planning, shaping rather than shaped by the proposals for regional transportation which in the end would largely determine future densities and the distribution of population.

THE CONTRIBUTION OF ROBERT MURRAY HAIG

In September of 1922 Professor Walter W. Stewart of Amherst had submitted his report on a suggested scope for the industrial and economic survey. Stewart called for a comprehensive investigation into fourteen specific fields of study:

I. Economic factors influencing the growth and character of population;

II. Influence of transit facilities on distribution and concentration of population:

III. Place of residence and place of work of population of Region;

IV. Economic and industrial activities of the Region;

V. Causes of localization of centers and economic and social activities;

VI. Character of manufacture within the Region;

VII. Building construction within the Region;

VIII. Extent and character of public works;

IX. The pressure for space – a study of causes and attempted methods of relief;

X. The real estate market and the development of new residence districts;

XI. The scale of incomes and the types of residence;

XII. Economics of the suburban community;

XIII. Influence of the automobile on transportation in the Region;

XIV. The integration of towns – a study in urban consolidation.[6]

Professor Stewart had neatly catagorized the salient development forces at work in the Region. Had the studies he proposed been undertaken, a sturdy foundation on which to erect the Plan might have been available to Thomas Adams and his staff. But Stewart's list of proposed studies was judged to be beyond the resources the Committee was willing to commit to the economic survey. Robert Murray Haig and Roswell McCrea, the Columbia University economists, suggested a less ambitious approach: study specific industries to determine the broad regional trends. Which industries were growing, which declining? Which were voluntarily moving out of Manhattan and which were staying, and why? How much open land would be required in the Plan for specific industries? Haig and McCrea proposed to provide the planners with solid economic answers on which to base their proposals. As a trial run, the printing industry was selected to determine whether an industry-by-industry survey would be productive and useful. Haig and McCrea noted that business enterprises would probably be helpful in providing information to supplement what was available from the factory-inspection agencies of the states of New York, New Jersey, and Connecticut. Such contracts, the economists suggested, would also inspire an interest on the part of the business community in the plan and its implementation.

The Committee on the Plan agreed, approving the Haig-McCrea memorandum on November 27, 1922. Haig would direct the survey and McCrea would be a consultant.

The inquiry concerning the printing industry yielded promising results, and on May 2, 1923, the Committee authorized Haig and McCrea to undertake twelve unit studies, nine of which were industrial surveys and three had to do with finance and distribution. These studies were carried to completion in the summer of 1923 and transmitted to the Committee on October 1, 1923. It was a remarkable achievement. Never before had the economic base of a large metropolitan area been analyzed in such detail. Using data from the factory-inspection agencies of the three states, some quarter-million cards prepared by hand recorded the character, location, and number of employees of each industrial establishment in the area for each of the four years, 1900, 1912, 1917, and 1922. The nine industrial studies covered 71.9 per cent of all the plants and 79.5 per cent of all the employees listed by the state agencies for the Region. These included chemicals, metal, wood, tobacco, printing, food, clothing, and textile industries. The three supplementary studies covered whole-sale markets, retail shopping, and financial districts. Detailed maps were prepared that graphically portrayed the changes which had occurred in industry and business over the first two decades of the century. Trends in each industry were analyzed in monographs prepared by specialists with the advice and supervision of Haig and McCrea.

Haig summarized the findings of the economic survey in two influential articles published in 1926. Extrapolating from the pathbreaking work of Edward A. Ross on the location on industries. Haig offered several hypotheses concerning the concentration of people and industry.[7] The metropolitan region was 'essentially a piece of productive economic machinery competing with other metropolitan machines . . . The great bulk of the population must work and must consume most of what they earn where they earn it . . .

consumption and production . . . must be carried on for the most part in the same place.'[8] Transportation advantages determine the location of production sites. 'The most favored spots are those from which the richest resources can be tapped with the lowest transportation costs. At such points would develop the great cities.'[9] And at these points consumption goods would be lowest in cost. This would have the effect, according to Haig, of exerting a powerful attraction on the entire 'foot-free' population to move to the urban areas. The question that Mumford and others had asked, 'Why live in the city?' Haig suggested should be changed to 'Why not live in the city?'[10] Haig acknowledged that some 'country mice' might prefer to sacrifice part of the rich assortment of consumption goods offered in the city to enjoy mountain lakes and rural open spaces. But, he concluded, 'country mice appear not to bulk large in the aggregate figures of the urban trend.'[11]

The Committee on the Regional Plan commissioned the economist Adna F. Weber to review the findings of the Economic Survey.[12] Weber, who had some twenty years earlier produced the monumental *The Growth of Cities in the Nineteenth Century*, disagreed with some of Haig's basic conclusions.[13] He concurred with Haig concerning the centralizing impact of transportation on the distribution of goods; only half in jest, he suggested that 'when the airplane comes into common use, a prophet may not go beyond the bounds of imagination who forecasts the monopoly of retail trade by the department stores of New York and Chicago!'[14] But Weber was not convinced that the large metropolitan region would similarly attract and concentrate manufacturing activity. The smaller city could furnish all the benefits of the large metropolis and, in addition, lower wages, lower rents, and less congestion. This, Weber thought, would explain, for example, the presence of General Electric in the small industrial cities of Schenectady and Pittsfield. Haig argued that such dispersion away from the largest centers was due to such factors as perishability or change in bulk of goods at point of manufacture, the availability of cheap woman and child labor as in the Pennsylvania mining towns, and, not least, the 'exactions' of trade unions which drive owners to some town where, as one manufacturer announced, 'he could tell the damn Bolshevists to go to hell.'[15]

These were distortions of Haig's ideal model in which all manufacturing would otherwise come to the metropolis. Haig did not pretend that he had demonstrated the soundness of the hypothesis behind his model. He advanced it 'in the hope that it may contribute toward an understanding of the phenomenon of metropolitan growth.'[16] The idea that all manufacturing might end up in the New York region (except for distortion due to the complicating factors mentioned) was a heady prediction for the business-oriented Committee and also for the staff. Industrial growth, if shunted to the outer areas, would produce the kind of controlled decentralization of population so avidly sought.

Haig's studies helped shed a good deal of light on which industries might be expected to be part of such decentralization. Hoping to find a 'scientific basis for city planning,' he proposed that eventually a formula would be devised which would show an industry's relative need for accessibility, i.e., its need to be at a high-rental, highly accessible, site, say in Manhattan, or alternatively, to be located at a cheaper, less accessible site further out. Armed with such a formula the process of entrepreneurial trial and error in finding the best site would be eliminated, and the planners, armed with such powerful equipment, would have a 'scientific basis for zoning.'[17]

Haig did not come up with the potent formula. What he did produce was the best scheme that had yet been devised for assessing the locational desiderata of industries. Rejecting Olmsted's proposal for division of economic activates into 'primary' and 'ancillary' categories, Haig constructed a list of factors affecting location and then checked off which were relevant to each specific industry or activity. One cluster of industries tended to occupy the center of the Region in Manhattan, and were characterized by small scale, highly-skilled, unstandardized work, with seasonal or changing market demand. These included such activities as women's outerwear, small job printing and high grade jewelry and plate-engraving. These were the industries which were rapidly growing in Manhattan, offsetting losses in a second category of industries characterized by large size, large ground area, and nuisance and pollution production. These industries were rapidly departing Manhattan for more convenient and cheaper sites in New Jersey or Long Island, with chemicals., textiles, slaughtering, and metal plants tending to go west of the Hudson, and clothing, baking, and furniture to sites across the East River. Some of these industries, Haig predicted, would in the future drift out of the New York Region altogether to such areas as the Pennsylvania coal fields, where the low-wage labor of women and children could be used.[18]

Haig's investigation showed that manufacturing employment in the Region had increased from 657,000 in 1900 to 1,206,000 in 1922, an increase of 83.6 per cent compared to a population increase of about 74 per cent.[19] The greatest rates of employment growth between 1900 and 1922 had occurred in the chemical (151.6 per cent), men's clothing (115.4 per cent), women's clothing (113.6 per cent), and metals industries (78.8 per cent). With the exception of the women's clothing category, the fastest-growing industries were those which sought sites away from the congested center.[20] This explained why central Manhattan's industrial employment had grown from 289,903 jobs in 1900 to 419,784 in 1922, an increase of only 44.8 per cent, while the rest of the inner industrial zone had gone from 301,746 to 661,960, an increase of 119.4 per cent. The remainder of the Region had gone from 65,338 to 124,379, an increase of 90.3 per cent. If past economic trends could be expected to continue, the planners would have to plan for a Manhattan with somewhat reduced industrial employment consisting of firms dealing in unstandardized production, surrounded by a twenty-mile belt of development containing the bulk of future industrial jobs, and, beyond this belt, an outlying area also of considerable industrial potential.

Haig did not provide specific projections of future industrial employment by industry and area, nor did he attempt to suggest the amount of open land in each part of the region to be allocated for industrial development, an input for the plan that the planners desperately needed. This part of the study was originally thought of as a later phase of the work. But the surveys had consumed most of the funds set aside for the economic studies and it is also probable that Haig did not wish to speculate on the future beyond the limits permitted by the information he had already gathered. In any event, it was left to the planners to incorporate Haig's conclusions into the plan. The most important of these were:

1. Manufacturing in the Region's center (Manhattan south of 59th Street) had peaked in employment in about 1917 and would continue to decline in total jobs.
2. Some kinds of manufacturing in the center would grow, however, notably those connected with style changes, skilled labor, or seasonal markets. In some industries, fabrication would be moved to the twenty-mile wide industrial belt around the center, often leaving behind offices and showrooms in the center.
3. Heavy manufacturing would grow in both the twenty-mile belt and the environs beyond it.
4. Wholesale markets would increasingly divide trading and goods handling functions, the former remaining in the center, the latter gravitating to waterfront and belt line railroad areas.
5. The Wall Street financial district would not shift its location.
6. The central retail shopping district would not move northward beyond 59th Street because of the barrier of Central Park. The 34th Street cluster of department stores would probably remain, though it might increasingly stress the price factor (i.e., serve less affluent groups).
7. Retail sub-centers in the growing residential areas would develop rapidly, particularly as standardization of goods increased.[21]

As it turned out, these were quite accurate forecasts of the economic future of the Region, albeit delayed by a depression and a war which were beyond the predictive power of economics. Haig had provided a great deal of valuable information to the planners. The question was whether they could use the information in a plan and then use the plan to help structure the physical environment to match the trends predicted by the economists.

Haig's most significant influence, however, was not so much on the Regional Plan as on the economic theory of urban growth. Until Haig, economists had almost universally looked on the city as a parasitic growth living off the agricultural surplus of rural areas. Haig turned the equation around by showing that the city could increase agricultural surplus through the production of labor-saving machines. Extending the concept further to include all goods made in the city, including consumer goods, Haig conjured up an image of the city as the great cornucopia of modern industrial society, a benevolent production and vending machine to which all who could leave the land would tend to gravitate to enjoy the bounty. For the machine to work efficiently enough to compete with other metropolitan areas, the internal frustration of moving goods and people had to be reduced as much as possible.

There was a large chink of stark reality between Haig's abstraction of the benevolent urban machine and the actual crowded city whose people would ensure daily personal discomfort and indignity for the sake of employment for themselves and sustenance for their families. People would go where the jobs went, and, as Adna Weber pointed out, all the jobs need not, perhaps should not, go to the metropolis or its suburbs. It was a point which Lewis Mumford also would forcibly make after the completion of the Plan. Haig's image of the ideal metropolis as a friction-less economic machine was diametrically opposite to Raymond Unwin's image of the city as a benign environment in which to live and work. It fell to Thomas Adams to choose one of these images or, alternatively, to try to reconcile them.

ZONING, TRAFFIC STUDIES AND PUBLIC RELATIONS

Through 1924, the Regional Plan staff moved ahead on three fronts, zoning, traffic studies, and public relations. Zoning, which had been conceived only eight years before, was at the time spreading rapidly across the Region and the country, often in ways which Bassett and his associates regarded as improper. State enabling legislation was often poorly written, and local ordinances too frequently were over-discriminatory in their exclusionary clauses. Bassett worried that too much bad zoning could jeopardize the whole zoning movement just as it was moving to an inevitable challenge in the Supreme Court. The growth of road traffic and congestion was also an issue of great moment to localities. The Regional Plan engineering staff, led by the youthful Harold Lewis, regarded the solution to automobile movement as one of its primary tasks. Above all, public relations appeared essential. When Charles Norton had sent out Flavel Shurtleff to ask what influential people were saying about the Regional Plan, the answer had come back: '. . . they are saying nothing about us.' Anonymity was, of course, a prescription for oblivion unless public awareness and involvement in the Plan could be increased. By moving forward in zoning, public relations, and traffic studies, the Regional Plan staff research would become topical and relevant to current issues. But the early emphasis on these issues, particularly the highway questions, worked to set the priorities of the Plan somewhat prematurely.

Bassett and Frank Backus Williams, his assistant in the Legal Survey, immersed themselves in an investigation of legal questions relating to the Plan. Bassett saw the Plan as a vehicle to achieve several central objectives of the zoning movement. The Plan would help spread zoning to the hundreds of communities in the Region. Their theory was that the more communities adopting zoning, the more likely the Supreme Court would be to accept its constitutionality when the inevitable challenge was made.[22] The work of the Regional Plan would also help to base zoning on rational overall planning. Bassett realized that with each community providing its own zoning ordinance, the overall effect would be a crazy quilt unless some kind of comprehensive plan could be devised transcending political boundaries. Bassett was particularly concerned that communities should not entirely zone out such uses as institutions and nuisance industry, which were locally undesirable but necessary to the life of the region as a whole. But he was most concerned about the effects of new transportation systems on density. He feared that the projected subways and parkways would simply engender new pockets of overbuilding, thereby losing whatever decentralizing benefits might be gained through better transportation. Zoning alone could not suggest what relationships between transportation capacity and building densities were proper, but the regional planning studies might well provide the guidelines Bassett thought essential, so that zoning maps would in reality constitute effective, compatible community plans.

By early 1924 Bassett, Frank B. Williams, and the Legal Survey staff had completed investigations into a variety of regional planning and zoning issues. Among the more interesting matters the staff analyzed were how to strengthen municipal planning powers, how to preserve the integrity and legality of the city plan, once adopted; how best to acquire open spaces and what authorities should be established to do so; how to ensure that state and town lands would be set aside for public uses; how to retain public title to fore-shore and under-water lands; how to acquire small parks and playground sites in urbanizing areas before they were built on and lost; how better to relate building codes to planning aims; and what authority should acquire open spaces to separate communities. Also significant was the work done by the Legal Division to help establish county planning commissions in Nassau, Westchester, Passaic, and Fairfield Counties.[23] But the most influential document that the Division produced was a small pamphlet issued in May of 1924 entitled, 'A Form of State Enabling Act for Zoning.' Following the swift spread of zoning in the eight years after the adoption of the first ordinance in 1916 in New York City, a piece-meal approach had been taken in the three states in the region. None had an adequate enabling law, Bassett asserted. To provide uniformity to what Bassett thought good practice, he devised a model code which set out clearly and simply the scope, purposes, and procedures for the application of zoning by localities.[24] It was this model code that the U.S. Department of Commerce's Advisory Committee on Zoning used in formulating its influential Standard State Zoning Enabling Act, which was published later in 1924. Bassett sat on this committee at the invitation of the Secretary of Commerce, Herbert Hoover. The Department of Commerce model code subsequently provided the basis for the legislation on zoning adopted by most of the states.[25]

One of Bassett's early assignments as head of the Legal Division was to study how the Regional Plan, once completed, could best be implemented. Charles Norton had thought in terms of a 'Plan of New York Authority' comparable to the Port of New York Authority to cope with the impediments of the three state boundaries. Bassett's opinion was that such an entity would be impractical and too difficult to attain politically. A crisis over proposed differential freight rates between New Jersey and New York had been the galvanizing force behind the creation of the Port Authority. No such crisis appeared available to the Regional Plan group. Bassett concluded that a better model for plan implementation would be a modification of the procedure he had used in gaining political acceptance for zoning in the neighborhoods of New York City in 1916: proselytize, provide information, emphasize local control, and help establish voluntary organizations to work with the staff. Recruit a committee of influential citizens from all parts of the Region who could go back to their communities and work for the goals of the Plan.[26] Bassett recommended against any expenditure of effort to create a new regional planning authority. It would be better, he thought, to develop as a successor to the Committee on the Regional Plan a private advisory body to work with local planning and zoning groups, free of political constraints.

Bassett's conclusions found acceptance among the Committee and its staff, and the information and public relations function was augmented. By May of 1924, Flavel Shurtleff could report that in the previous twelve months he had visited 150 communities in the Region, including all those over 10,000 in population, to acquaint local groups with the work of the Regional Plan. Some of these visits bore fruit. A meeting organized by Shurtleff on March 13 at Paterson, New Jersey, resulted in the formation of a Passaic County Planning Association, and a similar meeting held in Bridgeport, Connecticut, on March 31, led to the creation of the Fairfield County Planning Association. The Region was beginning to know and talk about the plan that was being prepared for it in Manhattan. But not all the comments were favorable. In early 1924, after much internal debate, the official title for the plan was adopted by the Committee. 'The Regional Plan for New York and Its Environs.' This irritated some New Jerseyans who took umbrage at the implicit suggestion that New Jersey was merely the environs of New York City. But the title was kept.[27]

Recognizing that the development of a constituency would be essential to the success of the Plan, the Regional Plan Committee arranged a major conference in Manhattan's Town Hall. Representatives from several hundred of the Region's local governments and organizations attended. The focus of the conference was on 'highway traffic problems of New York and Its Environs,' a topic of great interest to the many localities inundated with an unexpected deluge of cars and trucks. Highway congestion was a topic of interest to most communities in the Region, large and small, and by isolating it from the wide array of other regional problems, the Regional Plan Committee hoped to demonstrate both that the work they were doing was immediately relevant to the real problems of the Region's communities, and that their staff and consultants were technically highly competent. Harold Lewis and Ernest Goodrich presented reports predicting ever-increasing automobile registration and consequent clamor for new roads. Thomas Adams identified the two central questions related to traffic congestion: the effect of high buildings on amounts of motor traffic and the need to provide for express motor trafficways bypassing congested areas.

Curiously, little attention was paid at the conference to the crucial relationship between public transit and highway traffic. The two systems were viewed as largely separate and complementary rather than competitive. By emphasizing the highway traffic problems and the engineering solutions to immediate problems of congestion, the Regional Plan Committee had tapped a vital public concern – but it had also implicitly given the highway problem a distinct and high priority in its planning research. This emphasis would later be reflected in the completed plan.[28]

The conference of May 20 produced another development which reflected the outlook of the Regional Plan Committee. A resolution was put before the conference authorizing the Chairman of the Committee to appoint a general advisory committee representing the communities of the region, which in turn would appoint an executive committee to collaborate with the Committee on the Regional Plan. The resolution was unanimously carried. Later, some 250 prominent citizens from all parts of the Region would be appointed as a 'Regional Council' and after meeting several times in 1925 and 1926, would be disbanded.

As an attempt to create a quasi-public regional assembly, the council proved a failure. The planning process as conceived by the Regional Plan Committee was a top-down process, where ideas were generated by experts and transmitted to the localities and agencies. Democratic planning in which ideas percolated up from below was not readily compatible with the regional systems outlook which increasingly pervaded the philosophy of the Committee and its staff.

OUTLINES OF A PLAN

In November of 1924, with the Advisory Planning Group reconnaissance studies completed and the four surveys well under way, it was apparent that a staff and Committee consensus on the proper scope and substance of the proposed Regional Plan was needed. To this end, Adams circulated among the staff a confidential draft outline of his ideas on the subject.[29] Adams' draft proposed a sequence of staff activities consistent with his view of the plan as a map of future uses of land. First, a basic map of existing physical conditions would be required showing topography, water courses, roads and buildings. In his planning work in England, Adams had relied on the superb British Army Ordnance Maps, which showed in great detail natural and man-made features, including structures. Similar maps did not exist for the New York Region. The closest approximation was the U.S. Coast and Geodetic Survey series, completed in 1900, at the far grosser scale of 2000 feet to the inch. Adams proposed that this series, updated by staff field surveys, serve as the basic map. The various proposals of the Regional Plan staff, official agencies, and citizens' groups would be assembled on this base map. These would then be accepted, rejected, or changed to produce the final Plan. Adams' approach was to be more synthetic and eclectic than analytic:

> We need to have these proposals considered in proper order and directed towards the end we have in view in logical sequence. The focus of all our work is the regional plan, and each study and proposal has to be moulded with the other so as to converge toward that point.[30]

Adams was explicit concerning the sequence of considering the various proposals in the development of the plan:

> Having before us a map of existing conditions, the next thing necessary is to show the framework of our plan. The first part of the Plan would consist of the transportation and rapid transit needs for a population of 20,000,000 people . . .
> The next step is to develop the plan of extensions of the highway system, and fit these in with the transportation and transit plans . . .
> The necessity for including in any modern plan adequate facilities for parkways and of having areas which are proposed to be set apart for parks and other kinds of open space accessible by railroad and highways makes it desirable to consider these in immediate connection with the transportation and highway system. The park areas should be selected as far as practicable in advance of building development.[31]

Reservation of watersheds and solutions to sewerage and drainage problems were also to be considered, but only in broad outlines.

With the proposed future infrastructure determined, Adams suggested that problems connected with the architectural treatment of civic and neighborhood centers, controls on future use, heights, and the proper placing of public buildings could be resolved.

With his draft proposal, Adams initiated the process by which the shape of the Plan began to crystallize. The Plan more and more was coming to be viewed as a map of proposals for the efficient future use of the land rather than as a set of policies directly aimed at the improvement of social and economic conditions.

The question of limiting urban population growth, so significant in the contemporary planning debates in London, had become somewhat obscured in the Regional Plan staff assumption of a projected 1965 population of 20,000,000. By the time of the writing of the draft proposal it was the general consensus of the staff that 20,000,000 could easily be accommodated on the land available for development in the Region. The crucial question became not how to stop growth, which seemed impossible anyway, but how to distribute growth in such a way as to realize the benefits of agglomeration without suffering the consequences of congestion. The reactions Adams received from his staff and consultants were thus concerned more with details and procedural questions that with the fundamental issues of the form and substance of the Plan and the desirability and shape of future expansion.

Like most of the staff and consultants, Edward Bassett reacted favorably, on the whole. But Bassett's rigid legalistic view of planning resulted in some conflict over the proper scope and character of the Plan. Bassett suggested that there were really two basic maps that should be prepared, one being the map proposed by Adams showing topography, buildings, roadways, piers, rail lines, and other tangibles in place, and the other showing 'intangibles,' which Bassett defined as those qualities of the land with which it had been endowed by the law. These would include boundaries, official map plans of streets and roads, zoning, and similar legal constraints. Bassett asserted that these constraints in fact constituted a regional plan:

> This is the present Regional Plan. It has many imperfections. It has never been studied as a whole. But it is truly a regional plan as will be our Regional Plan for 20,000,000 inhabitants.[32]

Bassett's strict view of planning excluded proposals for buildings or civic centers. He did not wish to see such proposals incorporated under the title of 'Plan.' The Plan was limited in his view to the legal 'intangibles.' He cited the accomplishment of the Chicago City Plan to support his contention:

> The essential part and the only part [of the Chicago Plan] that has been carried out was the intangibles. Even here let me admit that some of the lake front structures resemble the illustrations in the Chicago City Plan. This is because landscaping and architecture there suggested were followed more or less closely, but architecture and landscaping are not city planning.[33]

Henry James disagreed vigorously with Bassett:

> One might also argue that interior decoration is not buildings or architecture. That would be right. But the man who is providing himself with a home is not going to omit the decorations from his plans and budget . . . Bassett . . . admits that it is as important to consider architecture and landscaping as what *he* calls

city planning. The process of including landscaping and architecture in the general scheme of things simply cannot be described in English by any convenient verb except the verb 'to plan.' It seems to me that Bassett ought not to object to the use of the word plan in the natural and convenient, though somewhat loose sense, until he can provide a suitable word for what he says is not truly 'planning.'[34]

James, obviously irritated by Bassett's narrow legalistic views, added that:

Bassett likes to make this conceptual distinction. That's all right if he doesn't consume time at staff meetings, etc., in arguing about it.[35]

In his rebuttal to James, Bassett persisted in his view that designs for buildings or groups were not appropriate parts of a plan. He outlined what he thought the plan should comprise, citing the inevitable Webster definition:

A plan is a graphic representation – Webster.

A graphic representation expresses distinction.

The plan of a city is the graphic representation of the distinctions created by the *city authority,* i.e. various legislatures.

City plan distinctions are different qualities of land areas created by law. There are no other permanent distinctions. I do not consider public structures city plan distinctions because they are not permanent.

City planning is therefore the determination of different legal qualities of land areas.

The determination of these different qualities of land areas depends on four needs of the inhabitants:
(1) Transfer from place to place of persons and property. (Movement)
(2) Health, safety, convenience, economy and welfare of the people in their work and living. (Zoning)
(3) Recreation.
(4) Public business.
There are no other.[36]

Within these categories Bassett listed the different legal qualities of land that were possible:

Due to movement: streets, highways, plazas, marginal ways, deep channels, foreshore, pierhead lines, bulkhead lines, ferries, canal, trunk railroads, terminal railroads, street railroads, urban rapid transit railroads, tunnels, bridges, water supply, sewer systems, gas supply, electricity supply, steam supply, telephone utility, telegraph utility, legalized omnibus routes.

Created by zoning: use districts, height districts, area districts, fire limits.

Recreation: parks, public buildings for recreation purposes.

Public business: government buildings, public institutions, buildings for public instruction.[37]

The Regional Plan, according to Bassett's rigid definition, should show land used for these purposes and these purposes only. It ought not to show private buildings (except as these would be reflected in zoning proposals), and designs for public structures definitely should not be incorporated in the plan, although suggested sites might be indicated.

Adams, always the conciliator, attempted to resolve the serious differences between Bassett and James. Adams noted that his outline for the Plan included all that Bassett recommended

> ... and some things that Mr. Bassett regards as (1) ancillary but necessary and proper, others that he regards as (2) ancillary but remote, and still others that he regards as (3) improper because they have no relation to regional planning inasmuch as they cannot be effected by any valid statute or ordinance. The question is whether classes (2) and (3) should for the sake of economy and precedent be eliminated.[38]

One of the key plan elements that fell into Bassett's 'improper' category was the concept of new satellite cities in the environs, which had been proposed by Nolen and other members of the Advisory Planning Group. While Britain and Europe had pioneered in building garden cities, nothing of the sort had been attempted in America outside of a handful of company towns. Adams was highly sympathetic to the concept but Bassett's conservative views gave him pause. No legal provisions existed to permit public development of new towns or garden cities, thus precluding their consideration under the Bassett formula. Adams realized that to push new ideas too fast or to appear to be attempting to foist British notions on America could jeopardize his and the Plan's credibility.

This did not prevent Clarence Perry from responding to Adams' outline for the Regional Plan with a method to achieve controlled new settlements within the American market system of land development as part of a positive policy of population decentralization. Shelby Harrison sent Perry's ideas to Adams with a note urging that the planning for transportation facilities be based on, rather than precede, planning for the possible distribution of population through the Region. Perry thought that he had a solution to the problem of moving too boldly on satellite cities:

> Before the framework of the ultimate Plan can be laid down it will be necessary to determine what principle is to be followed in predicting the future distribution of the population of the Region. There are two alternatives: *(a)* gradual congestion and extension of existing population centers [present tendency if undisturbed]. *(b)* creation of new regulated population centers [artificial stimulation of satellite cities]. Manifestly, however much we desire to promote decentralization, we should be regarded as highly visionary if we went ahead and based the final plan upon the satellite principle. It is feasible, however, to ascertain the wishes of the public in this matter. We could prepare rapid sketches of *(a)* the Region as it will probably be if present growths continue and *(b)* the Region if the increase might be distributed among a certain number of well placed satellite cities. In connection with such sketch maps we could present tentative data showing the transportational, recreational, and social conditions which may be expected in connection with each mode of development. There could also be submitted simultaneously a tentative legislative program for

putting the satellite system into effect, should that be decided. These two sketch plans would be confessedly theoretical and tentative but they could be nevertheless fairly authoritative representations of what will or of what might happen. They could be given the widest publicity in the press and submitted directly to local bodies already cooperating with the Plan. After local and general discussion of these two principles it would not be difficult, in time, to determine with fair accuracy which the public would favor and the elaboration of the final plan could then proceed on the basis indicated by this referendum.[39]

Perry was realist enough to know that satellite cities would not occur spontaneously, even after a publicity campaign. Incentives were required. In a supplementary memorandum he wrote:

We know enough about the suitability of the various districts in the region to say, theoretically, where certain satellite cities ought to go. We could easily picture the Region laid out with a system of satellite cities and one of the latter we could picture in detail.

The legislative procedure for giving desire for a satellite development might well follow these lines. There should be devised a new form of city charter which the legislature would grant under certain conditions, upon application of a body of property-owners of a given area. The provisions of the charter would come into effect progressively, each new provision becoming operative after certain conditions had been met. The basic condition for granting the charter would be the acceptance of the property-owners [of a given per cent of them of the area to be occupied by the proposed city] of certain specified conditions as to the plan of the future city. Chief among these conditions should be a park reservation completely surrounding the proposed city limits, this to be reserved and bought in time by the municipality and the state at a figure which would not be regarded as confiscatory by the owners. Other conditions of the charter should provide for comprehensive and continuous planning of the future development of the city.

I cannot of course, draft such a charter but I believe it is within the powers of citizens to secure for themselves many benefits which so far they have not considered practicable. The procedure here involved is this. Suppose Nanuet, New York, were a site indicated by our Plan as well suited for a satellite city. Today land around Nanuet is worth, say, $300 an acre. Once a city is fixed for that district immediately land values double or triple. The new city charter law would say – on such and such conditions – property-owners representing 70 per cent of the area of the proposed city can, upon their application receive charter rights. Then a local group who learned of these opportunities would seek signatures from the other property-owners. To get their signatures it would be necessary to assure them of provision in the charter for equalizing or pooling property value so that the new increment of value would be spread equitably over the whole area. By signing, by accepting the conditions, they assure themselves a chance at the new values. If they withhold their signatures, the new city project may go elsewhere. The force of the present opportunity would secure generally the acceptance of the charter conditions. Once a charter was granted the incorporators could go ahead and offer inducements to industries to locate there and the city would be started.

If a feasible legislative program could be prepared along with the pictures of the satellite city undoubtedly a voluntary association of public spirited citizens would immediately form to promote the passage of the desired legislation and the education of the public as to the merits of the satellite scheme for the future development of this Region.[40]

Perry's ingenious idea made little headway with Adams. Adams was naturally inclined towards a cautious, conservative approach, and Perry's proposal appeared too innovative to be credible. Moreover, Adams was urged not only by Bassett but also by Henry James to take a realistic point of view. James counseled Adams to orient his plans, particularly for transportation and transit, to long-range general conditions in 1960 but to make those plans immediately usable. A blueprint for action was far preferable to a formula for utopia if results were to be achieved. 'Only then,' James cautioned, 'can we produce a plan which we can hope to "put across" – which will be realizable as opposed to academic.'

James' views probably reinforced Adams' reluctance to investigate the possibilities of the innovative conceptions that Perry proposed and that George Ford had found so conspicuously absent in the efforts of the Advisory Planning Group. Increasingly, Adams viewed his task as one of steering a middle course between the pragmatic activists and the visionary theorists. The Plan should certainly stretch the public's vision of what could be done. It need not be confined to Bassett's narrow options within the existing legal constraints. But neither could it appear too boldly visionary. There were limits to the public's willingness to absorb new ideas.

Through 1925 the studies of the four survey groups moved ahead, largely independently of one another. Little, however, was accomplished on the Physical Plan because Adams and his staff had become preoccupied with several immediate and controversial regional development issues. Conflicts with the Port of New York Authority arose over a projected rail tunnel across the Narrows. And Long Island proposals by Robert Moses for new parkways were not in harmony with the premises of the Committee on the Regional Plan.[41] While Adams was diverted from the main work on the Plan by these immediate issues, their effect was to reinforce his propensity to view the Plan as more of a graphic agenda of realizable projects than as a strategy for long-term regional development.

During 1925 the staff was also occupied with several important national conferences which had been attracted to New York as a result of the work on the Regional Plan. In May of 1925 the International Garden Cities and Town Planning Federation met at the Hotel Pennsylvania. The meeting attracted the most renowned American and British planners and urbanists of the period, including Ebenezer Howard, Raymond Unwin, C.B. Purdom, Henry Wright, and Lewis Mumford. The growing division between the garden city, anti-metropolitan protagonists and the pro-metropolitan-growth proponents was heightened as a result of this conference.[42]

In the fall of 1925 two other conferences were held to discuss regional planning. The Third National Conference on the Science of Politics, held in

September, devoted seven sessions to problems of metropolitan planning. And on October 30, the American Statistical Association convened in New York at the suggestion of Shelby Harrison to discuss problems of population and economic forecasting for metropolitan areas.

Preoccupation with the fluid political scene in New York City in the fall of 1925 and the winter of 1926 also absorbed the Regional Plan Committee and its staff. The amiable James V. Walker was elected mayor on November 3, the incumbent, Hylan having been denied the nomination because of embarrassing conflicts with Governor Alfred E. Smith over a proposed rail tunnel to Staten Island. The Walker administration seemed to promise an opportunity for the various civic groups, including the Regional Plan Committee, to establish the permanent planning agency to deal with broad problems of city growth which the reformers had sought in 1913 during the Mitchel administration. An offer to assist Walker was proffered by the Committee on the Regional Plan in January of 1926. Though a Tammany Democrat, Walker, unlike Hylan, welcomed the support of the Wall Street reformers. He responded several months later with an invitation to the entire Committee to become members of a Committee of Five Hundred on Plan and Survey of the City of New York. Harold M. Lewis of the Regional Plan staff was also invited to become a member.[43] As the name of the group suggests, many of the members of the City Committee on Plan and Survey were closely connected with the Regional Plan. Vice-Chairmen of the Committee were Columbia University President Nicholas Murray Butler, and *New York Times* Editor John H. Finley, formerly President of the City College of New York, both of whom had close ties to the members of the Committee on the Regional Plan. Edward Bassett chaired the subcommittee on zoning and Harold M. Lewis contributed to the traffic and highway studies.

The City Committee would issue its report in 1928, calling for a permanent New York City planning body to cooperate closely with the Committee on the Regional Plan of New York.[44] But the drive for a city planning commission would be aborted in Albany in 1929 with the defeat of a proposed enabling bill in the legislature at the hands of borough interests fearing a loss of power. Eventually a New York City Planning Commission would be established, but not until 1936, when it was created as part of a general charter revision adopted by referendum. The efforts of the Committee on the Regional Plan and of its successor, the Regional Plan Association, together with those of other reform groups, including the City Club and the Citizens Union, were instrumental in finally realizing the establishment of the Commission. But if the Committee on Regional Plan had been counting heavily on the presence of an official, cooperative counterpart agency to plan for the development of New York City in detail beyond the means and scope of the Regional Plan, its hopes would be disappointed for more than a decade after the original initiative had been taken in 1926. However, the promise of a future City Planning Commission and the existence between 1926 and 1928 of the seven subcommittees of the City Committee on Plan and Survey seem to have further spurred the attention of Adams and his Regional Plan staff toward a concern for immediate projects for New York City.

By the end of 1926, with relatively little accomplished on the physical plan for the Region and with the Russell Sage funds scheduled to run out in 1927, Adams realized that a major effort on the Plan could not be postponed. Colonel William J. Wilgus, the Plan's consultant on transportation, had submitted his scheme for railroad consolidation and belt line development, which reaffirmed most of the proposals made in the 1921 Port Authority Comprehensive Plan. And Harold Lewis had assembled on a single map most of the highway proposals that the three states and other jurisdictions had proposed. But much remained before the fragments could be titled a 'Plan'. On November 23, Adams presented to the staff a preliminary set of recommendations for the substance of the Plan:

- The staff would develop proposals for an area within a twenty mile radius of Manhattan in more detail than for the rest of the Region.

- A population of 20,000,000 would be accepted as the probable population of the Region in 1965.

- That while the use of the terms 'centralization' and 'decentralization' should be avoided, the staff should point out the desirability and means of securing a more even and better balanced distribution of buildings, more space about buildings for all purposes, and reduction of the friction of space between home and place of employment.

- Any condemnation of high buildings should not, as a rule, be in respect of height in itself, but in respect of lack of proper scale between height and open areas surrounding buildings.

- That the standard of open space for public recreation and for general amenity for the whole Region be that which has already been attained in Westchester County.

- That the general plan of belt-line transportation, originally proposed by Colonel William J. Wilgus and revised by the staff, be approved in principle, but that it be put on the Plan only as a diagrammatic presentation of the general lines on which a system of transportation should or might be laid out, and not as a definite scheme propounded by the staff for the guidance of the railroads.

- That the proposals of the staff for development of Hackensack Meadows and Jamaica Bay be approved in principle.[45]

A month later, on December 30, Adams' guidelines were accepted with minor revisions by the Committee on the Regional Plan. Adams' 'basic general assumptions underlying the Regional Plan' constituted an attempt to synthesize the work and conclusions of the separate economic, engineering, social, and legal studies. Haig's economic studies had been completed, Bassett had provided much new thinking on zoning and land use controls, and Harold Lewis and William Wilgus had respectively developed regional highway and railroad schemes. The Social Survey had yielded up little of regional import. Clarence Perry had presented his Neighborhood Concept in 1926, and Wayne Heydecker had presented a survey of population densities and had proposed to develop a low-cost model demonstration house based on the 'sunshine' plan, which set minimum standards for light and air. The Social Division also had proposed other ideas for studies: water and air pollution, garbage disposal, and selection of future sites for schools and prisons. Except for Perry's ideas on neighborhood design, the Social Division's proposals were rather bland. The difficult issues had been avoided, such as how to get more and better housing for the poor and how to increase the income and stability of poor families. Thus the Social Division offered little counterweight to the industry-oriented ideas of Haig, the conservative legalisms of Bassett, or the engineering systems approach of Lewis and Wilgus. It fell to Adams to bring his British garden cities experience and sensibilities to leaven the various technical inputs from the surveys. But the result was timid and disappointing. In his list of general underlying assumptions Adams did emphasize the question of housing, calling for the 'betterment of living conditions' as a primary goal of the Plan. But this he qualified (Adams constantly qualified his original statements) by adding that better living conditions were to be achieved, 'so far as this can be promoted by improved environment of dwellings, by saving of waste in land development, and by adequate facilities for transportation and outdoor recreation.' Adams also suggested that the preferred solution to the problem of overcrowded, deteriorated, central city slums would be to erect dwellings on cheap land in suburban areas made accessible by means of transit and roadways and planned so as to provide open surroundings and recreational facilities. Deteriorated central areas would be replanned to open up more traffic ways and provide more open spaces 'with a view to creating new values . . . '[46]

Under the heading of living conditions Adams rather startlingly called for special consideration for industry and business:

> Where the needs of industry or business conflict with those of healthy living, a balance may have to be struck. For instance some degree of congestion may be a necessary concomitant to reasonable business concentration.[47]

Further on. Adams described what reasonable business concentration implied: 'that which will enable industry and business to function efficiently.'[48]

Adams constantly sought, in his own words, 'the middle course.' He called for spacious housing and at the same time concentration of housing near business; neither centralization nor decentralization, but 're-centralization,' a better balance between industry and residence, and for the skyscraper problem, an espousal of Delano's formula: to scatter the skyscrapers around the downtown so that clusters did not form, blocking out light and air and producing congestion on sidewalks and streets. Height in itself was not to be condemned.

In his proposals for the development of port facilities, Adams emphasized development of the existing harbor, reserving Newark and Jamaica Bay for later development. He also proposed that a grade-separated highway system with bypasses around congested areas be built in the Region. At the same time transit and rail passenger service should be improved. Adams saw no fundamental conflict or competitive relationship between the transit and highway alternatives.[49] In a 'balanced' system, both would be necessary.

Even in the question of population, Adams chose a flexible position: 'It is being assumed that the population of the Region will not exceed 20,000,000 in 1965. Whether such a number is reached in that year or ten years later is not a matter of great moment.'[50]

The Plan itself was to be flexible by being purposely indefinite:

Unlike a formal plan prepared for a city, town or village, the Regional Plan must not be hampered by having to conform to what is immediately practicable under existing laws. It should visualize possibilities and indicate opportunities that are rational even if new legislation is required to carry them out. Its disadvantages from indefiniteness are offset by advantages in elasticity. It is an elastic outline for the purpose of guiding definite action by public authorities, private corporations and individuals.[51]

For Adams the idea of balance was a necessary counterpart to the idea of compromise, and compromise was the secret of success in carrying out plans. But too often the result was ambiguity of meaning and qualification of statements so severe as to obscure what was intended. It may well be that Adams' qualifications were due to the conservative views of the members of the Committee on the Regional Plan. Adams had constantly to take into account those views as he worked toward the final version of the Plan. For example, he managed to gain the Committee's acceptance of the concept of satellite and neighborhood communities as a basis for planning (noting that the open wedges between the suburban rail lines would provide good sites). But one of his justifications for satellite towns was that they would encourage the 'Americanization of the body of immigrant labor which is still crowded in Manhattan . . .'[52] The percolating of the melting pot was a preoccupation of the patrician-reformers of the time. If anything would sell new towns, this argument would.

Efficiency in public spending and a cautious view of government enterprise were also recurrent themes. The fiscally conservative Committee was undoubtedly responsible for the 'general assumption' which required that all

of the Regional Plan proposals be premised on the recognition of two categories of public services: profit-making and non-profit-making. Any subsidies for activities which might be made self-supporting would in effect be
withdrawn from other non-profit but related activities because taxing capacities were limited or fixed.[53]

The broad outlines of the Regional Plan were now clearly in view. Rather
than pressing a strategy for radically shifting the course of regional development, the Plan would ride with the trends. Population growth of several
millions was regarded as inevitable. New jobs, factories, and business centers
would be created. The problem as Adams saw it was not to halt growth but
to harness and guide it into desirable forms and locations. Not everyone on
the staff agreed with Adams' basic assumptions concerning growth, particularly those based on Haig's conclusions. In response, Adams had agreed to
ask the eminent economist Adna F. Weber to comment on Haig's studies. But
Weber's reactions would come too late to alter the broad outlines already laid
down.

Though his title was General Director of Plans and Surveys, Adams saw
his task as one of synthesis rather than command, and his commission from
the Committee was to pull together the conclusions of the separate surveys
and studies. From Pearl and Reed he had the probable future population size.
From Haig he took the notions of reducing the transportation frictions of the
business economy and the easing of industry relocation to appropriate places
in the region. From the Port Authority and Colonel William J. Wilgus he had
his regional rail schemes, and from Harold Lewis, a plan for a grid of new
highways to bypass the congested centers. The Regional Plan was emerging
as an agglomeration of separate proposals rather than a set of strategies aimed
at specific goals.

With the pieces of the Plan seemingly falling into place, Adams felt
confident that he could meet the deadline for completion set by the Committee for September 30, 1928. In October of 1927 Adams announced final
publication plans. There would be nine survey volumes, which would present
the work of the Physical, Economic. Legal, and Social surveys, and two Plan
volumes. As an alternative, the ninth survey volume could be a Plan volume,
Adams suggested.[54]

Ultimately only eight survey and two plan volumes would be published.
The ninth volume, important enough to Adams to merit consideration as one
of the Plan volumes, apparently would have treated the important topic of
housing and new town development. But on November 14, 1927, the Committee on the Regional Plan came to a fateful decision concerning the manner
in which the Plan would deal with housing:

> Proposals regarding housing should avoid controversial matters and consist
> mainly of concrete suggestions illustrating the application of sound principles
> of planning.[55]

In effect this meant that the Plan would make no substantive proposals for building new towns or for rebuilding the deteriorated housing in the central city. It was a default of considerable significance, particularly in light of the intense efforts of various housing and social welfare groups to convince government of its responsibilities in providing more and better housing for low and middle income families. Undoubtedly, the Committee felt they could not get too far out in front of public opinion on controversial issues. But by defaulting on the question of housing, they in fact set back the thrust towards publicly-assisted housing. Ironically, the Committee, dominated by the leaders of the American zoning movement, had eagerly brought back from Europe the zoning idea but had rejected its counterpart there, government responsibility for the planning and development of residential districts for workers. In America, the *laissez-faire* market would provide such housing, or so the conservative members of the Committee assumed. The failure of the Regional Plan to come to terms with the underlying dilemma of housing was its most serious defect. If Adams was distressed over the Committee's regressive decision, he gave little evidence of it. His position required him to be, too often, a reed bending in the wind.

A hopeful way out of the housing problem came two months later, when Adams was invited by the developer, Alexander Bing, to be a consultant on a model industrial community which the private City Housing Corporation proposed to build on 1050 acres it had acquired in Fairlawn, New Jersey. The new community, to be called Radburn, was exactly what Adams had in mind when he had called for new towns in the green wedges between the rail corridors, close enough to have ready access to the metropolitan center in Manhattan, yet large enough and sufficiently far to have an independent community life of its own (see figure 5.7). It seemed the perfect compromise to the needs of the motor age. It was, however, not the isolated new town that the American proponents of garden cities had in mind as a means to halt city growth. Rather, it was suburban growth, but of a superior kind.[56]

The Radburn project brought Adams together with the architects Clarence Stein and Henry Wright, members of the Regional Planning Association of America (RPAA), an informal group dedicated to a re-creation of community through new town development and neighborhood planning.[57] Clarence Perry, who was both a staff member of the Regional Plan and a member of the RPAA, had since 1922 been researching the effects of street patterns and building relationships on neighborhood social structure. Perry had lived for several years as an observer in the Russell Sage Foundation model community at Forest Hills.[58] Community relationships, he observed, were determined largely by the location of arterial streets and boulevards and by the location of the elementary school.

Perry proposed that new neighborhood units be consciously created in the Region according to the following set of principles:

- The neighborhood should consist of the population required to support one elementary school, or, typically, between 4,800 and 9,000 people for schools ranging from 800 to 1500 pupils. The land area required would depend on residential density. The neighborhood unit principles, Perry suggested, could be applied to both high-density apartment districts and single-family suburban areas.

- The neighborhood unit should be bounded by arterial streets and boulevards. Placing the busy streets at the edge of the neighborhood would serve to enhance its identity and reduce the hazard of accidents to the residents.

- A system of internal small parks and recreation spaces should be provided.

- The neighborhood school and other local institutions should be grouped together at a central point.

- A local neighborhood shopping district should be located at the circumference, perhaps at an arterial traffic junction.

- The internal street system should be laid out to discourage through traffic.[59]

Perry saw the neighborhood units as a means of providing a safe, healthful, and pleasant setting for family life in the city, of the sort associated with rural villages and small towns (see figure 5.8). He also hoped that the neighborhood units might provide a political weapon against the 'selfish political machine.'

> The only place where a social movement affecting local government can arise is among the residents of the locality. Conversely, if the people who have a common interest in a specific section are not in face-to-face contact with each other, the natural method of protecting or improving that interest through spontaneous concerted effort is not available.[60]

The neighborhood unit, by permitting face-to-face contact, would encourage political reform and civic virtue:

> Suppose a prominent citizen ... [proposes] a reform scheme. His only points of contact are within his own profession or social circle ... At once the ... movement ... gains the tag of 'silk-stocking,' 'capitalists' or 'labor' and thereafter it is discredited by all other classes and groups having different interests.[61]

By substituting a residential for an economic basis for the organization of political life, Perry hoped that the polarization of issues would decline and the 'mass of politically inert tissue' of the cities would come alive.

Perry's neighborhood unit concept provided the basis for the vastly influential Radburn Plan, which grouped clusters of houses on culs-de-sac around common green spaces. The focal point of the community was the school, which could be reached on foot without crossing major thoroughfares. Adams, who was very active in the planning of Radburn, warmly endorsed the Radburn concept as a model for similar communities in the Region.[62] The Radburn project seemed to offer hope in the economically bountiful years of the late 1920s that privately financed new communities could without governmental assistance provide residential environments of high quality for the nine million additional people who would have to be housed in the next three or four decades in the New York Region. But Radburn was never completed. The City Housing Corporation, bankrupted by the crash of 1929, was dissolved, and the two-thirds of the project's land which remained undeveloped was sold. Radburn was regarded by the RPAA architects and planners as a feasible experiment, a first step toward realizing the Garden City ideal with protective greenbelt and self-contained employment. Adams viewed Radburn as a prototype for regional suburban development. As Clarence Stein later observed, Radburn failed financially but as an idea it was an enormous success, influencing subsequent development in many countries.[63] The Radburn project brought together for a short period the two antagonistic philosophies of community development of the 1920s: the growth orientation of the Regional Plan and the new communities ideas of the RPAA. The result was a compromise between Adams' view of what was economically and politically feasible within existing metropolitan constraints and the grand vision of the RPAA group. But it was the vision which became the enduring legacy. Adams' hope for the spread of other Radburns through the New York Metropolitan Region went unfulfilled. Though influential throughout the world, Radburn remained an isolated, fascinating experiment in its own Region.

NOTES

1. For a review of the development of regional population projection, see: Dorn, Harold F. (1956) Pitfalls in population forecasts and projections, in Spengler, Joseph J. and Dudley, Otis (eds.) *Demographic Analysis*. Glencoe: Free Press, pp. 69–90; Jones, Barclay G. (1965) Land uses in the United States in the year 2000, in Weiss, Charles M. (ed.) *Man's Environment in the Twenty-First Century*. Chapel Hill: School of Public Health, University of North Carolina, pp. 171–195; and Isard, Walter (1960) *Methods of Regional Analysis*. Cambridge: MIT Press, pp. 5–50.

2. Committee on the Regional Plan of New York and Its Environs (1929e) *Regional Survey of New York and Its Environs*. Vol II. *Population, Land Values and Government*. New York: Regional Plan of New York and Its Environs, pp. 89, 109.

3. *Proceedings of the National Academy of Sciences*, VI, June 15, 1920, pp. 275–288.

4. Goodrich, Ernest P. (1925) The statistical relationship between population and the city plan. *Papers and Proceedings, American Sociological Society*, **XX**, pp. 123–128.

5. *Ibid.*

6. Regional Plan of New York and Its Environs (1923) *Report of Progress, May, 1922–February, 1923*. pp. 32–41

7. Ross, Edward A. (1896) The location of industries. *Quarterly Journal of Economics*, April.

8. Haig, Robert Murray (1927) The economic basis of urban concentration. Reprinted in the Committee on the Regional Plan of New York and Its Environs (1927) *Regional Survey of New York and Its Environs*. Vol I. *Economic Factors in Metropolitan Growth*. New York: Regional Plan of New York and Its Environs, p.21.

9. *Ibid.*

10. *Ibid., p.22.*

11. *Ibid.*

12. Weber, Adna F. Comments on Professor Haig's 'Essays in the Economics of Regional Planning'. Unpublished report to the Committee on the Regional Plan, March 24, 1927, Regional Plan Papers.

13. Weber, Adna, F. (1899) *The Growth of Cities in the Nineteenth Century: A Study in Statistics*. New York: The Macmillan Co.

14. Weber, Comments . . ., *op. cit.*

15. Haig (1927) *op. cit.*, p.25.

16. *Ibid.*

17. *Ibid.*, pp. 104–107.

18. *Ibid.*

19. *Ibid.* p.23. Haig noted a population increase of 66.8 per cent based on census figures for 1900 to 1922. The adjusted figure of 74 per cent for 1900 to 1922 was suggested by Adna F. Weber in his 'Comments . . .', *op. cit.*

20. *Ibid.*, pp.23, 34.

21. *Ibid.*, pp. 9–12.

22. The challenge, which was successfully met, came two years later in the famous Village of Euclid vs. Ambler Realty Company case, 272 U.S. 36 (1926).

23. Subjects for Investigation. Unpublished report of Legal Survey, January 4, 1922 to July 27, 1925, Regional Plan Papers.

24. Committee on the Regional Plan of New York and Its Environs (1924a) A Form of State Enabling Act for Zoning. New York: Regional Plan of New York and Its Environs, May.

25. U.S. Department of Commerce, Advisory Committee on Zoning (1924) A Standard Zoning Enabling Act. Washington.

26. Report of E.M. Bassett, with supplement by Frank B. Williams, on 'Best Planning Authority for Carrying Out the Regional Plan'. Unpublished report of meeting of April 6, 1923, Regional Plan Papers.

27. Minutes of meeting, Committee on the Regional Plan, February 19, 1924, Regional Plan Papers.

28. Committee on the Regional Plan of New York and Its Environs (1924) Second Report of Progress, February 1923 to May 1924; also Committee on the Regional Plan of New York and Its Environs (1924b) Traffic Problems in their Relation to the Regional Plan of New York and Its Environs – Report of a Conference Held in the

Town Hall, New York City, May 24, 1924. New York: Regional Plan of New York and Its Environs.

29. 'Draft Regional Plan'. Confidential staff memorandum, November 10, 1924, Regional Plan Papers.

30. *Ibid.*, p.2.

31. *Ibid.*, pp. 3–5.

32. Edward M. Bassett to Thomas Adams, November 11, 1924, Regional Plan Papers.

33. *Ibid.*

34. Notes by Henry James on letter from Edward M. Bassett to Thomas Adams, Regional Plan Papers.

35. *Ibid.*

36. Edward M. Bassett, 'Response to Mr. Adams on Regional Planning', December 12, 1924, Regional Plan Papers.

37. *Ibid.*

38. Thomas Adams, 'Notes as to Changes Suggested by Mr. Bassett', December 13, 1924, Regional Plan Papers.

39. Clarence Perry to Shelby Harrison, November 13, 1924, Regional Plan Papers.

40. Clarence Perry, 'Supplementary memorandum on the Proposed Referendum'. November 13, 1924, Regional Plan Papers.

41. See *infra.*, pp. 225–236

42. *The Survey*, May 15, 1925, p.216.

43. Minutes of meeting, Committee on the Regional Plan, January 19, 1926; May 18, 1926, Regional Plan Papers.

44. Report of the New York City Committee on Plan and Survey, June 5, 1927. The influence of the Regional Plan Committee can be seen even in its report format, which closely resembled that of the Russell Sage group's publications.

45. Minutes of meeting, Committee on the Regional Plan, November 27, 1926, Regional Plan Papers.

46. *Ibid.*, p.2.

47. *Ibid.*

48. *Ibid.*

49. *Ibid.*, pp. 2–4.

50. *Ibid.*, p.6.

51. *Ibid.*, p.7.

52. *Ibid.*, p.5.

53. *Ibid.*

54. Staff minutes, October 27, 1927, Regional Plan Papers.

55. Minutes of meeting, Committee on the Regional Plan, November 14, 1927, Regional Plan Papers.

56. Minutes of meeting, Committee on the Regional Plan, January 24, 1928, Regional Plan Papers.

57. Lubove, Roy (1963) *Community Planning in the 1920s: The Contribution of the*

Regional Planning Association of America. Pittsburgh: University of Pittsburgh Press, pp. 62–66.

58. Staff minutes, December 13, 1922, Regional Plan Papers.

59. Committee on the Regional Plan of New York and Its Environs (1929) *Regional Survey of New York and its Environs.* Vol VII. *Neighborhood and Community Planning.* New York: Regional Plan of New York and Its Environs, pp. 34–35.

60. *Ibid.,* p.125.

61. *Ibid.*

62. Interview with Lawrence M. Orton, September 10, 1972.

63. Stein, Clarence (1966) Toward New Towns for America, revised edition. Cambridge: MIT Press, p.67.

7

FROM SURVEY TO PLAN

TRANSPORTATION: RAILS OR RUBBER

Nowhere did the ambiguities of Adams' 'balanced' approach to the Regional Plan show up more strongly than in the development of the transportation element. Adams must surely have appreciated that the private motor vehicle and public transportation were competitive, not complementary, for many kinds of trips, especially the journey to work. Yet the nature of that competition and the necessity for the Plan to take a position on whether rubber or rail was to be emphasized was barely acknowledged. In his prospectus to the Plan Adams had cautioned the staff to 'avoid putting forward concrete proposals that conflict with the proposals of public authorities who have the power to carry them into effect.'[1] Since public authorities had been established to plan for both rail and highways, Adams ultimately incorporated the programs, somewhat modified, of both groups in the Plan.

The failure to consider the relationship between highways and public transportation was the result of several factors. Throughout the studies, highway traffic was considered a problem separate from that of 'transportation', which included only public and quasi-public carriers on fixed routes, such as rail passenger and freight operations, and subways, trolleys, and buses. Highway traffic was regarded not as a transportation matter, but largely as a problem of congestion relief. Consequently, separate studies were conducted of the two issue areas with the result that the problem of competition was never adequately explored.

Colonel William J. Wilgus, the Committee's consultant on transportation, presented his final report and recommendations on rail operations and surface systems at the April 1925 meeting of the International City and Regional Planning Conference in New York City. Wilgus took a bold, sweeping view of the overall planning problem. He saw the Plan as having three important elements: transportation, recreation, and industry, in that order. Transportation shaped the location and development of recreation and industry and thus formed the framework of the Plan. Transportation he regarded as consisting of four elements.

(a) Through and suburban passenger and freight over trunk rail lines.
(b) Urban passengers over rapid transit and surface railways and distribution of freight within the city.

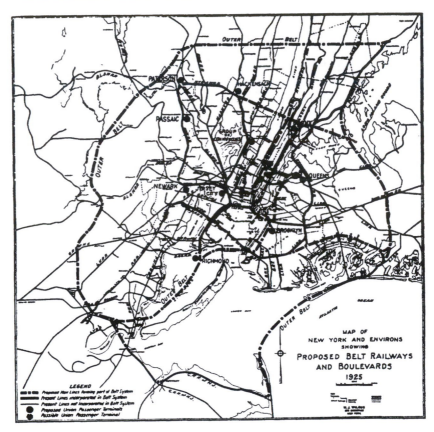

Figure 7.1. Modification of Port Authority rail plan proposed for the Regional Plan of New York by W.J. Wilgus, 1925. (*Source:* Regional Plan Papers)

(c) Trackless passenger and freight vehicles on streets and highways.

(d) Waterborne commerce.[2]

Wilgus' proposals for rail freight and passenger lines emphasized the development of circumferential belts to bypass the congested central areas and to permit easier interchange among the various rail systems serving the Region (figure 7.1). Colonel Wilgus also emphasized the importance of belt systems in wartime, citing the role of the Grande Ceinture around Paris in saving the cause of the Allies in World War I.[3] In 1916 Wilgus had helped devise the original Port of New York Authority rail plan, and his rail recommendations to the Regional Plan group were based largely on the earlier conception (figure 7.2). Wilgus called for an outer belt at a radius from Manhattan of roughly twenty miles. In New Jersey, the conception was nearly identical to what the Port Authority had proposed. But Wilgus called for a complete belt

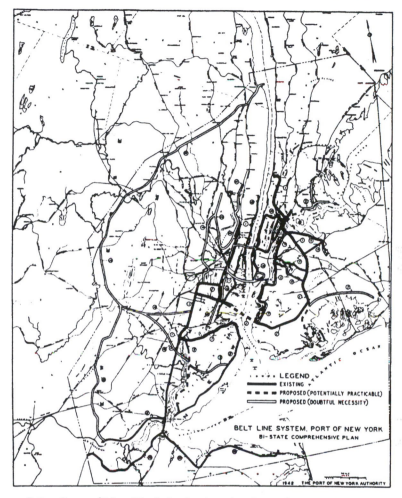

Figure 7.2. Port of New York Authority plan for rail system improvement, 1942 (adopted 1921). (*Source:* Bard (1942))

around the Region with new rail tunnels or bridges crossing the Hudson at three points: Yonkers, 178th Street in Manhattan, and at the Narrows. He also called for a Lower Bay crossing between Sandy Hook in New Jersey and Breezy Point in Queens via dramatic causeways and a tunnel under the ship entrance to the harbor.

Wilgus, who was responsible for the masterful, integrative engineering of New York's Grand Central Terminal, proposed that with the outer rail belt a circumferential boulevard be built providing access to recreation areas on the shores and in the nearby mountains. Wilgus' comprehensive concept of a multiple-use outer belt in which transportation, industry, and recreation would be developed together, was to become a major feature of the final plan.

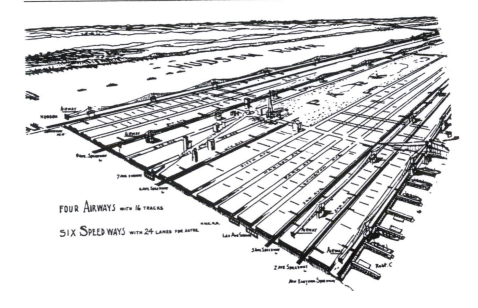

FOUR AIRWAYS with 16 tracks

SIX SPEEDWAYS with 24 lanes for autos

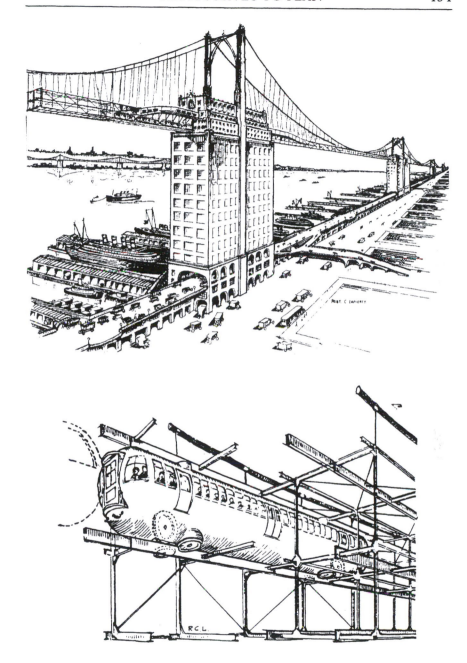

Figure 7.3. Studies for West Side highway development.

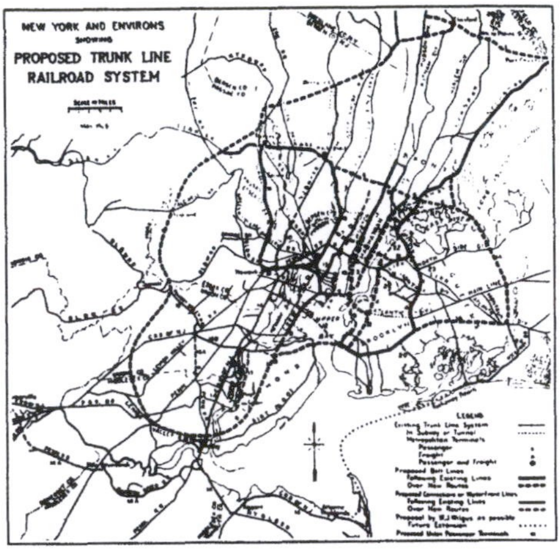

Figure 7.4. (top) Plan: Proposed
trunk line rail system, Regional
Plan of New York and Its Environs,
1928. (*Source:* Committee on the
Regional Plan of New York and Its
Environs (1929*d*))

Figure 7.5. (right) Plan: Proposed
rapid transit system, Regional Plan
of New York and Its Environs,
1928. (*Source:* Committee on the
Regional Plan of New York and Its
Environs (1929*d*))

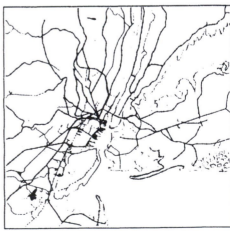

Figure 7.6. Reality: Railroad
system, 1965. (*Source:* Regional
Plan Association)

The concept meshed nicely with the finding of Robert Haig, the economic consultant, that the Region should reduce the frictions of movement and make provision for industrial decentralization.

In addition to the Outer Belt, Wilgus proposed several new inner rail belts to facilitate transfers and the bypassing of congested points. One such belt was proposed for the west side of Manhattan, to the Battery, and thence up the east side to a connection in the Bronx with existing routes. Another would provide a waterfront link in Queens and Brooklyn and had been suggested in the 1921 Port Authority plan. Additional inner connections were proposed in New Jersey, mostly along existing routes.

Wilgus' proposed regional rail system was intended for use not only by freight but also by passenger service, of which he identified three categories: long distance trunk line passengers, suburban rail commuters, and rapid transit passengers. Wilgus called for unified control of rail operations within the Region to permit integration of these services and to operate joint union passenger terminals, much in the manner that Grand Central Terminal had integrated the terminal services of the New York Central and the New York, New Haven, and Hartford Railroads. Wilgus proposed thirteen new or expanded union terminals in various parts of the Region where major rail lines intersected, and a possible major new terminal on Manhattan's West Side near 59th Street, to supplement Pennsylvania Station and Grand Central. Several of these new termini, such as Mott Haven in the Bronx and Sunnyside in Queens, would make use of air rights over existing railroad yards, a concept advanced for its time, although Wilgus had already demonstrated its feasibility at Grand Central Terminal.

Long-distance trunk line services would be facilitated by the proposed belt lines and Hudson River tunnels, particularly for those roads which terminated in New Jersey. But trunkline traffic was not the major issue. Suburban commuter and rapid transit service were the major problems. As the developed Region spread to the suburbs, the question arose of whether and how suburban rail service should penetrate Manhattan's business districts. Could commuter rail and city subway service be integrated and coordinated? Technical problems existed but were not insurmountable, and track widths were uniform. Official transit commissions had been established in Westchester in 1921 and in North Jersey in 1922 to investigate how best to serve those growing suburban areas by rail rapid transit, possibly linked to the New York subway system in Manhattan. New York City itself had, after years of controversy, determined in 1927 on a broad program of new construction involving new city-owned lines under Sixth, Eighth, and First or Second Avenues in Manhattan, with additional new extensions planned for the outer boroughs.

Wilgus and his associate, consulting engineer Daniel L. Turner, proposed a fully integrated network of rapid transit lines for the area within the outer

Figure 7.7.   Passenger rapid transit plan, W.J. Wilgus, 1925. (*Source*: Committee on the Regional Plan of New York and Its Environs (1929*a*))

loop (figure 7.7). Under their scheme almost no neighborhood within twenty miles of Manhattan would be more than a half-mile from a transit stop. In Queens alone, it was proposed that ten new parallel lines be built. In Northern New Jersey a similar network of fifteen parallel lines would run east-west from the outer belt to Manhattan. Six additional transit tunnels under the Hudson between New Jersey and Manhattan were projected. The whole system was to be integrated with both city subways and the rail system, with transfers possible at many intersecting points.[4]

Other independent experts had proposed more modest schemes. Henry Brinckerhoff, a consulting engineer, had proposed in 1920 a far less elaborate regional system to serve New York and New Jersey. Under this system five major east-west cross-Region routes and a single north-south route along the New Jersey shore of the Hudson would be constructed.[5]

In 1926 and 1927 the North Jersey Transit Commission had made proposals similar to Brinckerhoff's, with the addition of what the Commission

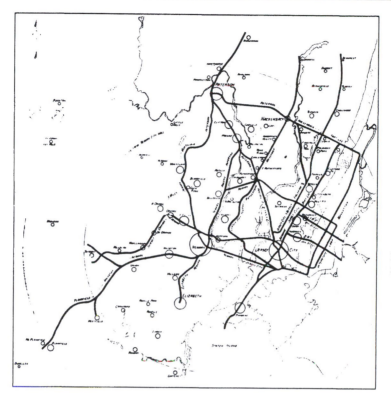

Figure 7.8. Proposed rapid transit system, North Jersey Transit Commission, 1925–1929. (*Source:* Regional Plan Papers)

termed an interstate loop in Midtown and Lower Manhattan (figure 7.8). The NJTC's proposals called for transit tracks to run on the 178th Street bridge and under the Hudson in tunnels at the Battery, 14th Street, and 41st Street, to be extensions of the New York City Subway system. In New Jersey the system would mostly use existing rail trackage.[6] New York City transit officials, however, were typically reluctant to consider the integration of suburban and city subway service. Their interest was largely in getting the new city-owned Independent System (IND) under construction and acquiring the privately-owned Brooklyn and Manhattan Transit (BMT) and Interborough Rapid Transit (IRT) systems.

In March of 1927 the engineering staff of Regional Plan, working closely with the North Jersey Transit Commission, had evolved a staged plan for regional rapid transit that did not require extensive integration with the city subway system, although some connections to the new Manhattan lines were contemplated (figures 7.9 and 7.10).[7] The immediate action plan called for completing the Independent System as approved by the New York City Board

Figure 7.9. Additions to the existing rapid transit system, proposed for completion by 1940. Engineering Division, Regional Plan of New York and Its Environs, 1927. (*Source:* Committee on the Regional Plan of New York and Its Environs 1929*a*))

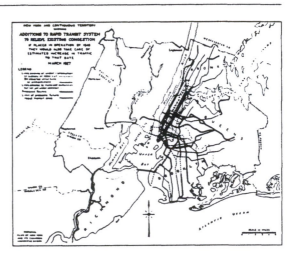

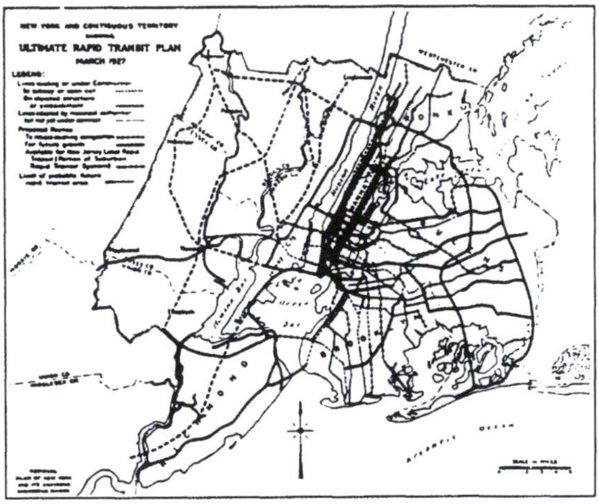

Figure 7.10. Proposed ultimate rapid transit plan. Engineering Division, Regional Plan of New York and Its Environs, 1927. (*Source:* Committee on the Regional Plan of New York and Its Environs 1929*a*))

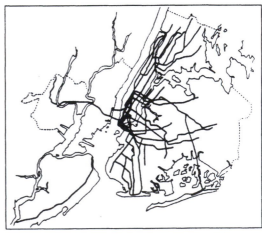

Figure 7.11. Reality: Operating rapid transit routes, 1963 (*Source:* Regional Plan Association)

of Estimate and Apportionment. A link between Manhattan and a proposed rail transfer point in the New Jersey Meadows was also suggested. The proposed ultimate suburban public transit system called for several additional subway routes through Queens, a loop system from the Rockaways passing along the eastern boundary of Queens, thence across the Bronx and Manhattan, on over the 178th Street Bridge to Hackensack and Paterson in New Jersey. Several other routes were proposed to serve metropolitan New Jersey, with tunnel links to Manhattan's business district. The 1927 staff Plan was thus far less extensive than the Wilgus Plan of 1925 and more closely reflected the plans proposed by the several official commissions at work on the problem of transit.[8]

By 1928 it had become clear that New York City transit officials would not consider the integration of suburban service with the city subway system. The new IND system had followed the principles of the Regional plan staff in Manhattan by emphasizing decentralizing routes closer to the edges of the Island, express service, and longer station spacing. But the City system did not provide enough capacity in Manhattan to handle additional suburban trains during the rush hour. Moreover, technical and administrative problems of coordinating operations across the city line appeared formidable. Political problems were raised as well: Why should the city help New Jersey and the suburban ring, with which it was in competition for new taxable growth? Wilgus had called for a unified administrative system for regional rail, subway, and surface transportation, a visionary proposal in light of the numerous public and private carriers operating in the three states. In the absence of such an entity, regional integration of transit and rail was patently impossible.

It was this situation that Adams and Harold Lewis, his chief engineer, faced in 1928 when they prepared to draft the final Regional Plan recommendations for rail and transit development. Adams had no choice but to accept the fact that the city subway system would not be part of a regional system. Consequently, the final Regional Plan contained no recommendations or discussion whatsoever regarding the crucial New York City subway component which had prompted Edward Bassett and George McAneny to initiate zoning in New York, and which in turn had stimulated the effort to undertake a regional plan. It was an extraordinary omission, considering the impact the new Independent Subway system under construction could be expected to have on the development of the city.

Adams focused his attention instead on the possibilities for development of a separate suburban rapid transit system that would operate mostly over trunk line routes. The Regional Plan proposal for trunk line rationalization was thus the key determinant of Adams' plan for rapid transit.[9] The Regional Plan for rail trunk lines that Adams finally adopted was basically the belt-line plan Wilgus had proposed in 1925, a modification of the original Port Authority Plan (figure 7.4). But there was one significant element omitted in the Regional Plan; in 1926 the Committee on the Regional Plan had approved the Wilgus plan in principle, but had balked at the bold proposal to link New Jersey and Long Island by means of a rail and boulevard causeway and tunnel under the outer harbor.[10] The Committee, fearful of appearing visionary and impractical, decided instead that the proposals be shown as a suggestion by Colonel Wilgus but not endorsed to be part of the Plan itself. Indeed, the Committee was reluctant to endorse the Wilgus plan at all, indicating instead that it should be regarded 'only as a diagrammatic presentation of the general lines on which a system of transportation should or might be laid out, and not as a definite scheme propounded by the staff for the guidance of the railroads.'[11] It was to Adams' credit that this diluting and ambiguous proviso was in the end not incorporated in the Plan.

Adams' final version of the trunk line rail plan differed from Wilgus' 1925 proposal in several other important particulars. Adams eliminated the idea for a new 59th Street Union Passenger Terminal on Manhattan's west side. A terminal at this location comparable to Grand Central and Pennsylvania Stations had long been discussed in connection with a proposed Hudson River bridge in the mid-1850s. But the Regional Plan opposed a bridge at this location on the grounds that it would add to the existing congestion on the west side of Midtown. The west side terminal was also opposed and dropped from the plan for the same reason. Adams did, however, accept the Wilgus proposals for union passenger terminals at other, decentralized points in the Region, such as Mott Haven in the Bronx and Sunnyside in Queens, envisioning these nodes as future centres of business as well as transportation.

Another Wilgus innovation, remarkable for its time, was also dismissed from the final regional plan for trunk line freight operations. Wilgus had proposed in 1908 a system of freight rapid transit 'to reduce the costs and delays of moving freight shipments by truck from the New Jersey railheads to Manhattan industries and businesses.' The large-capacity freight car, Wilgus suggested, should be excluded from the congested sections of the Region. Instead, a system of small, electrically operated car bodies on which demountable containers would be placed could carry freight via a new set of tunnels under the Hudson and the Manhattan business areas to points where unloading could take place and transfer made to trucks for short local hauls to final destinations. The problem, of course, was that two transfers were required under the Wilgus scheme, one from standard freight cars to the small containerized trains, and a second to surface motor trucks.[12] Wilgus' automatic electric system for distribution of freight to Manhattan had been incorporated in the Port Authority Comprehensive Plan of 1921, but by 1928 serious doubts had arisen concerning the cost of tunnels in Manhattan's impervious gneiss rock. Moreover, heavy industry was departing Manhattan for less congested areas.[13] And new vehicular crossings such as the Holland Tunnel and the 178th Street Bridge suggested that trucks could adequately carry Manhattan's freight. Furthermore, the eight private trunk line railroads had obstinately opposed any cooperation with the Port Authority in carrying out its Comprehensive Plan.[14] The Wilgus automatic electric scheme, had it been implemented, might well have been integrated with the containerization system adopted in the 1950s and 1960s, thus relieving Manhattan's street congestion problem. But its defects and expense seemed too formidable in the 1920s and it was dropped from the final recommendations of the Regional Plan.

Adams' 'Ultimate Suburban Rapid Transit Plan' (figure 7.5) was essentially a plan for improved suburban commuter rail operating on existing lines, rather than a proposal for a new separate system of closely-spaced subways and surface lines. The rapid transit plan was therefore closely related to the proposals for trunk line operations just described. As a first step Adams adopted a proposal put forward by the North Jersey Transit Commission in 1925 for an 'interstate loop', which would bring commuter trains from Jersey City across to Manhattan at the Battery, up Third Avenue to 57th Street to meet another cross-Hudson route from Weehawken. The ultimate plan envisioned the electrification of many of the existing New Jersey trunk lines within the projected outer belt rail line. The outer belt itself was regarded as an important part of the rail plan and was projected to cross the Hudson over the 178th Street (George Washington) Bridge. The Regional Plan Committee and its engineers were largely responsible for convincing the Port Authority to provide structural capacity for a future second level in the bridge to be used for rail and transit service.

The rapid transit section of the Regional Plan had its basis in the 1921 Port Authority Plan for belt rail lines, a plan that by 1928 was generally regarded as defunct because of the Neanderthal attitudes of the eight railroads, who adamantly refused to cooperate with each other for the public good. The railroads remained institutions imbued with nineteenth century *laissez-faire* competitiveness. Unified operation within the Port area would obviously be essential to realizing any rationalization of rail passenger and freight service. But the railroads were not willing to risk the loss of any small advantages each enjoyed for the benefit of the system as a whole. Only an act of Congress could force interstate consolidation of operations, and despite numerous calls for such legislation, the Congress was not willing to act. Not even the Port Authority could force the railroads into cooperation. This situation, together with the reluctance of New York City to participate in planning for transit on an interstate regional basis meant that Adams' transit proposals were largely academic exercises, a fact of which Adams was well aware. It was not surprising then that Adams and his staff looked to the highway system and the motor vehicle to solve the Region's transportation problems. A new technology unencumbered by established institutions and interests offered many more possibilities for new routes than the old, fossilized private railroad system. Adams suggested that highways could in many cases replace rail and transit development:

> If a bold and comprehensive treatment of the highway system is pursued, in advance of actual need, instead of following far behind such need, a great deal of the expense in railroad and transit line construction may be avoided and the plan of those latter facilities may stop short of what is proposed.[15]

This was, in fact, what happened. The motor vehicle undoubtedly seemed the way of future transportation to Adams and his associates. In the six years between 1920 and 1926 motor vehicle registrations in the twenty-two county Region had tripled, from 475,000 to 1.33 million vehicles, and the ratio of population per vehicle had gone from 19.1 to 7.6. The engineering staff predicted that by 1965 there would be about 6.7 million vehicles, or one for every three persons, a prediction that turned out to be fairly accurate. The old residential streets and colonial highway systems were totally unsuited to the new demands placed on them. A new arterial network was essential if total chaos was not to ensue. Mass automobile ownership was not to be denied in a democracy. The sole question was how the public authorities would respond to mounting congestion and an appalling accident rate.

Nelson Lewis had articulated the highway needs of the future Region in his early work on the Plan. His son, Harold Lewis, carried that work to completion. Working closely with his engineer colleagues in the growing state highway departments, Lewis developed a systematic approach to the Region's highway development. He called for a radial-concentric network of roads, largely based on existing routes to be upgraded and widened (figure 7.12).

Lewis was assisted by Ernest P. Goodrich, whom General Hugh L. Scott, Chairman of the New Jersey State Highway Commission, called the "first traffic engineer in the country." Together they pioneered in techniques of counting traffic, predicting travel volumes, and proposing engineering solutions to problems of moving vast numbers of vehicles.[16] Their proposal for long-distance expressways was certainly one of the earliest, though the general idea of grade separation was not new as a means of solving localized congestion problems.[17]

Lewis' 1927 Regional Survey volume, *Highway Traffic*, did not present a final plan for highway development. Instead, Lewis presented a summary of the proposals made by the various public authorities.[18] Out of these proposals, some of which were redundant or conflicting, Lewis developed a rational network of highways as the basis for the Regional Plan. By assembling the pieces and forcing them into a coherent regional pattern, Lewis performed a coordinating role for which no public agency was responsible at the time.

Many of the highway proposals incorporated in the Regional Plan two years later had long been under consideration and were really not innovations of the Regional Plan engineering staff. Several of these had been conceived by Nelson Lewis in his years as Chief Engineer of the Board of Estimate shortly after the turn of the century. These included the notion of building express highways around Manhattan along the two waterfronts. Other important proposals were even older, such as Olmsted's proposals for a belt system of parkways in Brooklyn and Queens. Burnham's proposals for highways on Long Island and the 1907 New York City Improvement Commission's plans, which among other projects called for a bridge between the Bronx and Queens, to which others later proposed a 'tri-borough' link to Manhattan. This collection of highway and parkway proposals had entered the public civic works consciousness in varying degrees. It was Harold Lewis' achievement to draw them into a coherent system.

Lewis' basic contribution was the conception of a metropolitan loop consisting of boulevards and express arterials which encircled New York City and the built-up portion of New Jersey. Prior to this time most road construction emphasized radial routes to the center of the Region. Lewis and Adams realized the need for regional circumferential routes. It was a step beyond the usual solution to congestion, which was to establish local bypasses around centers of traffic concentration.

The Metropolitan Loop, which in several areas closely paralleled William Wilgus' outer belt rail line, was to be the Plan's key structural element for the development of the suburban ring (figure 7.13). The Loop crossed the Hudson at the 178th Street Bridge, then under construction, traversed the lower Bronx to a proposed new bridge to Queens at Whitestone, crossed Queens along the eastern boundary of the City, and then went west along Jamaica Bay through Brooklyn to the Narrows, where another bridge or tunnel crossing was proposed. Then it looped across Staten Island, around Newark, north to Paterson and east to the 178th Street Bridge.[19]

Where the Metropolitan Loop was routed through relatively undeveloped areas in New Jersey and Queens it was proposed that it be integrated with the Outer Belt rail line, which would run in the highway median strip. At strategic points, sites for future industrial development would be reserved. The Metropolitan Loop was an advanced conception, which, had it been effected in the way envisioned by Adams and Lewis, might have anticipated the circumferential industrial belts that developed around some American cities in the 1950s and 1960s.

Within the Metropolitan Loop, the Regional Plan called for a grid of north-south routes roughly paralleling the Hudson, crossed by a set of east-west routes. In addition to the two waterfront highways on the Hudson and East Rivers, the Plan called for a Lower Manhattan expressway to link the Holland Tunnel with the East River Bridges and a mid-Manhattan through route at about 38th Street to link proposed tunnels under the Hudson and East Rivers. A Brooklyn-Queens express highway to connect the projected Triborough Bridge to downtown Brooklyn was also proposed, an idea first put forth

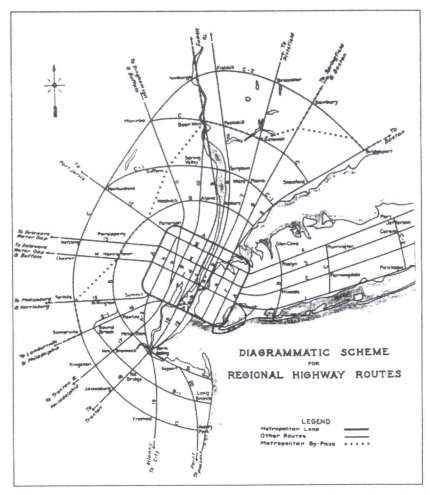

Figure 7.12. Diagramatic scheme for highways, Regional Plan of New York and Its Environs, 1928. (*Source:* Committee on the Regional Plan of New York and Its Environs (1929*d*)

in the New York City Improvement Commission Plan of 1907. Several north-south routes were also proposed in New Jersey to link Newark and Jersey to the 178th Street Bridge.

Intercity routes connecting the New York Region to Philadelphia and Boston were proposed. The idea of a national express highway system was also not new. Lester P. Barlow, who was sculptor Gutzon Borglum's chief engineer, had called in 1925 for a network of federal toll roads linking Boston, New York, Washington, and Philadelphia to Omaha, an early vision of an interstate expressway system.[20] The Regional Plan called for an expressway between Newark and Philadelphia and a parkway north from

Figure 7.13. Key plan for highways, Regional Plan of New York and Its Environs, 1928. (Metropolitan Loop is 'A') (*Source:* Committee on the Regional Plan of New York and Its Environs (1929*d*)

Westchester County to Bridgeport, Connecticut. This route, later named the Merritt Parkway, was the result of collaboration between the Regional Plan engineering staff and the Fairfield County Planning Association and was subsequently incorporated into the Regional Plan.[21] Parkways were an important component of the Regional Plan's proposals for coping with the demands of the motor vehicle. The worst traffic jams in the Region in the 1920s occurred on summer weekends when city residents sought relief at suburban beaches and resort areas. The automobile was regarded by the engineering staff as primarily a pleasure vehicle, and the parkways were a response to recreational demands.[22] The concept of a regional parkway

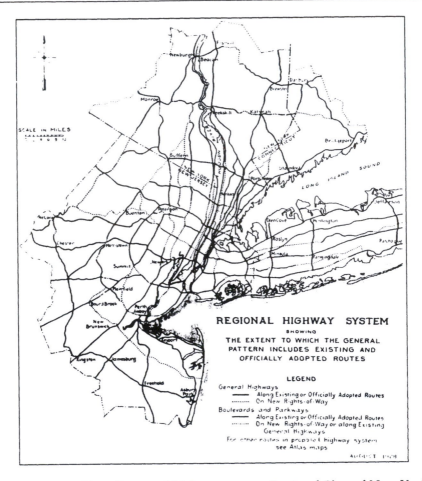

Figure 7.14. Plan: Proposed highway system, Regional Plan of New York and Its Environs, 1928. (*Source:* Committee on the Regional Plan of New York and Its Environs (1929d)

system linking the metropolitan area's large green spaces had originated with Frederick Law Olmsted, Sr., in the mid-nineteenth century and was continued by the Olmsted Brothers' firm in their work for the New York City Improvement Commission in 1907. The concept was adopted in the 1920s by the Westchester County Park Commission under Jay Downer, and on Long Island by Robert Moses, who in the mid-1920s was acquiring park and parkway land for a state system there. The Regional Plan staff worked closely with both groups and incorporated many of their proposals into the Plan. The parkway proposals for New York City contained in the Regional Plan were taken almost directly from the 1907 New York City Improvement Plan. The parkway plan for the New Jersey portion of the Region was more original and

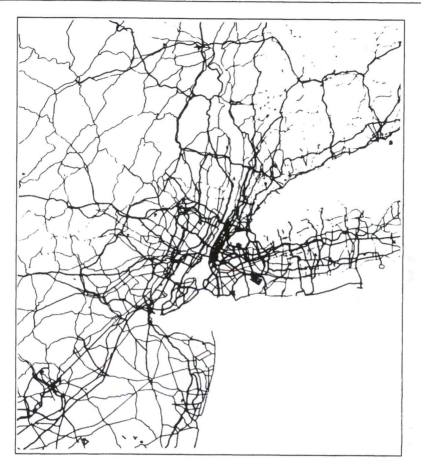

Figure 7.15. Reality: Major expressways, parkways and state highways, 1965. (*Source:* Regional Plan Association)

called for new routes along many of the stream valleys which laced the area. An important parkway proposal which originated in the Plan was a project for a route to link metropolitan New Jersey with Atlantic shore points.

The motor parkway idea was a happy vestige of the days when elegant horse-drawn carriages brought the wealthy from their homes to landscaped city gardens and parks. The Regional Plan staff adapted the idea to fit the automobile, but continued to assume that the drive itself was part of the experience and that slow speeds over meandering routes were what was desired. Others such as Robert Moses saw that this conception of the parkway was doomed. The motoring public wanted pleasant roads away from commercial traffic, but it also wanted to get to the shore and the mountains rapidly and in large volumes. Few at the time, however, realized that the parkways would eventually play a significant role in the journey to work and would become primary traffic carriers from future suburban residential areas back to the city.

AIRPORTS

The airplane symbolized for the 1920s the seemingly limitless possibilities of technology. Indeed, the emerging popular image of the metropolis as a region was in no small measure a result of the aerial photographic techniques perfected in World War I. By the end of the 1920s the dramatic potential of the air age had become evident to many. Charles A. Lindbergh's Paris flight in May of 1927 from Roosevelt field on Long Island was quickly followed by lesser known flights from the same field to the French coast by Richard A. Byrd and to Germany by Clarence D. Chamberlain and Charles A. Levine. In the following months the City of Newark commenced construction of its airport near Newark Bay, and New York City began building a new municipal airport in south Brooklyn. By 1929 the New York Region possessed twenty-two hard-surface airports.[23]

Leadership in regional airport planning at this time came not from the Committee on the Regional Plan but from a 'Fact-Finding Committee on Suitable Airport Facilities for the New York Metropolitan District', created in 1927 by Department of Commerce Secretary Herbert Hoover. This group studied some seventy-two sites, finally selecting six for recommendation, located in the following areas:

1. Flushing Bay – Queens;
2. Newark Bay area;
3. Bronx – East River area;
4. Hackensack Meadows;
5. Jamaica Bay area;
6. Wall Street – Brooklyn area.[24]

The Regional Survey generally endorsed the recommendations of the Department of Commerce committee, urging New York City to acquire three sites in addition to the Floyd Bennett development. The Regional Survey, quoting the prescient Ernest P. Goodrich, forecast the development of the helicopter and STOL aircraft. But the idea of rooftop airfields, which were much in discussion at the time, was discarded as being generally impractical.[25]

Adams' proposal for a regional system of airports, published in 1929 as part of the Graphic Regional Plan, included the proposals of the Hoover Committee. But Adams called for not six but sixteen new fields to be added to the thirty-nine sea and land plane facilities available in 1929. Adams emphasized provisions for light aircraft through the acquisition of space for fields close to the Region's centers and integrated with other forms of transportation. Acquire the land while it can be had, Adams urged public officials. If the sites purchased prove to be more than are needed, they can always be used for parks. And if they need not be developed immediately, they can be put to temporary park use. Adams' advice was advanced for its time, but rapid changes in aviation would render the airport plan obsolete just a few years after its publication.[26]

OPEN SPACE AND RECREATION

The biological analogy of the city often invoked in the nineteenth century saw transportation as the veins and arteries of the urban corpus. The lungs were the open spaces. And in an era of high incidence of tuberculosis and pneumonia, reformers generally felt that there could never be enough urban open space. New York City was in particularly desperate straits. New York was more deficient in open space than almost every other large American city, despite the achievements of the elder Olmsted. Boston in 1926 had, for example, 219 persons per acre of park land, whereas New York had 601 and Jersey City, 901.[27] Deficiencies in the New York Region were greatest in the older industrial counties surrounding the harbor. Little could be done in these dense areas to provide large open spaces. But the failure to capture adequate green space was an error that the planners of the 1920s did not want to see repeated in newly developing areas. The drive for open space at the fringe was greatly spurred by the stark contrast of the gray, crowded, industrial city and the green of the suburbs. This contrast between asphalt and green led some reformers to imbue open space with moral attributes. Open spaces were spiritually uplifting as well as healthful for the body, a counter to the degrading influences of the city.

The Regional Plan staff did not curse the industrial city to applaud nature, wedded as they were to the idea that the two were complementary and capable of integration. Open space for them was not a denial of the city but a means to making the city more livable. In their conception, one did not escape the city to go to open spaces; open spaces were extensions of the city and city living. A hierarchy of open space suited to the surroundings was thus conceptually possible, ranging from the small city playground or park to the large regional park at the edge of the metropolis. The focus was on man's use and manipulation of the land rather than on protection of the land for its own sake. Consequently the regional survey for open space focused largely, though not entirely, on its uses for public recreation.

Lee F. Hanmer, the recreation expert on loan from the Sage Foundation staff, carried out a number of helpful empirical studies on the recreation use of open space in the Region. These were gathered together and published in 1928 as Volume V of the Regional Survey.[28] In his preface to this volume, Adams argued that more open space in the dense areas would help keep wealthy families from moving out of the city, and, contrary to popular belief, would reduce rather than increase congested areas, and would furthermore enhance total property values rather than lessen them through loss of taxable land. Adams pointed to the effect of Central Park on Manhattan's land values, noting that the increase in values over what might have been expected without the park more than compensated for the loss of the park's land area for economic uses.[29]

Pointing out that the automobile had changed patterns of park use, Adams called for the acquisition of more open space throughout the Region. Distribution was important and the parks should be where the people could get to them. Adams emphasized the need to buy parks at the fringe in advance of the land speculators who would drive prices to a level where acquisition costs would be prohibitive. Mountains, lakes, and stream valleys, in all parts of the Region, and Long Island's unique bays and barrier reef were particularly vulnerable and required immediate action.[30]

In the congested parts of the city, the problem was more difficult. Easy access for central city dwellers to new regional facilities at the edge of the ubanized area offered only part of the solution, for not everyone could make the trip, especially the poor who lacked cars to travel the parkways. Within the city more playgrounds were desperately needed, though this was not a new observation. More innovative were proposals to recapture city waterfronts long lost to railroad, industrial, and harbor uses. The Harlem River with its obsolete, low-intensity waterfront uses offered special opportunities of this kind. The Harlem River, Adams suggested, could become the Seine of New York.

Imaginative use of rooftops was another neglected possibility for open space, Adams pointed out. Additionally, more open spaces could be provided in privately-sponsored redevelopment projects, as had been done by the City Housing Corporation at its Sunnyside Houses and at Tudor City in Manhattan. The city, Adams observed, had legal authority to require more use of the courtyard principle in the design of private residential complexes. Special opportunities also existed, Adams noted, in the two largely undeveloped boroughs, Queens and Staten Island, and on Welfare, Randall's, and Wards Islands in the East River.

Adams reaffirmed the principle established by the elder Olmsted that large open spaces should be connected by ribbons of green in which parkways, trails, or paths, might be placed. The resultant network of green would work to relieve the endless urbanization which characterized such places as Brooklyn and Jersey City and would help provide identity to individual neighborhoods.

It was on the basis of these principles and concepts that Adams devised his general plan for the park system of the New York Region (figure 7.16). Adams proposed that the Region look to Westchester County for a model, with its extensive park and parkway system developed in the 1920s. The Regional Plan for parks consisted of some eighty-eight major proposals for large acquisitions and ribbon parks along stream valleys. Among these the Plan called for a doubling of the area of the Harriman-Bear Mountain Park, capturing of the marshlands and islands in Long Island's Great South Bay, acquisition of Long Island's barrier reef at Jones Beach, Fire Island, and Montauk, additions to the protected stretches of the spectacular Palisades along the Hudson, acquisition of the two Watchung ranges and numerous stream valleys in northern New Jersey, and protection of the historic Highlands of the Navesink near Sandy Hook.[31]

Of course, not all of these proposals were original with the Regional Plan. In New York City, for example, the proposals closely followed the ideas put forward in the McClellan Plan of 1907. On Long Island the plans of the Long Island State Park Commission were used as a general guide. Other opportunities, however, were first identified by Adams and his staff. But the real contribution of the Regional Park Plan was that for the first time open space was treated as a regional system, closely related to proposals for housing, jobs, and transportation.

URBAN DEVELOPMENT

In the Graphic Regional Plan Adams distinguished between 'open' and 'closed' development, the latter category comprising industry, residence, and business of an urban character, the former including parks, airports, watersheds, and military reservations (figure 7.18).[32]

Adams' plan for new industrial areas reflected the findings of Robert Murray Haig and Roswell McCrea that heavy manufacturing would decentralize from its concentrations in the old cities. The Plan proposed that extensive new industrial areas be developed in New Jersey around Newark Bay, the Hackensack Meadows, and the Raritan River. In New York City new areas were proposed for Newtown Creek in Queens and in the southeastern part of the Bronx. An extensive industrial ribbon was also proposed along the New Jersey portion of the rail belt line suggested by Colonel William Wilgus and adopted as part of the Plan. Smaller industrial areas were proposed at sites distributed throughout the Region.

If the Committee on the Regional Plan was dominated by New York City industrial interests, it was not particularly evident in the industrial proposals made in the Plan. By far the largest share of proposed new industrial development was for the New Jersey side of the Region. Very little new industrial land was suggested for Long Island or the northern sector of the Region in New York State. Particularly noteworthy was the substantial reduction of new industrial land proposed for Jamaica Bay in Queens. In effect, Adams had repudiated the Jamaica Bay port scheme which for years had been sought

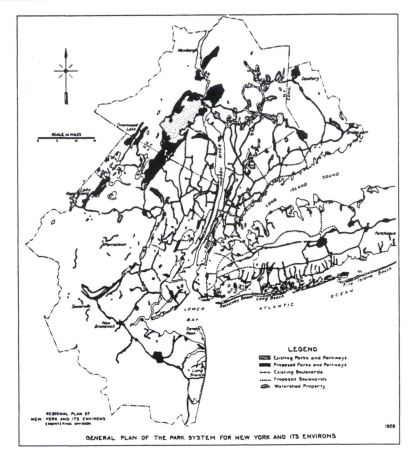

GENERAL PLAN OF THE PARK SYSTEM FOR NEW YORK AND ITS ENVIRONS

Figure 7.16. Plan: Existing and proposed parks and parkways, Regional Plan of New York and Its Environs, 1928. (*Source:* Committee on the Regional Plan of New York and Its Environs (1929*d*))

by many New York City industrialists, including some closely associated with the Plan. Adams determined that a great harbor at Jamaica Bay was unnecessary and that, in fact, the amount of waterfront zoned for wharfage in the Region was three times as large as would be needed. Far better, Adams suggested, would be to return a large part of this potential amenity to recreation and residence.[33]

The treatment of new residential areas in the Plan reflected Adams' assumption that New Jersey would attract a major share of new industrial employment. Bergen, Essex, and Union Countries, large parts of which were undeveloped in 1929, were projected to be completely filled with residence by 1965. Substantial corridor growth was predicted for Passaic, Morris, Somerset, and Middlesex Counties. On the New York side, Staten Island,

Figure 7.17. Reality: Open space and watersheds, 1965. (Source: Regional Plan Association)

Queens, the Bronx, southern Westchester, and Nassau (except for the North Shore) were planned to be filled with residences, relieved only by the proposed green ribbons and parks. Adams purposely did not specify future densities for this new residential development – that was, he thought (quite diplomatically), a matter for local planning. It is nevertheless evident from the area of land allocated to residence for the nine million additional people expected that he was thinking of fairly compact growth for the developing fringe – of the order of fifteen to twenty persons per gross acre, which was a density considerably lower than most of Brooklyn, for example, but higher than many of the newer suburbs in Westchester.[34]

The compact, contiguous residential development that Adams proposed in the Regional Plan was at variance with the Garden City principles he had followed in his work with Ebenezer Howard on Letchworth and Welwyn. It

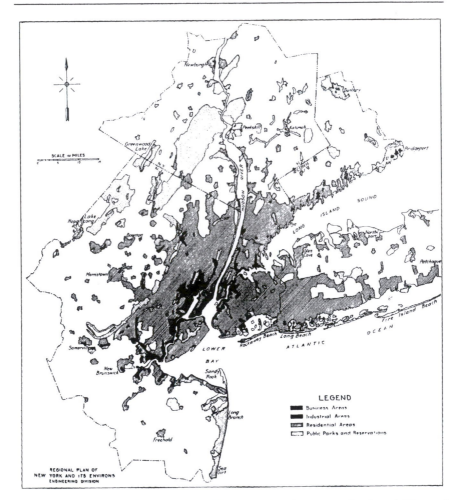

Figure 7.18. Plan: Projected 1965 urban development, Regional Plan of New York and Its Environs, 1928. *(Source:* Committee on the Regional Plan of New York and Its Environs (1929d))

differed also from the composite sector plan he had developed in 1925 with the consultants of the Advisory Planning Group. But those schemes seemed inappropriate when viewed in terms of the realities of American real estate development practices. Adams had little choice but to take a pragmatic approach, hoping somehow that local planning and zoning commissions and enlightened developers would create desirable patterns within the broad framework he had developed. It was a large hope, indeed.

Business centers, Adams correctly adduced, followed population growth, and therefore could also be regarded as local concerns, beyond the scope of a regional plan. Only one major retail center was therefore proposed in the

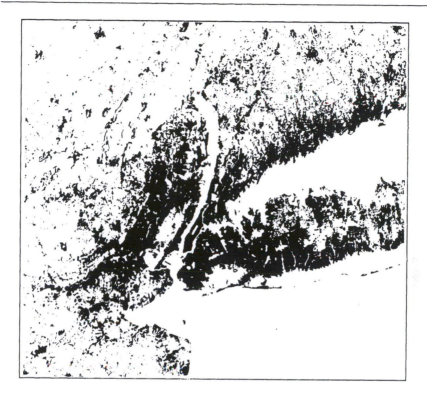

Figure 7.19. Reality: Actual extent of developed area, 1962. (*Source:* Regional Plan Association)

Graphic Plan, to be located in the residential community slated for the Hackensack Meadows. Other retail growth would go to expansions of existing centers, or so the Plan implied by the absence of alternative proposals. But Adams was not unaware of new patterns of shopping emerging as a result of the influence of the automobile. One of the reasons new business centers were not shown on the Graphic Regional Plan, Adams wrote, was that 'tendencies towards change in the distribution of business is [*sic*] so pronounced as to make it impossible to give any approximately accurate forecast as to what is going to happen even in the next few years.'[35] Adams noted that some department stores were talking about opening new branches in places having a high degree of accessibility and yet in comparatively open areas where ample space would be available for circulation and parking.[36] Here was a hint of the shopping centers and endless commercial strips that were to come in twenty-five years. The problem of planning for changing patterns of retail business was in reality an opportunity within the power of imagination and design in 1929, but Adams chose not to address it. At a period when he might have been extremely influential in shaping subsequent developments, this decision was a default of considerable magnitude.

SYNTHESIS: THE GRAPHIC REGIONAL PLAN

Adams overlaid the various Plan elements on a single canvas to produce the summary Graphic Regional Plan: the Wilgus belt systems for rail and transit derived from Port Authority proposals; the highway network synthesized by Harold Lewis from the ideas of the rising state highway bureaucracies; park and parkway schemes, some original but many dating from much earlier planning studies; the new decentralized industrial areas hung on the scaffolding of rail and highway transportation; and new residential areas reflecting the push of the urban area outward to the suburban counties. Adams had synthesized a collage of trends, forecasts, old proposals, and approved projects. The overall strategy was clear: ride the forces of change, channeling them where possible into more efficient or more amenable patterns. Avoid the impractical and the excessively visionary. Provide a plan to be used as an immediate guide to action yet one based on a more distant but not altogether opaque future. The Plan that Adams produced met all of these objectives. His synthesis was an adroit blend of most of the proposals, insights, and forecasts of the various consultants and staff experts. But this was the Plan's weakness as well as its strength. An accumulation of pragmatic wisdom expressed in a set of combined overlays of regional systems, the Plan provided no clear set of objectives or strategies to guide decision-makers or protagonists. In their dedication to balance, common sense, and compromise, the planners did not clearly convey what they thought the Region should become and what social goals were most important. The vision and dream had been blurred by abstractions made concrete in the graphic atlas of the future. Adams hoped to make that vision clearer in his forthcoming second Plan volume. Meanwhile, the Graphic Regional Plan was complete and ready for presentation to the public.

The Graphic Regional Plan was published in 1929. Charles Norton's advice about the importance of fine printing was followed. The Plan was a superlative example of the printer's art, bound between red covers reminiscent of a large bible. The frontispiece was an air view of the New York Region by Jules Guerin of Paris, who had provided the watercolour views for the 1909 Burnham Plan of Chicago.

The Plan was presented to the public at a dinner meeting on May 27 in the Engineering Societies Building in Manhattan. Representatives of New York City and the three states accepted the Plan for their jurisdictions in a ceremony reminiscent of that autumn day in Chicago two decades earlier, when Burnham's Plan had been presented to Chicago city officials by Charles Norton and Frederic A. Delano. Twenty years later Delano was repeating his role, this time as Chairman of the Committee on the Regional Plan. But a new dimension had been added, symbolic, in a way, of the extraordinary changes in technology that had occurred in the period between the two plans: the proceedings were broadcast in an hour-long radio program over the facilities of the National Broadcasting Company. The first speaker was Mayor James J. Walker, who accepted the Plan on behalf of the City of New York. Delano then read messages from President Herbert Hoover and New York Governor Franklin D. Roosevelt, Delano's nephew.

George McAneny, who had been appointed to the Regional Plan Committee in 1927, outlined the findings and recommendations of the Graphic Regional Plan. After this, the Plan was accepted for New York State by the Lieutenant Governor, Herbert H. Lehman, for New Jersey by J. Raymond Tiffany, the State Attorney General, and for Connecticut by Daniel S. Sanford, Vice President of the Fairfield County Planning Association.

Following the dinner presentation, the select assemblage adjourned to an adjacent auditorium where an overflow crowd of 2,000 persons had gathered to hear McAneny provide a descriptive talk on the Plan, illustrated with lantern slides. The final presentation was made by Eugenius H. Outerbridge, former chairman of the Port of New York Authority, who told of a new association that had been formed to carry out the Regional Plan and which he had agreed to chair. The evening ended on a note of tremendous optimism and mutual congratulation. To the assembled civic leaders and industrialists, the destiny of the Region seemed more secure than it had ever been before. Few in that audience had any thought that five months later New York's economy would lie strewn in the national financial wreckage of Wall Street's Black Thursday.

The Plan was complete, but who would carry it out? Informal acceptance by the Governors of the three states and the Mayor of New York was hardly a guarantee that the Plan would be followed. The Committee on the Regional Plan had been aware of this dilemma throughout the eight years of survey and planning work. Charles Norton had in 1922 urged a 'Plan of New York Authority,' but Edward M. Bassett argued against the idea as politically impossible.[37]

In 1923, Frederic A. Delano, in a talk before the Chicago Regional Planning Association, a private association patterned after the New York Committee on the Regional Plan, had described the Regional Plan as more of a 'bureau of planning service which the City of New York and the cities and towns outside can avail themselves of.'[38]

The Regional Council of influential citizens formed by the Committee on the Regional Plan in 1925 was viewed as a vehicle to disseminate the Plan's proposals through a process of leadership osmosis. It had become increasingly clear, however, as the Plan neared completion, that a more formal group to promote the Plan's objectives would be required after the Sage Foundation funding ran out. Consequently, in late 1927 Edward Bassett and Lawson Purdy were appointed to consider and report on the organization of the work of the Committee on the Regional Plan after September 30, 1928.[39] Purdy recommended that a private corporation with the name, 'Regional Plan of New York, Inc.,' be established to 'promote regional planning in general harmony with the Regional Plan.' A twenty-one member board of directors was proposed, which would include the ten members of the Russell Sage Committee on the Regional Plan. Noting that nine of the ten members of the existing Committee were residents of Manhattan, Bassett and Purdy recommended that six of the new directors be residents of suburban counties. A list of distinguished names were proposed, including Mrs. Franklin D. Roosevelt, Arthur Sulzberger, Lillian Wald, Richard S. Childs, and Homer Folks. Purdy proposed that directors serve for staggered seven year terms.

He also proposed that any interested person or civic group with fewer than ten members be permitted to become a member of the Corporation by paying the sum of $100 a year, or a life fee of $2,000.[40] The staff urged a greater regional representation, stronger participation by the membership in the selection of the directors, and avoidance of an appearance of a closed, tightly knit corporation. Purdy eventually came around to this viewpoint and his final draft of the constitution of the new group called for three year terms.

Purdy's proposals were endorsed by the Sage Trustees, who were well aware of the difficulties which might arise were the Foundation to undertake promotion of the Plan's projects among the various public authorities. An independent corporation would have much more freedom to work with officials and legislative bodies. The Sage Trustees agreed to underwrite the new corporation with an initial grant of $25,000, but urged that it become self-supporting as soon as possible. Meanwhile, the Russell Sage Committee on the Regional Plan would be continued for a short period with a small staff 'to show and interpret the Plan material to anyone who might have need of it and to supplement the Plan as far as necessary to keep it up to date.'[41]

The new association met for the first time on April 4, 1929, with Purdy presiding. Eugenius Outerbridge was offered the presidency but declined because of age and failing health. He accepted instead the chairmanship of the Board. After Outerbridge declined, the presidency was offered to George McAneny, a position he would subsequently hold for the next eleven years.

In addition to McAneny and Outerbridge, seventeen other prominent men accepted directorships, seven of whom were members of the original Russell Sage Committee on the Regional Plan. Four of the original committee members did not assume directorships: Frederic Delano, Robert DeForest, John Glenn, and Dwight Morrow. Delano had become preoccupied with the planning of Washington.[42] DeForest and Glenn probably declined out of a desire to reduce identification of the new Association with the Sage Foundation.

The remaining six directors were influential businessmen, bankers, or lawyers. These included: Charles G. Meyer, Alexander M. Bing, and Robert E. Simon, real estate developers; DeWitt Van Buskirk, a New Jersey banker; Garrison Norton, a New York attorney and the son of Charles Norton; Bertram Saunders, president of a New Jersey bleachery; and Percy S. Straus, the president of R.H. Macy, Inc. The original board was thus heavily oriented to business and finance. None of the individuals proposed as directors in 1928 who were prominent in social welfare or were elected officials became directors. It is not clear whether these individuals declined membership or were simply not invited in the end because of some change in policy. Whatever the reason, the board at its outset became clearly identified with private business and development leadership rather than with the public sector and social reform.[43]

Four of the original members of the Board were active staff members of the Russell Sage Foundation or the Committee on the Regional Plan: Shelby Harrison, Wayne Heydecker, Laurence Orton, and Flavel Shurtleff. Harrison, Heydecker, and Shurtleff resigned a few months after the Association was created in order to become members of its staff, and Orton did likewise in 1931.

At the first meeting of the board on April 4, 1929, the constitution prepared by Purdy was approved, and in place of the originally proposed title 'Regional Plan of New York, Inc.,' the title 'Regional Plan Association, Inc.' was adopted as a compromise, after members from New Jersey expressed a desire to have the name of their state included.[44]

Through 1929, the new board of the Regional Plan Association worked to add directors, hire a professional staff, and promote membership in a large 'regional advisory council', which, it was hoped, would provide a base of support for the Regional Plan. By January of 1930 the board had narrowed its choice for General Director down to two names: John Nolen and George B. Ford, both of whom had served as consultants to the Regional Plan. Thomas Adams, who would have been the logical choice, wished to return to England and was reluctant to take the position. By 1930, Nolen, whose office was in Cambridge, Massachusetts, had emerged as one of the few planners with a national practice. Ford, an engineer and architect, had also prepared plans for numerous cities around the country but was better known than Nolen in New York. Nolen expressed a willingness to accept the post but felt that because of prior commitments he could spend only three-fifths of his time in New York. Largely because of this condition, the board selected George B. Ford. Adams submitted his resignation, to take effect on March 31, 1930, but agreed to continue as a consultant to the Committee on the Regional Plan in order to complete the second volume of the Plan. Ford became General Director of the Association on the following day, April 1, 1930.

Ford, who shared a keen interest in housing with his brother, James, an expert in the subject at Harvard University, was dissatisfied with the Regional Plan, particularly with its failure to come to grips with the problem of housing. Not long after taking over as General Director he proposed that the housing element of the Plan be restudied, and suggested that the entire Plan might have to be scrapped and a new plan prepared.[45] After eight years of preparation this suggestion was hardly a desirable prospect for the new Association; the Plan had taken on a symbolic importance transcending its substance. Though it had come to be viewed as a flexible document subject to revision as new conditions developed, to abandon it so soon would have been tantamount to admitting failure.

Ford might have been able to effect major revisions after a reasonable period had passed, but four months after assuming the Directorship, he died, in August, 1930, at the age of fifty-one. Once again, death had played an unanticipated part in the development of the Regional Plan.

Ford's position was not immediately filled. Instead, McAneny took over his responsibilities, serving until 1933, when he was appointed New York City's Sanitation Commissioner. After Ford's death, technical studies and the updating of the Plan were given second priority to building membership and interest in the Association. By mid-1930 the Association had established a regional advisory committee comprised of 215 men, and an adjunct 'Women's Advisory Council' with sixty-five members, mostly club women or wives of socially prominent men who were not, for one reason or other, members of the male group. The men came from a variety of occupations and activities, though business clearly dominated (table 7.1).

Table 7.1. Composition of the regional advisory committee membership, 1930.[46]

Industry	43
Insurance, finance, banking	28
Public officials	26
Attorneys	22
Publishers or editors	15
Architects	14
Businessmen's associations	10
Civic, philanthropic groups	10
Education	8
Engineers	6
Religious leaders	6
Retailing executives	5
Railroad executives	5
Unidentified	18
Total	215

The Regional Advisory Committee list included many of the most influential and distinguished citizens of the Region. Absent, however, was any representation of labor groups or ethnic organizations. Most of those on the list were never active in the affairs of the Association and merely agreed to the use of their names out of sympathy with the general objectives of the Regional Plan. The Regional Advisory Committee was never thought of, nor could it have been, a substitute for a regional body through which the Plan would be implemented. Rather, it was intended to buttress the claims of the new Association to broad support and legitimacy.

Between 1929 and 1932 the Russell Sage Committee on the Regional Plan and the Regional Plan Association co-existed, the latter gradually assuming the functions and the staff of the former. The Committee on the Regional Plan saw its purposes nearly fulfilled with the creation of the Regional Plan Association. By February of 1930 several publications remained to be finished, and the Committee determined not to disband until these were in hand. One of the unfinished works was Adams' second Plan volume, which he proposed to complete in England in the capacity of consultant to the Committee, following his resignation as General Director. Another outstanding work was the final volume of the Regional Survey on building and site design examples for the developing parts of the Region. A third publication project was a popularized version of the Regional Plan, which the Committee felt would be necessary to communicate to the lay public the many complex proposals and ideas of the Plan. A textbook for schools modeled on the 1920 Wacker's Manual of the Plan of Chicago was proposed. Dr. Rexford of the New York City Board of Education was mentioned as a possible author. The textbook project, however, was postponed and instead a more sophisticated book aimed directly at the adult population was commissioned.

After a brief search for a professional writer capable of synthesizing and simplifying the complexities of the Plan, the Committee selected Robert L. Duffus, a professional writer. Though new to the techniques and concerns of planning, Duffus adroitly captured the essentials of the Plan in his book, which was published in 1930 under the title, *Mastering a Metropolis*.[47] Duffus breathed life and interest into the rather dry technical proposals, successfully conveying Adams' abstract argument for 'recentralization' while painting vivid pictures of the Plan's proposed transportation and open space systems. He portrayed the Plan as a natural evolution in the history of the Region's development and emphasized that the various projects would have to be built in any event in some form, and that a plan would simply coordinate development, resulting in greater fiscal efficiency. It was the same argument that Charles Norton had made years before in Chicago to counter the image of the staggeringly large capital sums that would be necessary to implement the proposals made in the Burnham plan.[48] There was, of course, no guarantee at all that the public sector would spend such sums, with or without a Plan, and a major purpose of both the Wacker Manual and Duffus' *Mastering a Metropolis* was to stimulate public support for capital program bond referenda. What effect Duffus' book had on voter propensity to support public capital programs is impossible to say, though it is likely that the impact was less than that of the Wacker Manual in Chicago. The New York Region was demographically far more heterogeneous and politically more complex than the City of Chicago. And by the time the Duffus book appeared in late 1930, unemployment due to the collapse of the economy had reached far more than a half-million in the Region. The times did not appear propitious for large public works bond issues. It would take far more than a Wacker Manual for New York to realize the Regional Plan.

HOUSING AND BUILDING THE CITY

In January of 1931, Adams completed his editing of the final volume of the Regional Survey, entitled *Buildings: Their Uses and the Spaces about Them*.[49] This volume dealt largely with the controversial topic of housing, but also treated the skyscraper problem, civic centers, public buildings, the relation of buildings to transportation facilities, zoning, and architectural controls. It was considerably more normative than the previous survey volumes, which were largely compilations of facts. Volume VI, instead, enunciated regional policies and principles for the location and control of new building development.

In his introduction to the volume, Adams summarized his conclusions concerning the most desirable patterns for new development. The chief social and economic defect in city building, he asserted, was the overcrowding of land with buildings.[50] This occurred in central areas, he argued, because builders were compelled to build tall buildings to cover high land costs. But high land values were a function of the value of construction the law permitted on a site. Reduce the permitted limits, land values would diminish, and new construction would spread itself, leaving more light and air and reducing congestion. Housing was crowded for similar reasons, and new subdivisions could be built at lower densities if zoning controls established more restrictive rules on site coverage and bulk. The most desirable form for skyscrapers, according to Adams, was a high tower on a low base, rather than a lower but bulkier shape. Such towers should be spread about the central business district, not crowded together as in lower Manhattan. Height, in itself, Adams concluded, was not an evil; the evil was to crowd high buildings. Adams pointed to the evolution of the isolated tower form of the Empire State Building, then nearing completion, as a model for other tall buildings. The Empire State Building, which as the world's tallest structure dramatically symbolized the power of commercial New York, had originally been designed as a much lower, bulkier building.[51] Adams' image of the future of Manhattan, then, was of a fairly low general profile punctuated by such isolated high towers. It was an approach typical of Adams: bend the trends to make the result better than it would otherwise have been; a permanent moratorium on new skyscraper construction was probably not possible in

Manhattan. Paris, London, and Washington might manage to control heights but the skyscraper had come to symbolize New York and could not be denied outright.

Adams' approach to housing was similar. New housing should not be so dispersed as to make travel difficult or to lose a sense of community. Neither should it be so crowded as to block out light and air. Every room should have some light and air. Adjacent structures should be placed so that from no window would the sky be obscured at more than a 45–degree angle. This was a higher standard than was currently being followed in the tens of thousands of cheap frame houses then being built in endless rows in Brooklyn and Queens.[52] Adams showed that it would not spread the urbanized area greatly to reduce average new densities in outlying areas from the typical twenty houses per acre to ten per acre. The reason was simple: cities grow in circumferential rings, and at the outer, ten-mile ring, one need go out only a few hundred yards to encompass a vast additional area.[53]

Adams called for better quality in lower-priced workers' housing and pointed to several schemes, such as those at Radburn, New Jersey, and Seaside Village in Bridgeport, Connecticut, as models to follow. In a companion monograph in the same volume, the architect Grosvenor Atterbury showed how factory prefabrication methods had been used to reduce costs in the Russell Sage project at Forest Hills.[54] But Forest Hills, for all its cost savings, had never been intended as residences for workers. And Adams could offer no new solutions as to how cheap but higher-quality housing could be provided at prices that the average worker could afford, though he did call for the formation of cooperative building societies and the easing of mortgage credit requirements, among several policy proposals.[55]

Interestingly, Adams spoke out strongly against the English policy of slum clearance and the erection of publicly assisted new housing for the poor and the working class. Slums might have to be cleared to protect the society at large, but not merely to provide sites for new low-income housing. Subsidized building did more harm than good. It interfered with the workings of the private housing market and could only be regarded as a last resort. Moreover, it was unfair to working men not eligible for housing for the poverty class. 'Why,' Adams asked, 'must the solution of the housing of the very poor consist of building new houses, when so many who are comparatively well off must live in old houses?'[56] If the poor were to be subsidized, far better, Adams believed, to do it through increases in wages than through subsidized housing. Adams held that the long-range answer to the problem of intolerable housing for the poor was a program of municipal enforcement of minimum standards, and a planned expansion of the total housing supply at the urban fringe of new higher priced dwellings to relieve the pressure on the existing stock of units. Slum clearance for new projects was expensive and ultimately self-defeating. Subsidized housing for workers who could be self-supporting was, Adams warned, 'a form of socialism,' which tended to lead to inequities in the distribution of public tax revenues.[57]

Adams' philosophical discourse on housing policy summarized the main points of contention over what proper government housing policy should be, a debate which has continued since the 1920s. Many of the points Adams raised were valid, but in the aggregate his position on housing was quite conservative, even for the period in which he was writing. His recommendations concerning housing for low-income groups simply avoided the problem. Adams had missed an opportunity to link housing policy for the workers and the poor to comprehensive regional planning. Instead, he merely reaffirmed the rights of property over those of people.

It may well be that Adams was speaking for the conservative members of the Committee on the Regional Plan in his espousal of the view that all housing 'should return a fair yield on the investment in buildings and land.'[58] But we cannot escape the conclusion that Adams himself was in considerable sympathy with the Committee's opposition to government-assisted housing.

With the completion of the eight volumes of the Regional Survey, the final task remaining for the Committee on the Regional Plan was the publication of the second volume of the Plan. Thomas Adams completed the draft of this work in England, and the Committee gave its approval for publication in 1931. The volume, a companion to the previously published *Graphic Regional Plan*, was entitled *The Building of the City*, and described the key projects proposed in the Plan, as well as principles for the construction of buildings to preserve light and air. The recommendations contained in *The Building of the City* were intended to provide the fabric to go on the armature of the Graphic Regional Plan. Specific important projects were described and general principles of good building outlined. There was, inevitably, considerable redundancy and repetition of the substance of the first volume, *The Graphic Regional Plan*. But *The Building of the City* was also Adams' personal, occasionally eloquent statement of what a large city-region should be and how it should look. Adams reiterated his ideas about opening up the city, pushing skyscrapers apart and providing more land surface for pedestrian and automobile. The image of the skyscraper tower on a platform base was pervasive. Adams did not want to scatter the components of the downtown but rather to open the city to the sky and to reduce the thrice-daily compaction of human bodies on the sidewalks beneath the office towers. Among other proposals, Adams urged the widening of congested streets and the construction of European-style sidewalk arcades. Double-decking of streets and sidewalks in extremely congested areas was also suggested.[59]

An extraordinary array of architectural images of the Manhattan of the future was incorporated, many from the studies of the volunteer architectural teams assembled by Charles Norton.[60] It was as if all the clashing styles of past and future had been gathered into one emporium for a gigantic sale. Here was Ernest Flagg's precise, delicate, very French, delineation of the multi-level towered city to come.[61] There were the charcoal sketches of Hugh Ferris so reminiscent of Edward Steichen's contemporary photographs of the city, the hard edges of stone softened into a vague, dark mist.[62] The shiny Art Deco with its curved bands of light and chrome was represented in several sketches, including one by the youthful E. Maxwell Fry.[63] Present also was the classicism of such firms as the one which practiced under the venerable names of McKim, Mead, and White, though all three had long since passed to their reward.[64] It was for architectural design a period of uncertainty and transition. Like the Regional Plan, architecture was struggling to acquire a modern manner of expression, but was unable to break all of its bonds with the past.

Nowhere was this more evident than in the work of Francis S. Swales, the architect who joined the Regional Plan staff to redesign with Adams the project areas first attempted by the several architectural teams.[65] The projects prepared by the teams varied widely in quality and sophistication and, in some instances, conflicted with each other. Adams sought a unified image of future possibilities, more integrated with the transportation systems which had been endorsed in the Graphic Regional Plan. Swales produced an extraordinary panorama of suggested waterfront developments along the East, Hudson, and Harlem Rivers.[66] The East River waterfront was particularly ripe for high-class residential and institutional development with the departure of many of the kosher slaughterhouses for other parts of the Region, and with the impending construction of the East River Drive. Swales and Adams proposed an attractive quayside development with the drive at water level, above which grand buildings would be set on a platform. The structures Swales delineated, while largely examples rather than concrete proposals, were mostly monumental, low masses, curiously reminiscent of Daniel Burnham's Beaux Arts edifices for the Chicago Plan of 1909. It was architecture founded on the new technology of the engineers though not yet subordinate to it. The City Beautiful movement re-emerged in these elegant fantasies.

Less happy was Swales' solution to the City Hall civic center problem in lower Manhattan, where he proposed a towering bulk to mark the seat of municipal government. Dwarfing the beautiful original City Hall as well as McKim, Mead, and White's adjoining Municipal Building, it would have risen nearly as high as the Empire State Building, then under construction. Swales' design was embarrassingly like the congesting, crowded skyscrapers condemned by Adams elsewhere in the Plan, and though Adams defended the concept, he felt obliged to prepare, with Chester B. Price, an alternative design more in keeping with his model for a tower on a platform. The result was less attractive than Swales' proposal, a crude municipal version of Shreve, Lamb and Harmon's Empire State Building.[67]

The Building of the City offered other specific development projects too numerous to describe here. Some are worth brief mention for their innovative concepts, such as the treatment of the various rail sub-termini in Manhattan, in the Bronx, and at Sunnyside in Queens, which proposed extensive use of air-rights over rail yards. The combined civic center and air terminal in Central Queens was a less realistic combination.[68] A fabulous obelisk was proposed for the tip of the Battery in Manhattan as a monument to the World War dead, after a design by Eric Gugler and Paul Manship. A civic center for Brooklyn at the foot of the Brooklyn Bridge was perhaps more realistic than the treatment proposed for Manhattan's City Hall area.[69] Less reasonable was Electus D. Litchfield's suggestion for massive waterfront reconstruction, with high apartment buildings, in the elegant townhouse neighborhood of Columbia Heights.[70]

Adams was less specific about proposals for the environs. Here he could only offer models for the desirable development of civic centers, public buildings, and park facilities. An important exception was an elaborate plan for the development of the 30,000 acres of the Hackensack Meadowlands. Two-thirds of this area was to be given over to new residential neighborhoods, 4,400 acres to parks, and 4,000 to industry. In one of its bolder suggestions, the Plan called for a public 'Meadowlands Reclamation Committee'. The Meadows was the only open area for which the Plan made specific design proposals.[71]

Except for the Meadowlands proposal, Adams made no specific suggestions for new satellite towns in the Region, despite his promise in 1929 that such proposals would be made in the final volume.[72] Adams did urge that such new towns be developed, but he declined to specify possible sites on the quite plausible grounds that to do so would unnecessarily drive up land prices at such locations. Orange, Rockland, upper Westchester, and Fairfield Counties all had potential areas where satellite towns could be established, he observed, but Long Island was less appropriate because it was unsuited to the industry an independent satellite town would require. This dubious argument had earlier been put forward by Frederick Law Olmsted, Jr., in his sector plan for Long Island and accepted unquestioningly by Adams.[73]

Edith Elmer Wood, the eminent housing expert, in her *Recent Trends in American Housing*, had severely criticized the Graphic Regional Plan for its failure to deal adequately with the problem of housing for low and moderate income groups. Her hope that Adams would keep his promise that the second volume of the Plan would make constructive suggestions for a housing policy went unfulfilled.[74] Adams offered little new or specific information concerning the basic issue of housing in his capstone work for the Committee on the Regional Plan. *The Building of the City* was a noteworthy achievement but deeply flawed by this omission.

The completion of the Regional Plan of New York and Its Environs was celebrated with a presentation dinner held on December 11, 1931, at the Hotel

Roosevelt in Manhattan. Delano, with Adams and McAneny, presided at the ceremonies. Wilbur D. Cross, Governor of Connecticut, and Franklin D. Roosevelt, Governor of New York, were present. Joseph G. Wolber, president of the New Jersey State Senate, represented that state. Roosevelt, in his short talk at the dinner, recalled the day twenty years earlier when Charles D. Norton had described to him the Plan of Chicago. From that moment on, said the Governor, he had been interested in the larger aspects of planning. Planning, Roosevelt thought, would be the way of the future:

> Out of the survey initiated by Mr. Norton in Chicago has developed something new, not a science, but a new understanding of the problems that affect not merely bricks and mortar, subways and streets; planning that affects also the economic and social life of a community, then of a county, then of a state; perhaps the day is not far distant when planning will become a part of the national life of this country.[75]

A little over a year later, Roosevelt, as President, would shape his early New Deal policies with these planning principles very much in mind.

With the public presentation of the final volume, the work of the Russell Sage Committee was complete. On March 20, 1932, the Committee disbanded and the staff operating under its direction was merged with the staff of the Regional Plan Association. The Plan was finally complete. The task was now to carry it out – and to defend it against its critics.[76]

REACTIONS TO THE PLAN

Reviews of the Plan volumes mostly repeated press release information and were almost unanimously favorable and uncritical. Exceptions were few, the most notable being those of Lewis Mumford and Benton MacKaye, both of whom had been members of an influential, informal group of architects and planners who had organized themselves in 1923 as the Regional Planning Association of America.

Mumford, a disciple of both Ebenezer Howard and Patrick Geddes, had expressed skepticism concerning the premises of the Russell Sage-sponsored Regional Plan as early as April of 1925, when the International Town, City, and Regional Planning and Garden Cities Congress convened in New York at the Hotel Pennsylvania. The conference, which brought together the generation's most renowned European and American planners, was held in New York largely through the efforts of Thomas Adams, a founder of the group. When the Regional Plan staff presented their preliminary maps and plans, the garden city proponents, including Mumford, were disappointed at the absence of proposals for new communities. Raymond Unwin, C.B. Purdom, and Ebenezer Howard, the patriarch of the Garden City movement in England, each expressed at the New York conference concern over the excessive growth of the metropolis and reiterated their theory of decantation of the over-crowded metropolis into self-sufficient garden cities beyond the periphery of development. The garden city could not simply be a planned suburb. It was necessarily a new method of urban development with quite different objectives from a mere suburban development. As Mumford wrote shortly after the conference, 'anyone who went away still believing that [Howard, Purdom, and Unwin] meant a fancy kind of suburban land subdivision or a particular variety of landscape gardening must have been both deaf and blind.'[77]

The Regional Plan premise of accepting and coping with growth was clearly at odds with the garden city ideal of stringent control and channelization. Much closer to the ideal was Henry Wright's sketch scheme of a future pattern of New York State, made for the State Housing and Regional Planning Commission [report of May 7, 1926]. Wright's scheme envisioned a far wider distribution of activities and transportation across all of New York State in hopes of reducing the economic denudation of rural areas and the over-concentration of population in New York City.[78]

'These plans,' Mumford wrote,

> stand symbolically at opposite poles: one assumes that technical ability can improve living conditions while our existing economic and social habits continue; the other holds that technical ability can achieve little that is fundamentally worth the effort until we reshape our institutions in such a way as to subordinate financial and property values to those of human welfare.[79]

By the time the first volume of the Plan was issued in 1929, Mumford's views had changed little. He was convinced that the Regional Plan promised a continuation of the worst trends toward over-centralization and concentration. In an article for *The New Republic*, he awarded a 'prize in "Applied Logic"', one of a number of 'Booby Prizes for 1929', to the Committee on the Regional Plan

> for its admirable demonstration that by providing for a population of 20,000,000 in the New York area, the problems of transportation which are now insoluble would become less so, and park areas and playgrounds, which are now non-existent or impossible to reach, would then be more numerous and easier to reach.[80]

Adams was deeply hurt by the attack and responded to Mumford by letter the day after publication of the article.

> The writing of that article in the New Republic must have given you great fun, but why direct a shaft at the Regional Plan, when you couldn't have time enough to study it to enable you to understand it?
>
> I am certain that anyone who takes the trouble to study our report on the Plan will be satisfied that we have both logic and good sense behind our proposals. They will do what we say they can do, if they are carried out. Patrick Geddes would give support to these proposals. I wish you would read the report because I know that then you would be one of the most ardent supporters of what the Regional Plan stands for. Unfortunately we cannot prevent the growth of New

York to 20,000,000, but we may do something to give that growth the right direction with more spaciousness.

I am sorry we cannot count on support from your able pen because, with all deference, your duty to the public is more important than your intellectual enjoyment as a critic.[81]

Mumford remained unconvinced that his public duty was to support a plan which seemed to him to guarantee an extension of the congested, inhuman urban fabric he deplored. Writing to Adams a few weeks later, he expressed admiration for the technical work of the survey but demurred about the basic assumptions underlying the Plan:

The chief difficulty is not with the Plan's conclusions but with its premises: namely, that continued growth at the present rate in the metropolitan area is inevitable, and that the first duty of the Plan is to facilitate such growth. I do not regard this notion as an axiom; far from it; yet all your elaborate provisions for future traffic and transportation system are based upon it. On the basis of past experience, I see no reason whatever for hoping that this growth and vast expenditure will be compatible with a sufficient and timely provision of parks, playgrounds, and housing facilities: so long as growth and the maintenance of land values are the ends in view, it is rather safe to say that these vital facilities will remain in 'embellishments' – scamped and squeezed in order to accommodate the budget. The emphasis that the Plan has so often laid upon 'available open space' and 'average building heights' seems to me to encourage false hopes and misplaced expectations, since it tends to distract attention from the impossibility, at present, of creating sufficient open space in the congested housing districts, or sufficient circulation of traffic and relief from the inhuman subway overcrowding in the skyscraper districts.

Unfortunately, all these points of difference flow from the original premises about the growth and distribution of population: they are not disagreements over mere matters of detail, but fundamental differences of principle and method, that cut at the very root of the whole matter. Since the chief function of the Regional Plan is educational, I cannot accept with any pleasure or equanimity a series of recommendations that seem to me wholly unsound in their general tendency, however appropriate or necessary any particular one may be. Remembering the disastrous work of the City Plan Commissioners of 1811, I had rather see a continuance of the present muddle and shortsightedness, than the general acceptance of an able and comprehensive plan which works in the wrong direction. When we discussed this matter in 1925, you urged that I be patient with my criticism until the work was finished and the final results could be examined. I genuinely regret that, from the present indications, I can feel no greater enthusiasm over the Regional Plan now than I did then. Believe me: it gives me no pleasure to take the opposite side in this matter, and were it not for a sense of public duty I would gladly remain silent.[82]

Shelby Harrison, who, of all the staff members was perhaps most oriented to a social welfare viewpoint, was asked by Adams for his interpretation of the Mumford critique. Harrison thought Mumford quite wrong in his reading of the Plan:

Mr. Mumford is apparently unwilling squarely to discuss with you the merits of the Plan's conclusions. They are the features which presumably will be most directly concerned with action, and if they point in the direction which Mr. Mumford thinks developments should take, why does he worry about false premises? But of course, he misstates the Plan's premises anyway.

As I see it, either the metropolitan area will grow at something like its present rate, or it will not. If its population does not grow any more at all a better distribution is desirable; and if it does grow, a better distribution is still more desirable. And, as I understand it, such better distribution is one of the major purposes of city and regional planning, and particularly the purpose of the New York Regional Plan. The only thing left in his implied criticism of premises seems to be to understand him as thinking the Regional Plan should somehow limit the number of persons who shall stay in the New York Region, or come to it in the future. I wonder how he would do that through the agency of City and Regional planning without making just about exactly the same recommend-ations for future development which the plan is making.[83]

Adams made one last attempt to convince Mumford by letter that their views were not irreconcilable. Adams argued that to plan for growth which in no way could be avoided was not to be condemned as encouraging such growth:

I can imagine that if you do not believe in the continued growth of the metro-politan area at some rate approximate to that which has been occurring in recent years, you will not be able to look upon the Regional Plan with favor. We have been forced as a result of our studies to face this growth as inevitable. I deprecate, however, your suggestion that we have regarded as our first duty to facilitate such growth. What we have regarded as our first duty is to facilitate such dispersal of the growth as will make it healthier than it will be if it is left to go on as at present. All our elaborate provisions for future traffic and transportation are put forward with the idea of spreading the growth, if and when it occurs. I remember when I was the first executive of the Garden City Company in England, I thought it possible—as you appear to do—that the building of garden cities would tend towards stopping the growth of London. What it has done is to make the growth of London better and to spread rather than contract the big city. We all wished it had been otherwise, but that has been the experience.

I agree with you that there is no reason for hoping that the increased growth and vast expenditure will be compatible with a sufficient provision of open spaces and housing facilities, *if* you judge solely from past experience. But we are of the opinion that past experience has little bearing on what will happen under the conditions of the next fifty years. I am surprised that you should say that we have the growth and maintenance of land values as an end in view because one of our chief ends has been to destroy the fallacy that land values matter at all when human values are at stake. I prefer to put it this way, however, that high land prices mean low value because it is the price situation with regard to land that presents the difficulty of getting ample spaces. I wish you would read the final chapter of the Regional Plan volume on open development and see how much we emphasize the question of openness. We have been disappointed in not getting more support to the views expressed as to the need of more country areas within the city. There is still a long way to go before we can have public opinion changed to see that the city may not need to be entirely devoted to buildings.

I think when we have completed our presentation of that portion of the Plan that relates to the building of the city, you will find that we are not encouraging false hopes or distracting attention from the immense difficulties of lessening existing congestion. I cannot possibly see any benefit from submitting a regional plan that will set up an impossible ideal or fails to accept facts as they are. A city must always possess the weaknesses of the human beings who inhabit it and of the governments that control it. We cannot assume perfection in the city any more than in human nature. I am inclined to defend the City Plan Commissioners of 1811 against those who criticize them because all the defects that have occurred in Manhattan are the result of not following the Plan and limiting the density of building to the street widths that were provided.

You will have plenty of opportunity of seeing a continuance of muddle and shortsightedness. There will always be a sufficient disregard of planning and sound principle, however much improvement may be made. It is right and proper that you should criticize the Plan in respect to what you conceive to be its defects. I hope, however, that in founding this criticism on the assumption that the city will cease to grow, you will show that you have a reasonable basis for this expectation. I confess that it seems to be a case in which you are prepared to let the wish become father to the thought. How happy I would be if I could do the same! I should be glad to see you present your views because I believe that no movement is healthy which is regarded with unanimous favor. The Regional Plan will have to be condemned by those whose interests or views conflict with it, and as G.K. Chesterton once said of the garden city movement, there is usually little good about anything that has no opponents. Nevertheless I feel that there is much between us that is the result of a misunderstanding. I hope some day we may be able to discuss our fundamental differences.[84]

Mumford responded by suggesting that Adams should have examined the reports of the Regional Planning Association of America in the *Survey Graphic* of May 1925 and Henry Wright's report to the New York State Housing and Regional Planning Commission of May 7, 1926. Now, four years later, it was too late for the decentrists' idea to have much impact on the Regional Plan. Intellectual and political commitments had obviously been made and could not be undone. A few days later Adams wrote back that he had reviewed the RPAA reports but noted that they had dealt with the subject of 'state regional planning and not of regional planning in relation to any community of the character of New York.'[85]

The positions of the two men became even less reconcilable with the appearance of another blast at the Plan in the editorial pages of *The New Republic*, unsigned but no doubt written by Mumford, who was a contributing editor. The editorial denounced the Regional Plan policy statement on skyscraper construction, which favoured continuation of high skyscrapers, provided that the towers occupied only 25 per cent of the lots. Also severely criticized was the gargantuan civic center building proposed by Thomas Adams and Francis Swales for the vicinity of City Hall, a structure which clearly violated the Regional Plan policy statement but which Adams defended as a necessary exception if the civic center was to dominate the area.[86]

Mumford's close associate, Benton MacKaye, the originator of the Appalachian Trail, took an even stronger stand against the Regional Plan in a review of R.L. Duffus' popularized version of the Plan, *Mastering a Metropolis*.[87] MacKaye's vision of regionalism was the open, balanced region in which town and country were in organic harmony. The underlying premise of the plan – that ten million people would be added by 1965 to the ten million already in the Region in 1930 – was not acceptable to MacKaye. Even if the additional ten million people were inevitable, it would be better, thought MacKaye, *not* to provide for them in advance. 'Why deliberately plan to achieve something that looks nothing like an asset and something like a liability? One way *not* to get [ten million more people] is *not* to make "swifter and less painful" subways,' MacKaye opined. Build some new cities, he suggested, down South, our West, anywhere but in the New York Region. 'The American city,' he observed, 'is no longer a city problem, it is a national problem.'[88]

MacKaye was wrong, of course, to assume that not building transportation would keep people out of New York. Only a few new subway lines were in fact built, and yet nearly nine million additional people did settle in the Region. MacKaye's notion of a national growth policy was far sounder, but perhaps too advanced a concept for its time. How could the nation as a whole agree on a desirable population distribution when individual large metropolitan areas were too fragmented to carry out plans on a regional basis? And if the ten million new people were therefore inevitable, why not provide in advance for their transportation and other needs? So the growth or non-growth arguments were drawn between the Regional Planning Association of America group and the Regional Plan Association.

The most memorable and detailed attack came two years later when in June of 1932 Mumford's long-awaited critique of the Regional Plan was published in the *New Republic*.[89] It was a devastating treatment serving only to show the very different premises upon which the two groups were operating. Yet Mumford's criticisms were frequently justified. Mumford labeled the plan a 'monumental' failure both as a 'specific enterprise for the benefit of New York' and as a model for other cities. Were its example to be widely followed, the results, Mumford thought, would be disastrous.

The Plan, according to Mumford, contained many internal contradictions. Proponents of garden cities as well as of concentration could find support for their positions at some point in the text. What the Plan lacked was a fertile theoretical base upon which concrete proposals might be made. What Adams had offered up was, for Mumford at least, a synthetic collage of concrete proposals from many sources, unrelated by a unified conception. Mumford thought that the Plan was characterized by its drift into the future and its unquestioning assumption of continued growth. There were other shortcomings: the geographic and historical studies which should have been basic to the Plan were perfunctory and arranged in no logical order in the survey series; the choice of a region as an area of metropolitan influence was contrary to geographic usage, and the boundaries chosen on the basis of an hour's commutation to the center were arbitrary and too close; the Pearl-Reed population projection modeled on fruit fly multiplication in a closed container was inappropriate to a metropolitan area.

Mumford noted that the peak of centralization had occurred about 1910 and was declining thereafter as the automobile and electricity transmission decreased the advantages of the center of the metropolis. The Plan and Survey, he asserted, ignored this trend and had been erroneously based on growth statistics from the period 1900–1912.

Mumford further criticized the Plan for offering solutions capable only of immediate fulfillment when what was needed was a plan flexible enough to be operative over thirty or forty years. He criticized the Plan's failure as a tool for education of the people in the 'reorientation of our civilization' necessary before many critical social problems might be solved:

> It may be more effective, as well as more clear-sighted and honest, to say that no comprehensive planning for the improvement of living conditions can be done as long as property values and private enterprise are looked upon as sacred, than it is to draw pictures of parks that may never be built . . . and garden cities that will never be financed.[90]

Mumford accused the staff of having absorbed the values of their elite employers at the Sage Foundation:

> The Russell Sage planners did not take advantage of their theoretical freedom: they were so eager to fasten to a viable solution, a solution acceptable to their committee full of illustrious names in financial and civic affairs, to the business community generally, to the public officials of the region, that they deliberately restricted the area of their questions.[91]

Mumford attacked the Plan for its willingness to compromise on a number of issues. It called for more light and air, and yet endorsed the skyscraper and proposed dense residential and institutional development along the city riverfront. It called for garden cities and yet proposed a denser concentration in the center, precisely the opposite, Mumford thought, of a prime objective of building garden cities. It called for better housing for low-income groups, but offered no new governmental or social techniques for achieving it. In essence, he contended, the Plan substituted heavy capital investment in transportation for a community building program.[92]

Mumford's sharpest criticism was directed at Adams' failure to look at alternative strategies which might have required far less investment in infrastructure. Mumford proposed an alternate solution: lessen the pressure of congestion in lower Manhattan by recentralizing the business districts of the metropolis; lay down new cities and direct the exodus of industries to these new cities *outside* the New York region; rebuild the blighted areas and take care of part of the increase in population by a process of 'intensive internal colonization', by which Mumford meant establishing denser neighborhoods with more open space. By diverting new growth to redevelopment inside the city boundaries, Mumford hoped that the suburban drain of resources and support for the civic institutions of the city could be avoided. Mumford's alternative regional conception, an extrapolation of the ideas of Ebenezer Howard, Patrick Geddes, and Henry Wright, was not a denial of the metropolis but of what Mumford deemed to be its unnecessary expansion at the expense of amenity, community, and the vitality of civic institutions.

Mumford further criticized the absence of a sound theoretical foundation for the Plan and the short time-horizons of the projects proposed. 'There is nothing more practical,' he declared, 'than a fertile theoretical attack; there is nothing less practical than a concrete proposal which, if not immediately carried out, becomes obsolete and must be replaced.'[93]

The Regional Survey he thought excellent in its compilation of facts and conditions, but he saw little evidence that the Plan had been based on the Survey. 'Maps, charts, tabulations, surveys, statistical analyses are useful accessories of thought: they do not take the place of it,' he concluded.

Mumford summed up his criticism by comparing the Regional Plan to the efforts of the previous generation of 'City Beautiful' planners. The latter were superficial, but at least they left parkways and civic centers on the American urban scene and a greater feeling of spaciousness and elegance.[94] The Regional Plan of their successors he thought even more shallow and unredeemed by aesthetic value. For Mumford, the Regional Plan was a badly-conceived pudding, into which many ingredients had been poured, some sound but many dubious, by a cook who

> tried to satisfy every appetite; . . . the guiding thought was that it should 'sell' one pudding to the diners, especially to those who paid the cook. The mixture is indigestible and tasteless: but here and there is a raisin or a large piece of citron that can be extracted and eaten with relish. In the long run, let us hope, this is how the pudding will be remembered.[95]

While other writers sharply criticized the Plan for its failure to come to grips with the housing problem, it was Mumford's general attack which aroused Adams to a written rebuttal.[96] Labeling Mumford an 'esthete-sociologist', whose ideas were 'pathetically immature', Adams denied that he or his staff had tried to find a solution 'acceptable to the committee consisting of a caste of bankers' or that they had deliberately restricted the area of their questions.[97]

Adams invoked his past personal association with Patrick Geddes and Ebenezer Howard, asserting that both would have approved the basic ideas in the Plan. Mumford's ideas, Adams acknowledged, were high, but unworkable. What was essential to progress in reform, Adams asserted, was 'movement'.[98] It was this 'movement' toward progress which Geddes would have applauded, he suggested, and not Mumford's unrealizable Garden City idea. As for Howard, Adams contended, he would have approved the notion of garden suburbs close to the city, for had he not sited his second Garden City, Welwyn, seventeen miles closer to London than the first, Letchworth?[99]

Adams denied categorically that skyscrapers were incompatible with garden cities, that the proposed highways and rail systems were substitutes for housing, rather than complementary to it, and that the boundaries chosen for the Region were too close in to allow for new town proposals in the fringe countryside. Adams vigorously rebutted many other detailed criticisms Mumford had made, but most vehemently the assertion that the Plan would add to congestion rather than reduce it. Because his criticism was based on a 'wrong diagnosis', Adams asked that Mumford's conclusions be dismissed.[100]

Adams and Mumford, committed reformers both, had sailed past each other like ships in the night. Their differing value premises precluded any communication on fundamentals. Mumford's words still stand tall after forty years, his vision of human community untarnished by the passage of time. By contrast, Adam's detailed plans and his arguments in defense of them seem more dated, embedded in an era and a place. For Adams the object of the Plan was to formulate a usable public agenda acceptable within the bounds of public opinion. To go beyond this was to risk failure and impotence. For Mumford, on the other hand, the object of a plan was to stretch the limits of public opinion itself, to provide new images of a humane community. Adams sought solid but incremental improvements in the city and region as it existed in reality. Mumford sought to change political and social reality. Mumford's words perhaps seem more durable because the realities are still in need of change. Adams' plans seem dated because they were fitted to the perceived needs of the time. If Adams had indeed concocted a raisin pudding by assembling in one place the ideas of a myriad of actors and agencies, he had fashioned it out of the fragmented regional political economy, which was itself a pudding even more indigestible.

Mumford and Adams epitomized the two strains of reform that have often appeared simultaneously on the American scene in periods of change. One radical and visionary, the other conservative and pragmatic, they have often clashed bitterly. But just as often, the first has prepared the way for the achievements of the second, though only after enough time has passed for the visionary to come to seem possible. Thus after forty years Mumford's ideas strike a responsive chord, while Adams' seem timid by comparison.

But the contrast is due not only to the passage of time and the difference in reform styles. Mumford's criticism of Adams was accurate in many particulars. The Plan was indeed timid on the crucial matter of housing, and this was a direct consequence of the pressure placed on Adams by the conservative members of the Committee he served. And certainly the images of Manhattan redevelopment proposed by the architectural teams conjured up environments more dense than the abstracted rhetoric of Adams' written version of the Plan. These, however, were matters largely beyond the control of Adams, who was by personality and position more synthesizer than commander. These failings of the Regional Plan of New York were so serious that Adams' successor, George Ford, had contemplated in 1930 abandoning the Plan and starting over. Yet Adams' achievement ought properly to be recognized. Mumford's vision of the future New York Region was in many ways more attractive than that which Adams had proposed in the Regional Plan. Nevertheless the Region became in some ways a better place for having had Adams' plan than it would have been without it.

CONTRIBUTION TO PLANNING EDUCATION

Work on the Regional Plan revealed a great deficiency in the numbers and quality of trained people in the field of city and regional planning. The Committee's staff and consultants, almost without exception, had entered planning through related disciplines. Adams was a surveyor-engineer, Olmsted, Jr., a landscape architect, Nelson and Harold Lewis were civil engineers. These men were largely self-trained in the field of city planning, building on their original disciplines. Adams had taught planning at MIT through the 1920s, but his students were architects seeking a broader knowledge of the city context. Harvard's program in planning, which dated from 1909, had grown out of its landscape architecture program, largely as a result of the efforts of James Sturgis Pray. A number of other universities followed suit, offering courses of one sort or another in town planning. In 1923 Harvard offered the first American degree in planning, Master of Landscape Architecture in City Planning, formalizing the course of instruction that had been available for fifteen years.[101]

The students emerging from these early programs were typically oriented to one or another of the traditional disciplines with a specialization in city planning. Partly as a result of his work on the Regional Plan, Thomas Adams saw a great need for professionals who were primarily broad city planners, oriented to solving city and regional problems.[102]

As a result of Adams' concern, Frederic Delano contacted Columbia University President, Nicholas Murray Butler, in early 1928 to organize a conference on a 'Project for Research and Instruction in City and Regional Planning'. Butler readily agreed to co-sponsor the conference with the Committee on the Regional Plan.

The conference, held at Columbia University on May 28, 1928, attracted the most prominent names in planning and social science of the period, including most of the consultants for the Regional Plan, and such luminaries as Robert M. MacIver, the sociologist, Paul Kellogg, editor of the *Survey*, Henry V. Hubbard, editor of *City Planning*, and Charles Merriam, the University of Chicago political scientist.

The conference appointed a committee, consisting of Henry V. Hubbard,

George B. Ford, and Henry James as chairman, to draft a report which was to be highly influential in the evolution of planning education in the United States. The report called for more 'fundamental research for the development of the profession' and for the establishment of an institute at one or more universities to carry on such research. It further stipulated that such an institute should not be part of an existing department such as architecture or engineering, but be a separate, independent unit. The committee recommended that the institute be established in one or more large cities where suitable 'classical' material would be readily available. Cooperation among the various universities was urged by Harvard Professor of Government, William B. Munro, though the committee stressed that it would be best not to scatter the effort and funds that might become available through too many institutions.[103]

While no particular institution was designated, it was logical that Harvard, the pioneer in planning education, should become the beneficiary of the committee's recommendations. A separate School of City Planning was subsequently established as a result of a grant from the Rockefeller Foundation, and a chair of Regional Planning in honor of Charles Dyer Norton was endowed by Norton's friend, James F. Curtis.[104] Adams, upon completion of his work for the Regional Plan Committee, taught for several years at the Harvard planning school he had helped establish. During this period he completed his summary statement of the work on the Regional Plan in the form of a textbook, *Outline of Town and City Planning: A Review of Past Efforts and Modern Aims.*[105]

The 1928 conference was a turning point in planning education, for it established the identity of a separate profession of planning and the need for trained planners independent of other disciplines. Following Harvard's lead, MIT, Cornell, and Columbia established professional programs in the 1930s.[106]

NOTES

1. Adams, Thomas (1927) *Planning the New York Region.* New York: Regional Plan of New York and Its Environs, p. 66.

2. Committee on the Regional Plan of New York and Its Environs (1929) *Regional Survey of New York and Its Environs.* Vol. IV. *Transit and Transportation.* New York: Regional Plan of New York and Its Environs, p. 6.

3. *Ibid.,* p. 164.

4. *Ibid.,* p. 171.

5. Henry M. Brinckerhoff, 'Urban and Suburban Transportation in the Metropolitan District of New York'. Address before the American Society of Civil Engineers, November 17, 1920, Regional Plan Papers.

6. North Jersey Transit Commission, 'Rapid Transit System Proposed by North Jersey

Transit Commission in 1925 to 1929 Reports'. Map, published in 1931, Regional Plan papers.

7. Committee on the Regional Plan of New York and its Environs (1929) *Transit and Transportation, op. cit.,* pp. 189–198.

8. *Ibid.,* p. 197.

9. Committee on the Regional Plan of New York and Its Environs (1929) *Regional Plan of New York and Its Environs.* Vol. I. *The Graphic Regional Plan.* New York: Regional Plan of New York and Its Environs, pp. 182–207.

10. Minutes of meeting, Committee on the Regional Plan, November 23, 1926, Regional Plan Papers.

11. *Ibid.*

12. Committee on the Regional Plan of New York and Its Environs (1929) *Transit and Transportation, op. cit.,* pp. 170–173.

13. Edward M. Bassett to Thomas Adams, February 28, 1928, Regional Plan Papers.

14. Bard, Erwin Wilkie (1942) *The Port of New York Authority.* New York: Columbia University Press, pp. 40–44.

15. Committee on the Regional Plan of New York and Its Environs (1929) *The Graphic Regional Plan,* p. 136.

16. Committee on the Regional Plan of New York and Its Environs (1927) *Regional Survey of New York and Its Environs.* Vol. III. *Highway Traffic* (by Harold M. Lewis with Ernest P. Goodrich). New York: Regional Plan of New York and Its Environs.

17. According to Harold M. Lewis, the Committee on the Regional Plan of New York and Its Environs was the first group to propose limited-access highways. Interview, June 21, 1971.

18. Committee on the Regional Plan of New York and Its Environs (1927) *Highway Traffic, op. cit.,* pp. 126–134.

19. Committee on the Regional Plan of New York and Its Environs (1929) *The Graphic Regional Plan, op. cit.,* pp. 221–226.

20. Lester P. Harlow, communication to the Regional Plan Committee, September 24, 1925, Regional Plan Papers. President Franklin D. Roosevelt later called for such a system in a message to Congress, April 27, 1939 (76th Congress 1st Session, House Doc. No. 272, 1939).

21. Interview with Harold M. Lewis, June 21, 1971.

22. *Ibid.*

23. Committee on the Regional Plan of New York and Its Environs (1929) *Transit and Transportation, op. cit.,* p. 200.

24. *Ibid.,* p. 201.

25. *Ibid.,* p. 203.

26. Committee on the Regional Plan of New York and Its Environs (1929) *The Graphic Regional Plan, op. cit.,* pp. 366–375.

27. Committee on the Regional Plan of New York and Its Environs (1928) *Regional Survey of New York and Its Environs.* Vol. V. *Public Recreation.* New York: Regional Plan of New York and Its Environs, p. 128.

28. *Ibid.*

29. *Ibid.,* pp. 20–21.

30. *Ibid.*, pp. 80–95, 187–198.

31. Committee on the Regional Plan of New York and Its Environs (1929) *The Graphic Regional Plan, op. cit.*, pp. 336–355.

32. *Ibid.*, pp. 318–319.

33. *Ibid.*, pp. 322–329.

34. *Ibid.*, pp. 331–336.

35. *Ibid.*, pp. 300–301.

36. *Ibid.*

37. Minutes of meeting, Committee on the Regional Plan, May 19, 1922, October 30, 1922, Regional Plan Papers.

38. Frederic A. Delano, 'Address at the inauguration of the Chicago Regional Planning Association at the City Club', November 2, 1923, Regional Plan Papers.

39. Minutes of meeting, Committee on the Regional Plan, November 14, 1927, Regional Plan Papers.

40. Lawson Purdy, 'Plan of Organization of Corporation to Take Over the Regional Plan of New York', memorandum, October 23, 1928, Regional Plan Papers.

41. Committee on the Regional Plan, 'Memorandum on Carrying Out the Regional Plan Paper', February 8, 1929, Regional Plan Papers.

42. Green, Constance McL. (1963) *Washington: Capital City, 1879–1950*. Princeton: Princeton University Press, pp. 288–289.

43. Hays, Forbes B. (1965) *Community Leadership: The Regional Plan Association of New York*. New York: Columbia University Press, pp. 45–46.

44. Minutes of meeting, Committee on the Regional Plan, April 16, 1929, Regional Plan Papers.

45. Interview with Lawrence M. Orton, September 10, 1972.

46. Letter of George McAneny to prospective members, April 14, 1930, Regional Plan Papers.

47. Duffus, R.L. (1930) *Mastering a Metropolis: Planning the Future of the New York Region*. New York: Harper and Row.

48. *Ibid.*, pp. 265–267.

49. Committee on the Regional Plan of New York and Its Environs (1931)) *Regional Survey of New York and Its Environs*. Vol. VI. *Buildings: Their Uses and the Spaces about Them*. New York Committee on the Regional Plan of New York and Its Environs. Volume VI was published two years after Volumes VII and VIII. The delay was probably due to Adams' preoccupation with the Graphic Regional Plan volume and possibly to its focus on the sensitive topic of housing.

50. *Ibid.*, p. 22.

51. *Ibid.*, p. 94.

52. *Ibid.*, p. 226.

53. *Ibid.*, pp. 226–228.

54. *Ibid.*, pp. 336–347.

55. *Ibid.*, p. 303.

56. *Ibid.*, pp. 281–283.

57. *Ibid.*, p. 281.

58. Committee on the Regional Plan of New York and Its Environs (1931) *Regional Plan of New York and Its Environs.* Vol. II. *The Building of the City* (by Thomas Adams assisted by Harold M. Lewis and Lawrence M. Orton). New York: Regional Plan of New York and Its Environs, p. 202.

59. *Ibid.*

60. See *supra*, pp. 108–111.

61. Committee on the Regional Plan of new York and Its Environs (1931) *The Building of the City., op. cit.,* pp. 314–315.

62. *Ibid.,* pp. 112–115, 307, 345.

63. *Ibid.,* pp. 152, 399. Fry also provided the sketches of the city skylines on pp. 110–111.

64. *Ibid.,* p. 446.

65. *Ibid.,* p. 228.

66. *Ibid.,* pp. 364ff.

67. *Ibid.,* p. 507.

68. *Ibid.,* pp. 377–381.

69. *Ibid.,* pp. 478–481.

70. *Ibid.,* pp. 485–487.

71. *Ibid.,* pp. 540–547.

72. Committee on the Regional Plan of New York and Its Environs (1929) *The Graphic Regional Plan, op. cit.,* p. 406.

73. Committee on the Regional Plan of New York and Its Environs (1931) *The Building of the City., op. cit.,* pp. 568–573.

74. Wood, Edith Elmer (1931) *Recent Trends in American Housing.* New York: Macmillan Co., pp. 146–147.

75. Roosevelt, Franklin D. (1932) Growing up by plan. *Survey,* LXVII, February 1, p. 483.

76. Minutes of the Committee on the Regional Plan of New York and Its Environs, March 20, 1932, Regional Plan Papers.

77. Mumford, Lewis (1925)) Realities or dreams. *Journal of the American Institute of Architects,* XIII, June, pp. 191–199. For another account of the 1925 International Town, City, and Regional Planning and Garden Cities Congress, see Anon. (1925) Bigger and better cities? *The Survey,* May 15, p. 216.

78. New York State Commission of Housing and Regional Planning (1926) *Report.* Albany, May 7.

79. Mumford (1925)) *op. cit.;* see also, Mumford, Lewis (1926) The intolerable city: Must it keep growing? *Harpers,* February, pp. 283–293.

80. Mumford, Lewis (1930) The booby prizes of 1929. *The New Republic,* January 8, pp. 190–191.

81. Thomas Adams to Lewis Mumford, January 9, 1930, Regional Plan Papers.

82. Lewis Mumford to Thomas Adams, January 18, 1930, Regional Plan Papers.

83. Shelby Harrison to Thomas Adams, January 24, 1930, Regional Plan Papers.

84. Thomas Adams to Lewis Mumford, January 27, 1930, Regional Plan Papers.

85. Lewis Mumford to Thomas Adams, January 31, 1930, Regional Plan Papers; Thomas Adams to Lewis Mumford, February 3, 1930, Regional Plan Papers.

86. Editorial, *The New Republic,* January 29, 1930, p. 262; Thomas Adams, letter to the Editor, *The New Republic,* March 5, 1930, pp. 75–76.

87. Duffus (1930) *op. cit.*

88. McKaye, Benton (1930) New York: A national peril. *Saturday Review of Literature,* August 23, p. 68.

89. Mumford, Lewis (1932) The Plan of New York. *The New Republic,* June 15, pp. 121–126; Mumford, Lewis (1932) The Plan of New York II. *The New Republic,* June 22, pp. 146–154.

90. Mumford (1932) The Plan of New York, p. 124.

91. *Ibid.,* p. 125.

92. *Ibid.*

93. *Ibid.*

94. Mumford (1932) The Plan of New York II, p. 154.

95. *Ibid.*

96. See, for example, Thomas, Norman and Blanshard, Paul (1932) *What's the Matter with New York: A National Problem.* New York: Macmillan Co., pp. 314–316; also Wood (1931) *op. cit.,* pp. 279–286.

97. Adams, Thomas (1932) A communication in defense of the Regional Plan. *The New Republic,* June 6, p. 207.

98. *Ibid.,* p. 208. Patrick Geddes was acquainted with both the Regional Plan Committee and its staff and Mumford's group, the Regional Planning Association of America. Geddes visited both groups on his last trip to America in the Spring of 1923.

99. *Ibid.*

100. *Ibid.,* p. 210.

101. Adams, Frederick J. and Hodge, Gerald (1965) City planning instruction in the United States: The pioneering days, 1900–1920. *Journal of the American Institute of Planners,* XXXI, February, pp. 43–51.

102. Adams, Thomas (1923) The architect and city planning, IV. *Journal of the American Institute of Architects,* XI, May, pp. 217–219.

103. Report of the Conference on a Project for Research and Instruction in City and Regional Planning, May 3, 1928, Regional Plan Papers.

104. Gaus, John M. (1943) *The Graduate School of Design and the Education of Planners.* Cambridge, Mass., privately printed, appendix.

105. Adams, Thomas (1936) *Outline of Town and City Planning: A Review of Past Efforts and Modern Aims.* New York: Russell Sage Foundation.

106. Adams and Hodge (1965) *op. cit.,* pp. 50–51.

8

CONFLICT AMIDST PLANNING: THREE DECISIONS

The physical development of the New York Region naturally did not halt pending completion of the Regional Plan. Quite the contrary, during most of the eight years between 1921 and 1929 in which the Plan was being prepared, economic prosperity stimulated both private and public capital development. Urbs and suburbs sprouted across the Region. New roads were called for to satisfy the newly affluent motoring minority. New parks were demanded as destinations for Sunday outings. But old development problems prevailed and intensified. The railroad situation around the port of New York was to most transportation experts irrational and chaotic. The subways were increasingly crowded as the office industry created congested skyscraper districts in downtown and midtown Manhattan.

Responses to demands for public action came from several directions, often pitting the administration of the City of New York against the State and the Port of New York Authority. In the same period another regional actor, Robert Moses, emerged as a significant force, beginning his transformation into a one-man regional development institution. These were the principal groups sharing whatever power existed to shape the Region, although none possessed enough political strength to accomplish much in the early 1920s. The Port Authority was just beginning to consolidate its power base. Moses was developing his adversarial approach to the accumulation of power, but was still far from his ultimate pinnacle. The New York State Governor's office, occupied for much of this period by a New York City Democrat, Alfred E. Smith, was counting on necessary regional action through his protégé, Robert Moses, and through the Port Authority, to which Smith had been appointed between his terms as Governor. Direct state intervention in regional concerns was thus unlikely, except where such concerns were solely within the confines of New York City, as in the volatile issue of public versus private control of the subway system. In such instances, the institutionalized and inevitable City-State conflict arose, with the City often the loser.

Into this fiery furnace of regional politics plunged the Committee on the Regional Plan and its staff. Lacking power itself, the Committee realized that to have any impact on development it would be necessary to influence and persuade those who did have power. Nor could such activity wait for the completion of the Plan. Major regional decisions were being made weekly, and the Regional Plan Committee, as the public became aware of its existence, could not avoid taking positions. Adams outlined the philosophy guiding the Committee's intervention on specific issues:

> There is a constant temptation to deal with urgent . . . problems because of [the] popular interest which they arouse. On the whole, it is not desirable to ignore these local interests, and, where we can, we try to influence the right policy and plan in dealing with them.
>
> An extreme policy on our part would be to give our whole attention to concrete proposals as they are made; and an opposite extreme would be to ignore all local questions and proceed with the general Regional Plan. It seems best however to take what may be described as a middle course and while devoting ourselves to our main object of making a regional Plan, to give attention to local problems as well, and in achieving that object, simultaneously keep up the popular interest in local movements and causes.[1]

One of the first of a number of stormy conflicts that arose after Adams became Director involved a controversial opera house and music and art center which New York City Mayor John Hylan wanted to erect in Central Park. In March of 1924, Hylan wrote a private note in reply to a request from the City Chamberlain, Philip Berolzheimer, for information about similar facilities in London. Much to Adams' dismay, his note was read at a public hearing on the project by the Hylan forces supporting the project, and it was generally assumed that the Committee on the Regional Plan supported the project. Its chairman, Robert DeForest, was furious, but Adams, chagrined and chastened, had been baptized in the ways of New York politics. He suffered in silence when he received a letter from the City Chamberlain thanking him for his help in getting the music and art center approved in the Board of Estimate.[2] Adams was thereafter considerably more cautious in his dealings with political groups and the press.

The music and art center controversy was but a prelude to other, more important conflicts which involved the Regional Plan Committee and its staff. The three most interesting and controversial such issues were the aborted Narrows Tunnel, the Hudson River Bridge controversy, and the fight with Robert Moses over the location of Long Island parkways. Each of these conflicts merits particular attention, for each reveals how the Regional Plan group saw its role and its relationship with the other regional actors.

In the Narrows Tunnel debate, the Committee espoused the position of the Hylan administration in opposition to the New York State legislature, and, indirectly, the Port Authority. The Hudson River Bridge controversy saw the Committee on the Regional Plan allied with the Port Authority against private entrepreneurship. In the conflict over Long Island parkways, the Regional Plan Committee was accused by Moses of protecting the special interests of its affluent members against the general public good for which Moses felt he spoke. The conflict marked the regional emergence of the protagonist Moses, whose use of orchestrated controversy non-plussed the patrician reformers of the Regional Plan Committee and its staff.

The composite picture that emerges from these case studies is that of a dynamic but politically fragmented region in which a number of regionally-oriented groups or individuals laid claim to the authority which in other, simpler circumstances would properly have been the domain of a general government. Only by narrowing the scope of functions could the Port Authority and Moses, the regional giants, as Robert Wood later termed them, amass the power to accomplish anything of regional significance.[3] The vacuum was partially occupied by these giants, but not filled, for no regional interstate government was politically possible (although Moses would later become in effect, if not title, a one-man regional development coordinator east of the Hudson).

The Regional Plan group, lacking any power, hoped to compensate by doing what none of the other regional actors could afford: to take the point of view of a general regional government, had one existed. Its values, though derived from the experiences and views of the Committee and staff members, were nevertheless far more broadly based than those of the Port Authority or Moses, or, for that matter, the several City administrations. But lacking power, it lacked focus. Its viewpoints were derived from abstract notions such as congestion and decentralization, rather than from the hard and immediate demands of day-to-day decision making. This was its virtue, of course, but its weakness as well. In the end, the Regional Plan group, as Moses had pointed out, was more able to block the proposals of others than to initiate and carry out ideas of its own.[4] A realization of this dilemma may well have warped the Plan into the conservative mold it ultimately took. Many of the proposals of the Port Authority, Moses, and other groups were eventually incorporated into the Plan. By doing so, the plan-makers were functioning as regional coordinators and information transmitters. They were also building political capital for future use. The tantalizing question is whether in so doing the would-be co-opters were in the end themselves co-opted.

THE ABORTED NARROWS TUNNEL

Staten Island has always been something of an anomaly. As a land mass, it is much nearer to New Jersey than to any part of New York. Its political attachment to New York rather than to New Jersey was supposedly the result in 1688 of the Duke of York's unusual method of settling the dispute between the two colonies over which should have possession. A sailing race around the island was held, which the New Yorkers won. When the Greater City was consolidated two hundred years later, Staten Island voted to join the City of New York. Connected politically, the Island was nevertheless physically isolated from the other boroughs. Only the gossamer thread of the shuttling ferries linked the Island to the city to which it had been joined. Consequently, many Staten Island groups looked to the day when a subway tunnel would link the remote borough to Brooklyn or Manhattan. Realtors, in particular, who viewed the verdant island as 'lying fallow', saw great benefits to be reaped from such an enterprise.

On the opposite side of the Narrows, influential Brooklynites had a complementary dream: direct rail access to the west, eliminating the cumbersome car-floating to the Jersey railheads of the major carriers serving the region. Brooklyn industrialists felt at a competitive disadvantage with New Jersey. Brooklyn piers could be reached by rail trackage only through the circuitous Hell Gate route of the New York Connecting Railroad and the Long Island Railroad. And if the dream of Brooklyn businessmen of a great new deep water harbor in Jamaica Bay was to be achieved, freight facilities connecting directly to the west were essential.

It was the genius of the consulting engineer, Colonel William J. Wilgus, to join these two dreams. Wilgus, who as chief engineer and vice-president of the New York Central Railroad was responsible for the extraordinary planning achievement of Grand Central Terminal, accepted the position of consulting engineer to the Committee on the Regional Plan in 1924. In 1922, prior to his affiliation with the Regional Plan, Wilgus had been consultant to the New York City Board of Estimate. As one of his proposals to the Board, Wilgus suggested that a combined rail and subway tunnel be built under the Narrows between Bay Ridge, Brooklyn, at the New York Connecting Railroad Terminal, and Arlington, Staten Island, where a spur would connect with the Baltimore and Ohio Railroad line, the only railroad on Staten Island. Following approval by the State Legislature the State Transit Commission officially adopted the project on October 3, 1922; on April 27, 1924, detailed plans were released by Arthur S. Tuttle, Chief Engineer of the Board of Estimate. The proposed tunnel, according to Tuttle, would require sixty-three months to build at a cost of $27 million. The whole project, including connecting tracks, was estimated to cost about $60 million. Ten miles long, it would be the world's longest sub-aqueous tunnel.[5] The plan called for two tubes of eighteen feet inside clearance, enough to accommodate the largest freight cars then in use as well as rail passenger and rapid transit coaches. Connections were planned to the Fourth Avenue subway line of the Brooklyn Manhattan Transit Company (BMT) and to the Long Island Railroad via the New York Connecting Railroad for rail freight and passenger service. An electric blocking system of the type in use by the Michigan Central Railroad under the Detroit River would be employed to permit the joint rail and subway use of the tunnel. Movement of freight would occur mostly at night when transit demands were light, thus maximizing utilization of the tunnel's capacity.

There were, it would appear, no insurmountable technical obstacles to the project. The compatibility of transit and freight service had been demonstrated in several American cities. Nor was the bore of the tunnel extraordinary. The proposed eighteen-foot diameter of the tunnel, while large for the period, had already been exceeded by the Holland vehicular tunnel, then under construction.

If the two types of traffic could be combined, it was argued, the project could be justified financially, whereas separate freight and transit facilities probably could not be, at that point in time. The borough of Richmond had a population of only 140,000 in 1925 not enough to generate much transit traffic in the immediate period after construction of a tunnel. But expected freight traffic could reach twelve million tons a year. By combining freight and transit, proponents argued that a tunnel could be financially self-supporting.[6] By providing direct rail connections the city engineers also hoped to reduce much of the street congestion in Manhattan and elsewhere, which they claimed was due largely to the need to truck freight through the streets from waterfront terminals.

The Hylan administration was motivated to support the Staten Island tunnel project for still another reason. It had spent some $30 million on cargo piers on Staten Island in response to heavy demands made on the port during the First World War, but by the time the piers were completed the war was over. Little used, they were a considerable embarrassment to Hylan. The Citizens Union labeled the piers 'a gigantic gamble, a war baby, which was born too late to ensure any returns to the city.[7]

Hylan, an old-line Tammany man supported by the Hearst papers, was an anathema to the patrician Wall Street financiers and the downtown merchants. Hylan appealed directly to the masses through the press, bypassing what he liked to call 'the interests'. His *bête noire* was the private transit companies, the BMT and the IRT, and his popularity rested on resisting their annual demands to raise the nickel subway fare. Hylan sought an independent subway system, publicaly-owned and controlled by the City, independent, that is, of 'the interests'. He also sought City acquisition of the private lines.[8]

Merchants and downtown businessmen demanded that the City move more rapidly to relieve the intolerable congestion building up on the Manhattan portion of the subway system as a result of the construction of skyscrapers and the general expansion of the activities of the central business district. Hylan was accused of substituting rhetoric for action in dealing with the Manhattan transit crisis. Hylan was reluctant, however, to assist the private companies with public monies. In any case, Hylan's adoption of the Narrows Tunnel project seemed to the Manhattan commercial interests to be a misplacement of priorities, particularly in view of the state's constitutional limits on the City's capacity to incur indebtedness.

The Hylan project offended other groups whose interests were threatened, most notably the Port of New York Authority. The Port Authority's plan for railroad coordination and development did not call for a connection under the Narrows.[9] The Authority was instead committed by its plan to a longer rail tunnel under the widest portion of the upper Bay, connecting the Pennsylvania and Lehigh Valley railheads at Bayonne to the same point in Bay Ridge, Brooklyn, that was to be reached by the Hylan tunnel. The Port Authority, struggling at this period to establish its position, could not help but feel its credibility threatened by the City's proposal. Nor could the Pennsylvania and other trunk railroads view favorably the preferential position that would have been accorded the Baltimore and Ohio by the Hylan tunnel.

Probably realizing its vulnerability, the City moved rapidly to achieve a *fait accompli*. Contracts totaling six million dollars were let for the first phase of construction: two deep shafts, one in Bay Ridge and one near St. George, Staten Island. The shafts, each nearly a hundred feet deep were required for construction of the tunnel and would later serve as ventilation sources; by April of 1924, the Brooklyn shaft was completed and the Staten Island shaft half finished.[10]

Two months later, opponents began to attack the concept. Leroy T. Harkness, speaking for the three member New York State Transit Commission, which had been created as a watchdog on city transit activities, condemned the idea as 'the grossest waste of public funds that I have seen in an experience of more than twenty years in municipal affairs,'conveniently forgetting that the Commission approved the tunnel in 1922. He claimed that the project would exhaust the City's credit, endangering the construction of lines elsewhere in the city. He also pointed out that the City had no assurance that the railroads would use the tunnel; on the contrary, he asserted, they had indicated that they would not.[11]

Arthur S. Tuttle, the City's Chief Engineer, supported by members of the New York City Board of Transportation, stoutly defended the tunnel project as necessary to afford Staten Island passenger service, to give Brooklyn a freight and passenger terminal, to connect Greater New York and Long Island with New Jersey trunk line railroads, and to decrease waterfront congestion through the Port.[12]

The *New York Times*, no friend of the Hearst-supported Hylan, added its editorial weight to the opposition, claiming that Hylan was using the Staten Island tunnel as 'a club to coerce the Port Authority into abandoning unification of the port.[13]

Governor Alfred E. Smith, though a Democrat, was also sympathetic to the Port Authority viewpoint. Smith had been one of the original Port Authority commissioners prior to his election and at that time had indicated his opposition to the freight feature of the tunnel. But Smith kept his silence on the matter, preferring to avoid an open break with Hylan, his fellow Tammany Democrat. On December 19, 1924, however, Smith gave his blessing to the initiation of a State transit investigation into the general transit situation in New York City, and appointed State Supreme Court Justice John V. McAvoy to conduct the inquiry. As McAvoy's appointment was announced, Harkness again attacked the tunnel project, charging that the connection to the Fourth Avenue line would require a series of 'ram's horns, twisting and doubling back and forth.' Harkness called for a rapid transit tunnel with steeper grades rather than a combined tunnel which required a more gentle gradient for freight movements.[14]

After six weeks of investigation, McAvoy delivered his report on February 9, 1925. The judge held Hylan responsible for the delay in building subways, and, as his principal recommendation, called for immediate legislation to change the Staten Island tunnel to a smaller-bore facility solely for rapid transit. The New York Times called the report 'simply annihilating', and suggested that it marked the political end of Mayor Hylan. The Herald Tribune proclaimed that on the basis of the report Hylan was obviously unfit for the job of mayor.[15]

Two days later, State Senator Courtland Nicoll and Assemblyman Samuel A. Hofstadter, both New York City Republicans, sponsored joint legislation to require that 'if a tunnel is built from Staten Island to Brooklyn, it must be a passenger tunnel.' This would mean early completion of the tunnel and a saving of $40 million, they claimed, though precisely why reducing the bore diameter by a few feet would result in such a large difference was not explained.[16] On February 17, Governor Smith dropped the other shoe and let it be known that he favored the McAvoy recommendations, including the proposed restriction of the tunnel to passenger service. The controversy simmered through March as the Nicoll-Hofstadter bill neared a vote in the legislature. Numerous Staten Island and Brooklyn civic groups and chambers of commerce backed Hylan. But the influential, Manhattan-oriented Merchants Association came out strongly against the combined tunnel and opposed Hylan's plan to establish an independent subway system. On March 10 1925 a public hearing on the Nicoll-Hofstadter bill was held in Albany, and on the 24th the Assembly passed the measure 83 to 64, generally along party lines, although ten Republicans, mostly from Staten Island and Long Island, broke ranks to support the Hylan tunnel, but in vain. The next day the Senate voted 28 to 22 to pass the bill.[17] When asked why upstate Republicans were so eager to prevent New York City from undertaking a project solely within its jurisdiction and well within its constitutional bonding authority, State Senator John Knight, the majority leader, replied that 'sometimes people have to be saved from themselves.'[18] But the opportunity to embarrass and divide the two Tammany Democrats in the Governor's Mansion and City Hall on the eve of a mayoral election could hardly have been far from the minds of the Republican majority.

Governor Smith had hoped that the Nicoll-Hofstadter Bill would be de-

feated, saving him from having to confront directly the tunnel issue and
Mayor Hylan. But with the passage of the bill, he had no choice. He could
veto the bill, thereby repudiating both his previous position and the recommendation of Judge McAvoy, his hand-picked transit investigator, and opening himself to charges of Tammany collusion. Or he could sign the bill,
forcing the City to modify the tunnel to serve only rapid transit. Facing one
of the most controversial conflicts of his tenure as Governor, Smith decided
to schedule a public hearing on April 19, 1925, so that both sides would have
their say in court. There could be little doubt at this point, however, where
his sympathies lay.

The battle lines were drawn in early April. The Port Authority, through its
consulting engineer, General George W. Goethals, known as 'the builder of
the Panama Canal', blasted the feasibility of a combined freight and transit
operation. Opponents pointed out that Goethals had previously stated that
such a combination of services would be practicable, but Goethals later
claimed that what he had said had been misinterpreted.[19]

Colonel Wilgus led the expert counterattack on the Port Authority's position. Backed up by some of the most prominent engineers in the country,
Wilgus categorically affirmed the practicability of combined operations in
the tunnel. He concluded in a letter to Governor Smith:

> . . . the throttling, the constricting, of the bore of the tunnel so as deliberately
> to bar its use for the greatest possible number of tenants will be a step backward
> for the port as a whole, as well as a disastrous blow to the New York side of the
> harbor and a grave injury to the taxpayers and commercial interests of the Port.
> In a word, the decreasing of the size of the tunnel, in this day and generation,
> will be utterly at variance with the tendency of modern times to plan broadly for
> the future. I cannot too emphatically urge the vetoing of the bill.[20]

The issue split not only the engineers and the Tammany organization, but
business and citizens groups as well. The Brooklyn and Staten Island Chambers of Commerce urged Smith to veto the bill. The Downtown League,
representing two thousand businesses in Manhattan, also came out in favor
of a veto.[21] The Merchants Association, however, urged Smith to sign, as did
the Citizen's Union.[22] However, the Committee on the Regional Plan, at the
urging of Colonel Wilgus, came out strongly against the bill in a statement
sent to the Governor on April 13. The statement, drawn up by Wilgus, was
also signed by Thomas Adams and Frederic A. Delano. It set out clearly the
arguments for going ahead with the combined service project.[23]

The Regional Plan statement evoked the immediate wrath of the Port
Authority leadership. E.H. Outerbridge, a Port Authority Commissioner,
wrote an outraged letter to Adams. Noting that the Chief Engineer of the Port
Authority sat on the Regional Plan Advisory Engineering Committee, and the
Counsel of the Authority sat on the Legal Advisory Committee, he asked why
no consultations on the issue had been held with the Port Authority. 'It is

most unfortunate,' Outerbridge concluded, 'that your organization should have been misled into taking the action that it has in throwing its weight behind a stubborn intention of the City Administration to fly in the face of the established laws of the States of New York and New Jersey and of Congress.' A similar protest was voiced to Adams by the Port Authority Chairman, Julian A. Gregory.[24]

With Delano in Washington and Wilgus on vacation in Vermont, Adams had to bear the full brunt of the onslaught, a situation which caused him considerable unease. He wrote to Delano of the controversy:

> Our difficulty in dealing with matters of this kind when they are really of public interest is that we get embroiled in political conflicts and the favor that we receive from one side is set off by the dissatisfaction we engender on the other side. I feel now that perhaps it would have been better to have taken no definite action although we cannot always be expected to have the same opinion as the Port Authority.[25]

The next day, Julius Henry Cohen, Counsel of the Port Authority, called Adams to protest the Regional Plan position and to notify the group of his intention to resign from its Legal Committee, chaired by Edward M. Bassett.[26] Adams panicked. The risk of losing the goodwill and cooperation of the Port Authority was too serious to merit a sustained fight over the tunnel. Unable to communicate with Delano, he prepared a supplementary letter to Governor Smith that greatly weakened the original Regional Plan position. Believing that Wilgus had provided him only with the engineering details of the tunnel controversy and had neglected the political and legal aspects, Adams retreated from full support of the combined tunnel.[27]

Learning of Adams' wavering support, Delano sent a telegram urging him to hold firm: 'Believe we are on solid ground and that our judgement is fully equal to Cohen's.' Wilgus also sent a telegram urging Adams not to give in to 'political expediency.'[28] But it was too late to halt the letter of capitulation Adams had sent to the Governor.

The extraordinary Albany public hearings on the bill, convened and chaired by Governor Smith on April 20th, witnessed an unusual parade of opponents and supporters. Mayor Hylan chartered a train carrying nearly five hundred supporters from Staten Island and led the march to the Capitol. At the hearings the Mayor denounced the Pennsylvania Railroad and the Port Authority for blocking the project. Judge McAvoy repeated his recommendations against the project. State Transit Commissioner George McAneny, who, significantly, was later to become Executive Director of the Regional Plan, attacked the combined tunnel as a public gift to the Baltimore and Ohio Railroad. Objections to the freight feature were advanced by the Port Authority, represented by Julian A. Gregory, Julius Henry Cohen, and General George W. Goethals. Smith listened to the testimony for almost five hours, revealing through his questioning his hostility to the combined tunnel. During Arthur Tuttle's testimony, the Governor observed that 'if the [City's] plan is carried out, the Port Authority plan falls to the ground.'

Tuttle replied, 'Well, there is nothing sacred about the Port Authority plan.' 'A contract with a sister state is involved, for one thing,' retorted the Governor. 'Well, what guarantee have we that the Port Authority tunnel will ever be built?' Tuttle asked. 'We have a going concern [and] are prepared to go ahead with construction and will open bids on a $28,000 construction contract next month.' But Tuttle's arguments were unpersuasive and Smith's view remained unchanged.[29]

Two days later Smith announced that he would sign the Nicoll-Hofstadter Bill, dealing the death blow to the combined tunnel. Accusing the New York City authorities of bad faith in dealing with the Port Authority, he urged that Staten Island be given its rapid transit tunnel at the earliest possible moment and that the freight feature be cared for under the comprehensive plan of the Port Authority.

Smith thus accepted the view that to run freight and rapid transit through the same tunnel would be impracticable. But the single most decisive factor was the threat to the Port Authority's domain. Acceptance of the freight feature could well have destroyed support for the Port Authority in the State of New Jersey, and this Smith would not tolerate after his strenuous efforts to develop the Authority's standing. The sound technical arguments of the Regional Plan and Wilgus could not overcome this obstacle.

Realizing that he would be finished politically by Smith's decision, Hylan made several futile gestures to save his project. A suit on grounds of violation of home-rule provisions in the State constitution was contemplated but later abandoned as hopeless.[30] An equally impossible ploy was attempted through a Board of Estimate vote to build a 'rapid transit tunnel' but with a bore large enough to accommodate freight cars. But a threatened taxpayers' suit soon halted this evasive strategy.

The battle was over, however, for the Regional Plan group, much to Adams' relief. 'We are confronted with the situation that it would be better for the Regional Plan that the matter be allowed to die,' he wrote to Delano after Smith had reached his decision.[31] To a request from Arthur Tuttle for support of the larger bore strategy, Adams responded with a proposal for an independent study by a competent group of engineers appointed by the Governors of New York and New Jersey, the Chairman of the Port Authority, and the Mayor of New York. The irony, of course, was that the Port Authority and the Regional Plan itself had supposedly been constituted as impartial, technically-oriented bodies. If these entities could not render an impartial judgement, how could another supposedly neutral group render an acceptable opinion? The proposal was ignored by both sides.

The Regional Plan group, realizing that the tunnel was a lost cause, turned its attention to mending fences with the Port Authority. If the Regional Plan was to be carried out, the Port Authority's good will would be essential.

Delano took special pains to clear the air. Writing to E.H. Outerbridge, Chairman of the Port Authority, he held to his support of the combined tunnel:

> I appreciate the trouble you have taken to fully state the basis of the decision of the Port Authority, and will cheerfully admit that your opinion is reinforced by the weight of greater testimony. I still believe that we were right in our views, but that is not a matter of particular importance for the time being, at least, as the Governor has decided in favor of your views. I need hardly say that if I were going to decide this question along political lines, I should always support the Governor as against the Mayor.[32]

In another letter he called for reconciliation:

> So far as the matter of difference of opinion between me, or members of the staff or consultants of the Regional Plan Committee, and the Port Authority is concerned, I am perfectly willing to let it drop. I trust we have honest differences of opinion on important questions, even involving policy, without jeopardizing friendly relations, or without making future cooperation impossible.[33]

Relations thereafter between the Regional Plan and the Port Authority were generally good. In fact, the tunnel controversy may well have strengthened communication between the two bodies, each having recognized the importance of cooperation with the other, and each having, at least in part, the same supporting constituency in financial, administrative, and technical circles as the other. Cohen, the Port Authority counsel, resigned from the Regional Plan Legal Committee, but Outerbridge later became closely identified with the Regional Plan and served on several of its committees.

When it was published, the Regional Plan cleverly showed a compromise on the tunnel issue, including both a rail facility at the Narrows (though not a transit link) and an ambiguous 'connection' where the Port Authority Greenville freight tunnel had been proposed. The 'connection' could have been interpreted as simply representing the extant car float service, or as a possible tunnel facility, though which was intended was intentionally left unclear.

None of the proposed tunnels for transit or for freight was ever realized, despite Governor Smith's urging of support for the Port Authority freight tunnel and a New York City transit tunnel in his decisive veto of the combined project. A private Narrows Development Corporation was formed by Brooklyn and Staten Island groups to undertake the venture, but nothing came of it.[34] In 1929 a vehicular tunnel was voted by the Board of Estimate for the Narrows as an alternative, though on a different right of way from that of the Hylan proposal. This project, which was also incorporated into the Regional Plan, was aborted by the collapse of the economy in November

1929, but was eventually realized as the Verrazano-Narrows Bridge by Robert Moses' Triborough Bridge and Tunnel Authority.

The Port Authority's proposed Greenville tunnel, the prime consideration in Smith's veto of Hylan's proposal, also was never realized. The railroads never looked favorably on the project, and the Port Authority, turning its attention to profit-making facilities for rubber-tired vehicles, had abandoned the concept by 1941.

The Hylan tunnel proposal has been criticized in analyses of the activities of the Port Authority as simply a politically motivated pork-barrel construction project.[35] But had the combined tunnel been completed, Staten Island would certainly have grown differently and earlier, though whether for better or worse it is impossible to say. And the industrial pattern in Brooklyn and Queens would probably have been different, with more plants and jobs located east of the Hudson, enhancing the economy of New York City.

But the two great ventilation shafts which still lie forgotten in Brooklyn and Staten Island have an importance transcending these lost options, for they symbolize the end of municipal entrepreneurship. Hylan was only repeating the kind of development leadership that Tweed had exercised in an earlier era in authorizing the Roeblings' Brooklyn Bridge. But Wilgus was not Roebling and Hylan was not Tweed. In the later generation technical expertise and political power could no longer be joined by a simple municipal decision. The reform movement had created in the form of the Port Authority an administrative intervenor, characterized by its supporters as technically competent and politically neutral. But whether too weak, unpersuasive, or unwilling to coerce the railroads into action, it could act only to block the municipal authorities who, in the tunnel instance, at least, sought to realize a project which promised benefits to the entire city. The Port Authority, by virtue of its narrow scope and its bonding requirements, could not take the view of a general government such as a municipal administration. Its regional jurisdiction was geographically greater than that of the City, but its regional scope was bought at the price of a severely limited mandate, although, given the state boundary in the Hudson, it probably could not have been otherwise.

The Regional Plan group, by contrast, was able to take both a regional and a comprehensive view; like a general government, it could consider long-term benefits and broad effects. But the price of this was even higher, for the Regional Plan Committee, a private advisory group, had no power except that of persuasion.

In supporting the Hylan tunnel, the Committee demonstrated that it could pursue its values of regional development and comprehensiveness even when this meant supporting an administration which it found distasteful and alien. Its support was due to the presence of two civic entrepreneurs, Wilgus and Delano, both established, confident hands in the old tradition, possessed of technical competence and the authority that comes from past personal achievement. But it was Adams who represented the emerging administrative tradition. Lacking both the technical confidence, at least in the tunnel matter, and the authority of wealth and position, he was the most reluctant of the three to do battle in the political arena. As planning moved from the hands of the enthusiastic civic entrepreneur to the bureaucratic professional, it also moved away from the centers where the hard decisions were shaped.

THE HUDSON RIVER BRIDGE CONTROVERSY

For waterborne commerce New York's greatest asset had always been its great bays and North River pierheads. But for overland transport, the river was a severe barrier to communication with the rest of the continent. The dream of spanning the river from Manhattan to New Jersey dates from as early as 1810, when a Thomas Pope conceived a 'flying pendant lever arch of timber of 3000 feet span.'[36] In 1868 two companies were incorporated in New Jersey, known, respectively, as the New York and New Jersey Bridge Company and the New Jersey and New York Bridge Company. Little progress was made until 1890, when by act of Congress a charter was granted to the North River Bridge Company authorizing construction of a combined rail, suburban transit, and vehicle-carrying span. The New York State Legislature also granted its authorization at about the same time.

The renewal of activities promoting the Hudson span in the 1890s was due largely to the efforts of the notable bridge designer Gustav Lindenthal (1850–1935), an Austrian engineer who had emigrated to the United States as a young man.

Lindenthal, who was New York City Commissioner of Bridges during the year 1902–1903, was responsible for the supervision of the design and erection of the Queensboro Bridge, begun in 1901, and the Hell Gate Railroad Bridge, begun in 1916. He was generally regarded as the dean of bridge engineers, and his support of the Hudson bridge project gave high promise to its successful accomplishment.

The North River Bridge, as it was first called, was proposed in the 1890s to link 22nd Street in Manhattan to Hoboken, New Jersey. Lindenthal's plans called for a span of some 3200 feet between piers, using an inverted arch rather than the suspension technique that had been used in the Brooklyn Bridge. Railroads which had hitherto terminated at the New Jersey edge of the Hudson would have gained access to Manhattan over fourteen tracks, carrying both freight and passengers. Provision was also made for suburban rapid transit, electric trolleys, roadways for rubber-tired vehicles, and pedestrian and bicycle ways.

The 1890s design for the bridge was architecturally powerful, manifesting that confident energy that characterized the Brooklyn Bridge design of two decades earlier (figure 8.1). Had the 22nd Street Bridge been built, it would

Figure 8.1. Proposed North River (Twenty-Second Street) Bridge, Gustav Lindenthal, Engineer, 1896. (*Source:* Harrison, 1896)

have provided a monumental urban image for New York, comparable, perhaps, to the Eiffel Tower, which had just been completed in Paris.[37]

Even more important than imagery was the effect a Hudson crossing at 22nd Street might have had on the subsequent development of New Jersey and the Region as a whole. The balance of accessibility advantage to Manhattan's downtown would have shifted away from Long Island and Westchester toward the west side of the Hudson. Connections to New Jersey would have been enhanced and the political integration of the metropolitan area more easily achieved.

But the 22nd Street Bridge was not to become a reality. The gestation period required for public acceptance and support of a major facility, if the East River crossings were any model, was of the order of fifteen or twenty years from first proposal to commitment to build. In the case of the Hudson River Bridge, a number of factors intervened during this period to reduce the likelihood of its construction. Tunneling techniques had been greatly improved, and, though tunnels could not offer the same capacity as bridges, the difficulties of fitting the approaches into the existing city were far less severe for tunnels than for bridges. Moreover, several alternative commitments to separate rail, transit, and vehicular tunnels under the Hudson were made during the first decade of the century at various locations south of 33rd Street, somewhat reducing the need for the span.

Several locational factors were also operative at this time. The Manhattan central business district continued its movement uptown, attracted by the new rail terminals at 33rd and 42nd Streets and also by the northward drift of the affluent population. This move, together with the opening of the Queensboro Bridge in 1909 over the East River at 59th Street, prompted the Lindenthal group to propose that the location of the Hudson River Bridge be shifted northward to 57th Street, to provide a direct cross-Manhattan route from New Jersey to Long Island. The higher shores on either side of the river at this point were more favorable for a bridge than for a tunnel, according to Lindenthal. Moreover, the bridge would provide capacity equivalent to ten vehicular tunnels and twelve single track railway tunnels at half the cost.[38]

The proposed 57th Street bridge was structurally identical to the proposed 22nd Street bridge, but was architecturally redesigned to reflect the new aesthetic of Beaux Arts classicism, losing in the process much of the robust strength of the original design (figure 8.2). But sensibilities had changed not only in architectural tastes. Congestion and concentration had reached unacceptable levels, and a reaction had set in to new developments which would concentrate vehicles and people in Manhattan. Merchants on 57th Street had no desire to see their elegant commercial thoroughfare converted into a clogged crosstown arterial. The Fifth Avenue Association, among a number of influential groups, also opposed the bridge at Midtown. This chorus of opposition was joined by the newly created Port of New York Authority in 1921, when Eugenius H. Outerbridge, Chairman of the Port Authority, issued a statement summarizing his agency's opposition.[39] Outerbridge listed ten reasons why the bridge was not included in the Authority's plan for rail-freight facilities. The chief objections centered around the private nature of the undertaking. The Port Authority clearly preferred to avoid competition

Figure 8.2. Proposed North River (Fifty-Seventh Street) Bridge, Gustav Lindenthal, Engineer, 1921. (*Source:* Regional Plan Papers)

Figure 8.3.   Proposed Hudson River Bridge at 178th Street, Cass Gilbert, Architect; O.H. Ammann, Engineer, 1927. (*Source:* Regional Plan Papers)

from outsiders and did not wish to risk a plan based in part on the uncertainties of private promotion. Technical objections were also raised on issues such as problems of providing adequate platform space for passenger terminals and the destruction of a number of sound structures on the riverfront. The possibility of intolerable vehicular congestion at the Manhattan approaches was also raised again.

When proponents of the bridge learned, in May of 1922, of the newly formed Committee on the Regional Plan, they hoped to gain a new and potent ally in their struggle. Little did they realize that the Regional Plan group would eventually become a principal foe of their proposal. Samuel Rea, President of the Pennsylvania Railroad Company, upon receiving the May 10 prospectus on the proposed plan, wrote to Charles Norton urging consideration of the North River Bridge. Rea was one of the sixteen original incorporators of the North River Bridge Company and had been promoting the concept since the 1880s, along with his predecessor at the Pennsylvania Railroad, Alexander J. Cassatt. When it became clear around 1900 that the other railroads were not interested in using the bridge, the Pennsylvania went forward and built its own tunnels and Pennsylvania Station in New York City. The tunnels were nearing capacity use, however, and Rea suggested that the bridge be used for short haul transit and highway traffic to relieve the congestion at Pennsylvania Station.[40]

The controversy over the bridge raged throughout 1922 and 1923. For example, R.S. Buck of the Brooklyn City Railroad Company offered a barrage of reasons for not constructing the bridge, in a letter to E.H. Outer-bridge:

(1)   The bridge as proposed is so unprecedented, colossal and complex, not only as an engineering and construction problem, but primarily as a problem in coordinating or recasting many more or less firmly established and incompatible lines of railroad development, and also as a staggering problem in finance and political economy and far-reaching metropolitan development, that it has apparently been beyond the grasp of mere practical minds.

(2) The bridge with all its collateral problems, seems rather a fantastic futurist picture of the possibilities of transcendent engineering and architectural genius, than a plan based on mathematical, physical, and economic laws.

(3)   The essential element of use for steam railway purposes for both freight and passenger traffic in a bridge at 57th Street seems clearly precluded by insurmountable practical considerations.

(4)   The consensus of opinion among engineers . . . is that the only logical means of entrance into lower Manhattan for steam roads is by tunnel . . .

(5)   . . . when consideration is given to the present, fast incoming traffic congestion for many blocks around Columbus Circle, it is impossible to conceive how 20 new lines of traffic can be poured through this zone on the streets.

(6)   The incoming number of large vessels now docking on the North River water front well up towards 57th Street . . . has naturally given rise to opposition on the part of the shipping interests to a bridge so far down the river with a clearance not capable of at least passing the funnels of the largest vessels.

(7)   Such a main artery in time of war would be most vulnerable from air attack . . . [41]

Buck urged a bridge be built instead at 178th Street and a tunnel between 42nd and 59th.[42]

Shortly thereafter the Port Authority held a hearing to consider arguments for and against the Bridge. D.L. Turner, Consulting Engineer for the New York Transit Commission and later a consultant to the Regional Plan, urged three tunnels: at 57th Street, at 125th Street, and at some point above Dyckman Street in Manhattan. The Central Mercantile Association asked for a vehicular tunnel from 14th Street to Hoboken. The 14th Street Association endorsed this proposal. Robert Moses, then Secretary of the New York State Association, suggested that the Port Authority should construct all facilities, if possible, but if not able to obtain such powers should at least have supervisory and regulatory power. Moses asked for additional facilities but did not specify the type. The U.S. Real Estate Association called for two or three additional vehicular tunnels, including 57th Street and 125th Street. It opposed bridges, which it felt would lower real estate values in the vicinity of their approaches. Other local interests, such as the Harlem Board of Trade, called for tunnels or bridges close to their areas.

Thomas Adams presented a statement on behalf of the Committee on the Plan of New York, which was signed by Frederic Delano and Nelson P. Lewis as well as himself. The statement expressed the Committee's opposition to the bridge, arguing that it would produce intolerable congestion both on the nearby north-south avenues and on the cross-town streets just south of Central Park. The Committee also argued that the 57th Street location would be poorly located on the west side of the Hudson to serve the needs of vehicular traffic originating in New Jersey.

> It is too far north for the traffic of Newark, Elizabeth, the Oranges and contiguous territory immediately tributary to Jersey City and the south end of Manhattan Island, while too far south for the growing region of north Jersey and Rockland and Orange Counties, New York.[43]

The Regional Plan statement also suggested that a single high capacity crossing would result in unnecessary lengthening of hauls both on the Jersey shore and on the Manhattan side, which might be avoided were several separated tunnels to be substituted for the bridge. The report urged that two additional vehicular tunnels be built 'at the most advantageous points between Canal Street and 59th Street,' and that a high-level vehicular bridge be built farther north, 'for example, at Fort Washington (198th Street).'[44]

Lindenthal was not deterred by the arguments of the Committee on the Regional Plan. Hoping to persuade the influential group to adopt his position, he asked for a conference with Adams, Harold Lewis, and Delano, which was held on October 17, 1924. Lindenthal was joined by the prominent architect, Thomas Hastings, and Colonel William W. Wilgus.

Lindenthal explained his plan, pointing out the main features: a main passenger terminal in New Jersey connected by rapid transit with the two main terminals in Manhattan, Grand Central Terminal and Pennsylvania Station. It was Lindenthal's opinion that the greater increase of population would take place in New Jersey and would be served by a new central station with a great freight distributing station in the Hackensack Meadows. He claimed that his scheme would drain traffic away from the city rather than increase centralization.

When Adams proposed that the bridge be limited to rail and transit traffic, excluding vehicles, Lindenthal objected on the grounds that the bridge could not pay for itself without revenues from vehicular tolls.[45]

After the meeting Adams indicated that, while he had serious doubts about certain features of the bridge, he could not rule it out as a possibility. He suggested that a bridge limited to rail and rapid transit might be feasible. Adams was intrigued with Lindenthal's idea for a great terminal in New Jersey which would bring together the existing scattered trunk and commuter rail lines that terminated at the Hudson. Adams added, however, that Lindenthal's point that commuting traffic was unprofitable to the railroads was a further argument for decentralization.[46] The question of whether to emphasize in the Plan improved rail accessibility to Manhattan or the decentralization of housing remained to be resolved.

Opposition to the 57th Street Bridge on the part of the Committee on the Regional Plan, the Port Authority, and influential merchant and shipping groups kept the proposal dormant for several years. But in 1927, a new effort was made to gain acceptance for the idea. Powerful support came from the Baltimore and Ohio Railroad, which had long sought direct rail access to the city, and from Samuel Rea, former president of the Pennsylvania Railroad. Considerable support was also evidenced by business groups in New Jersey. The North River Bridge Company achieved something of a victory when the New York City Board of Estimate approved the plans for the bridge, subject, however, to the condition that the center line ship clearance be raised from 155 to 175 feet and that any possible traffic problems be resolved before a final franchise could be granted.

The War Department, whose approval was required by law because of possible obstruction to navigation, held a hearing in New York on September 9, at which Lindenthal presented his case. Maritime interests spoke in opposition. The Port Authority 'withheld definite opinion, but called attention to the need of leaving navigation free from interference and preventing congestion in the harbor.'[47] Thomas Adams transmitted to the hearing the original Regional Plan statement of 1923 and recommended that several tunnels rather than a single bridge be built.[48]

By September of 1929 Lindenthal had regained sufficient momentum to persuade the chief engineers of the Lehigh Valley, the Delaware and Lackawanna, the Erie, and the Baltimore and Ohio Railroads to attend a series of meetings. Representatives of the Port Authority were invited. Harold Lewis attended for the Regional Plan group.

Lindenthal revealed at the meeting that he had revised his thinking about the principal traffic that the bridge should serve. Buttressed by the support of the Baltimore and Ohio, and tacitly acquiescing in the arguments against massive rubber-tired traffic pouring into Manhattan, he proposed a bridge to serve rapid transit and rail passenger and freight traffic. The revised scheme called for four tracks for suburban rail transit, four for long-distance passenger trains, and two for freight. Provision for the later addition of surfaced lanes for vehicular traffic would be made, but the primary purpose of the bridge would initially be for rail traffic.[49]

But by September of 1929 the interested groups had strong commitments to projects which were not altogether compatible with the Lindenthal bridge. The 178th Street Bridge (George Washington Bridge) had been approved and was under construction by the Port of New York Authority (figure 8.3). The Port Authority had also made a commitment to a vehicular tunnel at 38th Street, the Lincoln Tunnel. The Graphic Regional Plan had been completed and published, calling for several tunnels south of 59th Street and recommending 178th Street as the best site for a bridge connection. A rail tunnel at 57th Street had been included in the Graphic Plan as a link in both the proposed suburban rapid transit system and the trunk line railroad system. The 57th Street crossing was planned to continue beyond Manhattan so as to connect with a five-borough system of new passenger terminals instead of a single large new terminal in Manhattan. It was also to connect to a loop through Manhattan to another tunnel located near the Battery. An important element in the Graphic Plan concept of decentralization was a proposal for a trunk line bypass route around the congested areas necessitating the placing of part of the required new trackage at a site considerably north of 57th Street. The Plan showed this trackage as traversing the lower deck of the 178th Street Bridge. The Port Authority had given its informal, if reluctant, approval to this concept and had designed the bridge to accommodate a lower deck for rail and transit traffic.[50]

Frederic Delano, who was strongly opposed to the 57th Street Bridge, was not, however, opposed to a bridge farther north in Manhattan, even though such a structure was not part of the Graphic Regional Plan. In a draft of a letter to Francis Lee Stuart, Lindenthal's assistant engineer, he suggested that the proponents of the bridge consider a site at 130th Street. Delano believed that the Manhattan central business district would continue its two-century drift northward by leaping over Central Park to the area between 110th and 125th Streets. With the construction of the Tri-borough Bridge at 125th Street, Delano felt that the business center would elect to settle at this future center of population of the four main boroughs of the City. In addition, this movement could serve another purpose: 'the Negro settlement just north of the Park between 110th and 125th Streets ought to be cleaned out and give way to a better development.'[51]

Harold Lewis expressed to Delano his reluctance to endorse the 130th Street idea, which he felt would create crossing problems through upper Manhattan. Delano, nevertheless, conveyed his thoughts to the North River Bridge Company.[52]

The controversy boiled through the Depression days of 1930 without resolution. Then word was passed that Hoover's Secretary of War, Patrick J. Hurley, would rule by April 1, 1931, on the requested approval of the bridge upon receipt of a report by the Army Chief of Engineers, Major General Lytle Brown.[53]

Delano asked Lewis to prepare a statement in opposition for his transmittal to Hurley. The statement repeated the 1923 Regional Plan arguments against a facility that would congest mid-town Manhattan and destroy property values near its approaches. The statement somewhat unfairly concentrated on the vehicular problems associated with the bridge, disregarding Lindenthal's revised emphasis on rail connections. It also urged that decentralizing rail by-pass connections were necessary before a centralized crossing was desirable. The statement achieved its purpose. Hurley delayed his decision pending further investigations.

With the rising unemployment of the early Depression years, the Hoover administration looked favorably on the prospect of the construction jobs that the 57th Street bridge would provide. In May of 1932 the papers reported that Secretary Hurley finally appeared ready to make a judgement, one which would be favorable.[54] However, Hurley was again persuaded to delay his ruling. He finally called a conference for December 14, 1932, with representatives of the Port Authority and the Regional Plan group. Delano presented a statement for the Regional Plan which he had prepared. Once again he put forward his view of a business center at 125th Street, with a bridge between 125th and 135th Streets:

> Fifty years ago the business center of the city was below Fourteenth Street, or Union Square. Today that business center is approximately Twenty-second Street. On account of the immense area of Central Park, when the business center has crowded up to Fifty-ninth Street, the next jump will be north to 110th Street. With the building of the Tri-borough Bridge at 125th Street, and the construction as may be expected of civic buildings at or near that point, it is likely that within the memory of men now living, 110th to 125th Street will represent the approximate center of the density of population and of business of Manhattan Island. It is not unlikely that this will come within a period of fifty years.
>
> It is not conceivable that the railroads would want or that financiers would finance the construction of a bridge at Fifty-seventh Street at this time nor in the near future. However, there is an argument for a bridge connection which will connect the trunk lines arriving from the West and South on the Jersey shore with the trunk lines radiating from Greater New York to the North, Northeast, and East. A bridge to effect this connection directly would be located not at Fifty-seventh Street, but at some convenient location between 125th and 135th Street.[55]

This was an extraordinary statement for the former chairman of the Committee on the Regional Plan to make. It completely ignored the rail proposals of the Plan and proposed instead Delano's own conceptions. It was, moreover, inconsistent in its basic arguments. If the problem was basically one of congesting the central business area, and that area was destined to move northward to 125th Street, then a bridge at 57th Street would have been decentralized with respect to the new centre. Similarly, a bridge at 125th Street could only congest the anticipated new center. Delano's argument was not only based on an improbable shift of the center, but was internally inconsistent and contrary to the notion of decentralization on which the Plan had been based.

When the administration of Franklin Delano Roosevelt took office in 1933, it inherited the 57th Street Bridge controversy. Lindenthal had conferred with Hoover in January of 1933, hoping to persuade the lame-duck engineer-President to endorse his request for $88 million in Reconstruction Finance Corporation loans to begin construction, but Hoover did not act on the request, and the issue was left to the incoming administration.[56] With Frederic Delano's nephew in the White House, Lindenthal's prospects were considerably dimmed. Roosevelt, like Hoover before him, was well acquainted with the work of the Russell Sage planners.

On November 16, 1933, Secretary of War George Dern announced the War Department's decision on the bridge company's application. It was rejected. Secretary Dern, in his statement to the company, noted the problems of obstruction to navigation, problems which were exaggerated by the opponents of the bridge since few piers were located north of 57th Street and the clearance under the proposed bridge at midstream was adequate to permit passage of all but the very largest transatlantic liners. The navigational problem was not, however, the major reason cited for rejection of the proposal. Rather, Dern emphasized the opposition of the Port Authority, which had been granted a loan of $37,500,000 by the Public Works Administration on August 29th to begin construction of a vehicular tunnel at 38th Street. The War Department accepted the Port Authority's contention that the 57th Street Bridge would compete with and threaten its own investment and that of the Federal Government in the proposed 38th Street tunnel and in the George Washington Bridge. Again, Lindenthal's emphasis on rail and transit use of his bridge was ignored.

The War Department's decision set two important precedents. It confirmed the Port Authority's claim to be the sole agency responsible for trans-Hudson crossings. And it greatly expanded the War Department's review power over river crossings, which formerly had been limited to questions of navigational obstruction. The War Department, through administrative decisions, extended its criteria to take account of local opposition and to protect decisions made by other federal agencies.

Proponents of the bridge attacked this administrative extension of executive review power as exceeding the authority Congress had delegated to the War Department. In an attempt to bypass the War Department, supporters of the bridge proposed that Congress establish an independent commission consisting of five 'disinterested expert engineers to be appointed by the President, one from the Army Corps of Engineers, one from the Navy, one from the Interstate Commerce Commission, and two from civil life.' Senator Royal S. Copeland of New York introduced the bill in the Senate and Representative Edward Kenney of Bergen County in the House.[57] The bill, which was supported by the Interstate Commerce Commission but opposed by the War and Navy Departments, was referred to the Senate Commerce Committee for hearings, which were held in June of 1934. The bill as written would have had the effect of forcing a decision in favor of the bridge, since it merely required the five-man commission to set an acceptable clearance height, not to judge the overall merits of the bridge. The bill would also have extended the life of the company's charter, due to expire in 1937, by five years, and, in the House version, would have enabled the commission to purchase the bridge company if it deemed it desirable to do so. The hearings on the bill brought out the usual parade of proponents and opponents. Lindenthal, now eighty-three, made his case and was supported by Representative Kenney. The opponents, led by the Port Authority, included representatives of the New York City administration, and the Fifth Avenue Association.[58] The Regional Plan Association was represented by Harold Lewis; interestingly, the Port Authority paid his expenses to Washington.[59]

The staffs of the Port Authority and of the Regional Plan Association worked closely in the subsequent months in their efforts to defeat the bridge. Delano, based in Washington, added his weight to the battle.

On June 6th the Senate Commerce Committee reported out the bill favorably. No action was taken by the House, however, and the bill remained bottled up until the next session.[60]

When Gustav Lindenthal died on July 31, 1935, the matter was still unresolved in Congress. His successor, F.H. Frankland, sought to gain the approval of the Regional Plan Association and to mute the Port Authority's fears of competition by proposing a change in the bridge design so that it provided facilities solely for rail, rapid transit, and pedestrians, with a major terminal and redevelopment project at 42nd Street between 9th and 10th Avenues. In a resubmission of the bills proposing the five-man federal commission, Kenney inserted a prohibition against providing any facilities for vehicles.[61]

Congressional opponents of the bridge responded with bills to repeal the charter of the bridge company, which in any event was due to expire at the end of 1937.

The prospect of vastly improved rapid transit resulted in a number of inquiries to the Regional Plan Association from citizens' groups and planning boards. Why did the Regional Plan group oppose a rapid rail crossing at 57th Street, when a rail tunnel crossing at that point was part of the Regional Plan? The vehicular congestion problem on local streets was eliminated with the conversion of the bridge to solely a rail facility. The navigation problem was finally deemed inconsequential, as nearly all the transatlantic lines indicated that they had no objection to the location of bridge piers or clearance heights. The objections of the Regional Plan group revolved on the issue of tunnels versus a bridge and on the abstract issue of concentration. Tunnels equivalent in capacity to the bridge would have been more expensive than the bridge. The Regional Plan staff, however, did not see demands for capacity to the west side of Manhattan requiring the six tracks for rail and four for transit that were included in the final proposal. Nor did they wish to see a new point of major accessibility established there. Dencentralization had become a dominant goal, and any proposal that seemed to concentrate urban activities was inconsistent with this fundamental principle of the plan.

In 1937 the charter of the North River Bridge Company expired and with it, though the Regional Plan Association could not appreciate this at the time, the principal opportunity to link metropolitan New Jersey with New York City in an effective rapid transit and commuter rail system. For all of their rhetorical espousal of rail transportation in their Plan, the Regional Plan group in their actions had inadvertently become a major factor in forcing the Region onto rubber tires.

The Hudson River Bridge controversy revealed the extent to which development controls had become institutionalized in the 1920s. The free-wheeling, innovative private entrepreneurial modalities inherited from the nineteenth century were subordinated to a public entrepreneurship, ostensibly more responsive and more responsible to the public weal. The era of the Roeblings and the Lindenthals was past. Engineering and promotional geniuses could no longer work directly through the political process simultaneously to articulate and to satisfy a latent societal demand, through incremental, though gigantic, additions to the urban armature. Bridges, tunnels, and other large urban projects, henceforward, were to be developed as part of comprehensive, rationalized systems. A bridge could no longer be viewed as simply connecting two points. It was seen as a crucial element in a larger system, and its location held consequences which ramified through the system.

The positive thrust toward increased rationality was not without its negative consequences, however. One such consequence was the loss of private entrepreneurial leadership in the creation of much-needed public capital improvements. It was by no means certain that the public entrepreneurs, such as the Port Authority, would be quite so willing to undertake innovative projects involving large risks as well as large payoffs as the capitalist innovators they supplanted. On the other hand, it was assumed that identification of societal needs and activity to meet those needs would no longer have to wait on the random appearance of a capable entrepreneur. An on-going review and development process would reduce the uncertainties of public sector responses.

Other potentially negative consequences arose from the very thrust toward increased rationality which motivated the creation of public and quasi-public regional institutions. The effective creation and operation of systems requires (1) a knowledge of the inter-relationships among system components, (2) a knowledge of the consequences of changes in system components both on other components of the system and on the system environments, (3) an ability to control all elements in the system, and (4) an ability to predict crucial changes in the environment.

Applying these criteria of rationality to the problem of the Hudson River Bridge leaves us with little confidence in the achievement of a higher rationality by the regional planners of the 1920s. They had limited capability in measuring the inter-relationships between rail and highway transportation. Nor were they equipped to measure the relationship between the provision of transportation accessibility and land development patterns.

Obviously, neither the Port Authority nor the Regional Plan group possessed the capability of controlling all elements in their systems. The Port Authority proved totally impotent in trying to control the railroads and only partly capable of controlling highway development. Even more important, the Regional Plan staff was completely without power to effect its proposals. Thus, it consistently lobbied against politically achievable but inferior schemes in hopes of achieving superior schemes which it was powerless to carry out. In the case of the Hudson River Bridge, the Regional Plan group would have gone far toward realizing its objectives had it embraced the final proposals of the bridge proponents. Instead, the Regional Plan Committee elected to pursue an alternative scheme only reluctantly endorsed by the Port Authority (a lower deck rail crossing on the George Washington Bridge and an even more remote transit crossing on 57th Street). Was it unreasonable for the Regional Plan Association people to assume that they would not be able to influence the Port Authority, in whom they had made a considerable political investment by allying themselves with the Port Authority on the bridge controversy? Wilgus and Lewis had, after all, convinced the Port Authority that they should provide for a lower deck for rail transit on the George Washington Bridge. And there was no reason to believe that the Port Authority had thought then of using that capacity for vehicular traffic rather than for transit. The problem lay in the inability of the Regional Plan Association group to predict the future environment with which they would have to cope. Had World War II not intervened, the drive for transit for North Jersey might have succeeded. But by the post-war period, the movement had lost its momentum. The Regional Plan staff could hardly have predicted the interlude of depression and war, though these profoundly affected the outcome of their proposals.

Had they elected to support the rail and transit bridge, a second-best solution, rather than holding out for Port Authority transit tunnels, they would perhaps have gone much farther in realizing their primary aims. The 57th Street bridge would have shifted population growth westward, as the Regional Plan had predicted, and away from Long Island. Improved rail service from New Jersey to Manhattan would have engendered more concentrated settlements oriented to rail stations, instead of the amorphous post-war pattern that emerged. The Regional Plan group disliked the terminal proposals of the North River Bridge Company because they did not mesh precisely with their architectural studies for the West Side. Yet nothing would have stimulated the development of an extension of the Manhattan central business district towards the west more than a third major rail terminal in this vicinity.

It is perhaps too easy to look back critically with the benefit of hindsight.

But it is an unavoidable conclusion that far more of the Regional Plan's objectives would have been achieved had they not been co-opted into supporting the Port Authority's efforts to protect its position.

ROBERT MOSES AND THE PARKWAY CONFLICTS

In the early 1920s, while the Regional Plan was under development, Robert Moses burst upon the New York development scene. It was inevitable that the paths of Moses and the Russell Sage planners would intersect. But few would have predicted at the time how stormy the relationship would be. In many ways the roots of Moses' career lay in the same patrician reform movement out of which the Regional Plan had sprung. A graduate of Yale and Oxford, Moses had written his doctoral dissertation on the civil service of Great Britain. But Moses was also keenly aware of the new sources of power emerging in the urban middle class, which his sponsor and friend, Alfred E. Smith, had mobilized in a successful quest for the governorship of New York.

Moses was willing to work with the wealthy philanthropic reformers backing the Regional Plan so long as they were helpful allies in his efforts. But he was deeply suspicious of the veracity of their rhetoric when their own personal interests came to be at stake. The Regional Plan Committee and staff, for their part, were eager to work through Moses, who commanded the resources to realize plans, while they could only propose and advise.

The first encounter between Moses and the Regional Plan Group began in 1922 over a parkway proposed to run from the Queensborough Bridge to Sagamore Hill, home and grave of Theodore Roosevelt at Oyster Bay. The Roosevelt Memorial Parkway project had been discussed ever since the former President's death in 1919, to cope with the crowds of motorists who were expected to make pilgrimages and pleasure trips to Sagamore. In 1922, the New York State Association, a prestigious citizens' group, endorsed the idea in its plan for State Parks and proposed that the route follow existing avenues and roads through Queens and Nassau. Nelson Lewis thought the route unsatisfactory and proposed to Frederick Keppel that the Regional Plan consider a new parkway through the Wheatley Hills, south of the New York State Association's proposed route. He argued that in the location he proposed the grades would be gentler, and that by going further south it would be possible to link up with the Grand Central Parkway, then under acquisition. Keppel forwarded the plan to Robert Moses, then Secretary of the New York State Association. Moses' reply was critical of the proposal, but noted that the issue of the choice of a right of way would have to await the hoped-for passage of the 1924 park bond issue.[62]

At about the same time, Dr. Charles P. Davenport, Director of the Carnegie Institute Cold Spring Harbor Station for Experimental Evolution, wrote to the

Russell Sage Foundation pleading for the preservation of the objects of special historical and scenic interest of Long Island, and specifically as part of the Roosevelt Parkway scheme, for protection of Cold Spring Harbor and a portion of the unique Hempstead Plains, a flat, tree-less area, parts of which 'appear never to have been plowed' and which 'reveal a flora the like of which is not found anywhere else in the United States.' Cold Spring Harbor Valley also was worthy of preservation, according to Dr. Davenport:

> . . . it represents a nearly straight valley about eight miles long of which two miles are occupied by a stream and series of lakes depressed nearly two hundred feet above the surrounding plateau . . .
> On the plateau are the homes of the late Colonel Roosevelt and the summer estates of New Yorkers of considerable means.[63]

Davenport also asked that measures be taken to protect the Harbor and its shores from an invasion of the 'cheapest sort of bath houses and so-called bungalows.' But he was most concerned about the beach at Cold Spring Harbor, for which his laboratory workers had located on maps the position of every significant plant as part of their ecological studies. Davenport pleaded for the preservation of this valley for all time as a sanctuary or public reservation. He added, 'Mr. Robert W. DeForest has his home on one side of Cold Spring Harbor opposite the barren beach and I believe he would approve this suggestion.'[64] DeForest, of course, was the President of the Russell Sage Foundation and a member of the Committee on the Regional Plan. His brother, Henry W. DeForest, who owned additional property around the harbor, agreed that the harbor should be preserved and indicated his willingness to turn over the larger part of his holdings to the state as a sanctuary 'under reasonable and appropriate restrictions as to use and occupation'.[65]

Davenport's plea to save Cold Spring Harbor was motivated by a desire to preserve 'some of the natural beauties of this country for all the people who are in a position to use it properly.'[66]

Cold Spring Harbor was undoubtedly a desirable feature to be preserved, but for whom and from whom? Mixed with the high environmental ideals was more than a trace of class interest. Did not the houses of the wealthy infringe on the estuarine ecology, even if their low densities rendered them less conspicuous than the 'so-called bungalows?' And if the wealthy sought waterside sites, why should those who could afford only bungalows not be permitted the same privilege? The result was an unavoidable merger of the worthy aims of the environmentalists and of protective privileges for the well-to-do. No proposal or proposition emanating from the philanthropic planning group, no matter how worthy or innocent, could escape the taint of ulterior motivation.

The Roosevelt Memorial Parkway and related matters remained quiet in the first months of 1924. Meanwhile, Moses had been appointed by Governor Smith as President of the Long Island State Park Commission and also chairman of the new State Council of Parks. The Roosevelt Parkway idea was not a high-priority project for Moses. He was most concerned with building his popular support in order to increase the funds available for later park and parkway development. To do this he needed a dramatic, quick, but inexpensive project. The shore near Montauk Point at the easternmost tip of Long Island looked very attractive to Moses, particularly since the Florida real estate promoter, Carl Fisher, was interested in acquiring it for a large resort hotel. As with Cold Spring Harbor, it happened that part of the Montauk shoreland that appeared most appropriate for beach and park development was in the hands of an advisory member of the Committee on the Regional Plan, Frederic B. Pratt, of the prominent Brooklyn family. Pratt was asked by Flavel Shurtleff, director of Public Relations for the Regional Plan, whether he would endorse the proposal as an owner with a close association with the Regional Plan group. Shurtleff, who sought the best possible relationship with Moses, was obviously aware that Moses would interpret anything but cooperation from the Regional Plan as protection of self-interest. Pratt declined, however, on the grounds that the Plan had not been completed and therefore it would be premature to endorse a specific site for park development.[67]

According to Shurtleff, Moses, when informed, reacted strongly to Pratt's position:

> The last chapter in this incident happened the morning when I saw Mr. Moses and told him Mr. Pratt's attitude . . . He has been rather pugnacious, has taken the stand that since Mr. Pratt was a member of the Regional Plan Committee he ought to be very helpful in pushing the program of the State Park Commission. Moses has gone so far as to say that if Mr. Pratt and Mr. DeForest, who is also an owner of land in the same general locality, weren't helpful they were saying things in public and doing inconsistent things in private, and that he [Moses] proposed to show up this inconsistency.[68]

'We haven't got to the end of this incident,' Shurtleff added. Indeed, they had not.

The matter was of sufficient importance for Frederic Delano to be asked to intercede. Writing to Moses, he suggested that Long Island was destined to be a playground for New York City, with fine homes, expensive resorts, and golf clubs, and with more modest resorts for the less affluent. Delano urged Moses to consider as an alternative the park potential of the large federal Camp Upton tract at Yaphank, a brushy, flat, and rather uninteresting site in the center of the Island.[69]

Moses caustically rejected Camp Upton as an unattractive site and one not likely to be given up by the federal government. Montauk was far preferable for park development, he concluded:

> We had hoped to obtain some of this [Montauk] area with the assistance of the people who have advocated large regional plans for the future. We have thought

that we would be doubly sure of obtaining their assistance where they happen themselves to be land owners.

If these assumptions are incorrect, we shall go ahead anyway . . . We do not propose to let this entire area get away from us. We do not have much in the way of funds at the present time, but I think we have enough funds and enough nerve and responsibility to see to it that the public is not entirely excluded by a selfish interest . . . It seems to us that this whole question presents a splendid opportunity for your committee to be of real lasting service to the state and to put yourselves in a position where public authorities will be under obligation to you . . . Neither the Suffolk County residents nor the general public will care much for the promise that we may get Yaphank some day as a substitute for taking action at Montauk now.[70]

Moses added a blast at the technical competence of the Plan staff. Referring to a visit he had made earlier to the Regional Plan offices for information on Staten Island he found that their maps

proved to be so vague and impractical that I could get nothing of value out of them. The trouble seemed to be that areas had been put on these maps simply on the basis of a topographical survey by an outsider who had no idea of any of the practical problems involved in obtaining land for public park purposes.

. . . if the Regional Plan Committee is going to be helpful and influential in the long run, it must face practical problems in the same way the public officials are bound to face them in order to obtain results.[71]

Writing to Henry James shortly after receiving the Moses blast, Delano agreed that there was little excuse for vague and impractical maps. But he disagreed about the Camp Upton site, which he felt could be forested and made attractive over fifteen or twenty years. His distinction between Moses' motives and those of Regional Plan are illuminating:

Moses wants to get early results and to that extent is an 'opportunist.' We are planning here more for the future than he. To us the securing of comparatively valueless land by gift or small expenses for future needs is of prime importance. People who can visualize immediate necessities are common, those who are wise enough to plan intelligently for the future are rare![72]

By July, Moses had acquired through condemnation about a fourth of the land he wanted at Montauk, 1800 acres, mostly from the Benson estate. Shortly thereafter, Henry James, a prominent lawyer who had volunteered to work with the Regional Plan staff, met with Moses to discuss the Montauk development and came away feeling rather resentful:

I don't feel much confidence in Moses; certainly none in his candor. He is picking up a number of bits of land which have a certain strategic value, but his proceedings suggest a desire to obtain newspaper notoriety as a commissioner who is forestalling the iniquitous schemes of the rich monopolizers.[73]

James added an ominous comment concerning Moses' attitude toward the Regional Plan Committee:

Moses seems for some unknown reason to want to give the public the impression that this Committee is failing to cooperate with him or is actually opposing him. A newspaper reporter has just been in who tells me that Moses named you and Mr. Pratt as members of this Committee who own Montauk land and are obstructing his plan.[74]

Despite the cooling of relations, when Moses invited a group of park officials and representatives of citizens' groups to inspect Montauk two months later, he asked Henry James to represent the Regional Plan Committee. After the inspections, James reported that Moses seemed not to have any particular use or development in mind for the 8,000 acres he sought at the tip of the Island. James assessed the purpose of Moses' drive to acquire Montauk as purely political:

> He expects to please Governor Smith and the newspaper public saying that he has made it certain that Montauk Point will not be monopolized by a rich man's development but will remain accessible to the poor. I don't understand that he has any money with which to build highways nor . . . did he indicate that he had any clear idea of how state land at Montauk would be made convenient for the public's use.[75]

James added, however, that he felt he had improved relations with Moses. 'For the present . . . our relations with him are very pleasant.'

With at least part of Montauk in Moses' domain, James became greatly concerned for the special ecological features of the area, which he felt Moses would destroy. He wrote to Olmsted of his doubts on August 11, 1924:

> . . . I suspect that the chairman of the Commission [Moses], is not very imaginative about this kind of opportunity. I recently spent a day with him at Montauk and he seemed to me to think chiefly in terms of autombobile picnicers [sic], large crowds of poor people, and facilities for recreation on a large popular scale. I suspect him of having a watchful eye for what the voting public will readily understand and quickly applaud. For instance, Dr. Higgins and I led him to one of the potholes east of the Inn, showing him what a curious and interesting botanical island it was, and he commented that it would be a great thing if it could be drained so that people could walk about it everywhere without getting wet feet.[76]

James proposed that Olmsted contact naturalists from the American Museum of Natural History and the Brooklyn Botanical Garden to unite on a recommendation to Moses for proper development of the Park. He repeated his proposal in another letter to Olmsted a few months later:

> . . . Adams gives me an account of a day he spent with Moses touring Long Island which includes a diatribe by Moses against the whole tribe of your profession toward whom he seems to harbor sentiments and opinions most regrettable and uncomplimentary. This diatribe was evoked by Adams' mild suggestion that some landscape problems with which Moses was dealing were worthy the attention of somebody such as yourself, or one of two or three other landscape architects whom he named.[77]

Norman Thomas, Director of the Brooklyn Botanical Garden, soon after

joined the battle to convince Moses to protect the vegetation from distur-
bance. The ecology-minded planners might have had little to fear from
Moses, who had grand plans for securing for the public 8,000 acres of
Montauk, all of Gardiner's Island, and a large part of Orient Point, more than
enough to preserve large areas in a relatively wild state.[78] But these plans
were thwarted by the purchase of nine thousand acres of the Montauk tip by
Carl G. Fisher, a Miami developer who hoped to duplicate his Florida
successes on Long Island. This was to be a gentlemen's resort and subdivision on a fabulous scale, with a channel and harbor for the yachts of the
wealthy, polo fields, and a grand hotel. Fisher anticipated an ultimate population of 100,000 affluent people in his development.[79]

Fisher's resort city plan was a metamorphosed fulfilment of Daniel Burnham's 1911 proposal for a great harbor development at Montauk, made to the
Brooklyn Committee on City Plan, a number of whose supporters were now
connected with the Regional Plan. Henry James was hopeful that Fisher
would develop the Point in a way that would preserve its natural features. The
Regional Plan group seemed to have more confidence in what the businessman, Fisher, would do than in what the public servant, Moses, intended.[80]
Fisher's resort city, of course, never materialized. Montauk's climate and the
stock market crash of 1929 undid all chances for what was probably an
unworkable scheme anyway.

The Fisher project temporarily blocked Moses from fully realizing his plan
for Montauk, but it did not deter him from proceeding with an integral feature
of his grand scheme for Long Island Park development: a parkway to run the
length of the Island to make his string of green beads more accessible to the
growing motoring public of New York City. This parkway conception,
eventually to be realized as the Northern State Parkway, was in fact a revised
version of the Roosevelt Memorial Parkway idea, routed, however, farther
south and envisioned as extending the entire length of Long Island. Ignoring
earlier proposals of his own New York State Association and those of Nelson
Lewis, Moses and his engineers selected a right-of-way through the Wheatley
Hills estate country, where DeForest had large holdings of land. The effect
was to rekindle the simmering controversy between the Regional Plan group
and Moses. The Regional Plan Committee vigorously opposed the Parkway's
alignment through the estates, publicly on grounds of aesthetic preservation,
though it is possible that DeForest was also interested in protecting his land
and the well-being of his fellow Long Island gentry. DeForest asked Adams
to go ahead on special studies of Long Island:

> Find out what Moses's plans are in order that the Committee's planning and
> studies may take due account of them. Do whatever would be in order for the
> Committee's own purposes and I will see what I can do in the way of getting up
> a citizen's invitation to you.[81]

'Citizen's invitation' referred to a proposed Long Island Regional Planning

Committee which would be established to bring rational planning to the Island and presumably to exert some control over Moses.

Edward Bassett, the Committee's counsel, was asked to look into the legislation creating the Park Commission to determine whether it possessed authority to build the parkway. Bassett opined that it did not have such powers, reasoning that taking land for a parkway without providing rights of access to adjacent owners would amount to a taking of property rights which would cost the state dearly in awards. Bassett, who had some influence in Albany, promised to bring this point to the attention of the Park Commission and also Governor Smith if Moses proceeded with his scheme.[82]

Bassett's argument was largely one of definition. The prevailing concept of a parkway was that which the elder Olmsted had devised in the era of horse carriages. Moses realized that the motoring middle class wanted to get to the beach or the lake through pleasant surroundings, but swiftly. But Bassett and the planners regarded such a road as a speedway or boulevard, not a parkway. Adams was inclined to accept the idea of a speedway for Long Island to serve as a spine though the center of the Island around which development could concentrate. In fact, such a road, the Long Island Motor Parkway, was already in existence. This was a thirty-five-mile private toll-road built principally for auto racing by the wealthy, but open to all for casual trips. Adams thought that Moses should take over and widen this more southerly route for a speedway which could then accommodate commercial vehicles as well as automobiles. He also supported Olmsted's plan for a supplementary parkway to be created out of existing roads through widening and landscaping changes. Adams was strongly opposed to Moses' alternative, a 'motor parkway' through the 'Gold-Coast' country of the North Shore, believing that the magnificient, well-landscaped estates were socially valuable and therefore worthy of protection.[83] Recalling his native Britain, he felt that many of these estates would eventually fall into the hands of the public or of institutions. Only in this indirect way was Adams concerned about the special privileges of the affluent over the motoring needs of the future middle-class park clientele.

Whatever his views, Adams was unfortunately and unknowingly drawn into the battle by the architect Thomas Hastings, who was a resident of the affected area and also a member of the Regional Plan architects' advisory committee. Hastings organized the local opposition to Moses, letting it be understood that Adams and the Regional Plan staff had been employed to draw up an alternative plan. This was not the case, but Moses, unaware of the truth, was enraged and attacked Adams in a vitriolic letter to Robert DeForest:

> You will doubtless agree with me it will be well if we all have a perfectly clear understanding at this time as to the relations which the [Russell Sage] Foundation wishes to have to the various official agencies working on programs

of this kind. We are very glad to have you submit any plans you may have to the Long Island State Park Commission. This, however, is a very different thing from cooperating with an organization which is aiming at the same time to offer assistance to a group of private individuals whose avowed purpose is to block the plan of this Commission with every weapon and facility at their command . . .

I need not point out to you how essential it is to the success of your work that the general public shall at no time be in doubt that you are on their side and that you are not working for any private or selfish interest or working to defeat the honest purpose of public officials. It is difficult enough for any foundation such as the Sage Foundation to avoid the hostility of uninformed or self-satisfied public officials, and it is even more difficult to overcome certain altogether natural, if unjustifiable prejudices on the part of the common run of people in New York City . . .

You are yourself a large landowner in the very section of the Northern Shore through which we are going and I know you would not want an impression created anywhere that the Sage Foundation is doing anything to influence the location of this parkway in one way or the other . . . Mr. Adams has not acted with complete candor in respect to the matter. At the very least, he has failed to inform us as to his relationship with Mr. Hastings . . . [84]

Adams countered with a point-by-point rebuttal to Moses' charges, stating that he had shown every desire to cooperate with Moses, which had indeed been the case, and that it was Moses who had lacked candor for refusing to reveal his plans. Adams had suffered an early version of the typical Moses blitz, an attack intended to wither opposition before it could gain any momentum. Moses was aware that his wealthy opponents would seize on any support at hand which could be credited as neutral and authoritative. There is no evidence, however, that the affluent members of the Russell Sage Committee had to convince Adams and the staff of the superiority of their alternative over that proposed by Moses. Indeed, their proposal antedated that of Moses. It was perfectly natural for these staff planners to assume that the fine North Shore estates, some owned by their employers and some designed by their colleagues as architects and landscape architects, should, as a matter of sound planning, be protected from the deleterious effects of a highway. These effects were of two kinds the immediate nuisance of traffic, and, more important to the planners, the change in character that would ensue from a change in accessibility.

Adams was strongly supported in his rebuttal to Moses by Delano. But Delano counseled Adams to make every effort to get along with Moses:

I am in receipt of your letter to Mr. Moses, which I entirely approve.

While I never believe in compromising on essentials, nor in dealing with a man who has proved himself dishonest, I am a strong believer in trying to get along with people, however disagreeable they may be, if they are endeavoring to do the right thing, even though one may seriously object to their methods. It has often been said that more flies are caught with molasses than with vinegar, but I have found that vinegar sweetened with sugar is even better. [85]

In mid-1925, James proposed a response to Moses in the form of a series of position papers on Long Island. Together with Olmsted's earlier work, these papers provided the basis on which Adams formulated a plan for the development of Nassau County.[86] The purpose of the plan and accompanying memoranda was to begin to build a constituency for planning and the broad view as a test for similar activities in the rest of the Region. James outlined his ideas to a receptive DeForest:

The purpose [of the publication] would be a combination of the following:

(a) To begin to inoculate the public with some of our ideas.

(b) To begin with the point over which the public is at the moment considerably interested and exercised.

(c) To learn something by this effort – which would undoubtedly produce some results that would be valuable to us, even if only in the form of disappointments.

(d) To inject ourselves into the Long Island discussion not as partisans, of the Park Commission or of anybody politically opposed to the Park Commission, but as what we are – an advisory body with a large point of view and a great deal of special knowledge and expert opinion that can be focused on particular phases of the question.

(e) To feel our way along toward the completion of the Long Island sector of our plan, using this sort of procedure as one means of putting our ideas to the test of discussion.[87]

Adams' plan indicated areas which he felt were suited for 'open' development and 'close' development, the open development confined largely to the North Shore estate country. In defense of this proposal, he wrote:

It would be difficult to put the land in the northern part of the county to any better than its present use, having regard to the character of the land, its degree of accessibility by any system of improved highways, the limitations of water supply and above all the general welfare of the inhabitants of Long Island.
Every great urban region must have provision for the kind of private estates that exist in Nassau County not primarily in the selfish interests of those who live upon them but in order to preserve a degree of open development and a character of pleasant environment that is economically prohibitive by any other means. No great city can afford to buy all the open land it needs as lung space, and therefore must have areas in its environs which have the openness of parks even though privately owned . . . Hence, the necessity to develop a system of highways which, without regard to private interests of property, as such, will perpetuate the desirable condition now prevailing in Nassau County.[88]

Adams repeated his proposal to develop a 'speedway' in the center of the Island with the open estate area served instead by improved and landscaped existing roads, which, however, would be left circuitous to keep speeds low.

Moses' reaction to the publications was remarkably favorable and conciliatory. This may have been due to the urgent appeal of Adams and the Regional Plan Committee for acquisition of more park land to serve the needs of the growing region. But to the basic premise that the estates should remain intact and the highways be rerouted closer to the center of the Island, Moses' reply was sharp and negative:

> I would suggest that you study the matter of property values in [the North Shore] and in the center of the island where practically all land is sold in lots and investigate the breaking up of big estates and study the city boulevard situation and the increasing population on the city border and ask your investigators to tell you how long they think that the big estates will have the open-ness of parks even though privately owned. I venture to say that five years from now – ten years at the outside – the arguments in favor of keeping all developments away from the Wheatley Hills will appear so ridiculous that no one will admit having made them.[89]

If the aim of the Committee on the Regional Plan in publishing 'crisis' documents was to evoke the creation of latent citizen support on Long Island, it was only partly successful. Interestingly, support did come from the very conservative Suffolk County Taxpayers' Association, which sought to block Moses' taking of taxable land from the rolls and oust him from his positions.[90] The Regional Plan staff wisely avoided the diminishing taxable land argument, though it did attempt to work through the taxpayers' group towards its own ends.

The controversy simmered for several years more without resolution. The wealthy landowners in the Wheatley Hills successfully stopped further progress on the Northern State Parkway. In the interim Moses completed a substantial part of the other east-west route in his scheme, the Southern State Parkway, and acquired Jones Beach and other large areas for park purposes. In the process he built both a reputation and a constituency, and, not incidentally, greatly aided the re-election of Governor Alfred E. Smith, a favor which Smith did not forget.

Adams and the Regional Plan group never deviated from their position on the Long Island parkway question and incorporated their original conceptions into the final *Graphic Regional Plan*, which was issued in 1929. But by the summer of that year Moses had assembled nearly two-thirds of the land for his preferred route, including fifty acres donated by Robert DeForest, which he had held in Suffolk. What remained was the missing section in the Nassau estate country.[91]

The landed gentry were not to be moved or bullied by the aggressive Moses. In May of 1929 they formed a Nassau County Citizens' Committee to oppose the routing of the parkway through their estates. Headed by Grenville Clark, a law partner of Elihu Root, they brought great pressure to bear on Moses and Governor Franklin D. Roosevelt, who had earlier publicly opposed the estate owners group.[92] Though this was hardly the kind of local civic organization the Regional Plan staff had hoped would evolve, the Citizens' Committee did not hesitate to use the Regional Plan as a basis for attacking Moses, terming his proposal 'unscientific and contrary to the views of the best qualified planning experts'.[93]

Moses assumed, quite naturally, that the Committee was an offshoot of the Regional Plan group, particularly since it was chaired by a partner of Elihu Root, who had been associated, if only indirectly, with the Regional Plan Committee from its inception. If he needed further conclusive evidence, it was that Olmsted, consultant to the Regional Plan, had been hired as a consultant to the citizens' group.

After a bitter public controversy, a compromise was reached on December 19, 1929, in the Empire State Building offices of former Governor Smith. With the elder August Hecksher acting as mediator, Moses accepted a settlement which detoured the parkway around the estates, adding some five miles of road. In compensation, the citizens' group agreed to contribute $175,000. The powerful estate owners had won. But the outcome was not what the Regional Plan had proposed. The Northern State Parkway was built according to the Moses plan except for the compromise detour around the Wheatley Hills.

The Northern State Parkway controversy clearly demonstrated the dilemmas facing the unofficial, advisory Regional Plan Committee. It also demonstrated the limitations on development imposed by organizational constraints. Let us, for the moment, discount the possibility, albeit a real one, that Adams and the rest of his staff had unconsciously absorbed the values of their affluent employers and assume that they were working on the basis of values derived from a professional and technical viewing of the issues. Their difficulty lay, then, with the level of abstraction with which they perceived the Region. How valuable in devising buildable projects were such ill-defined notions as 'openness', 'homogeneous corridors', and 'decentralization'?

On what basis could such coarse-grained conceptions be evaluated for their intrinsic desirability? Moreover, how could they possibly serve as criteria by which to judge the import of specific proposals such as the speedway or parkway? Inevitably, the planners' intuitions and imagery furnished the ultimate basis of their proposals, a basis hardly sufficient to justify great confidence.

This lack of confidence perhaps explains the modesty of their proposals. Moses was attempting to maximize production of a tangible, if limited, product in response to a latent demand that he was perceptive enough to recognize. The regional planners, on the other hand, were attempting to optimize some undefined, comprehensive public welfare function. But since they could not easily define what precisely was to be optimized (the 'best use of land'), they were inclined to be more timid than the public entrepreneur, Moses. Moses was far more perceptive about the future significance of the automobile. While the regional planners predicted some 350,000 cars to be registered in Nassau by 1965, Moses, who made no such precise prediction, nevertheless was planning boldly for what eventually occurred, about four times that many. That we may dislike the consequences is beside the point. Those cars would have come to Nassau, parkways or not. Moses simply accelerated the process of reliance on private vehicles. He saw his market in advance and responded to it.

Moses could not have been faulted for choosing the less expensive more direct northern right of way over the possibly superior but more expensive route proposed by the planners. He was maximizing the particular product he had to offer: fast parkways. He realized that he could do far less towards his mission were he to divert resources toward broader, and to him, dubious, goals.

In the end, the Regional Plan staff, unable to convert the prestige of their backers and their own technical expertise into tangible power, gave the appearance of being co-opted by the estate owners, when the planners' objective had been, instead, to recruit a larger constituency for their Plan.

Moses' later judgment that DeForest had made 'unconscionable use of his position as head of the Sage Foundaton' seems unjustified.[94] There is no evidence that Adams and his colleagues consciously let themselves be used by DeForest or the estate owners.

In the last analysis, neither Adams nor Moses was culpable. Moses' decisions were forged in the hard realities of governmental possibility. In the Long Island State Park Commission he had created a new public entity, albeit with severely limited powers and narrow mandate. Adams' proposals implied the eventual evolution of a far broader governmental entity capable of coordinating and controlling land development and transportation. The State of New York was constitutionally capable of providing such leadership. But in practice it could not. Even the ingenious and aggressive Moses could not have consolidated the political power required, had he wished to do so. He had difficulties enough simply convincing the courts of the legality of the Park Commission's acquisitions. The private land ethic and the popularity of local home rule effectively precluded broad regional development control by the State.

It was a false hope that the planners raised when they believed that good ideas based on sound study combined with local cooperation would substitute for effective, formal governmental leadership. The visions of the Regional Plan Committee and its staff for Long Island were consequently doomed to failure. The planners' battle with Moses, though ending in a partial victory, was costly, for other regional campaigns lay ahead in which Moses would be the commanding general.

THE METROPOLITAN POLITICAL VACUUM

The three cases just described demonstrate how the technologically stimulated growth of the metropolitan area beyond the bounds of New York City had created a power vacuum demanding to be filled. The failure of the Hylan administration to complete the Narrows Tunnel revealed the decline of New York City's political ability to carry out regional-scale projects in the face of conservative business opposition. By contrast, the thwarting of the Hudson River Bridge connection to midtown Manhattan marked the end of the individual entrepreneurial sponsorship of incremental but regionally significant projects, which had marked the era of dominance by the railroads and of the city political machines, an era which nevertheless had created much of the transportation infrastructure upon which the New York Region had been built.

Into the vacuum came the Port Authority, the Robert Moses conglomerate of commissions, and, far less potently, the Regional Plan group. Each sought to influence regional decision-making transcending city and state lines. But each drew power from different sources and used its power in quite different styles. The Port Authority epitomized the developing alliance between conservative business interests and a technical and finance-oriented bureaucracy.

The Port Authority's power was derived from the state legislatures of New York and New Jersey and more directly from its own independent bonding authority. Legally constrained by its financial obligations, the Port Authority tended to pursue the profitable regional projects, such as highways and airports, avoiding the more difficult and risky problems of rail passenger, freight, and transit improvements, even though these were, on paper at least, its original mandate. The Port Authority thus only partially and imperfectly filled the regional decision vacuum. Unlike the occasional visionary private entrepreneur, for whose rarity and uncertainty it was intended as a more dependable substitute, the Authority was unwilling to take large risks in pursuit of large visions. At the same time, its scope of activities, limited by its legal constitution, but even more by its financial set-up, kept the Port Authority from acting as the comprehensive transportation planning and development agency that the Region so desperately needed.

The emergence of Robert Moses as a regional development force was due to similar conditions east of Manhattan, with the difference that, with no state boundaries involved, Moses drew his power largely from Albany in his early career, principally from his sponsor and friend, Governor Smith. But Moses' constituency was quite different from that of the Port Authority; his was the newly affluent middle classes, motoring from the city to the sea-shore on green parkways or settling in the suburban counties of Long Island. Accordingly, unlike the commission-like Port Authority, Moses worked in a style reminiscent of that of the old-time political bosses, who got things done by providing what many wanted. The difference, of course, was that while the bosses appealed to immigrant workers, Moses recognized and made use of the growing political strength of an emergent, mobile middle class. In place of Christmas turkeys, he used the media to establish, through an unequaled combination of trenchant wit and scorn, an identity as the man who got things done. Moses also embodied the new efficient, administrative, bureaucratic style. His skilful and unique combination of the old and new models resulted in an intrinsically ambivalent attitude on his part toward the Regional Plan. Privately he valued the technical studies of the planners and welcomed their support when it was helpful. But as the so-called 'Builder for Democracy', his public response to the patrician sponsors of the Regional Plan was frequently negative, even vitriolic. Nevertheless, despite his disclaimers to the contrary, the evidence suggests that many of the projects carried out under Moses' development leadership were assisted by having been incorporated into the Regional Plan, even if some ideas such as the Triborough Bridge and the Long Island parkways were not original contributions of the Plan. Moses never expressed much enthusiasm for public plans and never revealed any overall regional conceptions of his own, but his copy of the Regional Plan provided a ready agenda of projects to which he must have referred often through the 1930s.[95]

Like the old political bosses, Moses got along well with the conservative business and financial interests in the community, but rather poorly with reform groups such as the Regional Plan Committee. And as with bosses, conflicts over one issue led to friction over other, unrelated issues. By contrast, conflicts between the Regional Plan and the Port Authority, whose model more closely resembled that of the Regional Plan, were more likely to be confined to single issues. Indeed, after the planners' initial defeat over the Narrows Tunnel, relationships became generally warmer between the Regional Plan Committee (and its successor, the Regional Plan Association)) and the Port Authority. This was in part due to the fact that the two groups shared many regional goals, maintained a strong consultative relationship between their engineering staffs, and subscribed to the idea of a comprehensive infrastructure plan as the basis for claims of technical competence and legitimacy. The foundation element of the Graphic Regional Plan was the rail plan originally promoted as the central objective of the Port Authority when it was created in 1921. That the consolidated rail plan had largely been given up as hopeless of achievement by the Port Authority made little difference. The Port Authority, still insecure in its status in the early 1920s, welcomed support from any quarter. The Port Authority Plan, though ceasing to have any real viability, retained symbolic significance, a common, tangible rallying point from which the regionalists could draw strength. For its part, the Regional Plan Committee (and later the Regional Plan Association) saw the Port Authority as one of the key vehicles through which its proposals could be achieved. While complete unanimity of positions between the two groups was not automatic, their mutual aims guaranteed a high level of cooperation and coordination in the years following the Narrows Tunnel decision. But as the Port Authority consolidated its position and filled its portfolio of capital projects, the partnership became increasingly unequal and the moral suasion and consent of the private, advisory, Regional Plan group became less salient to the needs of the Authority. Nevertheless, a cordial working relationship continued, in striking contrast to the deterioration of the relationship between the Regional Plan Association and Robert Moses.

The picture that emerges from this analysis of the thrust toward metropolitan regionalism in New York in the 1920s supports the views of neither the theorists of elitism nor of those who favor the pluralist model. It would, perhaps, be more accurate to speak of a pluralism of elites competing for the opportunities for regional power and responsibility created by the spread of development across the boundaries of the old central cities. But even this model is only partially accurate, for the regional groups contending for authority were generally careful to avoid direct competition. A better description of the pattern is Norton Long's concept of the metropolitan policy as an 'ecology of games', in which a variety of games are played in the territorial system: a political game, a public works game, a newspaper game, an ecclesiastical game, and many others. 'Within each game,' Long suggests, 'there is a well-established set of goals whose achievement indicates success or failure for the participant, a set of strategies handed down through experience, an elite public whose approbation is appreciated, and finally a general public which has some appreciation for the standing of the players.'[96]

In the new regional game that emerged in the 1920s, the players to whom regional power accrued were those who focused on well-defined objects and not on the general problems of regional governance. Metropolitan growth created markets for new public services, particularly highways and air transportation facilities. But growth also created new regional problems of coordination. The regional development bodies (the Port Authority and Moses) focused their attention on serving the new markets, because of their narrow mandate and because organizationally it was far more profitable to do so than to attack more complex development issues and the negative externalities of new technologies. Existing state and municipal governments were unwilling or unable to address such issues, but were also unwilling or unable to delegate the authority and direct the regional bodies to undertake unprofitable but essential ventures, such as rail consolidation, transit development, and housing for low-income groups. The authorities, concentrating on narrow functions, particularly highways and parkway development, exacerbated some of the problems which concerned the planners of the 1920s, while solving others. The 'recentralization' of new development into a compact, transit-oriented region was transmuted into a highway-dominated spread city of low densities, resulting in an entirely new set of social and development problems.

The Regional Plan Association, by supporting the construction of the public highway elements without being able to force the construction of the counterbalancing transit component, in a sense violated its own dictum of comprehensiveness and balance. The regional planners, however, really had little choice. Had Charles Norton's 'Plan of New York Authority' become a reality, the ecology of development games in the New York Region might have been different, and a more compact, better balanced region achieved. But Edward Bassett was probably correct in doubting the political feasibility of such a proposal. All the regional planners could hope to do was raise the level of political and technical discourse, and this was not enough to accomplish the broad goals they had set forth in the Plan.

The immediate regional decisions the planners were forced to make while the Regional Plan was under study demonstrated the need to create an agency to carry out the Committee's proposals. The mere existence of the Plan as a document would do little to ensure that regional proposals became part of the public agenda. As a result, the Plan increasingly came to be viewed as a tangible symbol of technical expertise, and less as a blueprint for specific actions.

NOTES

1. Thomas Adams, *Preliminary Report on the Plan of Nassau County*, February 10, 1925 (unpublished memorandum), Regional Plan Papers.

2. Philip Berolzheimer to Thomas Adams, April 2, 1924, Regional Plan Papers. The project was never carried out.

3. Wood, Robert C. (1961) *1400 Governments*. Cambridge: Harvard University Press, pp. 114–172.

4. Interview with Robert Moses, July 6, 1971.

5. *New York Times*, April 27, 1924, IX, p.4.

6. *Ibid.* The Port district at this time was handling about 63 million tons per year (exclusive of freight simply passing through). Of this amount about 40 million tons was carried by marine equipment to waterfront plants and terminals.

7. *New York Times,* April 21, 1925, p.1.

8. Both of these steps were eventually taken by later municipal administrations, but when Hylan first proposed them he was bitterly denounced by Wall Street and merchants groups.

9. See pp. 41–46 above for a description of the development of this plan.

10. *New York Times*, April 27, 1924, IX, p.4.

11. *New York Times,* July 12, 1924, p.16. The other two Commission members were George McAneny and General John F. O'Ryan.

12. *Ibid.*

13. *New York Times,* July 15, 1924, p.8.

14. *New York Times,* December 29, 1924, p.1.

15. As reported in the *New York Times,* February 9, 1925, pp. 1–3.

16. *New York Times,* February 11, 1925, p.2.

17. *New York Times,* March 25, 1925, p.1; March 26, 1925, p.2

18. *New York Times,* March, 26, 1925, p.2.

19. *New York Times,* March, 25, 1925, p. 1; April 9, 1925.

20. *New York Times,* April 6, 1925, p.3.

21. *New York Times,* April 11, 1925, p.14; April 14, 1925, p. 25.

22. *New York Times,* April 20, 1925, p. 8.

23. Letter from Frederic A. Delano, William J. Wilgus, and Thomas Adams to Governor Alfred E. Smith, April 13, 1925, Regional Plan Papers.

24. E.H. Outerbridge to Thomas Adams, April 16, 1925; Julian A. Gregory to Thomas Adams, April 26, 1925, Regional Plan Papers.

25. Thomas Adams to Frederic A. Delano, April 16, 1925, Regional Plan Papers.

26. Julius Henry Cohen to Thomas Adams, April 17, 1925, Regional Plan Papers.

27. Thomas Adams to Governor Alfred E. Smith, April 17, 1925, Regional Plan Papers.

28. Frederic A. Delano to Thomas Adams, April 17, 1925. William J. Wilgus to Thomas Adams, April 17, 1925, Regional Plan Papers.

29. *New York Times,* April 21, 1925, p. 1; April 23, 1925, p.1.

30. *New York Times,* April 22, 1925, p. 5; April 29, 1925, p. 1.

31. Thomas Adams to Frederic A. Delano, May 1, 1925, Regional Plan Papers.

32. Frederic A. Delano to Eugenius H. Outerbridge, May 16, 1925, Regional Plan Papers.

33. Frederic A. Delano to Eugenius H. Outerbridge, May 5, 1925, Regional Plan Papers.

34. *New York Times,* July 1, 1926, p. 40; September 21, 1926, p. 48.

35. Bard, Erwin W. (1942) *The Port of New York Authority.* New York: Columbia University Press, pp. 50–52.

36. Couillard, Ada S. (1924)) Bridging the Hudson River at New York City. *Municipal Reference Library Notes,* X, No. 6, February 6, p. 21. Also see *Municipal Reference Library Notes,* X, Nos. 7–10, pp. 22–39, for an extensive bibliography on Hudson crossings.

37. Harrison, Mrs Burton (1896) *History of the City of New York: Externals of Modern New York.* New York: D.S. Barnes and Co., pp. 812–813.

38. Gustav A. Lindenthal, 'The Hudson River Bridge', pamphlet prepared for The Hudson River Bridge and Terminal Association, 1921, Regional Plan Papers.

39. Eugenius H. Outerbridge, 'Statement to the Advisory Council of the Port of New York Authority – The Hudson River Bridge and Highway Development', December 8, 1921, Regional Plan Papers.

40. Samuel Rea to Charles D. Norton, May 19, 1922, Regional Plan Papers.

41. R.S. Buck to Eugenius H. Outerbridge, February 11, 1923, Regional Plan Papers.

42. *Ibid.*

43. *Plan of New York and Its Environs,* Statement to be submitted to the Port of New York Authority at the Hearing on December 5, 1923, Regional Plan Papers.

44. *Ibid.*

45. 'Interview with Mr. Lindenthal and Mr. Hastings', October 17, 1924, Regional Plan Papers.

46. Thomas Adams to Harold Lewis, October 22, 1924, Regional Plan Papers.

47. *New York Times,* September 10, 1927.

48. Thomas Adams to Col. F.C. Boggs, September 8, 1927, Regional Plan Papers.

49. Memorandum of Gustav Lindenthal, September 18, 1929, Regional Plan Papers.

50. The actual site selected for the 178th Street Bridge apparently was first suggested by the staff of the Regional Plan. Lawrence Orton remembers when 'I went with Adams and picked the place where the bridge should be on Washington Heights.' (Interview with Lawrence M. Orton, September 10, 1972.) The award of the architectural commission for the bridge to Cass Gilbert was probably partly due to the efforts of the Regional Plan group. Gilbert's design for masonry-clad towers was subsequently abandoned, leaving the superstructure exposed.

51. Draft of letter of Frederic A. Delano to Francis Lee Stuart, November 15, 1929. The final version of the letter softened this sentiment to read' . . . there is much to be said in favor of 110th to 125th Streets, because what is now a blighted Negro settlement might well give way to a far better development.' Delano to Stuart, November 27, 1929, Regional Plan Papers.

52. Frederic A. Delano to Francis Lee Stuart, November 27, 1929, Regional Plan Papers.

53. *New York Sun,* March 10, 1931.

54. *New York Times,* May 21, 1932.

55. Statement of Frederic A. Delano to the Secretary of War, December 14, 1932, Regional Plan Papers.

56. *New York Times,* November, 16, 1933.

57. 73rd Congress, 2d Session, Calendar No 1167, 53553, HR 9201, April 26, 1934.

58. *New York Times,* June 5, 1934.

59. Harold M. Lewis to Billings Wilson, Assistant General Manager, Port of New York Authority, June 11, 1934, Regional Plan Papers.

60. *New York Sun,* June 13, 1936.

61. 75th Congress, 1st Session, HR 4107, February 1, 1937.

62. Robert Moses to Frederick P. Keppel, April 5, 1923, Regional Plan Papers.

63. Charles P. Davenport to Russell Sage Foundation, March 13, 1923, Regional Plan Papers.

64. *Ibid.*

65. Henry W. DeForest to Robert W. DeForest, January 26, 1924, Regional Plan Papers.

66. Charles P. Davenport to Thomas Adams, February 1, 1924, Regional Plan Papers.

67. Flavel Shurtleff, conference notes, June 25, 1924, Regional Plan Papers; Flavel Shurtleff to Frederic A. Delano, June 26, 1924, Regional Plan Papers.

68. Flavel Shurtleff to Thomas Adams, June 26, 1924, Regional Plan Papers.

69. Frederic A. Delano to Robert Moses, January 16, 1924, Regional Plan Papers.

70. Robert Moses to Frederic A. Delano, June 20, 1924, Regional Plan Papers.

71. *Ibid.*

72. Frederic A. Delano to Henry James, July 4, 1924, Regional Plan Papers.

73. Henry James to Robert W. DeForest, July 31, 1924, Regional Plan Papers.

74. *Ibid.*

75. Henry James, Report of Meeting of Long Island State Park Commission at Montauk, September 28, 1924, Regional Plan Papers.

76. Henry James to Frederic Law Olmsted, Jr., August 11, 1924, Regional Plan Papers.

77. Henry James to Frederic Law Olmsted, Jr., November 6, 1924, Regional Plan Papers.

78. Moses, Robert (1970) *Public Works: A Dangerous Trade.* New York: McGraw-Hill, p. 107.

79. Henry James, Memorandum of an interview with Carl Fisher, October 8, 1925, Regional Plan Papers.

80. Henry James to Carl G. Fisher, September 25, 1925, Regional Plan Papers.

81. Quoted in Henry James to Thomas Adams, December 5, 1924, Regional Plan Papers.

82. Edward Bassett to Thomas Adams, January 13, 1925, Regional Plan Papers.

83. Thomas Adams to Henry James, January 14, 1925, Regional Plan Papers.

84. Robert Moses to Robert W. DeForest, January 19, 1925, Regional Plan Papers.

85. Frederic A. Delano to Thomas Adams, May 23, 1925, Regional Plan Papers.

86. Thomas Adams, 'A Plan for Nassau County, Long Island, May 18, 1925. Henry James, 'The Present Critical Situation on Long Island', 'Parks on Long Island', 'East and West Highways on Long Island', 1925, Regional Plan Papers.

87. Henry James to Robert W. DeForest, May 25, 1925, Regional Plan Papers.

88. Thomas Adams, 'A Plan for Nassau County, Long Island', *loc. cit.*

89. Robert Moses to Thomas Adams, December 9, 1925, Regional Plan Papers. Moses turned out to be fairly accurate in his prediction, though the process took closer to forty years. Many of the estates have since been subdivided or turned over to institutions.

90. Marvin Shiebler, Secretary, Suffolk County Conservative Taxpayers' Association, 'Park Memorandum', August 24, 1925, Regional Plan Papers.

91. *New York Times,* May 7, 1929; March 11; April 15, 1929.

92. *Ibid.,* April 13, 1929.

93. *Ibid.,* May 15, 1929.

94. Moses (1970), *op. cit.,* p. 136.

95. In an interview in 1971, Moses declined to credit the Regional Plan group with assistance in his development program. An indirect acknowledgement, however, came in his 1970 reminiscences, in the form of a tribute to Thomas Adams. See Moses (1970) *op. cit.,* pp. 97–98.

96. Long, Norton E. (1958) The local community as an ecology of games. *American Journal of Sociology*, LXIV, No. 3, November, pp. 251–261.

9

CARRYING OUT THE PLAN:
1929 TO 1941

EARLY MOMENTUM: 1929–1932

What impact did the Regional Plan have? How much of it was carried out and by whom? What elements were not carried out, and why? How accurate were the economic and population forecasts on which the Plan was based? Who benefited from the Plan?

Answers to these questions are needed if an accurate assessment of the significance of the Plan is to be made. But the answers are not easily divined. It is difficult to separate forecasts of events that would have occurred, plan or no plan, from events whose occurrence is attributable to the Plan. And what of long-standing proposals which predated the Plan and were simply incorporated into it? To what extent can the fact of their being part of the Plan be credited with their realization? Each specific project or proposal needs to be analyzed as an individual case study if definitive judgements are to be made about the causal relationships of plan and reality. Plans as artifacts do not carry themselves out. Groups, institutions, and individuals do the implementing. The plan can serve only as a source of reference and information and a legitimizing device for those who can support its recommendations. Only a study of the interaction of groups or individuals who have played a role in specific decisions can reveal what part plans play in determining outcomes.

There is another level on which plans may have influence, and here the problem of cause and effect is further observed. This is the level of the acceptance by decision-makers of general policy prescriptions as distinct from proposals for specific projects. For example, should decentralization be encouraged or discouraged? Or, should highways be emphasized over transit? General policy reveals itself in the making of specific decisions, but it is itself subject to modification and influence by plans, among other factors. But the extent to which plans as paradigms influence general policy is usually difficult to ascertain. The plan, if it embodies accepted policy, can reinforce that policy, but the strength of that reinforcement can only be a matter of speculation. Where the plan breaks new ground or attempts to alter accepted policy assumptions, it may be a simpler task to estimate impact by reference to points at which policy changes.

The Regional Plan was used by the Regional Plan Association both as a compendium source for new projects and as a guide to general regional policy between its completion in 1929 and the entry of the United States into World War II in 1941. Assessments of progress towards the realization of the Plan's proposals were made by the Association in 1932, 1936, and 1941 and published under the title, *From Plan to Reality*.[1] On the basis of these reports it is possible to assess the degree to which the Plan's proposals were carried out. 'Progress' was defined by the Association as a significant advance made toward realization of a project in the Plan. Minor differences in execution were acceptable since the Plan was regarded as a broad framework for suggestions and guidance rather than a set of detailed working drawings.[2]

The Graphic Regional Plan contained some 47 specific projects, 51 of which were designated as high-priority projects.[3] By 1932 the Association could report considerable progress in two issue areas: highways and parks. Of the 2,527 miles of major new highways proposed in the Plan, 555 miles had been constructed or were under construction. Another 349 miles were in the planning or adoption stage. Progress had thus been made on 36 per cent of the highway mileage proposed. In 1928 there were 3.5 miles of limited access expressways in existence; by 1932, 103 miles were in place or under construction, and another 179 miles had been officially adopted or planned. The expressway or freeway concept had spread so rapidly that several additional routes not contemplated in the Plan had been officially approved. Much of this mileage was located in New Jersey, where state highway policy emphasized industrial routes. America's first cloverleaf interchange was completed in 1932 in Woodbridge, New Jersey. Greatest highway progress was made in the four years after the release of the Plan on Radial Highways, Inner Routes and the Metropolitan Loop. The George Washington Bridge was completed in 1931, the Triborough Bridge was under construction, and the bridge proposed in the Plan between Whitestone, Queens, and the Bronx had been officially adopted.

On Long Island the emphasis was on parkway construction. The Northern State Parkway right-of-way had been acquired and sections of the Southern State Parkway had been completed by Robert Moses' Long Island State Park Commission. These routes substantially followed the proposals in the Regional Plan. The Eastern State Parkway (later the Taconic State Parkway)) was under development in Westchester and Putnam Counties. A 300–foot right-of-way had been acquired in Connecticut for the Merritt Parkway. With this new expressway and parkway development the New York Region had become the national leader in providing fast through routes for motor vehicles.[4]

Park acquisition proceeded nearly as rapidly as highway development. Between 1927 and 1932 the New York Region added 26,000 acres of open space to its existing 90,000 acres. This was, however, a lower rate of acqui-

sition than had prevailed between 1922 and 1927. Nevertheless, the Region
had reduced its population per acre of park land from 119 in 1921 to 103 in
1932, achieving the same ratio as the well-endowed Boston Metropolitan
Park District.[5] Ninety per cent of the 22,000 acres of park land acquired
between 1927 and 1932 were in the New York State portion of the Region.
The New Jersey counties lagged considerably behind the New York counties
in acquiring open space.

Little progress could be reported towards a suburban transit system. Several improvements were noted, however, in the trunk rail system, including
the electrification of several sections of the Lackawanna and Pennsylvania
railroads and commencement of the 150–million-dollar relocation of the New
York Central tracks on Manhattan's West Side.[6]

The summary tally of progress on the 51 projects classified as urgent in the
Plan was impressive. Fifteen were under construction or had been completed
and another thirteen were under official study or had been adopted. On
twenty-three, no official action had been taken. Progress was also reported in
the establishment of county and local planning agencies. Six county planning
commissions and forty-four new local planning and zoning boards were
created in the Region between 1928 and 1933.[7] While applauding the spread
of the zoning device, the Association warned of the growing use of zoning to
preserve the exclusiveness of some communities through excessive lot size
requirements, up to three acres in some instances. Such use of zoning was
held to be only 'remotely connected with public health or safety'.[8]

DEPRESSION AND PUBLIC WORKS: 1932 – 1936

Much of the progress towards realization of the Plan between 1929 and 1932
could be ascribed to the adoption of numerous proposals made independently
by official agencies prior to 1929. Many of these projects were budgeted
before the collapse of the economy in 1929 and went forward in spite of
declining public revenues. But progress on the Plan after 1932 seemed far
from assured. Work on the Triborough Bridge had been halted in that year
because financing could not be arranged. Other important projects had been
postponed indefinitely. Thousands of workers were out of jobs. Home mortgage foreclosures soared. Skyscrapers such as the new Empire State Building
stood half empty. It was not the image of the Region foreseen in the Plan. In
1933 the Regional Plan Association called for a public works program to get
the unemployed back to work.[9] Under the Hoover administration a Reconstruction Finance Administration was established in February, 1932, empow-
ered to make loans to banks, railroads, and insurance companies. But Hoover
moved timidly towards the public works concept, fearful that public budgets
would become excessively unbalanced.[10] Hoover's successor in 1933, Franklin D. Roosevelt, was far less fearful and far more committed to planning. In

the first hundred days of the Roosevelt administration, legislation was pushed through Congress creating a Public Works Administration. Roosevelt appointed Interior Secretary Harold L. Ickes, administrator. With Roosevelt's blessing, Ickes created the National Planning Board to help plan for the expenditure of $3,300,000 for public works. Ickes chose a board composed of Wesley C. Mitchell, the economist, Charles E. Merriam, a political scientist, and Frederic A. Delano, the President's uncle and former chairman of the Committee on the Regional Plan of New York. The National Planning Board (later the National Resource Planning Board) encouraged the formation of State Planning Boards and by 1936 every state but Delaware had a board. George McAneny, President of the Regional Plan Association, served on the New York State Planning Board.[11]

Through these appointments the experience gained in the preparation of the Regional Plan was applied to the problems of national and state planning in the early New Deal. More important for the New York Region was the immediate availability of the Regional Plan's agenda of urgent projects and, in Delano and McAneny, of sympathetic administrators in strategic positions. The New York Region accordingly received its share, and more, of the Roosevelt administration's public works appropriations.

The boon of pump-priming federal funds was evident in *From Plan to Reality: II*, which reported on the accomplishment of Regional Plan proposals during the years from 1932 to 1936. The chief beneficiaries of such funds were highways and park and playground development. The acquisition of new park lands slowed considerably, however, even though land prices had plummeted and new parks could be had far less dearly than in the 1920s. Land acquisition created no new jobs and was therefore not part of the federal public works program.[12]

By 1936, progress could be reported on 40 per cent of the Region's proposed highway network. 789 miles, or nearly a third of the projected 2547 miles, were under construction or completed, and another 236 miles were in the planning stage. Twice as much progress was reported on the proposed radial routes as on the outer circumferential routes urged in the Regional Plan. However, nearly half of the Metropolitan Loop was in place or under active consideration; but most of this was located east of the Hudson. Little had been built in New Jersey. Of all the types of highways, the expressways had been pushed ahead most rapidly. More than 135 miles of the Plan's proposed 313.5 miles of expressways had been completed and another 65 miles were on the drawing boards. The stalled Triborough Bridge project was resumed with the help of the Reconstruction Finance Administration. Expressway construction was pushed partly because it permitted extensive use of steel in bridges and viaducts, thus helping to stimulate the Midwestern coal and steel industries.[13]

Airport construction also benefited greatly from federal public works expenditures. The sum of $3,400,000 was allocated in 1935 by the Works Progress Administration for the improvement of the Newark Metropolitan Airport. And New York City proceeded with federal assistance in the construction of municipal airports at Floyd Bennett Field in Brooklyn and at the North Beach airport (later LaGuardia Airport) in Queens.[14]

Park acquisition in the Region between 1932 and 1936 slowed to 8,379 new acres, compared with the previous four years, when 22,000 acres had been acquired. New York City was an exception to the general slowdown, adding 3,250 acres, an increase of 23 per cent over what had existed in 1932. Most of this new park land was located in Queens, the largest tract being the Flushing Creek Meadows, acquired as a site for a great World's Fair proposed to open in 1939.[15]

Considerable progress was made in publicly-assisted housing in the Region between 1932 and 1936. The principle of subsidized housing for low-income families had gained wide acceptance in the Region and nationally, despite Thomas Adams' reservations about subsidies, expressed in the Regional Plan. Several publicly-assisted slum clearance projects were begun in New York City with financial help from the federal Public Works Administration. Some of these garden apartment projects followed Clarence Perry's principles of neighborhood design and the principles for maximizing light and air that had been promoted in the Plan.[16]

Less happy was the fate of Greenbrook, a planned industrial suburb for 4,000 families, modeled on Radburn, scheduled for a 4,200–acre site in Franklin Township, Somerset County, New Jersey. Greenbrook was one of six new garden suburbs proposed for development by the federal Resettlement Administration, which was under the direction of Rexford G. Tugwell, a Roosevelt brain-truster committed to the planning movement. Work on Greenbrook was halted in May of 1936 by a legal controversy that threatened to hold up other Resettlement Administration greenbelt projects in Maryland, Ohio, and Wisconsin. Rather than risk the entire program, the Administration scuttled Greenbrook, and the New York Region was denied a model community at its urban fringe.[17]

Planning organizations in the Region multiplied in the period between 1933 and 1937, largely because of federal assistance and the stimulation of State Planning Boards which had been established in each of the states in the Region. Twenty-nine new municipal planning boards were established in this period, bringing the number in the Region to 139, about a fourth of the 496 municipalities in the Region. Zoning proved more popular than planning, 308 municipalities having adopted ordinances by 1937.[18] In 1936, after years of struggle by the Regional Plan Association and other civic groups, a New York City Planning Commission became a permanent part of the city's governmental structure. Lawrence Orton, the general director of the Regional

Plan Association, was appointed by Mayor Fiorello LaGuardia as one of the four members of the original Commission.[19]

The character of early New Deal thought on planning and development was to no little extent influenced by the people and concepts of the New York Regional Plan of the 1920s. Roosevelt accepted the idea of planning partly as a result of his exposure to the work of his uncle, Frederic Delano. The New York Region received in return the fruits of federal support for planning. But the enduring heritage of this relationship lay in the Regional Plan proposals realized through the various federal public works programs. The results of the Depression were not all positive, however. If economic slump spurred public sector activities, most notably the development of highways, it completely stalled progress on private sector projects. Few accomplishments could be reported on trunk rail and suburban transit proposals. Even in the best of times, persuasion and coordination of the competing private railroads was difficult; under the harsh constraints of the mid-1930s, the task became impossible. The New Deal program had inadvertently pushed the Region onto rubber tires, more than the Plan had intended. But the Region's decision-makers were hardly unwilling recipients of the federal highway largess that provided much-needed employment. The result, however, was to accelerate the deterioration of rail services.

DIMINISHING IMPACT: 1936–1941

The third and final progress report in the 'From Plan to Reality' series was published in August, 1942, eight months after US entry into World War II. Again, most progress was reported in highway and parkway construction, with some additional park acquisitions made. Between 1936 and 1940, 225 more miles of highway were completed. Of the 2,600 miles in the revised Plan, 979, or about 37 per cent of the total, were in place or committed. The Metropolitan Loop was 41 per cent complete, with New Jersey continuing to lag. Radial routes continued to dominate construction, while the outer circumferential routes were neglected. The 1929 Plan had called for only 235 miles of expressway, but the 1941 revised version of the Plan proposed 732 miles, reflecting the insatiable demand for unrestricted motor vehicle routes.

New proposals for motor vehicle crossings not in the original Plan were added to the revised version, most notably the Brooklyn-Battery Tunnel project, originally conceived by Robert Moses as a bridge. After a bitter struggle with Moses, led by the Regional Plan Association, the bridge, whose approaches would have been greatly destructive in lower Manhattan, was redesigned as a tunnel, and construction begun in 1940.[20] The Lincoln and Queens Midtown Tunnels, both of which were in the 1929 Regional Plan, were opened to traffic in 1937 and 1940, respectively. The Whitestone Bridge, also a Plan proposal, was opened in 1939. A Narrows vehicular tunnel, proposed in the Plan to link Brooklyn and Staten Island, was officially adopted by the New York City Planning Commission. Also adopted were routes through lower Manhattan at Canal Street and at 38th Street linking the Queens-Midtown Tunnel and the Lincoln Tunnel. Much had been accomplished toward realizing the Plan's highway proposals. But by 1941 it had become clear that the 1929 Plan had been far too modest in its highways proposals to cope with growing traffic volumes. The Plan had become obsolete, in this category at least, after only ten years.

This obsolescence was due partly to the failure to make any headway on the suburban transit plan. Discussions and studies by the Port Authority for service to New Jersey had been conducted, but by 1941 little of substance had been accomplished. The same could be said of proposals for trunk line railroads, with the exception of the completion of the massive West Side Improvement in Manhattan.[21]

Airports were another matter. Air travel increased greatly between 1936 and 1941, with the opening of LaGuardia Field in Queens. A second major airport, Idlewild, was begun in the southeast corner of Queens in 1941. Floyd Bennett Field, however, was purchased by the federal government in the same year for military use.

Park acquisition continued at a reduced rate, although an additional 9,400 acres were acquired in the Region between 1936 and 1940, bringing the total to 134,282 acres. This was about 25,000 acres more than had existed in 1930, though it was still far short of the 358,000 acres envisioned in the 1929 Plan.

With the advent of the federal Public Housing Administration in 1937, some sixty subsidized projects were started in the Region between that year and 1941. These projects contained nearly 37,000 units, a major step forward in the effort to provide decent low-cost housing for families of modest means.[22]

Between 1937 and 1941 planning and zoning activities further permeated the Region with an additional 61 municipalities establishing planning boards. By 1941, 96 per cent of the Region's population lived in areas controlled by zoning ordinances.[23]

The World's Fair in Flushing Meadows opened in 1939 and closed the following year. For a brief period it had captured the imagination of millions, offering a glimpse of future technologies. The Regional Plan Association had prepared an enormous three-dimensional model of the proposals in the 1929 Plan, which was displayed in the New York City Building at the Fair (figure 9.1). With the closing of the Fair at the outbreak of hostilities in Europe, the model was loaned to the First Army Headquarters at Governor's Island for the duration of the war. The gesture was somehow fitting; peacetime plans were put aside, for the moment, throughout the country. And by 1941, twelve years after it had been completed, the Regional Plan had become largely obsolete. It belonged to the past, its assumptions and imageries rooted in a

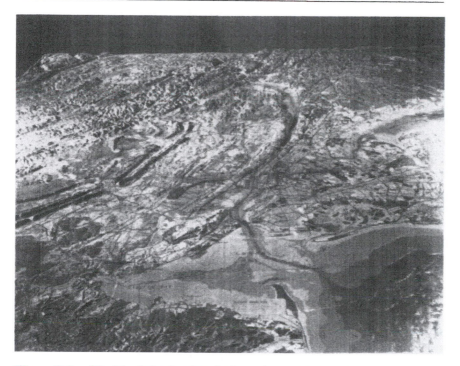

Figure 9.1. Model of the Regional Plan of New York and Its Environs on display at the New York World's Fair, 1939–1940. (*Source:* Regional Plan Papers)

distant, fading era. For better or worse, the Plan had helped to carry the Region to a new threshold. It had done its work, and except for a few residual projects that would remain in the civic consciousness, it would have little significance for the post-war period. The Regional Plan, a program for forty years of development, had lost its viability after only twelve years. Its lingering heritage was embedded in the organizations it had fostered: the Regional Plan Association, the New York City Plan Commission, and numerous county and local planning commissions. It had also left a heritage of trained men who knew the Region and the Plan and who went out to many influential positions where the concepts and projects of the Plan were never entirely forgotten.

NOTES

1. Regional Plan Association (1933) *From Plan to Reality I;* (1938) *From Plan to Reality II;* (1942) *From Plan to Reality III.* New York: Regional Plan Association.

2. Regional Plan Association (1933), p. 14.

3. Committee on the Regional Plan of New York and Its Environs (1929) *Regional*

Plan of New York and Its Environs. Vol. I. *The Graphic Regional Plan*. New York: Regional Plan of New York and Its Environs, pp. 399–407.

4. Regional Plan Association (1933) *op. cit.*, p. 16.

5. *Ibid.*, p. 69.

6. *Ibid.*, p. 19.

7. *Ibid.*, pp. 102, 112.

8. *Ibid.*, p. 103.

9. *Ibid.*, p. 140.

10. Schlesinger, Arthur M. Jr. (1957) *The Crisis of the Old Order, 1919–1933*. Boston: Houghton Mifflin, pp. 236–238.

11. Scott, Mel (1969) *American City Planning Since 1890*. Berkeley: University of California Press, p. 304.

12. Regional Plan Association (1942), p. v.

13. *Ibid.*, pp. II-1 ff.

14. *Ibid.*, pp. IV-10–11.

15. *Ibid.*, p. V-9. I.N. Phelps Stokes credits Frederic Delano and George McAneny with the idea for the Fair. See Stokes, I.N. Phelps (1939) *New York Past and Present: Its History and Landmarks 1524–1939*. New York: Plantin Press, p. 29. Robert Moses takes a dissenting view, crediting the idea to Joseph Shagden, a Belgian engineer, and Col. Edward Roosevelt, who 'sold it to McAneny'. See Moses, Robert (1970) *Public Works: A Dangerous Trade*. New York: McGraw-Hill, p. 538.

16. Regional Plan Association (1942), p. VIII-1. In 1933, Perry discussed the application of the neighborhood concept to slum clearance in an influential publication of the Regional Plan Association: Perry, Clarence Arthur (1933) *The Rebuilding of Blighted Areas*. New York: Regional Plan Association.

17. Regional Plan Association (1942)), p. VIII-1.

18. *Ibid.*, p. VII-2.

19. Makielski, S.J. (1966) *The Politics of Zoning: The New York Experience*. New York: Columbia University Press., pp. 54–56.

20. Regional Plan Association (1942), p. II-7.

21. *Ibid.*, pp. IV-2-3.

22. *Ibid.*, IV-12.

23. *Ibid.*, pp. V-2, VI-4.

10

PLAN AND REALITY: 1965

FORECASTS, PROPHECIES AND PLANS

The Regional Plan emphasized immediate action projects, and by 1941 many of these projects had been realized. Any residual value it might have retained thereafter as an agenda for public capital development was lost in the building hiatus of World War II. The effective life of the Plan thus amounted to ten or twelve years, considerably less than the forty-year time horizon that Norton and DeForest had envisioned in 1922. Adams and his staff, however, were never under any illusion that a static regional plan could remain relevant for more than a decade. The Plan was conceived as a moving program for action expressed in space and time, periodically revised to reflect changing circumstances. At the same time, Adams knew that major regional improvements endured for at least a generation, perhaps several generations, and to ensure that such improvements retained suitability and usefulness over their lifetimes, assumptions concerning the long-term development of the Region were necessary. The year 1965 was thus selected as the benchmark time horizon on which regional development assumptions might be made. There was nothing major or celebratory about the year 1965. It was simply forty years in the future from 1925, and presumably by 1940 an updated Regional Plan, had one been prepared, would similarly have looked ahead forty years to a target date of 1980. The distant target date selected for the Regional Plan raises the intriguing question of just how different the Region of 1965 turned out to be compared with the forecasts and proposals of the Plan. Comparison of 1965 reality and Plan are easily made. More difficult is to respond to the question of why deviations between Plan and reality arose. Elements of the plan may stand independently of other elements, but more often the parts are connected sequentially, one outcome depending on whether an earlier necessary outcome had occurred. For example, the location of jobs determines the location of residences, and both are determined in part by the availability of transportation. Deviations from plan in one portion of the cycle result in deviations in other parts, and the entire conception, to the extent of the functional interdependency, may fall like a house of cards.

Other plan elements are more in the nature of independent variables – birth rates, for example – and the question in comparing plan and reality for such elements is simply to ask how accurate the forecasts were. There are, however, probably no purely independent elements. Even birth rates may be influenced by the availability of housing, jobs, and transportation infrastructure. The distribution of population growth through a region is another example where forecasts may be made but outcomes are at least somewhat dependent on decisions affecting the urban infrastructure. In such cases the line between forecast and self-fulfilling prophecy becomes blurred.

It is also possible that the broad distributions of population and jobs assumed in the plan may not be realized because there may exist internal contradictions within the plan itself. A proposed infrastructure may not 'match' the assumed distributions which it is supposed to reflect and support, either because the nature of the relationship is not predictable, or because the planners simply erred.

Some or all of these sources of deviation between plan and reality may occur and it is not always possible to determine which have been most responsible for divergence in a particular plan. With this caveat in mind, we can reasonably ask what the long-term score card of a plan is. Did development happen in the way it was intended, and if not, why not?

Twenty-four years of development ensued between 1941, when the Regional Plan was in effect obsolete, and the Plan's target year of 1965: four years of war, a short period of recession, then a sustained post-war development boom followed by intermittent recessions amidst generally high levels of economic activity. In the years following World War II this growth occurred on the physical armature built up prior to 1941, much of which had been suggested or incorporated in the Graphic Regional Plan. After about 1947 public infrastructure development resumed in the metropolitan area to serve the spreading industrial developments that had been postponed for half a decade or more. Middle-class and wealthy families departed the central cities for sprawling, automobile-oriented suburban developments. Inner city densities declined, even while poor black and Puerto Rican families came from outside the Region to take the places of those who had moved to the suburbs. Industrial plants and shopping centers followed the trek to the metropolitan fringe. The Region of 1965 turned out to be quite different from the region envisioned in 1929 by Thomas Adams and his colleagues. Many of the ills and dangers foreseen by the regional planners occurred, most notably excessive decentralization (later dubbed sprawl and 'spread city'), rather than the balanced 'recentralization' urged in the Plan. In some important ways, however, the reality of 1965 closely resembled the Plan of 1929. This can be seen in the analysis that follows, which contrasts 1929 proposals and 1965 outcomes in several important categories: population size and distribution, extent and character of urbanization, transportation infrastructure, open space, and project proposals.

DIFFERENCES BETWEEN POPULATION PROJECTIONS AND OUTCOMES

The Graphic Regional Plan was developed on the assumption that there would be about 21 million people in the Region by 1965, a projected increase of about 12 million over the 1920 census total of 9.0 million. The actual 1965 total turned out to be about 17.3 million, or an increase of 8.4 million (tables 10.1 and 10.2). The 1965 projection was thus overestimated by some 3.6 million people, an error of 21 per cent.[1]

Table 10.1. Comparison of Regional Plan of New York and Its Environs population projections with actual outcomes.

County	Projections (000's)			Actual (000's)		
	1940	1960	1965	1940	1960	1965
Manhattan	2,300	2,280	2,280	1,890	1,698	1,595
Bronx	1,410	2,140	2,380	1,395	1,425	1,528
Brooklyn	2,900	3,860	4,090	2,698	2,627	2,699
Queens	1,050	1,700	1,900	1,298	1,810	1,942
Richmond	260	540	628	174	222	258
Hudson	848	1,072	1,150	652	611	613
Newark	555	703	740	430	405	411
Group1	9,323	12,295	13,168	8,537	8,798	9,016
Nassau	270	550	622	407	1,300	1,397
Westchester	620	1,220	1,400	574	809	853
Essex, exc. Newark	495	1,097	1,230	408	518	553
Union	380	740	830	328	504	540
Passaic So.	362	578	640	300	382	403
Bergen	420	840	951	410	780	849
Group 2	2,547	5,025	5,673	2,427	4,293	4,595
Suffolk	135	160	170	197	667	927
Fairfield[a]	515	890	929	418	654	724
Dutchess[a]	18	19	19	121	176	210
Putnam	11	12	12	17	32	42
Orange[a]	67	70	72	140	184	206
Rockland	46	48	49	74	137	187
Passaic N.	38	62	69	9	25	32
Morris	105	120	127	126	262	319
Somerset	63	72	76	74	144	175
Middlesex	255	367	419	217	434	493
Monmouth[a]	130	158	167	161	334	399
Group 3	1,383	1,975	2,109	1,554	3,049	3,714
Totals	13,253	19,295	20,950	12,518	16,140	17,325

(a) Projections are for parts of counties of Metropolitan as defined by the Regional Plan of New York and Its Environs; actual numbers are for whole counties. The differences are not so great as to alter the impact of comparisons between projected and actual populations.
Source: see table 10.2.

Table 10.2. Comparison of population projection with outcomes – by percentage

	Projection (per cent)			Actual (per cent)		
	1940	*1960*	*1965*	*1940*	*1960*	*1965*
Group 1	70.35	63.72	62.85	68.20	54.51	52.04
Group 2	19.22	26.04	27.08	19.39	26.60	26.52
Group 3	10.44	10.24	10.07	12.41	18.89	21.44
Region	100.00	100.00	100.00	100.00	100.00	100.00

Source: Computed from Table XV p. 119, Vol II, *Regional Survey of New York and Its Environs* and from *The Region's Growth*, May 1967, Table A–22, p. 140.

The population for 1940, the year by which the effective life of the Plan was over, was considerably more accurate, despite an unexpected lowering of the birth rate during the Depression. The Plan's 1940 forecast was 13.3 million, compared with an actual total of 12.5 million, an error of only 5.9 per cent.[2] Thus, during the decade in which the Plan remained relevant, the population projections on which it was based were not seriously in error. Whether the sizable error in the long-term population forecast resulted in the overdesign of Plan elements such as transportation and related infrastructure is difficult to determine, though the likelihood is that it did not.

The population forecasts diverged from what actually occurred not only in the gross regional totals, but also in its distribution through the Region. The most significant distribution error was a serious overestimate of the increase in the older counties at the center (New York City, Hudson County, and the City of Newark). Manhattan, which was expected to remain stable in population from 1920 to 1965, actually lost three-quarter million people. In the same period the Bronx and Brooklyn together were expected to add 3.7 million, but actually gained only 1.5 million, most of which growth occurred before 1940. Between 1920 and 1940 Queens grew slightly faster than had been expected, though the prediction for 1965 of 1.9 million turned out to be surprisingly accurate. Across the Narrows, Richmond also grew, but only at half the rate that was forecast. Hudson County and Newark, it was predicted, would both nearly double their populations between 1920 and 1965, but in fact each lost slightly.

In contrast to the predictions for the old core countries, the forecasts for the inner suburban counties (Group 2) turned out to be somewhat more accurate. By 1940 this group was expected to have 2.5 million, and in fact had 2.4 million. The estimate for 1965, 5.6 million, however, was high by about a million. But the relative accuracy attained for the group as a whole did not apply to the counties comprising it. Except for Bergen County, whose growth was accurately forecast, the New Jersey counties' growth was considerably overestimated, but the most serious discrepancy in this group occurred in the forecast of the direction of growth on the New York side. Development was expected to go northward to Westchester, rather than eastward into Long Island. Westchester was to have 1.4 million in 1965, Nassau, 0.6 million. Actually, by 1965 the results were nearly the opposite: Nassau, had 1.4 million and Westchester only 0.85 million.

Population in the outermost counties (Group 3) was generally underestimated. As a group the outer counties gained a million and a half more than had been expected in 1965. However, most of this growth took place after 1945. The projections for the period 1920 to 1940 were remarkably accurate. For example, while the enormous growth of Suffolk County to nearly a million by 1965 was entirely unanticipated, the 1940 prediction for that county was low by only 62,000.

To summarize, then, the prognosticators looking ahead forty years to 1965 failed to predict Manhattan's substantial population decrease; vastly overestimated the increase that was to occur in the other old core counties; were reasonably accurate in their prediction for the inner suburban ring; underestimated the growth of the outer counties; and missed the dominant direction of growth to the east, to Long Island, expecting much more to go northward to Westchester and to close-in New Jersey counties across the Hudson.

It would be unfair to call these discrepancies errors. Had the suburban transit element of the Plan been carried out, the predictions might have proved more accurate. However, it is possible to fault these early planners for not recognizing trends already observable while they were at work on their forecasts and plans. For example, a special New York State census taken in 1925 showed that Manhattan was losing population and that Nassau was already gaining at a spectacular rate, far faster than had been predicted. This census also showed that the outermost New York Counties – Dutchess, Orange, Rockland, and Suffolk – had by 1925 already reached their 1940 forecast.[3]

We may fault these early planners also for extrapolating the growth rates of the old core counties on a straight line basis when their own graphs revealed a declining rate of growth. Had they merely extrapolated their declining curves rather than projecting straight lines, their results would have been closer to what actually occurred.

And we may fault them for not comprehending what their high estimates for the core counties implied in terms of intensification, rebuilding and densities. Table 10.3 shows the density implications of the projections accepted by the staff. The densities for close-in, built-up counties, such as Brooklyn, the Bronx, and Hudson, could only have been attained by tearing down vast areas and rebuilding higher structures or by building at very high densities on the limited amount of undeveloped land in the less accessible, previously bypassed enclaves. Neither of these possibilities was likely, even from the vantage point of the 1920s.

Table 10.3. 1965 predicted and actual gross population densities – counties (thousands per square mile).

	1929 Regional Plan Prediction for 1965	Actual 1965
Manhattan	103.6	69.4
Bronx	56.7	36.4
Brooklyn	59.3	39.1
Queens	17.6	18.0
Richmond	11.0	4.5
Hudson	26.1	13.9
Newark	31.4	23.4
Group 1 excl. Manhattan	31.7	21.6
Total Group 1	36.0	24.6
Nassau	2.3	5.1
Westchester	3.1	1.9
Union	8.0	5.2
Passaic	3.5	2.2
Essex excl. Newark	13.1	4.4
Bergen	4.0	3.6
Group 2	4.2	3.4
Suffolk	0.18	1.01
Fairfield (part)	2.36	n.a.
Dutchess	0.16	0.3
Putnam	0.05	0.17
Orange	0.17	0.2
Rockland	0.26	1.02
Morris	0.26	0.66
Somerset	0.24	0.57
Middlesex	0.80	1.59
Monmouth	0.39	0.90
Group 3	0.55	0.97
Total Region	3.78	3.13

Source: Computed from Table XV, p. 119, Vol II, *Regional Survey of New York and Its Environs* and from *The Region's Growth*, May 1967, Table A–22, p. 140.

We do not know whether these errors were the result of a conscious desire to centralize population growth in the core counties to accord with a prevalent image of what constituted a 'good' city or a 'good' region; or whether they were the result of an overly-simple, mechanical approach to population forecasting, a faulty substructure upon which the Plan was ultimately raised. In any event, the distribution forecasts must have weighed heavily in Thomas Adams' development of the key elements of the Regional Plan. His choice was either to attempt to discourage through the Plan's proposals whatever detrimental effects he might discern in the growth forecasts, or to accommodate his plan to fit the forecasts. He chose to do the latter.

URBANIZED LAND

If the 1965 population projections were seriously in error, the forecasts of the amount of land that would be developed by 1965 turned out to be remarkably accurate. Figures 7.18 and 7.19 show the great similarities between what was indicated in the Plan and what actually occurred. A comparison with figure 2.2 which shows development in 1935, suggests how great an area was developed between the completion of the Plan in 1929 and 1965. Developed land in 1965 amounted to roughly two-and-a-half times that developed by 1935, whereas population had increased by only 44 per cent. This was, of course, a reflection of the greatly reduced densities at which the new development was taking place.

The near identity of the urbanization pattern proposed in the Plan and the actual pattern meant that the 5.3 million people added to the Region between 1930 and 1965 occupied newly developed land that the Regional Plan staff had thought would provide for 10.1 million. The Region had thus urbanized much as the planners had thought it would, but at considerably lower densities. It is intriguing to ask whether the Plan contributed to the impulse to sprawl by encouraging transportation development to serve a larger population than actually settled in the suburban areas, and also by residential images that emphasized the desirability of light and air. One can only speculate on the possible influence of the Plan on residential densities in the New York Metropolitan Region. It is true, however, that post-war densities in the New York suburbs were, on the average, lower than in most other U.S. metropolitan areas.

While the 1965 developed land pattern in the Plan and in reality generally corresponded, there were some local exceptions. Long Island, as we have noted, received considerably more population and was somewhat more urbanized than the Plan had forecast. Rockland County in New York and Fairfield County in Connecticut also underwent more land development than anticipated. The New Jersey pattern was about as expected, except for the failure of the extensive Meadowlands to be developed. Staten Island was far less developed than had been projected, as a result of delays in the provision of tunnel or bridge connections.

In general, though, Plan and reality were not greatly divergent insofar as the general development pattern was concerned.

TRUNK RAIL LINES AND SUBURBAN TRANSIT SYSTEMS

The 1929 Regional Plan for the trunk-line rail system was, as we have seen, based largely on the 1920 Port of New York Authority Plan, which by 1941 was moribund. The railroad companies, persisting in their dedication to nineteenth-century *laissez-faire* competition, saw little reason to cooperate with each other or with the Port Authority. The competitive game had become habitual and the railroads would play it to the bitter end. Thomas Adams was quite aware of the dilemma. There was no alternative, however, but to recognize the existence of the irrational rail situation and respond to it, as Wilgus had so valiantly attempted to do. Adams' rail plan was modest enough: more electrification of the radials, new connectors in places, better service on the industrial waterfronts, and building of the important belt line. Total new trackage proposed in the Plan was no more than three hundred miles, an increase of less than ten per cent over the 3,435 miles in operation in 1925.

None of the rail proposals was realized by 1965, with the exception of the electrification of several lines and the construction of the Manhattan West Side improvement. A comparison of the proposals for the trunk rail systems and the network as it existed in 1965 (figures 7.4 and 7.6), shows clearly the retrogression that took place. In the forty years between 1925 and 1965 trackage in the Region actually decreased by 750 route miles.[4]

If the railroads were willing to trim routes because of the diminishing importance of railway freight haulage, they were even happier to cast off unprofitable passenger service. The Regional Plan for suburban transit had been based on utilization of existing rail facilities rather than on the development of new systems (figure 7.5). No significant progress was made here either. On the eve of US entry into World War II the Port Authority made an attempt to bring the railroads together in the matter of transit. But coordination of the seven carriers was difficult; it was far easier to look to flexible motor vehicles for a solution. The rationalization and improvement of suburban rail transit was for all purposes politically a dead issue by the time the great suburban building boom occurred in the 1950s. The greatest setback was in New Jersey. Westchester, Connecticut, and Long Island enjoyed considerable electrified rail passenger service, whereas New Jersey had only two such lines. New Jersey suburban development consequently became largely dependent on the automobile and on bus service.

HIGHWAYS AND PARKWAYS

If by 1965 the rail and transit elements of the Regional Plan had largely failed to achieve results, the contrary was true of the highway and parkway components. The Regional Plan had called for 2,500 miles of new and improved major routes, of which 878 miles were to be on new rights of way; 235 miles of new grade-separated freeways were included in the latter category, and the remainder was to consist of highways and boulevards at grade.[5] Figures 7.14 and 7.15 show the Regional Plan for highways and the configuration of highways as they actually existed in 1965. Since much of the radial-circumferential network proposed in the Plan consisted of state or county highways already in place but for which upgrading was proposed, it is not surprising that much of the proposed highway system was in place in 1965. What is most noteworthy in comparing Plan and reality is the large addition in freeways not originally proposed in 1929. The Plan proposed some 253 miles of freeway, but by 1965 there were, in fact, 1,368 miles of freeway, resulting largely from the federally supported Interstate Highway System program, which was initiated in 1956 by the Eisenhower Administration.[6]

Nearly all of the freeway routes proposed in the Plan were carried out, including the marginal highways around Manhattan, the Brooklyn-Queens Expressway, and the Cross Island Parkway in Queens. Other proposed routes were never built but remained as official but controversial proposals in 1965, such as the Lower Manhattan, Mid-Manhattan, and Cross Brooklyn Expressways.

The Metropolitan Loop, not all of which was originally proposed for expressway standards, was completed by 1965 except for several sections in New Jersey. Much of the New York portion was built as high capacity expressways, including the Narrows (Verrazano) Bridge and its approaches, a key crossing which had originally been proposed in the Plan as a tunnel.

Most of the freeway proposals that were realized were built in the decade immediately after the publication of the Plan. A few proposals became reality after World War II, most notably the Garden State Parkway, the alignment for which was laid out by Harold M. Lewis, serving in the capacity of consultant to the State of New Jersey. Most of the major post-World War II freeways, however, were not conceptions of the Regional Plan, though often these corresponded to routes proposed for general highways. These included the New York State Thruway sections in the Region, the New Jersey Turnpike, and the Long Island Expressway.

The 1929 Regional Plan for highways was partly based on a set of predictions of future motor vehicle registrations computed by Harold Lewis in 1927 (Table 10.4). Lewis found that between 1920 and 1926 the number of motor vehicles in the Region had nearly tripled, growing from 476,000 to 1,330,000 over the six-year period. Lewis predicted that by 1935 there would be some 3.15 million motor vehicles registered in the Region, and by 1965, nearly 6.72 million. The 1935 prediction turned out to be high by about a million vehicles, because of the Depression. The 1965 prediction was high by about 800,000 vehicles. Interestingly, Lewis' 1965 estimates for the Region excluding New York City turned out to be remarkably accurate – a predicted 4.46 million vehicles compared with an actual registration of 4.23 million. The 1965 prediction for New York City, however, was considerably high: 2.26 million vehicles predicted, compared with an actual count of 1.69 million. The overestimate for New York City was due mostly to the fact that the City's population grew far more slowly than had been expected. The predicted ratio of persons to motor vehicles was remarkably accurate, as table

10.5 shows. Lewis predicted that in 1965 in the Region as a whole there would be three persons per vehicle. The actual figure turned out to be 2.94. The separate predictions for ratios for New York City and for the environs also turned out to be close to what actually occurred. Lewis' 40–year forecasts for vehicle registrations must rank as one of the more accurate long-range prognostications in the annals of planning.

Table 10.4. Motor vehicle registrations (thousands).

	Actual 1920	*Actual 1926*	*Predicted in 1927 for 1935*	*Actual 1940*	*Predicted in 1927 for 1965*	*Actual 1965*
New York City	223.2	573.0	1190.0	994.8	2260.0	1693.5
Rest of Region	252.6	757.0	1960.0	1442.3	4460.0	4227.3
Total – 22-County Region	475.8	1330.0	3150.0	2437.1	6720.0	5920.8

Sources: Predictions: Committee on the Regional Plan of New York and Its Environs (1927) *Regional Survey of New York and Its Environs.* Vol. III. *Highway Traffic* (by Harold M. Lewis with Ernest P. Goodrich). New York: Regional Plan of New York and Its Environs, pp. 48–52. Actual registration: Regional Plan Association, unpublished table from Department of Motor Vehicle figures issued by New York, New Jersey, and Connecticut.

Table 10.5. Persons per motor vehicle.

	Actual 1922	*Actual 1926*	*Predicted in 1927 for 1965*	*Actual 1965*
New York City	18.5	10.8	5	4.75
Environs	9.3	5.2	2	2.21
22–County Region	13.4	7.6	3	2.94

Sources: Predictions: Committee on the Regional Plan of New York and Its Environs (1927) *Regional Survey of New York and Its Environs.* Vol. III. *Highway Traffic* (by Harold M. Lewis with Ernest P. Goodrich). New York: Regional Plan of New York and Its Environs, pp. 48–52. Actual registration: Regional Plan Association, unpublished table from Department of Motor Vehicle figures issued by New York, New Jersey, and Connecticut.

But if Lewis's forecasts were accurate, why then was the highway network proposed in the Plan so considerably smaller in capacity than what was eventually required? Why was the Plan so grossly underdesigned for what we, retrospectively, can see would be needed? There are several explanations. First, there was the planners' expectation that transit, existing and proposed, would be adequate for a large share of the Region's work trips. It was assumed, at least implicitly, that the automobile would continue to be used largely for recreation trips rather than for the journey to work. But even if these assumptions were correct it would appear that the relatively modest highway network proposed was quite out of scale with a projected five-fold increase in the number of motor vehicles in the Region. The planners were either unwilling to face up to the long-term implications of their projections, or, more likely, they preferred to offer a regional highway plan for immediate action rather than for 1965, forty years away. A realistic highway plan that would have satisfied projected 1965 traffic demands would undoubtedly have appeared rather fantastic in 1929. The planners could not afford to jeopardize their credibility by proposing what might appear outrageously extravagant. Whatever the reason, the Plan had built into it a bias toward underdesign rather than overdesign, at least as a guide to long-term development. The useful life of the highway portion of the Plan was thus less than a decade. The Plan nevertheless helped spur the acceptability of the freeway concept and aided the growth of highway departments in the three states. As a result, freeways and parkways came earlier and in greater mileage to the New York Region than to other American metropolitan areas.

PARKS AND OPEN SPACES

In 1921 there were 53,071 acres of publicly owned parkland or accessible open space in the Region. By 1928 the Region had 94,131 acres.[7] The Regional Plan for parks and open space proposed a 1965 target of 352,037 acres.[8] By 1958, with 189,000 publicly-owned acres, open space was nearly double the area available when the Plan was completed. By 1965, however, the total park acreage had fallen short of the target by about 150,000 acres.[9] Nevertheless, the quadrupling of the Region's park land between 1921 and 1965 was a considerable achievement, which can be credited partly to the efforts of the Regional Plan Committee and staff and to the various county agencies which the Committee had helped to organize and support.

Not all the open space acquired corresponded to the proposals made in the Regional Plan. Gifts from individuals, unforeseen opportunities, and the attractiveness of large parcels in single ownership resulted in deviations from the 1929 Plan. Figures 7.16 and 7.17 contrast the configuration of the proposed open space with what had actually been acquired by 1965. Except for the failure to realize the park and parkway system proposed for northern New Jersey, there is a high degree of similarity between Plan and reality. Of the eighty-nine major proposals in the Plan, about half were carried out in whole or in part. Table 10.6 shows where the successes in park acquisition were greatest.

New York City and Long Island followed the Regional Plan more closely than other sectors of the Region. But this was partly due to the fact that the Regional Plan itself incorporated many of the standing proposals for parks made by the New York City Improvement Commission plan and the Long Island State Park Commission under the chairmanship of Robert Moses. The New Jersey counties in the Region and the five New York counties north of New York City, Westchester, Putnam, Orange, Rockland, and Dutchess, carried out far fewer of the Plan's open space proposals. Westchester and

Table 10.6. Number of proposed major open spaces in the 1929 Regional Plan acquired by 1965.

Sector of Region	Fully acquired	Partly acquired	Not acquired	Total numbers of proposals in the Regional Plan	Percent of total acquired in full or in part
Connecticut	0	5	2	7	72%
New Jersey	5	6	21	32	34%
New York, excluding N.Y.C. and L.I.	1	0	6	7	14%
Long Island (Nassau–Suffolk)	2	5	3	10	70%
New York City	12	9	12	33	63%
Total	20	25	44	89	56%
Percent	22	29	49	100	

Source: Regional Plan Association maps.

Rockland by 1929 already had sizable areas of open space, thanks to gifts of the Harriman and Rockefeller families, and probably perceived the need for additional acquisition as not very pressing. Orange, Putnam, and Dutchess Counties were largely rural in character until the post-World War II period and felt under no great compulsion to develop county programs. In New Jersey, Essex and Union Counties developed active park programs, and acquisitions there closely followed the Regional Plan. But the other seven New Jersey counties moved slowly or not at all. Bergen County's failure to acquire large open spaces in anticipation of the development spurred by the George Washington Bridge was particularly regrettable. Very little of the Plan's extensive scheme for parks and parkways for northern New Jersey was carried out.

Despite these failures the open space successes of the Plan were among its most notable achievements. By demonstrating the regional importance of parks and the benefits that would accrue to the outlying jurisdictions when they accepted state and county parks to serve populations beyond their own boundaries, the Regional Plan helped generate strong public opinion in favor of open space programs. The greatest successes were obtained where strong county and state agencies were established. The Plan provided a powerful reference from which the agencies could draw arguments for their programs. But also significant were the parallel gifts by the wealthy, which undoubtedly were stimulated by the Plan. The patricians who held extensive lands at the urban fringe were aware of the planning work of their acquaintances and colleagues on the Regional Plan Committee. The Regional Plan was criticized for its elite basis, but the significant parkland gifts made by the elite were a positive outcome of the social origins of the Plan.

Not all of the important proposals made in the Plan were realized. Miles of seashore, lakefront, and stream valleys were lost to private development; the lower Palisades, the Watchungs, the Shawun-gunks, the Highlands of the Navesink, and acres of wetlands remained unacquired and vulnerable to despoliation. But much open space was acquired as called for in the Plan: the great barrier beach parks at Jones Beach and Fire Island on the southern shore of Long Island, additions to the Palisade Interstate Park system, the extensive park system of Staten Island, and numerous smaller parks in other counties in the Region. These essential open spaces are undoubtedly among the most significant and enduring legacies of the 1929 Regional Plan.

DEVELOPMENT PROJECTS

The Regional Plan included a number of specific development and redevelopment projects, mostly for the dense central areas. A remarkable proportion of these projects were eventually carried out and a few are still under active consideration. The Regional Plan group constantly emphasized redevelopment for parks, residences, and trafficways along obsolescent industrial waterfronts in the older cities. The Plan called for intensive rebuilding of the East and West Sides of Manhattan and along the shores of the Harlem River in upper Manhattan and The Bronx. Redevelopment of the Harlem River waterfront was not carried out, although plans for a park and related development have been discussed. The Regional Plan proposals for the West Side went unrealized largely because of the regrettable character of the West Side Highway and New York Central Railroad improvements that effectively cut the riverfront off from the city. The Regional Plan's opposition to the elevated design for the West Side Highway has been borne out fifty years later. It appears now that the existing highway has deteriorated beyond repair and will be replaced by a facility integrated with surrounding development, much as proposed in the Plan.

The redevelopment of the East Side more closely followed the recommendations of the Plan. Here the marginal highway was constructed at grade level and a narrow park strip provided at the water's edge. The principle, emphasized in the Plan, of integrating buildings and highway, was followed in several places on the East River, where new construction used air rights over the East River (F.D.R.) Drive. With the removal of obsolete waterfront slaughterhouses and other industries, new complexes such as the United Nations headquarters, the Rockefeller Institute, and luxury apartments were constructed at the water's edge. The designs laid out in the Regional Plan were, of course, not precisely followed, but the essential principles were. The Regional Plan called attention to an attractive opportunity and the developers and institutions had responded. While the result was not the magnificent quayside envisioned by Charles Norton, the integration of park, highway, and building design on the East River was far superior to the chaos of the West Side waterfront. Even more successful was the similar treatment of the Brooklyn-Queens Expressway in Brooklyn Heights, where the roadway was double-decked to provide an attractive promenade overlooking the harbor, much as the Plan had proposed.

One of the key proposals in the Plan for Manhattan's West Side near the river was an art and cultural center at 60th Street. The Lincoln Center for the Performing Arts, completed in the 1960s, though three blocks east of the suggested site, was a fulfillment of that concept. Indeed, the design and layout of the court at Lincoln Center bears a striking similarity to the renderings in the Plan.[10]

Another important project in the Plan that was later partly carried out was the civic center proposal for lower Manhattan. The Regional Plan's concept for a new Municipal Building directly behind the City Hall was not followed, though the proposal is again under discussion. The general scheme of developing a civic complex north of City Hall was, however, realized with the construction of state and federal buildings in that vicinity.[11]

In Brooklyn the civic center proposal made in the Plan for the area at the approach to the Brooklyn Bridge was followed quite closely.[12] The Newark civic center proposed for the vicinity of the Pennsylvania Railroad terminal was not realized, although a major office redevelopment project was begun there in 1970.[13]

North of Newark lie the 30,000 acres of the Hackensack Meadows. The Regional Plan called for development there of a self-contained community for nearly 100,000 people, with a major new business center and an industrial area of about 4,000 acres. The Plan called for a Meadowlands Reclamation Commission to carry out the integral development of the Meadows. The State of New Jersey established such a commission in the 1960s, which has now carried out the development of this resource somewhat along the lines proposed in the Regional Plan.[14]

Although some of the project proposals in the Plan were realized, others were not. The decentralized rail terminals and office centers over the Mott Haven and Sunnyside yards were never really feasible because of the declining utilization of the rail passenger system. The idea of using the air rights over these vast rail consolidation yards was, however, later employed at Mott Haven for several residential and public buildings, and a similar project has been discussed for Sunnyside.

The idea of spreading office buildings about rail-oriented subcenters and also within the Manhattan uptown business district was perhaps a weak conception, for it ignored the natural tendency of offices to concentrate in a vicinity to facilitate face-to-face contacts. If the concept failed to be realized in sub-centers in the Bronx and Queens, it did have an effect in the late 1920s on the location of isolated office towers in Midtown Manhattan. In particular, the Empire State Building followed the principle laid out in the Regional Plan to build separated tall towers. Other examples were the McGraw Hill Building and the New York Daily News Building, both of which were designed by the architect Raymond Hood and located at opposite ends of Forty-Second Street. Such towers, separated from the main concentration of office buildings for reasons of aesthetics and reduced congestion, experienced considerable financial difficulty in the 1930s. The Empire State Building in its first five years had an especially high vacancy rate, partly because of its location, but also because of an overbuilding of office space in the late 1920s, a phenomenon to which the Regional Plan may have contributed through its images of a multitowered office landscape in mid-Manhattan.

For the environs the Plan mostly put forward prototypical proposals for residential layouts and public buildings, rather than specific designs. The extent to which these prototypes influenced development can only be conjectured, though surely here and there the advice was followed. Garden cities and new communities were not part of the Plan, but proposals for satellite industrial communities along the proposed belt railway were suggested.

These did not materialize because the belt line was never built. But even had it been constructed, it seems unlikely that the proposed satellite communities would have followed, since there were no public development agencies proposed or in existence to carry out the task.

THE SIGNIFICANCE OF THE REGIONAL PLAN: A SUMMARY

The 1929 Regional Plan of New York and Its Environs left a profound imprint on urban America and metropolitan New York. The physical fabric of the Region was altered by the carrying out of many of the proposals made in the Plan. Important new planning agencies and institutions were established or greatly assisted by the existence of the Plan and the work of the Regional Plan staff. Most important, perhaps, was the impact of the Regional Plan and Survey on urban theory and urban ideology. The ideas generated in the course of making the Plan altered the way American urbanists looked at their large cities and imagined their futures.

The Plan's basic physical planning conceptions were reflected in the subsequent development of the Region. The great bridges and tunnels that knitted together the pieces of the Region were located according to the recentralizing principles laid out by Thomas Adams and were accelerated in their construction by the existence of the Plan. The circumferential highways urged in the Plan were adopted by engineers and state highways departments. New grade-separated freeways were originated or accelerated by the Plan. The Merritt and Garden State Parkways had their origins in the Plan. The acquisition of parklands was also spurred by the proposals contained in the Regional Plan. Waterfronts in the cities were rebuilt along the principles of the Plan, though their use for highways took more priority over their amenity and recreational value than was envisioned in the Plan. In the growing centers of the cities, and especially in Manhattan, new structures were spread further apart to allow for better circulation and more light and air, in accordance with the images and ideas of the Plan. If many of these projects and concepts were not original with the Regional Plan, the Plan nevertheless brought them together in a unified presentation, making them far more widely known and accepted. Many such proposals, of course, might have been realized had there never been a Regional Plan. The raw materials of regional planning in the form of long-standing proposals and evolving principles existed independently of the Plan. But as a coordinating device the Plan accelerated the realization of these proposals and principles and thereby changed the face of the New York Region.

The Plan resulted in many positive successes, but it also must be charged with serious failures, both for what it failed to attempt and for what it attempted but failed to achieve. The Plan failed to address the long-term implications of vastly increased automobile ownership, despite the accurate predictions of the increase. It failed to address the problem of providing housing for low and lower-middle income families. And it was ambiguous in its support of new communities, supporting the concept, on one hand, and yet reluctant to indicate where or how new communities might be built.

The Plan also failed to realize its bold rail proposals, thanks largely to the neanderthal attitudes of the private rail companies. It failed to realize its too modest proposals for rail transit for several reasons: the problem of coordination across state boundaries, the reluctance of the Port of New York Authority to assume a leadership role in a financially unattractive venture, and the reluctance of New York City transit officials to permit suburban trains on the city subway system tracks. The result was progress in public highway construction without parallel development of transit facilities, resulting in a greatly decentralized Region by 1965 rather than the 'recentralized' Region envisioned in the Plan. The Plan also failed to make adequate provision for new or expanded business centers, even though it was quite apparent that a considerably increased and recentralized population would require such centers. Despite its failures, the Regional Plan clearly had a significant effect on the physical development of the Region.

The Plan also brought important changes in the institutional and public bodies concerned with Regional development. Numerous planning and zoning agencies were established at the county and municipal level as a direct result of proselytization by the staff of the Regional Plan. State policies toward regional development were also augmented and enhanced. The Port of New York Authority, an agency of New York and New Jersey, was greatly aided in its uncertain early years by the support of the Regional Plan Committee. Differences occurred, of course, but the influence of the Regional Plan on the Port Authority was usually salutary and broadening, as in the convincing case made in the Plan for providing rapid transit capacity in the design of the George Washington Bridge.

Robert Moses in his capacities as New York City Park Commissioner and chairman of both the Long Island State Park Commission and the Triborough Bridge Authority carried many of the Plan's highway and park proposals for New York City and Long Island to completion. The Regional Plan undoubtedly provided Moses with an agenda of public works. But more important, it created for Moses a climate of opinion among the business and political leadership in New York favorable to his program. Though the reformers might later regret it, the ascendancy of Robert Moses to power was considerably aided by this climate.

Much of the progress made toward the partial though considerable realization of the Plan between 1929 and 1941 was due to the vigorous efforts of the Regional Plan Association, which pressed local governments and the special authorities to undertake park and transportation projects. In a number of instances the Association provided detailed design proposals based on the

Plan, such as those for Great Kills Park in Staten Island and Jacob Riis Park in Queens, which directly resulted in acquisition or development.

The establishment of the Regional Plan Association, created to carry out the proposals of the Regional Plan, is perhaps the most enduring and significant institutional heritage of the efforts of the Russell Sage Committee. The Association continues to play a unique watchdog and research role in the planning and development of the New York Metropolitan Region.[15]

The Plan's impact on the theory and technique of urban planning was also important. The Regional Survey considerably advanced the development of population projection methods. Economic base theory had its beginnings in the work of Frederick Law Olmsted, Jr., for the Regional Survey. Robert Murray Haig and Roswell McCrea radically altered economists' theories of intraurban location of economic activity through their pathbreaking empirical studies of the accessibility requirements of firms and households. Haig and McCrea also demonstrated the validity of the view that the city was important as a production unit as well as a consumption unit in the national economy.

Clarence Perry's Neighborhood Theory had a great impact on planning thought and practice both here and abroad, and has enjoyed a revival of interest in recent years. Bassett, in his work on the Regional Plan, refined the zoning tool he had helped devise earlier. As a consequence of the Plan, local zoning was adopted earlier and more widely in the New York Region than elsewhere. Bassett also significantly developed the law of public open space and shorefront rights in connection with his work for the Plan. The definition of the freeway concept and the word 'freeway' itself were products of Bassett's efforts.

The Plan also gave early warning of special urban problems that continue to be serious: the pollution of air and water, the inequitable social effects of large-lot zoning, and the destruction of public investment in highways by marginal commercial development. But perhaps its most important contribution was to articulate the connections between the physical framework of the city and its social and economic conditions. No longer could engineering or architectural projects be promoted solely on narrow grounds of efficiency or aesthetics. Relationships between public investments in infrastructure and the distribution of jobs and people had to be taken into account. The Plan and Survey demonstrated clearly the need to take into account the complex connections among the basic regional systems.

These new ideas and principles spread rapidly through the culture of urban planning in the decades following the publication of the Plan in 1929. Former members and consultants of the Regional Plan staff took up important positions and tasks, not only in the New York area, but in other American cities as well, carrying with them the ideas and principles evolved in their studies for the Regional Plan Committee. Some, like Thomas Adams and Henry Hubbard, taught what they had learned in the new academic planning programs such as those at Harvard University and MIT. The evolution of planning as a separate academic discipline and profession was in considerable measure a byproduct of the Regional Plan. American urban planning, for better or worse, assumed its identity in the 1920s and was influenced greatly by the experiences and activities connected with the making of the Regional Plan of New York and Its Environs. Long after the Plan became only of historic interest, the values and imageries, the premises and goals of urban planners continued to be those embodied in the Plan.

The Regional Plan obviously had considerable impact on the New York Region and on the development of American urban planning. But the tantalizing question remains: impact for whom and on whom? Whose values were embedded in the Regional Plan, and who actually benefited from it? These questions are considered in the next chapter.

NOTES

1. The Regional Plan staff used the Nelson Lewis projection (which was supported by the later Pearl-Reed series). The alternative projections of Goodrich and Wilson-Luyten forecast a 1965 population of about 14.5 million, considerably lower than the actual outcome. Interestingly, had all the projection series available to the Regional Plan staff been averaged, the resulting figure would have been very close to the 1965 population total. High forecasts, however, have always been attractive to planners making a case for increased spending for public capital improvements.

2. This is the error in projecting total population levels. The errors in projecting the population growth increment were, of course, considerably higher: 16.6 per cent for the period 1920–1940 and 30.0 per cent for 1920–1965.

3. Results of the 1925 New York State Census were reported in Committee on the Regional Plan of New York and Its Environs (1929) *Regional Survey of New York and Its Environs. Vol II. Population, Land Values and Government.* New York: Regional Plan of New York and Its Environs, p. 71.

4. Regional Plan Association, Unpublished tabulations, 1965.

5. Regional Plan Association (1933) *From Plan to Reality I.* New York: Regional Plan Association, p. 23.

6. Nearly 1,000 miles of this were built between 1950 and 1965. Source: unpublished figures of the Regional Plan Association, 1965.

7. Committee on the Regional Plan of New York and Its Environs (1928) *Regional Survey of New York and Its Environs. Vol. V. Public Recreation.* New York: Regional Plan of New York and Its Environs, p. 237.

8. Regional Plan Association (1933), p. 69.

9. Regional Plan Association (1960) *The Race for Open Space.* New York: Regional Plan Association, p. 9. The total for 1970 was about 270,000 acres, as reported by the Tri-State Regional Planning Commission (1973) *Outdoor Recreation in a Crowded Region.* New York: Tri-State Regional Planning Commission, pp. 8–10.

10. Committee on the Regional Plan of New York and Its Environs (1931) *Regional Plan of New York and Its Environs. Vol. II. The Building of the City* (by Thomas

Adams assisted by Harold M. Lewis and Lawrence M. Orton). New York: Regional Plan of New York and Its Environs, p. 115.

11. *Ibid.*, pp. 381–388.

12. *Ibid.*, pp. 475–482.

13. *Ibid.*, pp. 535–539.

14. *Ibid.*, pp. 540–547.

15. In 1968, the Regional Plan Association completed the Second Regional Plan, a successor to the original Plan of New York and Its Environs. Regional Plan Association (1968) *The Second Regional Plan: A Draft for Discussion.* New York: Regional Plan Association.

11

THE REGIONAL PLAN AS ARTIFACT AND PROCESS

VALUES AND POWER: WHO BENEFITED FROM THE PLAN?

The Regional Plan was an attempt to articulate, coordinate, and expand the public agenda, and through the public agenda to influence private decisions. This process is summarized in the model shown in figure 11.1. Many kinds of organizations attempt to shape the public agenda in pursuit of their values. These values are derived from a variety of sources: behavioral norms, ideologies, utopian constructs, professional values, client group interests, and, not least important, from a need to perpetuate the organization. The values which motivate an organization's activities may be inherently conflicting and may shift from one period to another. The organization will have little success in imposing its values on the public agenda if it lacks power. An organization's power may be derived from a number of sources: its wealth, its prestige, its location in some hierarchy which itself possesses power, and through identification with members who possess power or influence from sources outside the organization. It should be noted that the acquisition of power may itself become a motivating value of the organization.

An organization succeeds in altering or adding to the public agenda if it is able to evoke a response from a relevant element of the apparatus of public decision making. Lacking an appropriate decision system or failing a hearing in the extant system, it may attempt to create a new system for its purposes. Public decision systems may take three kinds of action: distributive, the apportionment of resources to competing groups roughly in proportion to their power; regulatory, the making of rules to ensure the efficient functioning of on-going systems; and redistributive, where resources are allocated disproportionately to their possession of wealth, power, or some other relevant characteristic. Redistribution may concentrate power or wealth or may reduce concentration.

Decisions result in outcomes whose consequences may or may not be anticipated. Outcomes may also be regarded as being manifest or latent.[1] That is, latent consequences of actions are those which produce vital social effects even though these purposes are not the stated intention of the actions. Perception and evaluation of outcomes by organizations and decision systems can result in a revision of organizational strategy or even values.

Distribution or redistribution of wealth or power may result in changes in the power of an organization to shape the public agenda in subsequent rounds of activity.

The public decision system, as described in this model, is dynamic and in constant flux, responding to changes in the norms of the encompassing society. Motivating values are altered, power relationships shift, and even the

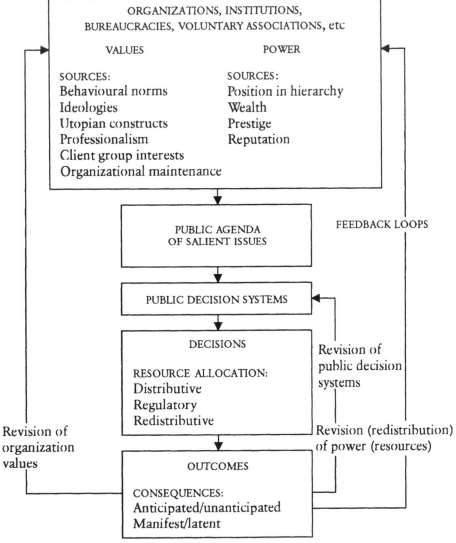

Figure 11.1.   A schematic model of the public decision process.

structure of the public decision process may change. A plan, by contrast, sits embedded in time, a crystallization of values and of assumptions about power and about the structure of the decision process. A plan attempts to capture in a single moment the way the present imagines its future. This was the dilemma of the Regional Plan. Its makers wanted it to be both artifact and process, both blueprint and propaganda tract. How, then, do we assess the Plan? Its goals were never stated explicitly. It served no well-defined client group. It offered no alternatives to be chosen by competing interest groups. Whose values did it express? Whose power did it augment?

Several scenarios are possible: The Regional Plan originated among the patrician class, bankers, business and professional men; was it an attempt by this group to wrest power from the unwashed immigrants and their political machine? Was it an attempt by industrialists to ensure a region fitted to their needs for land and labor? Was it an instrument of the new middle class, with their automobiles and potentially limitless mobility? Or was it a creation of a segment of the middle class, the new administrative class, bureaucrat-technicians seeking to achieve their own narrow systemic goals while claiming to speak for the public interest? The Regional Plan was motivated by all of these forces. But which was dominant? Here the model is suggestive: if decisional outcomes are a function of an organization's values and its influence, then an evaluation of outcomes may provide insights into the inherent values and the power orientations underlying the Plan. Systematic evaluation of metropolitan plans, however, is not in a very advanced stage. A few attempts have been made to devise *ex ante* evaluation schemes to judge the quality of alternative metropolitan plans and planning processes. *Ex post* evaluation of metropolitan plans is even more rare.

Several sets of criteria have been proposed as bases for the *ex ante* evaluation of alternative metropolitan plans. For example, Boyce, Day, and McDonald have suggested eight salient characteristics for judging plans.[2]

1. Feasibility: satisfaction of technological and fiscal constraints.
2. Distributional effects: equity of alternatives for groups in the population.
3. Conservation: limitations on the use, exploitation of natural and human resources.
4. Flexibility: capability of the regional system and plan to respond or adapt to a change in conditions.
5. Levels of service and system performance: technical specification of system performance and user requirements.
6. Economic efficiency: difference between gross benefits and costs.
7. Organization of facilities and services: spatial arrangement and operation of metropolitan facility service systems.
8. Interaction: ability of persons to interact spatially and socially in the metropolitan area.

This useful set of criteria was devised to compare alternative metropolitan plans, but it may also be used for subjective evaluation of priorities in the Regional Plan, as shown in table 11.1. The Plan set a high priority on feasibility, economic efficiency and interaction, and a low priority on distributional effects. The remaining criteria fall into an intermediate position.

The Boyce-Day-McDonald Criteria provide a means for the subjective evaluation of metropolitan plans. But they shed little light on a plan's distribution of benefits among population groups in a region. Table 11.2 addresses this question for the Regional Plan. It offers an impressionistic view of the benefits potentially derived from the several elements of the Plan, such as housing, the location of employment and the potential service of proposed transportation systems. Benefits are subjectively evaluated in table 11.2 on a scale of 0 to 3. A regional plan can affect population groups according to their location in the Region, their socio-economic status, and their generation. Benefits potentially realized by these distinct groups are estimated in the table.

Table 11.1. Evaluation of the Regional Plan of New York and Its Environs.

Plan evaluation criteria	Estimate of priority in Regional Plan
Feasibility	High
Economic efficiency	High
Interaction	High
Conservation	Medium
Levels of service and systems performance	Medium
Organization of facilities and services	Medium
Flexibility	Medium
Distributional effects	Low

The analysis in table 11.2 suggests that the expected outcomes of the Regional Plan would most have benefited groups located in or near the Manhattan business district and the other major centers and those in the suburbs. By socio-economic status, the beneficiaries were to be the upper-middle income and upper income groups. This should not seem surprising, for the Plan concentrated its attention on the two areas of greatest physical change, the center of the Region, Manhattan, and the suburban fringe. New housing, in the absence of subsidy programs, can help only those who can afford it. Transportation systems proposed in the Plan were geared to the affluent suburbanites or the city dweller able to afford an automobile. For the mass of people living in the older neighborhoods in the cities, the Plan offered little relief, nor, with its concentration on the areas of greatest physical change, the center and the fringe, could it have been expected to do so. The Plan, then, was imbued with the values of the emerging middle class in their quest for more spacious living and greater mobility. It was less a plan supportive of upper class values than an assertion of middle class needs. The

Table 11.2. Estimated distribution of potential benefits of Regional Plan proposals.

	Housing	Employment location	Passenger rail transportation	Highways	Recreation and open space	Amenities and environment	Total
Spatial distribution							
Center City	+++	+++	+++	+	+	+++	14
Mature core	+	++	++	++	++	++	11
Suburbs	+++	++	+++	+++	+++	+++	17
Fringe	++	+	+	+	+++	++	10
Rural	0	0	0	+	+	+	3
Income level							
Upper	++	+++	+++	+++	+	++	14
Upper middle	+++	+++	++	+++	+++	+++	18
Lower middle	++	++	+	++	+++	++	12
Lower	+	++	+	+	++	+	8
Poverty level	0	0	+	0	++	+	4
Time frame							
Contemporary	+	++	+	+++	++	+	10
Next generation	++	+++	++	++	+++	++	14
Secular	+	+	++	++	+++	+	10

upper class could, after all, purchase amenity and accessibility; the rising middle class could not so easily buy the environment they wanted. This group required the aid of the regulatory and allocative mechanisms of government. The framers of the Regional Plan appreciated the potency of the growing middle class and merged their goals with those of the upper class. But they also espoused the aims of the business leadership: an economically competitive and efficient Region, whose decision environment would be stabilized and rationalized. The values embedded in the Regional Plan were those of the dominant groups in the society. The Regional Plan, seeking legitimacy and power, had necessarily to embrace the values of those groups that could endow it with those attributes. Lacking authority and power of its own, it was designed to achieve influence by appealing to those who possessed influence.

Power could, however, come through another route as well: claims of expertise and research. Technicians and administrators with specialized knowledge and skills could control, at least partially, the development and implementation of the public agenda. There were, however, limits to the independence with which staff technicians could develop and pursue their own innovative ideas about urban systems. Approval of the Regional Plan Committee was required for all significant proposals. The Committee's views could not help but reflect the views of what it conceived its constituency to be. And similarly the staff technicians and planners tended to absorb the values of the Committee, a process abetted by the natural desire of the staff for social mobility upward to the levels of the prestigious members of the Committee. The result was inevitably a propensity toward conservative policy and a 'safe' Plan. The Regional Plan was trapped in a dilemma: it could acquire influence only by gaining the support of those who possessed influence, but it could only gain this support by appealing to the values of those with power or wealth. Thus the Regional Plan, initially motivated by a rhetoric linking aesthetic and redistributive goals, ended by being dominated by a concern for engineering efficiency and for perpetuation of an administrative organization. By the time of its completion the Plan was conceived of less as a hortatory and visionary document than as a device to secure legitimacy and authority for its authors and sponsors. It was soon realized that it was a continuing process of intervention, rather than the existence of a Plan, that would affect the future of the Region.

As realists and pragmatists, the Regional Plan Committee recognized that the potential to effect public programs resided largely in the diffuse business community. The business community was clearly not a monolithic, organized entity but a cluster of sometimes cooperating, sometimes competing interests. The Regional Plan sought to focus and harness these interests. By the joining of less attractive or profitable objectives, such as the provision of amenities or the amelioration of slum conditions, to proposals more attractive to the dominant business sector, it was hoped that the latter would carry the former to realization.

What happened to a considerable degree was just the reverse. Efficiency and growth-related elements of the Plan were enhanced in their acceptability by being linked to a rhetoric of concern for amenity and redistributive objectives. Thus massive public intervention for new highways was endorsed, and ultimately realized, far beyond the expectations of the Regional Planners, but public intervention for housing was unacceptable. Images of what constituted good housing and neighborhoods were incorporated in the Plan, but proposals for new programs and institutions for their realization were conspicuously absent. The Plan's *modus operandi* was thus inverted from its original conception as a mechanism to pull less feasible social programs along with those more readily acceptable, to a device that enhanced the acceptability of efficiency-related projects by linking them to social objectives. In its quest for influence, the Regional Plan group was thus forced to sacrifice some of its freedom to identify with and work for programs beneficial to the relatively powerless groups in the Region.

Had the Plan been more democratically based, its value premises might have been more broad and representative of the populace at large. But the Plan was modeled on national precedents, notably the establishment of the Federal Reserve System, which were not democratic but centralist innovations. The increasing complexity of industrial society precluded the involvement of the average citizen, who could not be expected to understand much about the intricacies of banking or of the metropolis, and who, besides, was probably not much interested in either. The Regional Plan was inevitably 'top-down' planning, with the technical experts, guided by the prestigious committee, delivering solutions to problems of regional growth. There was little feedback from the populace at large. The Regional Council, a group of distinguished citizens who met several times in 1925 and 1926, might have played this role but ultimately had little influence on the proposals adopted in the Plan. The Council was viewed more as a means of disseminating information and gaining acceptance for the Plan than as a source of ideas. Moreover, it was not at all representative of the Region's population. The Council was comprised of individuals who in their local communities played the same role and possessed the same elite status as members of the Committee on the Regional Plan did in the larger New York scene.

There was no way that the values or needs of the black and immigrant poor could filter into the process by which the Regional Plan was made. On the contrary, records of the Committee are permeated with distrust and misunderstanding of the newcomers. Concern for the Americanization of the immigrants and fear of Bolshevism were themes that appeared from time to time in Committee and staff discussions. And how can one explain the proposal of Frederic Delano, a decent and far-sighted man, to demolish the Harlem of the 1920s, which was then enjoying a renaissance as the center of American black culture? How explain Thomas Adams' proposals for lower densities and higher standards for housing for the working middle class without a recognition that higher standards inevitably meant higher prices, prices that many could not afford? How explain the eagerness of Adams to help city industries relocate to the suburbs so that they might avoid a union shop? But perhaps the supreme irony of values came with the Committee's selection of a Philadelphia firm to print the Regional Plan volumes. The printing industry of New York, which economist Robert Murray Haig had studied so closely and used as a model for his series of industries studies, was highly unionized, whereas Philadelphia firms were not. The Plan for the New York Region was printed outside the Region solely to avoid the higher costs of a union shop.[3]

For its contemporary generation the Plan offered far less than its originator, Charles Norton, had sought for the poor families of the city. The Plan encouraged the departure of industrial jobs from the centers, where the poor could reach them, to the less accessible suburban ring. The transportation systems proposed in the Plan, both for rail and highways, were drawn to suit the needs and resources of the middle class, not those of the urban poor. Fares on the proposed suburban rail transit system would necessarily be beyond the means of the city's poor. (No subsidies were proposed of the kind London had provided for its workers.) The proposed highways could only be used by those who could afford to own and operate a car. And in 1926 nearly half the families in the Region did not have a car.

By its very scale and its emphasis on abstract systems the Plan tended to skew the attention of the Region's civic leadership away from local needs such as schools, health centers, and playgrounds, and towards regional needs such as highways and large outlying parks, even though there was need for both regional and local facilities. A regional plan could obviously not deal with local matters in detail. But local facilities and services most affected the urban poor, as Charles Norton had pointed out. By emphasizing metropolitanism, the regional planners ultimately lost sight of that true comprehensiveness based on the needs of individuals and families in their immediate environments. The comprehensiveness of the Regional Plan was merely a comprehensiveness of systems.

Had Norton survived, his humane instincts might well have guided the Plan towards a greater concern for the needs of people and less for the needs of industry and the demands of the emergent automobile technology. With Norton gone, the engineering orientation of Delano, Adams, and the younger Lewis dominated the formulation of the Plan. With its emphasis on highway systems and the development of the suburban fringe, the Plan set the stage for the ascendancy of the undemocratic, unaccountable authorities – Robert Moses and the Port of New York Authority – as the ultimate shapers of the

Region whose projects catered to the needs of the powerful and the middle class, often to the detriment of the welfare of the poor in the cities.

If the Plan did not significantly benefit its contemporary generation of poor and working families, its proposals may have benefited their offspring. When large numbers of the children of the lower groups moved upward in socio-economic status, it became possible for this next generation to enjoy the parks and highway system realized in part through the Plan. The Regional Plan implicitly assumed a significant relative expansion of the middle class. The substantial metropolitan growth for which the Plan had made provision was to be the driving engine behind an expanded Regional economy and an enlarged middle class. To those who were able to participate in the upward social movement, the Plan offered potential benefits in the form of open space, parkways, and better suburbs, as table 11.2 suggests.

But many were left behind and there always seemed to be more poor from beyond the bounds of the Region to take the places of those who were able to move upward economically and outward geographically. For these groups, the Plan offered little. The assumption was that the physical patterns in the areas where such people lived had been fixed and were not easily altered. And because the Plan was oriented largely to physical change, it could say little about ways of providing needed social services and economic opportunity.

The Regional Plan may have combined the values and the political ambitions of an increasingly impotent, established patrician class and a growing upper-middle class and promoted the virtues of a centralized administrative bureaucracy. But in those parts of the Region where the Plan was influential, it also demonstrated the effectiveness of strong leadership at the sub-regional level, supported by positive state action. Counties such as Westchester and to a lesser degree Essex and Union were able to carry out development plans that were reinforced by their inclusion in the context of the Regional Plan. This was also true to some degree of New York City and the Long Island counties of Nassau and Suffolk. In these areas superior development patterns were achieved through governmental agencies able to transcend the local parochialism and small scale of individual villages and towns. With few exceptions, local parochialism and a failure in state leadership most characterized the New Jersey counties in the Region. The result was a development pattern considerably inferior to the patterns that evolved in the Region east of the Hudson. And it was in New Jersey that the unbridled nineteenth-century *laissez faire* attitudes of the railroad companies posed an insurmountable obstacle to the provision of adequate levels of passenger and freight service. So long as the metropolitan area was expanding, some form of centralization of authority and responsibility was essential. The old forms of local self-determination were totally inadequate to the demands of the metropolis. The notion that smaller units of government and of business were necessarily more responsive to local needs is not supported by the evidence. What was more likely to happen was that the smaller units simply failed to address the local implications of Region-wide problems and issues, often with detrimental consequences for the locality, or, at least, with opportunities missed.

But for all the reality of regional problems, the fact remains that the Regional Plan attempted to substitute a larger parochialism for the local variety. The Regional Plan grew out of a long tradition of American reform linked by heritage to such diverse enterprises as the abolitionist movement, the American Red Cross, and the Federal Reserve System. Optimistic, pragmatic, rationalist, and middle-class in its values, it was basically conservative. The Plan was a response to the industrial maturing of America's largest metropolis, the growing ownership of the automobile, and the spread of the city beyond its political boundaries. But it was more than that. It was a kind of funnel flared at both ends, into which were poured a variety of hopes and causes – from Charles Norton's dream of a beautiful city in which a poor man could live comfortably, to Edward Bassett's system of benign zoning, to megalopolitan, futuristic images of skyscrapers and freeways. Brought together for a moment in the Plan, these elements soon separated again as unrelated policies from among which the future could choose.

The Plan was a bridge between the eras of Theodore Roosevelt and Franklin Roosevelt, though there was perhaps more of the spirit of Teddy than of Franklin in it. In many ways, the Plan looked back more than ahead. It was socially timid where it should have been bold, and perhaps too technologically mechanistic where it should have been more humane. The reformers behind the Regional Plan occupied a position strategic for the influencing of urban social change and innovation. Accepted by their peers in the business and industrial structure, yet by contrast oriented not to the preservation of the *status quo* but to societal improvement, they nevertheless set their sights too low and realized far less than they were capable of. Reform groups have frequently served as the cutting edge of social change by adapting and legitimizing ideas and proposals that would appear extreme if proposed by groups outside the mainstream of respectability. In the case of the Regional Plan, however, the quest for acceptance and authority dulled the cutting edge of alternative values and potential innovations, especially for the poor.

The unresolvable conflict faced by the metropolitan reformers were those of America as a nation: the demands of an expansive industrial society versus the human need for community and the venerated traditions of democratic rule. Unable and perhaps unwilling to change the national political and economic context, the reform planners accepted its imperatives and sought balanced, ameliorative solutions to problems of metropolitan development. It was not surprising, then, that the Regional Plan as artifact and as process proved quite unequal to the laudable aspirations with which it had begun. The conflicts still endure much in the form in which they were originally encountered by the Regional Plan Committee and staff. But also enduring are the tangible legacies of the Plan such as open spaces and parkways, as well as a continuing endeavor to achieve a regional community in the face of immense political diversity and diffuse interests. It is more for these legacies that the Regional Plan should be remembered than for its failures.

CONCLUSION: SOME HYPOTHESES OF REFORM BEHAVIOR

The Regional Plan of New York and Its Environs was but one of many reform activities whose roots lay in the Progressive era, but which culminated in the 1920s and subsequently influenced social and legislative activity in the New Deal period. A single case study of regional planning is hardly an adequate basis for the proof or refutation of hypotheses concerning the American reform phenomenon. However, an individual case study may legitimately suggest tentative hypotheses for subsequent testing in other situations. The following hypotheses concerning reform and metropolitan planning summarize the foregoing analysis of the Regional Plan of New York:

1. Reform groups have tended to come from the upwardly mobile, upper-middle-class income stratum, of which they are a relatively small subset. Such groups are oriented to change and possess the resources to work outside the established economy and polity. Since this group has been concentrated in areas where the industrial economy is mature, such as the urban areas of the Northeast and the Midwest, reform activity has occurred earliest and most intensely in those locales.

2. Reform groups have focused their attention on a wide variety of issues and topics that have a common thrust toward enhanced societal efficiency and integration. Upper and middle income class-reform proponents have moved freely among such issue areas. Regional planning has been only one such issue area.

3. Reform groups often have several distinct interests: they have tended to view growth positively, as a means to social betterment for all groups; they have tended to use alterations in the *status quo* to attain and coalesce power to achieve their interpretation of broad societal goals, and, what often amounts to the same thing, their own desires and ends, which are urged on the society as appropriate for all groups.

4. Reform-based plans have typically been undertaken as ends in themselves embodying high purposes and goals; but ultimately such plans have tended to become a means to achieve legitimacy for the organization established to make the plan.

5. Values and goals of the upper class and the upper middle class have found more support in reform plans than have values and goals of

lower and lower middle classes. Consequently, efficiency goals have tended to take priority over equity goals.

6. Reform-minded plans have been premised on optimistic assumptions concerning growth and upward mobility.

7. Reform planning activity has tended to be more intense and better funded in times of affluence.

8. Reform plans have relied heavily on easily understood images to convey alternative possible futures. Such images are readily absorbed and adopted by public and private development decision-makers, but these images have not usually deviated radically from current norms.

9. Reform planning groups have viewed themselves as bridges between the controlling economic interests in the society and the public at large. Seeking to preserve the reality and the appearance of neutrality, reform planners typically have attempted to bypass existing political structures by creating independent quasi-public institutions to carry on their work.

10. Reform planning groups also have tried to convey a posture of neutrality by claiming impartial technical competence, which they contrast with the usually uninformed partisan conflict of the political arena. The rise of an American planning profession was in part a response to this stimulus.

11. The quest for a neutral posture as a basis for achieving legitimacy among competing groups has been linked to the planners' embrace of the abstract themes of comprehensiveness and regionalism. By escalating debate to higher levels of generality, existing arenas of concrete conflict were bypassed and claims for neutral technical competence more easily made.

12. Control of information flows has been crucial to the success of reform organizations, in or out of government. Enough general information is supplied, usually in the form of attractive reports, to assure attribution of technical competence and prestige. Such information is often of value to private development interests, thereby eliciting the support of such powerful groups. However, such information is rarely crucial to private decision-makers and can often be obtained from other sources, so the monopoly can be only partial and of limited value in protecting organizational power and prestige.

13. Physical plans have tended to be focused on growth areas, notably the urbanizing fringe and the central business district, since the possibility of controlling change is greatest there. Controlled change in such areas

has usually benefited property owners, typically from upper and upper-middle income groups.

14. However, long-term inter-generational and interclass benefits have resulted where downward filtering and change in the composition of population groups have occurred in areas developed according to plans.

Though these hypotheses have been derived from the present analysis of the Regional Plan of New York and Its Environs, I suspect that they typify many other kinds of urban reform activities and movements. Whether they accurately describe the characteristics of the American reform cycle, both past and emerging, must be left as a matter for further investigation.

NOTES

1. Merton, Robert (1957) *Social Theory and Social Structure*. New York: Free Press (rev. encl. ed), pp. 73 ff.

2. Boyce, David E., Day, Norman D. and McDonald, Chris (1970) *Metropolitan Plan Making*. Philadelphia: Regional Science Research Institution Monograph Series, pp. 121–124. For a similar list of criteria, see: Hufschmidt, Maynard M. (1970) *The Metropolitan Planning Process: An Exploratory Study*. Chapel Hill: University of North Carolina, Department of City and Regional Planning, pp. A78–A85.

3. The Plan was printed by William F. Fell Company of Philadelphia, a non-union shop.

BIBLIOGRAPHY

Adams, Frederic J. and Hodge, Gerald (1965) City planning instruction in the United States: The pioneering days, 1900–1920. *Journal of the American Institute of Planners*, XXXI, February, pp. 43–51.

Adams, Thomas (1923) The architect and city planning, IV. *Journal of the American Institute of Architects*, XI, May, pp. 217–219.

Adams, Thomas (1927) *Planning the New York Region.* New York: Regional Plan of New York and Its Environs.

Adams, Thomas (1932) A communication in defense of the Regional Plan. *The New Republic*, June 6.

Adams, Thomas (1936) *Outline of Town and City Planning: A Review of Past Efforts and Modern Aims.* New York: Russell Sage Foundation.

American Society of Civil Engineers (1924) Memoirs of Nelson Lewis. *Transactions of the American Society of Civil Engineers*, March 30.

Bachrach, Peter (1967) *The Theory of Democratic Elitism.* Boston: Little Brown.

Bard, Erwin Wilkie (1942) *The Port of New York Authority.* New York: Columbia University Press.

Bassett, Edward M. (1936) *Zoning: The Laws, Administration and Court Decisions during the First Twenty Years.* New York: Russell Sage Foundation.

Bottomore, T.B. (1964) *Elites and Society.* Baltimore: Penguin Books.

Boyce, David E., Day, Norman D. and McDonald, Chris (1970) *Metropolitan Plan Making.* Philadelphia: Regional Science Research Institution Monograph Series.

Brearly, Harvey (1914) *The Problem of Greater New York and Its Solution.* New York: Committee on Industrial Advancement of the Brooklyn League.

Carr, Edward Hallett (1961) *What is History?* New York: Vintage Books.

City Plan Commission, Newark (1915) *Comprehensive Plan of Newark.* Newark: City Plan Commission.

City of New York Board of Estimate and Apportionment: Committee on the City Plan (1914) *Development and Present Status of City Planning in New York City.* New York.

Committee on the Regional Plan of New York and Its Environs (1924a) A Form of State Enabling Act for Zoning. New York: Regional Plan of New York and Its Environs, May.

Committee on the Regional Plan of New York and Its Environs (1924b) Traffic Problems in their Relation to the Regional Plan of New York and Its Environs – Report of a Conference Held in the Town Hall, New York City, May 24, 1924. New York: Regional Plan of New York and Its Environs.

Committee on the Regional Plan of New York and Its Environs (1927a) *Regional Survey of New York and Its Environs.* Vol I. *Economic Factors in Metropolitan Growth.* New York: Regional Plan of New York and Its Environs.

Committee on the Regional Plan of New York and Its Environs (1927b) *Regional Survey of New York and Its Environs.* Vol. III. *Highway Traffic* (by Harold M. Lewis with Ernest P. Goodrich). New York: Regional Plan of New York and Its Environs.

Committee on the Regional Plan of New York and Its Environs (1928) *Regional*

Survey of New York and Its Environs. Vol. V. *Public Recreation.* New York: Regional Plan of New York and Its Environs.

Committee on the Regional Plan of New York and Its Environs (1929a) *Regional Survey of New York and Its Environs.* Vol. IV. *Transit and Transportation.* New York: Regional Plan of New York and Its Environs.

Committee on the Regional Plan of New York and Its Environs (1929b) *Regional Survey of New York and Its Environs.* Vol VII. *Neighborhood and Community Planning.* New York: Regional Plan of New York and Its Environs.

Committee on the Regional Plan of New York and Its Environs (1929c) *Regional Survey of New York and Its Environs.* Vol. VIII. *Physical Conditions and Public Services.* New York: Committee on the Regional Plan of New York and Its Environs.

Committee on the Regional Plan of New York and Its Environs (1929d) *Regional Plan of New York and Its Environs.* Vol. I. *The Graphic Regional Plan.* New York: Regional Plan of New York and Its Environs.

Committee on the Regional Plan of New York and Its Environs (1929e) *Regional Survey of New York and Its Environs.* Vol II. *Population, Land Values and Government.* New York: Regional Plan of New York and Its Environs.

Committee on the Regional Plan of New York and Its Environs (1931a) *Regional Plan of New York and Its Environs.* Vol. II. *The Building of the City* (by Thomas Adams assisted by Harold M. Lewis and Lawrence M. Orton). New York: Regional Plan of New York and Its Environs.

Committee on the Regional Plan of New York and Its Environs (1931b) *Regional Survey of New York and Its Environs.* Vol. VI. *Buildings: Their Uses and the Spaces about Them.* New York: Committee on the Regional Plan of New York and Its Environs.

Condit, Carl, W. (1964) *The Chicago School of Architecture.* Chicago: University of Chicago Press.

Couillard, Ada S. (1924) Bridging the Hudson River at New York City. *Municipal Reference Library Notes,* **X**, No. 6, February 6.

Creese, Walter L. (1967) *The Legacy of Raymond Unwin: A Pattern for Planning.* Cambridge: MIT Press.

Dahl, Robert A. (1960) *Who Governs? Democracy and Power in an American City.* New Haven: Yale University Press.

Dorn, Harold F. (1956) Pitfalls in population forecasts and projections, in Spengler, Joseph J. and Dudley, Otis (eds). *Demographic Analysis.* Glencoe: Free Press, pp. 69–90.

Dror, Yehezkel (1971) Planning in the United States – Some reactions as a foreign observer. *Public Administration Review,* **XXXI**, May-June, p. 402.

Duffus, R.L. (1930) *Mastering Metropolis: Planning the Future of the New York Region.* New York: Harper and Row.

Epstein, Jason (1992) The tragical history of New York. *New York Review of Books,* April 9, pp. 45–52.

Faulkner, Harold U. (1931) *The Quest for Social Justice, 1898–1914.* New York: The Macmillan Co.

Fein, Albert (ed.) (1968) *Landscape into Cityscape: Frederick Law Olmsted's Plan for a Greater New York City.* Ithaca: Cornell University Press.

Fitch, Robert (1993) *The Assassination of New York.* London and New York: Verso.

Gaus, John M. (1943)) *The Graduate School of Design and the Education of Planners.* Cambridge, Mass.

Glenn, John M. (1947) *Russell Sage Foundation, II, 1907–1926*. New York: Russell Sage Foundation.

Goldman, Eric F. (1952) *Rendezvous with Destiny: A History of Modern American Reform*. New York: Alfred A. Knopf.

Goodrich, Ernest P. (1925) The statistical relationship between population and the city plan. *Papers and Proceedings, American Sociological Society*, XX, pp. 123–128.

Green, Constance McL. (1963) *Washington: Capital City, 1879–1950*. Princeton: Princeton University Press.

Haig, Robert Murray (1927) The economic basis of urban concentration. Reprinted in Committee on the Regional Plan of New York and Its Environs (1927) *Regional Survey of New York and Its Environs*. Vol I. *Economic Factors in Metropolitan Growth*. New York: Regional Plan of New York and Its Environs.

Harrison, Mrs Burton (1896) *History of the City of New York: Externals of Modern New York*. New York: D.S. Barnes and Co.

Harvey, Kantor A. (1973) Charles Dyer Norton and the origins of the Regional Plan of New York. *Journal of the American Institute of Planners*, XXXIX, No. 3, pp. 35–41.

Hawley, Willis D. and Wirt, Frederich M. (1968) *The Search for Community Power*. Englewood Cliffs: Prentice-Hall.

Hays, Forbes B. (1965) *Community Leadership: The Regional Plan Association of New York*. New York: Columbia University Press.

Heiman, Michael K. (1988) *The Quiet Evolution: Power, Planning, and Profits in New York State*. New York: Praeger.

Hofstadter, Richard (1955a) *The Age of Reform*. New York: Vintage.

Hofstadter, Richard (1955b) *Social Darwinism in American Thought*. Boston: Beacon Press.

Hufschmidt, Maynard M. (1970) *The Metropolitan Planning Process: An Exploratory Study*. Chapel Hill: University of North Carolina, Department of City and Regional Planning.

Hunter, Floyd (1953) *Community Power Structure*. Chapel Hill: University of North Carolina Press.

Isard, Walter (1960) *Methods of Regional Analysis*. Cambridge: MIT Press.

Jones, Barclay G. (1965) Land uses in the United States in the year 2000, in Weiss, Charles M. (ed.) *Man's Environment in the Twenty-First Century*. Chapel Hill: School of Public Health, University of North Carolina, pp. 171–195.

Julien, Claude (1971) *America's Empire*. New York: Random House.

Kolko, Gabriel (1963) *The Triumph of Conservatism*. New York: The Free Press.

Lewis, Nelson P. (1916) *The Planning of the Modern City*. New York: John Wiley and Sons.

Long, Norton E. (1958) The local community as an ecology of games. *American Journal of Sociology*, LXIV, No. 3, November, pp. 251–261.

Lowi, Theodore J. (1964) *At the Pleasure of the Mayor*. New York: The Free Press of Glencoe.

Lubove, Roy (1962) *The Progressives and the Slums*. Pittsburgh: University of Pittsburgh Press.

Lubove, Roy (1963) *Community Planning in the 1920s: The Contribution of the Regional Planning Association of America*. Pittsburgh: University of Pittsburgh Press.

McKaye, Benton (1930) New York: A national peril. *Saturday Review of Literature*, August 23.

Makielski, S.J. (1966) *The Politics of Zoning: The New York Experience.* New York: Columbia University Press.

Mandelbaum, Seymour J. (1965) *Boss Tweed's New York.* New York: John Wiley.

Merton, Robert (1957) *Social Theory and Social Structure.* New York: Free Press (rev. encl. ed).

Mills, C. Wright (1956) *The Power Elite.* New York: Oxford University Press.

Moody, Walter D. (1919) *What of the City?* Chicago: A.C. McClurg and Co.

Moody, Walter D. (1920) *Wacker's Manual of the Plan of Chicago,* 3rd ed. Chicago: Chicago Plan Commission.

Moses, Robert (1970) *Public Works: A Dangerous Trade.* New York: McGraw-Hill.

Mumford, Lewis (1925) Realities or dreams. *Journal of the American Institute of Architects,* **XIII,** June, pp. 191–199.

Mumford, Lewis (1926) The intolerable city: Must it keep growing? *Harpers,* February, pp. 283–293.

Mumford, Lewis (1930) The booby prizes of 1929. *New Republic,* January 8, pp. 190–191.

Mumford, Lewis (1932*a*) The Plan of New York. *The New Republic,* **LXXI,** June 15, pp. 121–126;

Mumford, Lewis (1932*b*) The Plan of New York, II. *The New Republic,* **LXX**I, June 22, pp. 146–153.

New York City Improvement Commission (1907) *Report to the Honorable George B. McClellan, Mayor of the City of New York.* New York: City Improvement Commission.

New York, New Jersey Port and Harbor Development Commission (1920) *Joint Report with Comprehensive Plan and Recommendations.* Albany: The Development Commission.

New York State Commission of Housing and Regional Planning (1926) *Report.* Albany, May 7.

Olmsted, Frederick Law (1914) The town planning movement in America. *Annals of the American Academy of Political and Social Sciences,* **LI,** January, pp. 172–181.

Olmsted, Frederick L. Jr and Kimball, Theodora (1922) *Frederick Law Olmsted, Landscape Architect, 1822–1903.* New York: G.P. Putman's Sons.

Pearl, Raymond and Reed, Lovell J. (1923) *Predicted Growth of Population of New York and Its Environs.* New York: Committee of the Regional Plan of New York and Its Environs.

Perry, Clarence Arthur (1933) *The Rebuilding of Blighted Areas.* New York: Regional Plan Association.

Polsby, Nelson W. (1963) *Community Power and Political Theory.* New Haven: Yale University Press.

Regional Plan Association (1933) *From Plan to Reality.* New York: Regional Plan Association.

Regional Plan Association (1938) *From Plan to Reality, II.* New York: Regional Plan Association.

Regional Plan Association (1941) *From Plan to Reality, III.* New York: Regional Plan Association.

Regional Plan Association (1960) *The Race for Open Space.* New York: Regional Plan Association.

Regional Plan Association (1968) *The Second Regional Plan: A Draft for Discussion.* New York: Regional Plan Association.

Riordon, William L. (1963) *Plunkett of Tammany Hall.* New York: E.P. Dutton (first published in 1905).

Roosevelt, Franklin D. (1932) Growing up by plan. *Survey,* **LXVII**, February 1.

Ross, Edward A. (1896) The location of industries. *Quarterly Journal of Economics,* April.

Rush, Thomas E. (1920) *The Port of New York.* Garden City: Doubleday, Page and Co.

Sayre, Wallace S. and Kaufman, Herbert (1960) *Governing New York City.* New York: Russell Sage Foundation.

Schlesinger, Arthur M. (1933) *The Rise of the City 1878–98.* New York: The Macmillan Co.

Schlesinger, Arthur M. Jr. (1957) *The Crisis of the Old Order, 1919–1933.* Boston: Houghton Mifflin.

Schnore, Leo F. and Fagan, Henry (1967) *Urban Research and Policy Planning.* Beverly Hills: Sage Publications.

Scott, Mel (1969) *American City Planning Since 1890.* Berkeley: University of California Press.

Shurtleff, Flavel (1914) *Carrying out the City Plan.* New York: Survey Associates.

Simpson, Michael (1985) *Thomas Adams and the Modern Planning Movement.* London: Mansell.

Soule, George (1947) *Prosperity Decade: From War to Depression, 1917–1929.* New York: Holt Rinehart and Winston.

Spengler, Joseph J. and Dudley, Otis (eds.)) (1956) *Demographic Analysis.* Glencoe: Free Press.

Stein, Clarence (1966) *Toward New Towns for America,* revised edition. Cambridge: MIT Press.

Stokes, I.N. Phelps (1939) *New York Past and Present: Its History and Landmarks 1524–1939.* New York: Plantin Press.

Thomas, Norman and Blanshard, Paul (1932) *What's the Matter with New York: A National Problem.* New York: Macmillan Co.

Toll, Seymour (1969) *Zoned America.* New York: Grossman Publishers.

Tri-State Regional Planning Commission (1973) *Outdoor Recreation in a Crowded Region.* New York: Tri-State Regional Planning Commission.

Tunnard, Christopher (1953) *The City of Man.* New York: Charles Scribner's Sons.

Tunnard, Christopher (1968) *The Modern American City.* Princeton: D. Van Nostrand.

U.S. Department of Commerce, Advisory Committee on Zoning (1924) *A Standard Zoning Enabling Act.* Washington.

Villard, Oswald Garrison (1939 *Memoirs of Liberal Editor.* New York: Harcourt Brace & Son.

Weber, Adna, F. (1899) *The Growth of Cities in the Nineteenth Century: A Study in Statistics.* New York: The Macmillan Co.

Weiss, Charles M. (ed.) (1965) *Man's Environment in the Twenty-First Century.* Chapel Hill: School of Public Health, University of North Carolina.

Wiebe, Robert H. (1962) *Businessmen and Reform.* Cambridge: Harvard University Press.

Weinstein, James (1968) *The Corporate Ideal in the Liberal State: 1900–1918.* Boston: Beacon Press.

Wood, Edith Elmer (1931) *Recent Trends in American Housing.* New York: Macmillan Co.

Wood, Robert C. (1961) *1400 Governments.* Cambridge: Harvard University Press.

INDEX